AEGEAN DREAM

AEGEAN DREAM

Dario Ciriello

PANVERSE

Panverse Publishing

The events in this book are as accurate a recounting as my memories and records allow. To protect the privacy of others, names have been changed, characters conflated, and some incidents condensed or altered.

Published by Panverse Publishing, 2207 Holbrook Dr., Concord, CA 94519

Front cover: Brigitte and Alexis at the *kástro*
Rear cover: the house and *mílos*

Cover layout by Janice Hardy
All photos by Dario Ciriello

Visit Panverse Publishing online at www.panversepublishing.com

Printed in the United States of America

ISBN 978-0-9837313-0-6

For Linda

Acknowledgments

This book is the culmination of circumstances and events in which many people played a part, and to whom I owe the most sincere thanks.

First and foremost are the good people of the Aegean island of Skópelos—the 'Mamma Mia!' island—who welcomed my wife and me into their lives, their families, and, in many cases, their hearts. They all appear in this book, and are constantly in our thoughts. Also our dear friend Brigitte on the neighboring island of Alónissos, without whose enormous kindness, encouragement, and support we would have been lost; and Mános, who of course started it all.

An immense debt of gratitude is also due to the many friends in the US and UK who helped and supported us in one way or another and who were there for us when things turned grim: Bryta; Scott and Gretchen; Tony; Charles; Blunt; Judith; Lois and Richard; David and Tom; April and David; Juliette and Tim; Sylvia, John, Jane, and Luke; Barbara; Ali and Jim; Jody and Hector; and all those who followed and supported our adventure via the original *Aegean Dream* blog.

I'm also profoundly grateful to this book's many first readers including the amazing 'Written in Blood' group, all of who provided helpful insight and comment; to Janice Hardy, for her work on the cover; and to Anne Devlin, who always believed in the project.

Finally, my deepest thanks of all to my wife, Linda, without whose support, patience, and sense of humor none of this would have been possible.

CONTENTS

I

THE DREAM

There are a thousand ways in which a heart can be broken.
This is a true story.

An Unexpectedly Persistent Dream

August 2004
Santa Cruz, California

WE'D BEEN BACK a month from our second vacation in Greece and were picking over the remains of dinner when our conversation turned again to the small island of Skópelos.

I looked at Linda and shook my head. "What are we doing here? We could be living on Skópelos."

My wife gave me a playful smile. "Sure. Let's go and live in Greece."

I blinked. "Are you serious?"

"Why not? We've been talking about leaving California for years. We could be Greeks."

Beneath me, the world stopped turning. If it's true—as some physicists assert—that our tiniest actions and decisions each conjure fresh histories, new alternate realities, I believe these generally pass unnoticed. This time, I was staring at a sudden, unanticipated off-ramp on the freeway of our frantic life.

The words, "we could be Greeks," hung in the air like neon.

"Well, I guess I could do my work anywhere," I said, going with the fantasy. My skills were portable. I'd been self-employed all my life, a faux painter fancifying the homes and furniture of the wealthy. "But what will *you* do?"

"I'm going to make soap!"

The notion took me by surprise. But I knew Linda well enough to never doubt her ability to follow through. She'd been making luxury soaps on a hobby basis for a year or more, and was extremely gifted at it.

"Do you think you could work for yourself, though?" I said.

"Maybe. I'm tired of making money for other people. It's time I did something for *me*."

"Amen to that." I'd always 'done it for me,' a self-employee to the point of burnout. Twenty-five years of producing art under construction site conditions will do that, especially if you're a perfectionist.

I was also a science fiction writer, with several short stories published. The money earned from these efforts was laughable, rarely enough for a good dinner for two, but I had hopes. Besides, if you're a writer, you write.

We were, then, a fine pair of professionals: painting, writing, and soapmaking. No problem, success assured! *Of course* we could make a living in a foreign country where we couldn't even speak the language.

I fully expected our little fantasy to evaporate with the dawn, a wraith of dreamstuff brought on by wine and the romantic imagination. We'd wake, shrug our shoulders, and get back to the grind.

Oddly, the idea persisted.

WE ALL DREAM of escaping. But from what?

It was Saturday morning, the promise of a warm Indian summer's day in the air. We were on our second cup of coffee. Our conversation about Greece had stayed with me.

"The other night… were you serious about Greece?"

Linda gave a shrug. "What's the point of having dreams if they just remain dreams? I don't want to have regrets when I grow old, like so many people do."

"Well, we don't have children or parents to take care of. And, God! I'd love to get away from California." It wasn't just the stress and crowded freeways. Even after twenty years in this bizarre frontier land, not a day passed without my heart yearning to return to Europe.

I went on, "But could you handle the insecurity?" Linda had always been the stable one with the steady job. She'd worked for years in the fast lane, lately in a number of startup companies. She was good, and commanded a healthy wage. But soapmaking—like Greece from California—was a world apart from her 'day job'.

"What's security?" she said. "Are we secure here? We earn over a hundred thousand a year between us and we still can't afford to buy a house. Neither of us is young, and we're not going to live forever."

She was right. We'd seen two fifty year-old friends in apparently excellent health drop dead in the last year, one from a stroke, one from a heart defect; a twenty-two year old co-worker of Linda's die crossing the road; one of my oldest friends die at forty-nine of lung cancer. Jobs, spouses, life itself, all could be taken from you at any moment, without warning.

Why then fear moving to another country, shooting for the moon? Life was to be lived, and they knew how to do that in southern Europe, where people had time for family and friends, and didn't measure their worth by how many hours they worked.

We knew there were risks. But the risk of growing old and having regrets because we'd been too timid to follow our dreams was the most frightening of all. What to others seemed like courage was, to us, necessity. It was survival.

I CALLED THE Greek Consulate in San Francisco. Consulates are hardly ever open and do all they can to discourage business, but if you are fortunate they will note your message and call you back.

To my surprise, the man who returned my call had an accent—a genuine Greek!

"My wife and I want to move to Greece," I explained. "I'm an EU citizen, she is American. What's the procedure?"

"Do you have a European Union passport?"

"Yes. I'm British."

He hesitated. My stomach fluttered.

"And you are thinking of moving when?"

"Oh—perhaps a year, or a little less."

"Well. Britain is not a Schengen agreement member, and there are some papers required. But in December the Greek laws will change, and non-Schengen members will have full residence rights. I do not think there would be a problem."

"That's fantastic!" I blurted.

"Eh, yes." I could see the smile flicker across his lips from ninety miles away. "Why do you want to move to Greece?"

"I've always wanted to return to Europe," I said. The US had been good to me in many ways, but my British-born Italian genes screamed to be taken home. I missed European culture, architecture, the sheer common sense of the place. Even after seventeen years here, I thought America very strange. The dreadful Puritanism, the endless national navel-gazing over rights and 'values' while the things which really mattered went to hell. How could an entire nation get so worked up over, say, abortion rights or gay marriage, when they should have been out rioting in the streets over the appalling mess in healthcare? Nero, at least, was doing something creative while his city burned.

"And," I went on, "we love Greece and the Greek people." I told the official about the time we'd spent on Skópelos, and that I had a dear old friend on Alónissos, the neighboring island.

He seemed to sigh. "Skópelos is very beautiful. It is one of the jewels of my country."

"Yes," I agreed. "It certainly is."

We had taken the first tiny step towards transforming our lives.

LINDA WAS AS surprised as I was that we might actually be able to live in Greece without huge bureaucratic impediments. I felt I might be sleepwalking. Could something so audacious really be possible?

"I think we need at least a year," she said. "We have to save as much as we can."

I snorted a laugh. "Not easy, living here." The San Francisco Bay Area was one of the most expensive places in the US. And our finances had taken a huge hit in 2002. With the local economy reeling from the dot-com bust and the aftermath of 9/11, Linda was unemployed for months before landing a job as Director of Operations at Warmboard, a company that manufactured a sophisticated radiant heating system. And my painting business had tanked.

Now, our financial position was finally improving. Linda had seen some generous salary increases and my work was showing a pulse again. We were chipping away at credit card debt. If we could just stay on track, I was confident a year would see us in fine shape. We were going to do this.

OF COURSE, LIFE happens.

The market for my work went flat again; Linda's daughter suffered major car and personal crises which sucked zeroes from Linda's bank balance like M&Ms; both our teeth clattered for dentistry to the tune of several thousand dollars. By early 2005, it was clear we wouldn't be able to move before at least the end of the year, and likelier Spring of 2006. Given the rate at which we were hemorrhaging cash, even that was optimistic.

Heart sinking, I kept trying for dates on calendars; Linda remained circumspect. "We need to see how the next few months go before we commit to a date," she said.

I tinkered with cashflows and what-ifs, looking for bottom lines. After searching the Skópelos island website, I contacted Láli Páppas, a local real estate agent, to see if she handled rentals as well. Getting a realistic idea of the rental market would be a big help.

Mrs. Páppas spoke good English, and seemed happy to take our inquiry. "Yes, I have some rentals," she said. "When are you thinking of coming?"

"Probably early next year. Certainly by Easter."

"Ah." A pause. "I must tell you this is not a good time to rent a house on the islands."

God. "Why not?"

"You must understand the Greek psychology," she said. She pronounced it *psee-cologhy*. "In the summer, everybody here on Skópelos works very hard. If they have a house to rent, they have new people coming every one or two weeks. From June to September they are like crazy people. So at the end of the summer, they are so tired that they will be very happy if somebody wants to rent this house for one or two years. They will make a little less money, but they will have peace. But then, after one or two months, certainly by November, they will be rested, and start to think of how much money they can make if they rent the house by the week for another summer. Do you understand, Mr. Ciriello?"

"Uh, yes. Yes."

"Yes, it is this way on the islands. So if you want to rent a house it is best that you come in September, or in any case before the middle of October."

The clang as this new wrench struck the works was almost audible. Spring wouldn't work. We'd have to postpone again, this time to the late summer of next year. I knew Linda would welcome the extra time; and I knew, despite my impatience, that she was right.

Greek Lessons

IT ALL STARTED in early 2003, when we were planning our first Greek vacation. Linda had gone online to find a summer rental, and discovered the so-called Ánesis *spítia* ('comfort houses'), a pair of charming little traditional cottages set in an olive grove opposite the harbor and the old village of Skópelos. But there was no email address or booking form, only a phone number and the owners' name: Spýros and Mára Balabánis.

With Greece ten hours ahead of Pacific Time, Linda called from home early one morning. Using our new Oxford Greek Dictionary, she'd rehearsed a short script with all the right keywords, such as 'house' and 'rent' and 'July'. She could do this, no problem.

Of course, when Mára answered the call, it became quickly apparent that not only did she not have a copy of Linda's script, but also that she was as challenged in English as Linda in Greek. After a minute or two of mangled syllables and desperately made-up words, Linda was crying with laughter, and so was Mára. Eventually, Mára was able to make Linda understand she should call back later when Spýros was home, as he spoke better English.

Later that morning, Linda called me from work.

"So did you get hold of the husband?" I said.

She chuckled. "Well, yes, I did."

"How was his English?"

"No better than his wife's." She made that cute little whimpering sound, *oooh*, that she reserves for moments of profound muddlement.

"And how did you do? Do we have a deal?"

"Well, we've either rented a place to stay, or agreed to buy a table."

"We *what?*"

"Yes. He asked if I could send him a hundred Euros deposit and I said that would be fine. I asked where, and he gave me series of numbers, which I think is his bank account."

"Great!" I said. Linda had learned her numerals all the way to ten, and was very proud of the fact.

"But when I asked him *which* bank, he started talking about tables. I tried again and he kept talking about a table. Oooh. I'm *so* confused!"

"Hm. But was he nice?"

"He was delightful! We had lots of laughs. I just don't get all this stuff about a table."

This was too bizarre. She had to be missing something. "Do you remember exactly what he said?"

"Well, I kept saying *banko* and he kept talking about a *trapézi* something—that's a table, right?"

It was my turn to laugh. The Greek for bank was not *banko*, and the time-honored Anglo trick of adding an 'o' on the end of an English word wasn't gonna work here. "*Trápeza!*" the word came back to me in a flash, "*trápeza* is the Greek for bank. *Trapézi* is a table. Different stress accent."

"Omigod! He must think I'm so retarded!"

"No, I'm sure—"

"You need to call him."

"Me? No, no, I'm sure you got it right."

"No, you call him!" she insisted. "I don't want to get to Skópelos and find we own a table but have no place to stay! You're the one who's been to Greece lots of times, and has history with these islands. And you speak French and Italian."

"Which are no use in dealing with Greeks!" I protested. "Okay, give me a half hour, I need to bond with the dictionary first. I'll call you back."

"Good. And make sure we haven't bought a table!"

I made more coffee, playing for time. Hopefully Mr. Balabánis would be out when I called. I got a notepad and opened the dictionary, squinting at the unfamiliar letter-shapes.

A few minutes later, with some hastily-scribbled keywords such as 'number', and 'wife' (for which the Greek was the same as the word for 'woman') before me, I dialed the long sequence of digits. To my dismay, the phone was answered almost immediately.

"*Emprós?*" Hallo, go ahead—I remembered that one.

"*Kýrie Balabánis?*"

"*Ne.*" Yes. I knew that one, too.

"My woman Linda, she talk you!" I blurted, in my best Greek.

"*Ne, ne!*" He sounded amused.

"My woman..." I fumbled for words. "The number bank. One hundred Euros."

"*Ne, ne!* I say her!" he added, in a flourish of craggy English.

"Number bank? Not table?"

"*Haaaa! Óhi trapézi! Trápeza!* Bank, bank, no *trapézi!*" A burst of muffled Greek as he turned from the phone to explain the joke, and a woman's laughter joined his own explosion of mirth. I started laughing too.

I called Linda back to reassure her we hadn't bought a table, and that the Balabánises appreciated the humor of the situation.

"He *laughed?* God, I love these people already… They have a sense of humor even when they're dealing with an idiot!"

Laughter, along with food, is one of the best ways to people's hearts, and this small incident served to endear Greece to her from the very beginning.

SEVERAL MONTHS LATER, on our first evening in Athens, Linda was further, and irrevocably, seduced by Greece. It didn't hurt that we'd chosen to stay in the St. George Lycabettus, a four-star boutique hotel in the city's stylish Kolonáki district.

We booked dinner for ten p.m., the normal dinner hour in Greece, at the hotel's famous rooftop restaurant, Le Grand Balcon. We held hands across the starched linen tablecloth, looking out through the sultry heat of the Athens night to the softly-lit ruins of the Acropolis less than a mile away. Occasional lights from shipping twinkled in the black expanse of the Saronic Gulf beyond.

When Linda spoke, her eyes were brimming with tears. "It's beautiful," she said. "It's exactly the way I imagined it."

WE ARRIVED IN Skópelos two days later.

Unlike the parched southern islands such as Mykonos and Santorini, the islands of the Northern Spórades—Skiáthos, Skópelos, Alónissos, and a number of uninhabited islets—are carpeted in lush forests of Aleppo pine, jewels of living emerald set on a backdrop of ultramarine, and boast waters more limpid than glass. The Ánesis cottage, set in a tranquil olive grove facing the harbor just a ten-minute walk from the tavernas and shops, proved a delightful location. It was quiet, and the view across the bay to the *hóra*, or old village, of Skópelos with its whitewashed houses, red-roofed and blue-shuttered, climbing the green hillside from the harbor, was magnificent.

The Balabánises proved as likeable in person as they had been on the phone. Despite the formidable language barrier, we had many laughs together, and Mára and Linda somehow managed a level of communication that transcended speech. They were like sisters.

By the end of the three weeks, both the island and its people had sunk honey-coated barbs deep into both her heart and mine. When, three years later, the blind workings of the world left us no choice but to tear free, the wounds would be irreparable.

LINDA WAS VERY clear about the need to learn Greek if we moved to the country. "I don't want to be the Ugly American. If we're going to start a business, we need to speak the language. And I want to be able to talk to Mára and Spýros, and to make friends."

We'd already started on the alphabet. I'm always puzzled that people who are able to learn, say, Windows Vista, find the notion of learning a new alphabet daunting. I mean, how difficult is it to absorb two or three new symbols a day for a week? It's certainly the easiest aspect of learning Greek, and one we both enjoyed: as we learned to trace the sinuous shapes of Greek cursives such as α (alpha) or δ (delta), we began to appreciate these letters as things of true beauty.

It's also impossible not to feel the connection to antiquity in the characters of the Greek alphabet; take the consonant ψ, or *psi*, (pronounced 'ps'): this is the first letter of the Greek word *psári*, which means 'fish', and you can be certain that this letter's trident shape—ψ— is not a coincidence. This is an old, old language, and the traces of ancient thought are sometimes very clear.

We found a software suite called 'The Rosetta Stone' and made good progress for a while. But the syntax was peculiar, and we began to bog down over verb conjugations. We were going to need a teacher.

Santa Cruz is a small place, but there was a Greek Orthodox church in town, and an annual Greek festival. After some inquiries, we discovered Jody and Hector, a delightful couple who'd developed a tag-team approach to teaching Greek.

The lessons were often hilarious. Jody was patient, creative, and methodical, and her strong Texas accent gave her Greek an unusual coloration. Though she freely admitted that her Greek was somewhat rudimentary, her practical teaching skills were terrific.

Enter Jody's partner, Hector, a retired industrial chemist and native Athenian. Hector supplied the perfect diction and pronunciation, but was prone to go off on wild and opaque tangents: a simple question on grammar would derail the lesson into a lecture on the evolution of a word over two millennia. Greeks are very fond of their history, and really do take every opportunity to remind one that Greek has contributed tens of thousands of words to the world's language base. On these occasions Jody would be visibly torn between the need to maintain an appearance of dignified professionalism in front of her students and the desire to strangle her erudite and garrulous partner.

The Greek language was also full of dreadful hazards, which we had only touched upon in the bank/table episode.

Like the word for 'answer' or 'solution', which differed only slightly from the word for 'rabies', making it terribly easy to tell someone you had rabies when you were discussing a problem.

Working one night through some vocabulary, we learned the Greek words for happy and worried, *eftihisménos* and *stenohoriménos*. As we practiced them in sentences, a sly smile crept across Hector's face. "You must be careful with 'I am happy'," he said. "It is not very different from the Greek for 'I am soiling myself.'"

Another night found us role-playing in Greek. Linda's assigned scenario was to pretend she needed to find the way to the town hall to obtain her driving license. Hector would be the policeman, and she would ask him the way.

The value of role-playing lay in forcing us to find workarounds to compensate for our limited grasp of the language. So when Linda failed to fully understand police officer Hector's directions, she hit on an idea: she would ask him to show her the way. She didn't know the verb for 'show', but she could say 'will you come with me?'

Unfortunately, the Greek word '*kimoúmai*' (to sleep) sounds a lot like 'come with me', and under pressure, wires will get crossed. In a precious, unforgettable burst of confidence, Linda gave officer Hector a big smile, made a gracious *lead on* gesture with her upturned palms, and said, in excellent Greek, "Please, will you sleep with me?"

It was an approach, I decided, that would probably take us far.

The Greek Island Soap, Decorative Painting, Radiant Heat Layout, and Science Fiction Writing Company

THE MONTHS PASSED and our Greek improved. We talked a lot about our plans, occasionally checking to make sure we were both still on the same page.

"In some ways it'd be so much easier to go and live in Italy or France," said Linda one evening.

"Well, I speak the languages," I said.

"But I really do love the Greek people. They're so warm; I felt so welcome there. I know we could make friends and be happy."

I nodded. "I think another good argument for Greece is that the economy isn't so mature, the niche markets already built-out. In Italy and France, there are probably already lots of little cottage industries making soaps and natural cosmetics. I think you—and I, for that matter—would find a lot less competition in Greece."

I began to research the market for natural cosmetics in Greece and discovered it was booming, especially at the luxury end. And Greece, along with much of mainland Europe, still enjoyed a strong native tradition of herbal and natural cures. 'Natural' was huge. This, coupled with Linda's desire to use as many locally-sourced products as possible, fueled my already fiery optimism.

LINDA'S OWN ANTICIPATION began to manifest in unexpected and delightful ways.

"My package arrived!" she said one evening, when I returned home. On the dining table was a mound of blue towels and a plastic zipper bag of blue and white linen. "I ordered towels and bed linens in the Greek colors. What do you think?"

I loved them. Blue and white are the Greek national colors, repeated to infinity throughout the country: white village houses set everywhere against the blue of the sea, which, in that land of crinkly coastlines and over 1,600 islands, is never far away.

Linda began to make *frappés*, the delightful, frothy iced coffee served throughout Greece, and mastered the cooking of lamb for gyros; her *tzatzíki* (yogurt dip) was better than most we'd had in Greece. Occasionally, we bought a bottle of *rétsina* to go with a Greek meal.

She also started to plan her soapmaking business. "I want to incorporate as many island products into my soap as I can. I'm going to use pure Skópelos olive oil, nothing else, as a base. Goat milk is a terrific moisturizer. I can use Skópelos honey, too."

"Can you use wild herbs for scents, or to infuse the olive oil?"

"Absolutely! I want to make the people of Skópelos even more proud of their island. I've been thinking of a design as well…" She took a pad and drew a rounded rectangle to represent a bar of soap, and inside that, a crinkly, elongated triangle.

I recognized the shape at once. "The outline of Skópelos!"

She beamed.

"Are you going to paint it on?"

"I'm thinking I'll stamp it on each bar. Can you see it?"

I could. I totally could.

KNOWING WE WERE leaving made the days both easier and more difficult. Linda seemed to cope well. The thought that before too long she'd be living in one of the most beautiful places on Earth made even trying days easier for her.

But I, with my damned artist's temperament, was struggling. Anticipation made it harder than ever for me to put up with the nonsense and stupidity of the workplace.

A decorative painter is one of the very last people on a job, as a good finish requires a clean environment with a minimum of traffic. But since most of the projects I worked on were large, complex homes, when time came for me to begin my work, the project was always well past deadline and way over budget, the inevitable end result of the delusional optimism and outright lies that are the universal currency of the construction industry.

So after a lifetime of trying to do delicate surface work that required dust-free conditions, while electricians hacked holes in panels I was trying to woodgrain and plumbers installed toilets in bathrooms where I was applying delicate gold leaf (a job sensitive even to minute air currents), I was primed like a demolition charge, and it took all my self-control not to go homicidal and start beating contractors to death with my heavy, 4" x 6" stippling brush.

But it was the pot-filler that really made me snap.

I'd gone to meet a designer to bid on a job. As she was showing me around the almost-finished project, I noticed a long-stemmed faucet on a swivel mount set in the sumptuous granite slab behind the stove.

"It's a pot-filler," the designer explained, "so they don't have to carry a pot of water from the sink to the stove."

I stared at her. The sink was barely six feet from the stove. And I knew from experience that the kitchens in many of the homes I worked in were destined to be severely underused. "Are you serious?"

She laughed. "Of course. We're putting them in most of the kitchens we're doing now."

Call me old-fashioned, idealistic, or Luddite, dear Reader—I've been called worse. But this was a gut punch, the moment in which I understood with the most terrible clarity just how terminally banal our society was, how skewed our values had become. In a world where a billion people went hungry every day, we had become so lazy that we'd spend several hundred dollars to avoid moving a pan of water six feet. I could stand no more.

WHILE LINDA'S BUSINESS plan was taking shape, there was little I could do at this end to further my own. Just get to Skópelos, market my painting skills, maybe buy or commission the occasional piece of traditional furniture, apply exciting finishes, try to resell it. Repeat.

Pretty thin stuff.

But in the summer of 2005 an opportunity presented itself which might provide me some telecommuting income in Greece.

Warmboard, the radiant heat company for whom Linda worked, had a growing need for outside designers, especially during the warm-weather months when most construction took place. And since plans could be emailed, the work was perfect for telecommuting. If I could acquire the skills, it didn't matter whether we lived six or six thousand miles away.

I received some in-house training and signed up for a community college CAD (computer-aided design) course. CAD was diametrically opposite to my traditional 'day job'; a thing of laser-fine accuracy and precision, all science and engineering, worlds apart from the shifting, hand-applied, clouds of subtly nuanced color from which I'd made my living for over two decades.

I loved it: I had discovered my inner engineer.

So we were now looking at 2006 for our move, and (I remembered Mrs. Páppas's caution, 'you must understand the Greek psee-cologhy') likely the end of summer. It seemed impossibly far away. Still, it gave us time to 'tuck in all the corners', as Linda put it, and make sure we didn't miss anything.

The thing we were most anxious to have absolutely covered was Linda's right to reside and work in the country; southern European countries have notoriously baroque and unwieldy bureaucracies, and it was critical to have all our paperwork in order. I decided to check in with the Greek consulate again.

This time I got a charming, young-sounding Greek woman. Yes, she assured me, the spouse of an EU citizen only had to present an application at the prefecture within ninety days of arrival, along with a marriage certificate and a few other papers, and they would be granted a five-year renewable residency. And of course, we would have to get our AFM, or *afimí*, the Greek equivalent of a social security number. "Without an *afimí*, you can not do anything in Greece," she said.

"Is it easy to get one?"

"Oh yes. Any accountant can do this for you."

I scribbled notes and went on to ask about shipping our belongings, customs regulations, and the like. "When you have your inventory, just bring it to the consulate. We will stamp it and issue a paper for the customs. It will cost you twenty dollars."

I thanked her very much in my best Greek, and was rewarded with a chuckle and a telephonic smile. I couldn't believe the process could be so simple, the bureaucracy so benign. Had we found our pre-ordained path to personal happiness, or were we being lulled into a sense of false security?

We wrote to Spýros and Mára in our terrible (but improving) Greek, telling them we loved their island and were planning to make it our home. Three weeks later we received an envelope in a hand unused to the Latin alphabet. It found us despite the town being written as 'Santa Crut'.

Linda opened the letter to find a dried wildflower folded inside, a token of blessing or welcome, a tangible connection to the dream we were working to realize. The letter itself was warm, joyous: they were very happy that we loved Skópelos and were going to make our home there.

THE MONTHS GROUND away. I took evening classes in CAD and endured a succession of jobs from hell in which I found myself trapped between criminally incompetent contractors and terminally frustrated clients.

Most weekends Linda made soap, experimenting and refining her skills. She worked on color and scent, packaging and presentation, until the house overflowed with soap in various stages of completion. It smelled wonderful.

We talked and dreamed about Greece. We bought guidebooks, read histories, and made lists.

"There are so many places we can visit once we're up and running," I said to Linda, as we pored over a large-scale map that covered half the dining table. "All those other islands. Mount Olympus, and the monasteries high on the crags at Metéora. The temple of Poseidon at Soúnion." My finger slid northward to Rumania. "Even the Transylvanian Alps—I always wanted to go to vampire country! And Ephesus, in Turkey. It's all so close."

"I *really* want to go to Turkey," said Linda. It wasn't the first time she'd expressed the desire to visit that exotic land. A comic pout, and, "Can we *please* go there?" she pleaded.

I hugged her. "Of course we'll go there! It can be the first place we go, if you like."

"I want to go to Turkey!" she repeated, stamping a foot for comic effect like the spoiled brat she so patently was not.

WE BEGAN TO TELL friends about our plans and the time grew wistful. When you move 6,000 miles, you know there are dear friends you may only see a handful of times in your life again, if that. Our already lively social calendar became intense, with dinners planned weeks and weeks ahead. They called us brave, and expressed admiration. "I'd *never* have the courage to do that!" was a frequent comment. I wondered what stopped people from living their dreams, and why everyone was so afraid of change. The illusion of security is strangely potent. Society relies on the herd instinct, and straying from the herd is invariably regarded as risky.

AS WINTER DEEPENED, our plans solidified. We would move in August and enjoy a few weeks of beach time before the weather broke. Winters in Northern Greece are wet and cool, and the season in the Spórades usually ends by mid-September. We could rent the little Ánesis cottage from Spýros and Mára while we looked for a house to rent and waited for our belongings to arrive.

"Once we have a workshop, I can be building my soap stock up through the winter," said Linda. "That way, when the tourist season begins, I'll be ready."

"I'll be able to help you," I said. "I can do the grunt work."

It was my intention from the beginning to help Linda with her soap business as much as she needed. Growing Linda's business was the key to success: that was where the real potential lay, and if it failed, it was hard to see how we could earn enough to make a life for ourselves.

"Wouldn't it be great," she said, "if we could work hard through the winter and be able to relax a little and enjoy the island during the summer, just delivering stock to shops and retailers? And if Warmboard sends you CAD work, it can only help our financial position."

"God, yes! And after the first summer, you could start expanding to other islands."

"That's what I'm thinking. I could have some more stamps made, one for every island."

"And get some high-end retailers in Athens and Thessaloniki. If we can do that, then you have year-round sales, rather than just during the tourist season."

Linda was cautiously optimistic; I was certain. This was going to work. It really was.

OUR TO-DO LIST grew daily. There were belongings to pack and inventory, my workshop to clear, a car and an SUV to sell, utilities and services and contracts to tie up, and a myriad of minor details.

In February we began to sort and pack, doing everything ourselves. We rented a big storage locker, and as things were boxed and inventoried, I moved them from the house.

I started to get shipping quotes, and had the good fortune to discover Aris Export in San Leandro, a small, long-established mover that specialized in the Balkans and Middle East. From my first conversation with them, I knew we'd found the right company. It would cost us about four thousand dollars to rent, load, and ship a twenty-foot container to Piraéus, the port of Athens; at the Athens end, there would probably be about two or three hundred dollars in customs clearance fees. I was happy.

The big question now was how to get our belongings from Piraéus to Skópelos; Aris couldn't help us there unless we wanted to involve a major international company, which would be prohibitively expensive.

I wrote another letter—slowly, with dictionary in hand—to Spýros and Mára, updating them on our plans and asking if they could keep an eye open for any rentals, and if they had any thoughts on how we could get our belongings from Piraéus to Skópelos.

They replied that they could not advise us on rentals, because how could they know we would like something they chose? But when we arrived they would try to help. Of transport, no mention was made.

I put these on my list of things to worry about. We had time.

IN MAY, AS we were finalizing plans for an August move, Linda's daughter Lisa announced she was going to wed and start a new life in Albuquerque.

"I really want you guys to be here for the wedding," she told Linda.

We wanted to be there too. We liked the fiancé, and were delighted Lisa had reached a solid place in the previously erratic trajectory of her life. Linda asked when they'd have the ceremony.

"July or August," said Lisa, "before you go."

Welcome as this news was, it slammed into our plans like a medium-sized meteorite: weddings cost money. But I knew how much it meant to Linda to see her formerly wayward daughter and her beloved grandson, Ben, finally become part of a 'real' family.

"Even keeping it simple, it's going to cost several thousand dollars," said Linda. "We're going to have to put our move back a few more months."

I groaned. "I really hate to do that. Christ, it's just one thing after another! At this rate, we'll never get to Greece." I was terrified of our dream slipping away from us in the dull grey onslaught of the ordinary. "We have to set a date, make a commitment."

We kicked dates around and settled on a move at the very beginning of October, as late as we dared leave it if we wanted to have a choice of houses still available for rent. We would miss our chance at a holiday before we began to work; but since the whole adventure was our dream bid for freedom, it seemed like a small thing to give up.

I KEPT ASKING Linda when she was planning to hand in her notice at work. I understood her reluctance: it was a huge step, an irrevocable stab through the heart of our security. But it had to be done, and she wanted to give a full ninety days' notice, to allow plenty of time to find and train her replacement.

One morning in early July, she went off to work, apprehensive but full of resolve.

"How did it go?" I asked her when she got home that night.

She laughed and shook her head. "The boss walked into my office this morning, and said, 'Linda, I'm afraid we're going to have to take your office away and build you a nice cube. We only have the three private offices, and with the new CEO starting soon …' He was so apologetic! So I said, You know, that's really okay, because I'm moving to Greece in three months, and I was going to hand in my notice anyway!'"

I burst out laughing. "God! That's hilarious!"

"I know! Anyway, he was very sweet. Said he understood, but that he'd really miss me. I told him I'd do everything I could to help the new guy settle in. I'm going to be working my butt off."

THE WEDDING CAME, and went off swimmingly. Everyone was happy; we'd managed to give 'the kids', as we affectionately thought of them, a good send-off, without entirely derailing our own plans. We booked our flights for early October.

I started a blog, opening it with a countdown calendar and photos of boxes piling up. There were dinners with friends, the first real goodbyes. We bobbed and tossed on a pitching sea of emotion, alternately sad and elated, nervous and overwhelmed. And all the while the siren call of a new life informed our waking hours.

But with only 35 days to go before our departure, Warmboard's newly-hired CEO asked Linda whether she'd consider staying on an extra month to ease the transition.

Another delay. I couldn't believe it!

Fortunately, Linda rolls with the punches better than I do. So when I stopped whimpering, we began to look for a win-win. Linda's boss would certainly compensate her, and the extra month's income plus bonus would be welcome. Perhaps I could still fly out as planned, using my original ticket. With transit times and local bus/ferry travel to

Skópelos, that would allow me nine full days on the island, which I hoped would be long enough to find a rental, sign a lease, then fly back to California and back out to Greece with Linda at the beginning of November. It meant I'd be entirely responsible for choosing our future residence, but Linda—bizarrely, I thought—had no qualms about that. I promised to email her pictures of possible rentals from the Internet café before I signed anything.

THE FIRST HINT that Greek bureaucracy was going to present some challenges came just before I left, when we made a return visit to the Greek consulate to pay the fee and obtain the necessary papers to get our belongings cleared by customs at Piraéus.

"Yes, we can do this," said Chrysoúla, the young woman assisting us, "but you must have something to show that you are living in Greece."

Linda and I looked at one another. "But… we don't live there yet," said Linda.

"You do not have a house?"

"Not yet. My husband's going out there in two weeks' time to try to rent one."

"Well, that is good. When you come back and you have the lease, you will return here with the papers and your inventory of boxes, and we can give you the permission."

"We had no idea that we needed to have a signed lease first" I said. Because you didn't bother to tell us, damn it.

"Eh, yes, of course. You must show that you are living there before you import your things."

I opened my mouth to deliver a little gentle sarcasm, but Linda squeezed my hand and thanked the young lady, promising we would be back around the twentieth of October.

All I had to do now was fly halfway around the world to a country where I barely spoke the language, and return with a signed lease.

House Hunting

TRAVEL TO SKÓPELOS in autumn is a very different experience than in summer.

To begin with, there are fewer connections. But an overnight stay in

Athens is never a hardship, especially if you can snag a special rate at the St. George Lycabettus.

I arrived early in the evening. After a shower and shave, I walked down the café-lined street to nearby Dexaméni square, where a group of six-to-eight year-olds appeared to be playing the same soccer game they'd been playing when Linda and I were last here, fourteen months earlier. It was around nine p.m. and there wasn't an adult in sight. The place felt at once familiar and utterly exotic; I wished Linda were there to share it.

The evening was balmy and I kept walking, one eye always on the sidewalk. When it comes to road repairs—or indeed any sort of construction—Greeks are more given to riffs of solo improvisation than to orchestrated effort. As a consequence, the sidewalks are not only patched and uneven, but include more textures and discontinuities than one would imagine possible even if you designed it that way. Add to that the occasional semi-basement, where the sidewalk has been cut away to accommodate a pair of deep steps dropping down to a five-foot tall door just below street level, and you begin to understand that some caution is in order when walking in Athens.

And this was the upscale part of the city.

I walked a while, letting the sights and sounds and smells of the culture drench my senses, then circled back around to Kolonáki Square. The place was noisy, hopping with rich kids and twenty-somethings in Beemers and Porsches, a *déja vu* of Beverly Hills.

Between the busier cafés, I saw an archway with a few stairs leading down to a vaulted semi-basement. A quiet, unpretentious dive, exactly what I wanted that evening. I ordered in Greek, and the waiter started a little casual conversation, which I was able to carry on. Later, as I ate, I felt a sudden, quiet swell of pride in my achievement: I'd managed this whole exchange in a difficult language without once resorting to English or fumbling for my dictionary. The year of lessons had certainly been worthwhile.

THERE WERE FIVE of us on the bus from Athens to the port of Ághios Kónstantinos, splashing along under mid-afternoon skies bleary with rain. Lightly cultivated fields rolled by on both sides, with here and there the white puffs of cotton plants. Bluish hills rose on our left; eastward, to the right, I caught occasional glimpses of steely water.

It's impossible for anyone of a certain sensibility to travel through the Greek landscape without feeling the presence of its Gods and Heroes, its battles and myths.

Alexander the Great surely camped hereabouts, perhaps taking a cup of wine under an old moon as he consulted with his commanders, or watching as his priests peered at steaming rabbit entrails to divine the outcome of his next battle. The pile of tumbled rocks at the bottom of that nearby hill might be the result of one of Zeus's thunderbolts gone astray.

An hour and a bit out of Athens we pulled off the road for the obligatory rest stop at a café-restaurant-gas station-gift store. In the summer, the place is a madhouse, with people crowding the long counters to buy a soda or snack and perhaps a selection from the innumerable varieties of sticky, oversweetened dainties of which the Greek palate is so notoriously fond, before the bus driver calls time. But this was the off-season, and there was all the time in the world. No tourists, only Turkish and Bulgarian truckers smoking cigarettes and drinking coffee.

I had a coffee and a *tirópita*, the famous Greek snack. Féta cheese wrapped in phýlo dough and deep fried: as Linda famously put it, fat wrapped in fat and fried in fat. It was wonderful stuff.

Sunset found me boarding the Flying Cat at Ághios Kónstantinos.

The Flying Cats, which supplement the traditional ferry fleet, are hydrofoil-supported catamarans powerful enough to carry over 300 passengers to the islands at a cruising speed of around 40mph.

Inside, the Cat is what airplanes ought to be—spacious, with plenty of leg room and a bar serving hot and cold drinks, alcohol, sodas, and food. Wonderful in every way except in rough seas, where the vehicle's speed intensifies the pitching and tossing. On these occasions, the crew hands out paper bags, just like they do on airplanes. I begged a couple of Dramamine tablets from the barman, washed them down with iced tea, and settled back in my seat.

THE CAT SLID into Skópelos harbor at ten p.m., and Spýros was there to meet me. We kissed one another on the cheek in the unselfconscious way of men in these parts. The tourists had almost all left. It had rained, and the air was damp and cool. I breathed in the salt smell of our soon-to-be island home.

Spýros dropped me off at the cottage and left me to settle in. By the time I'd unpacked—a habit of mine as soon I arrive anywhere, even for a day—it was eleven-thirty. I was a little hungry, but most of all I needed to celebrate my arrival and unwind from all the traveling. I pulled on my hat and jacket and went off into the blustery night, braving the spray from the waves along the road to the village.

To my delight, I found not only the glass of *oúzo* I so deserved, but a meal too—and this at midnight on a Sunday at the end of the season! These people had their priorities right. Greeks knew how to live.

The next morning I walked into town under heavy skies, breakfasted at the Internet café, sent Linda an email to announce my safe arrival, and began to make calls.

The first of these was to Láli Páppas, the real estate agent. She only had one property available for me to look at; we'd seen it online, a two-storey, traditional stone house too large to be properly termed a *kalívi*, or country cottage. The monthly rental was 600 Euros (now about $780 with the worsening exchange rate), the very top of our price range; but we were prepared to pay that for the right property, especially if there was enough room for us to have our workshop there. I arranged to see the property that afternoon.

It turned out a complete bust. Despite lovely views and rustic, glowing pine floors and ceilings, there was no space we could use as a workshop, and the kitchen—a corner of the living area with zero counter space, a pair of electric rings, and a tiny portable oven set beside an even smaller sink—was a joke. A very junior London estate agent might have enthused about such a setup, calling it 'rustic', or perhaps 'functionally compact'. But we love to cook and entertain. It would not do.

Back at the cottage I resized a few digital pictures I'd taken and transferred them to a CD-ROM to send to Linda and post on our blog. I made a cup of tea, put my feet up, and read.

That evening I braved the elements again.

I love walking in any weather, and throughout my entire seventeen years in California had missed the wild gales and blustery showers of my native England. Skópelos did not disappoint in this regard. My fedora, which had grown dusty on its shelf during the dry California summer, got a good wetting on the ten-minute walk from the cottage to the

Internet café. I ordered an *oúzo*, dashed off an email to Linda, and set up a Skype account before setting off for Spýros and Mára's house.

Skópelos houses have no addresses, and I'd only been to Spýros and Mára's once before. The home, near the top of the *hóra*, or old village—took a little finding in the dark, and some care in negotiating the rain-slicked stone streets. But between memory and Spýros's directions, I somehow found my way there. Damp, windblown, high on the feeling that our dreams were finally close to becoming a reality, I was greeted with hugs and joy.

The Balabánises' home is bright and full of laughter. Guests are welcome at any hour. And Mára—in keeping with the traditions of Skopelitan women—keeps the place spotless.

I was handed a drink, and managed a lively conversation despite our language handicaps and the constant chatter from the television. I inquired if they knew of any properties we could rent; they didn't.

Linda had bought four sweatshirts from our favorite coffee house in Santa Cruz for me to bring as gifts: it is impossible to out-gift a Greek, but one tries anyway, and the gesture is invariably appreciated.

Rígas and Anna, Spýros and Mára's adult children, soon arrived. Rígas was leaving in a few weeks to begin his military service; Anna worked for a courier company and was on her way to becoming engaged.

I'd not previously been impressed by Greek cuisine, but my low expectations were happily confounded as Mára served up one excellent dish after another: a selection of appetizers including a perfectly-balanced *tzatzíki* (yogurt dip), mouth-watering *keftedákia* (meatballs), tomatoes, olives, cheeses, and *kalamári* (fried squid). After that came a plate of spaghetti with a pork ragoût that an Italian would have been proud of.

Once Mára starts serving food, it keeps coming, wave after wave after wave, until the guests turn glassy-eyed and start to whimper. And since I was brought up in the days when parents would encourage children to eat by repeating the *finish-your-food-because-the-children-are-starving-in-India* mantra, it's my habit to clean my plate.

I eventually learned that in Greece finishing your food is taken to mean you could eat more but are too polite to ask; the same is true of draining your wineglass. But on that evening, I kept cleaning my plate, and Mára kept feeding me. When eventually I reached a point where I simply *couldn't* finish what was put before me, the food stopped coming.

There's one Greek table custom that foreigners—including myself—often find difficult: bowls and serving dishes are set out family-style, but without serving implements. Diners simply use their forks or spoons to pick at the dish, a mouthful at a time. To someone who's at all concerned about hygiene and matters bacterial, this is deeply disturbing[1].

So I surreptitiously noted where my hosts—all apparently healthy, but one can never tell—inserted their utensils into the various dishes, and tried to serve myself from in-between these 'hot spots'.

At first, it was easy, like keeping a mental count of the last few numbers that come up on a roulette wheel. But between the growing number of dishes, the shifting patterns of spoon- and fork-insertion as gaps appeared on the plates, the difficulty of keeping up a conversation in a language which I only vaguely grasped the outlines of, and my frequently-replenished wineglass, I was soon forced to abandon my efforts at guarding against Balkan bugs, and simply hoped for the best. I was in Greece, and would have to learn Greek ways.

THE NEXT MORNING I rented a car and spent much of the day following up a lead on a property in Glóssa, at the far end of the island. After an hour of driving flooded roads in a violent rainstorm and another hour of polite coffee-drinking with the owner, I was finally shown the property. Even more stunning views than the stone house, and even less of a kitchen. And the exterior wall of one bedroom hadn't even been built yet!

With no local paper and no Craigslist, renting anything on a small Greek island is a word-of-mouth process, and I'd already exhausted my direct contacts. I had only another week, and was beginning to appreciate the true difficulty of the undertaking. If I failed to return with a signed lease, the Greek consulate wouldn't give us an exemption to ship our belongings into the country.

It occurred to me to panic, but I decided to explore one other option first: I would call on the Balabánises again and see if they could be of any help.

---

[1] To illustrate my own fussiness in these matters, I confess to holding my breath whenever anyone near me sneezes, and to always washing my hands whenever I've been around children, all of whom are notorious germ factories.

They came to the cottage later that evening. I'd prepared some snacks and a cheat sheet of Greek phrases like 'we can pay for three months in advance' and 'we also need a space to use as a studio or workshop'.

They listened, and asked questions, and thought and chatted for a time. When they asked how much we wanted to pay, I decided to lowball it and see what they said: we could, I suggested, go as high as five hundred or five-fifty for a really nice place, but would prefer something in the four hundred Euro region.

"We do have a house," said Mára, "which will be Anna's when she gets married." They explained that since Anna had only just entered what sounded like some kind of pre-engagement, the wedding would be at least a couple of years off—which was exactly the timeframe we had in mind for renting a property while we got established and decided where on the island we would like to settle.

I dared to hope. We arranged a viewing for five p.m. the following day.

THE HOUSE WAS on a sharp bend of the Ring Road, where it circled the top of the village. Built on a slope, the place looked huge, a curving rampart of whitewashed stucco rising from the road to a pair of arch-topped balconies; the roof terrace above was encircled by a balustrade, with a squat, cylindrical tower rising from the center of the terrace. A short stair led from street level to a landing by the front door, and thence to the roof terrace.

Inside, the house that appeared so large from the street really consisted of a flat, a single habitable floor in a large structure. A tiny kitchen faced the front door, with an even tinier bathroom to the left; to the right, a narrow hallway led past the dining room, and beyond that, a small living room; at the end was the master bedroom, the largest room in the house.

Despite its small size, the house had an undeniable charm. I liked it immediately, and said so. Spýros explained he'd just finished renovating it. Marble tile floors and blue-shuttered windows gave it a traditional feel; French windows in the kitchen, dining, and living rooms opened onto the arched balconies I'd seen from the street. All the walls were freshly whitewashed.

I snapped a few pictures for Linda, then returned to the kitchen.

The kitchen *had* to work. And it really was minute, and oddly-shaped because of the curving outer wall: a small, squished pentagon of a kitchen, the cabinets barely adequate, the counter space minimal. A single sink and no appliances, though there were hookups for a washing machine and stove.

"Will there be a stove and fridge?" I asked Spýros. He nodded, pointing to an electrical cover plate in the wall by the window. The fridge would go next to the door, and a washing machine beside it in the corner. Appliances would reduce free floor space to a four-by-six foot area, but we could live with that. A dishwasher, though, was out of the question, and the single sink would be a pain.

I reminded myself this wasn't America, and that people had managed without dishwashers and double sinks for most of human history.

"*Páme sto balcóni,*" said Spýros: let's go to the terrace.

The evening was cold and wet. But even with the wind snatching at us and ruffling the puddles on the flagstones, one look at the roof terrace sold me: we had to rent this place!

The terrace was vast. You could have hosted a wedding for two hundred people up there, with room over for a band. To the right, the hills of the island's interior rose green and lush; on the left, past the concrete balustrade, stretched an incomparable view of the entire village down to the harbor and the bay beyond. And in the middle of this great, airy expanse of stone stood a three-story, whitewashed tower inset with small, blue-shuttered windows, such as might have belonged on a castle.

"This was the mill," Spýros explained. "My grandfather built it." He pointed to the circular, pebble-paved area on the harbor side of the terrace. The small hole in the center must have been the insertion of the fulcrum for the horse-drawn shaft supporting the mill-wheel. The exposed location would have ensured the chaff was carried away on the wind.

I looked at the tower. Not itself a mill, but likelier a granary.

"In the summer we rent it out," said Spýros, "but just for a few weeks, when the Ánesis cottages and our *kalívi* are full. You would still have all the terrace."

I took more pictures and we walked to the railing. In the summer, we'd be able to see the ferry or hydrofoil carrying visiting friends, and trot down to the quay in time to greet them as they docked.

"I like it very much, Spýros," I said, the Greek words tumbling out with no effort. "I think Linda will also like it. How much do you want each month?"

Spýros was tentative. "Three hundred? Would that be alright?"

Less than four hundred dollars. It was a steal, postage-stamp kitchen and all. And with a terrace and view like this, we could live with a small kitchen; at least we'd have a full-sized stove, unlike the laughable, twin electric-ring setups I'd seen in the other two rentals.

"I will send Linda pictures with the computer. I think it will be very good."

I was pretty sure she would like it; with very limited options and my time running out, I hoped she'd love it.

LINDA'S REPLY WAS ecstatic. "I've shown everyone at work the pictures," she said. "The place is amazing! I'm going to *live* on that terrace in the summer!"

"I'd like to offer Spýros another fifty a month," I said. "I think he's being more than generous, and they're friends. I want to be fair to them."

Linda agreed. "Do it. It's still a great deal!"

Spýros was delighted. "But," I said, "I must leave here with a lease to make the papers for the Greek consulate. Otherwise we will have problems with our belongings."

"What day are you leaving?"

"Monday. In six days."

"It will be difficult. But I'll call Chrýsa and make an appointment for tomorrow night."

"Chrýsa?"

"The accountant."

"You need an accountant to make the lease?"

"Of course. You *must* have an accountant to do this."

CHRÝSA WAS FORTYISH, bony, and darkly intense. An open bottle of aspirin sat among the scattered folders and papers on her desk, along with a half-used blister pack of tablets. Tranquilizers, I decided, from her look and manner.

She asked Spýros a series of questions, taking notes all the while. She turned to me. Her eyes had a haunted quality that made you want to duck when they swung towards you. "Passport?" she said.

I handed it over. More scribbling.

Chrýsa pushed a paper—of which I couldn't read a word—across the desk and pointed out a couple of fields, explaining in fragmented English what I was signing. When I was done, she smiled for the first time since our arrival. The action transformed her, a blaze of sun through storm clouds. I didn't know what to make of this woman.

She turned to Spýros, all business again. "The lease will be ready on Friday."

I thanked her. "When I come with my wife, can you help us with *afimí?*"

Another startling smile. "Of course. You can telephone me."

I bought Spýros an *oúzo* at one of the nearby cafés on the *paralía*, or waterfront. They had clear plastic windbreaks up, and we sat outside in the cool evening air.

" Chrýsa is very serious," I ventured.

"She is very good. The best." He said something else, which I understood as "Her husband jumped…"

Something in the way he said it and let his words trail off made me think it was the prelude to a funny anecdote; I smiled and nodded, waiting for more.

Spýros peered at me over his drink. "Eh, you understand what *pethéni* means?"

It was the word he'd just used, and the way he asked made me realize I'd got it entirely wrong. "No, I don't think so."

Spýros folded his hands over his chest and rolled up his eyes. "*Kaput!*" he said, "*Éna kárkino.*"

Dead. A cancer. I felt terrible.

"When he die?" I said.

"Seven or eight years ago. He was thirty-five."

I shook my head. The senseless cruelty of this world, to take someone's partner at such a young age. No wonder Chrýsa seemed so intense.

After a moment of respectful silence, we moved on to other subjects. I asked if Spýros had any ideas about how we could get *ta prágmata mas*, our belongings, to Skópelos from Piraéus. Maybe on the Evagelístria, the ship that brought supplies to the island every week?

Spýros thought a moment, then got out his cellphone.

A few moments later we were joined by a serious young man in a bomber jacket. Spýros introduced him as Andréas. "He is a truck driver," said Spýros.

Andréas spoke no English. After a short conversation, during which I supplied approximate dates and the 'cube', or volume, of our belongings, Andréas said, "*Hilía.*" A thousand.

Spýros tilted his head, as if he hadn't quite understood. "Nine hundred?"

A firm 'no' from the trucker. "I will need two men to unload the container then load it all on the truck."

The price seemed fair to me. I agreed, we shook hands, and Andréas gave me his cellphone number, with instructions to let him know as soon as possible the exact date of arrival. The whole business took less than ten minutes.

MY MISSION ACCOMPLISHED, it was time to visit the widow of my old friend Mános on the neighboring island of Alónissos, just a twenty-minute journey by hydrofoil.

Brigitte met me at the dock, and drove me up the rutted, twisty road to the old Artemis rooms. She had a fire going, and a meal and *retsína* ready.

Back in the 1960s, when Mános built his little resort, named Artemis after the moon goddess, on the bluff overlooking the small harbor at Patitíri on Alónissos, he had chosen what might be the most perfect view on an island of perfect views set in an archipelago of the same. The terrace at Artemis faced directly toward the *Dío Adelfí*, or Two Brothers, a pair of low islands sculpted to classical proportions by Apollo's own hand and set at just the right distance beyond the turquoise waters of Patitíri harbor so as to be perfectly framed by the pair of leaning pines at the front of the Artemis terrace. I had begun to call it the 'Million-Dollar View' back in the 'seventies, when a million dollars was still worth something.

Artemis closed to tourists in 1990. The main building, about a thousand square feet, which had once served as an office/reception area had been turned into a cozy home. The large stone fireplace dominating one wall of the big living area made it particularly welcoming in the damp Alónissos winters.

Several of the fifteen or so guest bungalows were now used as storage, but Brigitte had converted the four terrace rooms at the far end of the compound to a warren-like, one-and-a-half bath apartment, complete with its own kitchen. It was imaginatively done, with open arches, splashes of bright tile, and color in unexpected places.

"You see?" said Brigitte, her German accent lending muscle and heft to the English words. She had a way of stressing every third or fourth word that freighted her sentences with energy and rhythm: "I was *inspired* when I saw the *website* of your *painting* work!"

In the bedroom was an electric heater; Brigitte showed me where the extra blankets were kept. "It is cold at night now, we are not in summer. Everybody thinks it is always hot in Greece, but we are in the North, and you see how the weather is now." She chuckled. "Maybe after tonight you will not like it so much."

I took this as a light-hearted prompt for me to air any last-minute doubts about our plans. "Oh, I think I'll like it," I said. "In California we don't see a single cloud in the sky for seven months of the year. Not a drop of rain, never a thunderstorm. It drives me crazy!"

AFTER LUNCH THE next day we visited Mános's grave in the tiny cemetery just outside the *hóra* of Alónissos.

The cemetery was high on a promontory overlooking the northern part of the island and the vast expanse of indigo stretching to distant, holy Mount Athos on the Athos peninsula, one of those three spits of land that trail like the fingers of a God into this revered sea. The cemetery was low-walled, its headstones lower still, as if to avoid the brawny winds typical of these islands[2].

Brigitte opened the little glass door of the shrine above Mános's grave. Inside was a framed photo of Mános, as well as the peaked Captain's cap he often wore. Beside those—as in every Greek shrine—stood a small oil lamp and a plastic bottle of olive oil. A whirlwind of images and memories of times we'd spent together on my past visits to Alónissos swept through me. Brigitte refilled the lamp, lit it, and closed the door.

As we turned to leave, a tiny old woman arrived. She was dressed in black and wore a shawl against the cold wind. Brigitte chatted to her and handed her a few Euros. "Her husband is dead and she is alone," Brigitte

---

[2] Seafarers have called the Northern Spórades 'The Gates of the Wind' for centuries, perhaps millennia.

explained, "so she takes care of the graves. Everyone gives her a little money, so everything is all right." I smiled. It was how things worked in these small communities.

Later, Brigitte drove me down to the harbor to catch the afternoon Dolphin back to Skópelos. "I am so happy we will be neighbors," she said. "I will be visiting Germany when you arrive, but you can come after Christmas, when I return."

"We're happy too, Brigitte. We can't wait to come and visit you as neighbors!" It wouldn't be long.

Back on Skópelos, I began composing the following blog entry, which I posted a few days later:

From the Aegean Dream blog:

Destiny and the Island Next Door
Friday, October 13th, 2006

Departure -24 days

Last Friday, I took the ferry across the four-mile strait of wine-dark sea to Alónissos, the neighboring island, to visit the wife of my dear, recently departed friend Mános. Mános and I go back 40 years, to 1966, when I first came to Alónissos with my parents. I was 14.

We'd just come from Athens. My father was a senior journalist for a prestigious Italian daily, and the shaky Greek government (which within a year would be toppled and replaced by a military junta) had put us up in a 5-star hotel and provided us a chauffeur-driven car and a guide in the hope, perhaps, of promoting tourism to Greece. When it was suggested we visit the islands, my mother said she wanted to see 'the real Greece', not the tourist places. Our guide thought about it a moment. "Alónissos," she said.

After a grueling bus and ferry journey we slid into the darkened harbor at 11 p.m. Alónissos had no electricity and no dock. The ferry simply dropped anchor in the bay and the local fishermen came to meet it in their caïques.

Memories: my parents and I, horrified, climbing down a rope ladder from the ferry into a small, pitching boat at 11 p.m. by lantern-light as our luggage was handed down over the side; a young, excited Mános meeting us on the quayside and strapping our suitcases to a donkey for the steep climb up to Artemis (the first tourist facility on Alónissos, consisting of six snug cinder-block cabins in a row); the rumble of the ancient truck engine Mános had rigged as a generator in a concrete bunker to provide evening electricity to the bare bulbs in the rooms; the iron beds with what looked like army-surplus blankets; my parents' vows to leave the island by the first ferry the next day.

Of course, in the morning everything looked different. We woke to the scent of pine and a breakfast of olives, féta, figs, fresh bread , goat butter, and honey on a terrace overlooking what I still think is one of the most idyllic views in the world. Discovered gorgeous beaches, limpid seas, and friendly people. Enjoyed magical, moonlit boat rides in waters rich in phosphorescent plankton. Astonishing night skies. No cars. We stayed ten days and never forgot the place.

Over the next several years Mános visited us in London and I returned to Alónissos several times. In 1989, the year I moved to the US, Mános suffered a severe stroke. We lost contact until 2004, when Linda and I decided to visit Greece and settled on Skópelos, the adjacent island, where Linda had found a charming rental advertised online.

I sent a letter to Mános, not sure whether he was even still alive. Two weeks later we received a reply from Brigitte, Mános's wife, whom I knew from my last visits in the late 1970s/early 1980s. They were still there, living at Artemis: although in poor health and bedridden, Mános was alive and sharp as a tack. They would be delighted to see us.

So Linda and I took a day trip over and an old friendship was renewed. I'll never forget Mános's face at our first meeting after so long.

Linda fell in love with the islands and the people, and I was reminded of how luminous life can be. The following summer found us once again in Greece.

Over dinner, a month after our return to the US, Linda and I asked ourselves 'what are we doing here?', and decided there and then to move to Skópelos.

Mános died peacefully in his bed, surrounded by loved ones, on July 23rd of this year.

Dario

I WENT TO the Balabánises' house to pick up the lease. It had been notarized and stamped on every page at the town hall. I gave Spýros three months' rent in advance, in cash. Mára poured us a little *tsípouro*, the fiery eau-de-vie which transcends mere *oúzo*, and the deal was sealed.

I'd originally planned to leave Monday, but there was a general election on Sunday. "You will not find a ferry or a Dolphin to take you," Brigitte had warned me. "All the Skopelítes who live on the mainland will return to the island to vote, and they will all leave Monday. There will not be any seats."

I was puzzled. "Why do they come back to Skópelos to vote? Can't they just register where they live?"

"Some do. But if you are registered somewhere else, the government pays for your ticket to go back and vote. So it is like a holiday for them."

I raised an eyebrow.

"Eh, yes. This is Greece."

Which made me laugh aloud. After twenty years of living in the government-phobic US, I was coming to a land where government played a role in every aspect of life; and while I may have disagreed on the issue of being legally obliged to vote, the fact that the state reimbursed any expenses, and that the individual could game the system by remaining registered in their hometown, amused me more than a little.

A few moments at the ferry office proved Brigitte right: not a single seat was available on Monday. I'd have to leave Sunday and spend two nights and a day in Athens to catch my flight back on Tuesday.

By Saturday afternoon, the island had undergone a remarkable transformation. Whereas the previous day everything had seemed empty and ready to close for the winter, the town was suddenly bustling with activity. Two big ferries, the Skiáthos Express and the Jet Ferry, sat at dock. The bars were full, with whole families taking up long tables and filling the air with music and laughter. Fashionably-dressed women and men in designer clothes drank and smoked with old friends and relations. Island children reunited with city cousins and friends played together. It was like an action replay of a summer afternoon.

I couldn't think of a better place to call home.

Papers and Prágmata

A FEW DAYS later, back in San Francisco, Linda and I returned to the Greek consulate with our new lease and every document we could think of. Scanning the inventory of our belongings, Chrysoúla stopped at,

BOX 27: MOTHER'S ASHES & PHOTO ALBUMS.

"Ah. This you can not bring into Greece."
I looked at her. "Why not?"
"It is not allowed to bring human remains. I am sorry."
"These are cremated *ashes*; my mother's ashes. Why can't I bring them?"
She looked uncomfortable. "It is the law. I will ask the Consul and call you. But I do not think this is possible."
I groaned inwardly. The mindlessness of bureaucracy.
With everything photocopied and the fee paid, we rose to leave. "When can we pick up the papers for customs?" I asked.
"When are you leaving?"
"November seventh," said Linda.
"And today is the twentieth," said Chrysoúla. "I do not think there will be a problem. Call me in a week and I will hope to have them ready for you."

I'D SOLD MY Isuzu Trooper before leaving for my trip, and we scrambled to find a buyer for Linda's beloved Acura. Parting with both cars was a shock, the final cut of the umbilical that bound us to this place and whatever security we had here. For the first time, I found myself awed at the magnitude of the step we were about to take. I pushed back anything that felt like fear and focused on the task at hand, and the new life that awaited us.

We'd pared down to what we could fit into our suitcases, plus a few extra items which we'd pack in a couple of boxes at the last moment and mail to ourselves.

On Friday twenty-seventh, with just over a week to go, I called Chrysoúla at the consulate. No, the Consul hadn't signed our papers yet. He was very busy and was leaving for a week on Tuesday. She would do her best. My stomach twitched in a nervous spasm. She didn't mention my Mum's ashes, and I didn't ask, as our goods were just about to be loaded onto a ship.

Our last week in California arrived. I cleared my workshop of shelving and ladders and surplus tools, and set everything out on the street with 'FREE!' labels. The stuff disappeared almost as fast as I put it out.

Chrysoúla called to say the papers were ready. I dropped Linda off at work on Wednesday and drove the ninety miles to San Francisco to collect the damn things.

We spent the weekend with friends, and on Monday afternoon we drove to Los Gatos for a night at a luxury spa, a farewell gift to Linda from her employer. Here was the perfect send-off: not just the perfect stress-buster, but a last night spent in the lap of luxury prior to the simpler, more modest life of our island idyll. It was at once real and surreal.

We were *so* ready.

TWENTY-FOUR HOURS later found us in the departure lounge at San Francisco International, waiting to board our flight. Sat in front of us were four Greek men. I guessed they were from the provinces, as their speech was laced with heavy accents and odd rhythms. We listened and listened and listened, trying to be discreet. A year of lessons and we could barely understand a word.

Linda summed up our mutual dismay with her trademark humor. She put her face in her hands; "Oh shit!" she said, chuckling and shaking her head, "I'm *totally* hosed!"

Cut to a few days later: a hydrofoil in the middle of the northern Aegean on a blustery November day, and us, a crazy couple about to start a new life on a tiny island of 5,000 people where we knew almost no-one and on which we'd spent just a few weeks in the summer tourist season.

II

THE AEGEAN

Not a day passes without my thinking about Skópelos. Technology adds an exquisite extra dimension to the loss by allowing me to bring up the Skópelos live webcam with a few keystrokes. By chance, the webcam is positioned not far from the mílos, giving almost the identical view of the harbor and the northern tip of Alónissos that we enjoyed from our glorious terrace. If I time it right, I can even see the ferries and Flying Dolphins arrive.

Scherzo with Teknítises

THE FLYING DOLPHIN—as the smaller hydrofoils are called—swung in to Skópelos harbor just before dusk. Anticipation, excitement, and apprehension roiled us both. I babbled non-stop, Linda was quiet. And then we were walking down the gangplank and our friend Spýros was there to meet us with his little red pickup and a big smile.

We hugged and kissed him on both cheeks, breath smoking in the cold. Spýros looked a little dismayed, as if not quite able to believe we were really here, this time to stay.

I hoisted our cases—heavy cases, which we would be living out of for at least a couple of weeks—into the bed of the pickup, and three minutes later we were at the house and walking up the front steps in a fizz of excitement.

The place was clean and ready for us, a blank, unsullied canvas for our new life. Every surface was fresh and clean, each room ready to welcome us. It was also freezing cold. And the kitchen was strangely empty, as in no stove or fridge.

My heart sank. I was certain that when I'd asked whether a stove and fridge would be included, Spýros had indicated they would. Now I wondered whether he'd just thought I was asking if the big gaps between the cabinetry and wall were *meant* for a stove and a fridge. Either way, he'd said yes, and I'd told Linda there would be appliances.

She was going to kill me.

Or maybe later—she would kill me later, I decided, as right now she just shrugged her shoulders. "We'll have to buy some."

We turned to the other surprise, which was that the house was freezing despite the newly-installed central heating system.

"There is no diesel in the roof tank," said Spýros. "Do you want to get some?"

Did we want heating? It was November, and decidedly cold.

Despite the fact that it was a Sunday afternoon, Spýros made a quick call and arranged a delivery for six p.m. "After, we would like you to come to our house for drinks," he told us.

"We'd like that very much," said Linda. "After we eat?"

Spýros patted the air: there was no hurry. "Nine, ten o'clock. Whenever you want."

He took his leave, and now here we were, after all the waiting and worry, the packing and form-filling, climbing the stairs to our roof to admire the view while we waited for the diesel delivery.

It was dusk, and lights were winking on in the village and out along the Stáfilos road that cuts across the island to the south coast beaches— rocky Stáfilos, cozy Agnóndas, sprawling Pánormos, peaceful Miliá. A light mist rose in the plain as the temperature sank toward freezing. Opposite us, across the bay from the harbor, steep, pine-clad slopes surrendered their color to the twilight, while beyond the headland at the eastern tip of the bay the dark bulk of neighboring Alónissos loomed across five miles of deep water.

We got the diesel tank filled, with me hauling up the business end of the heavy hose hand-over-hand with a rope slung over the roof balustrade while the tanker owner controlled the hose reel on the truck below. A manly business, male bonding across language barriers.

But even with the tank brimful of diesel, the furnace wouldn't fire up. I called Spýros from the payphone across the road and he assured me he'd have a *teknítis* (sometimes Greek is really easy) look at it first thing in the morning.

Spýros and Mára had loaned us a bed, linens, a rickety wardrobe, and a couple of blankets to get us through until our belongings arrived, but other than those and the contents of our suitcases, that was it. Fortunately, we discovered that the wall-mounted air conditioners in the bedroom and dining room also had a heat setting. We stole batteries from our clip-on book light, figured out the remote, and *voilá*, heat. Not a great deal of it, but enough. We'd be comfortable.

Hungry and eager to experience our new surroundings, we set off to find some food. The street was empty, the village quiet. Across the ring road, asphalt gave way to stone paving, transporting us back a century as we entered the seductive maze of narrow lanes and snug stone houses that comprise the old village. Even without knowing the exact way, we had only to keep going downhill to emerge on the *paralía*, or waterfront.

The *hóra's* lanes and alleys are a liability lawyer's dream—a treacherous, undulating marriage of smooth stones set in a coarse mortar, and more than a little steep in places. There are no sidewalks, and many of the streets are barely wide enough for the tiniest Eurocar; flights of slick stone stairs are common, with knee-torturing, uneven risers up to a foot high in places. The older Skopelítes all walk with sticks, and cautiously.

Linda and I strolled hand-in hand down the lanes toward the harbor, entranced by the sheer, wonderful fact of actually having made it here after all the months of planning and worry. We'd only experienced the island in high season, and marveled at the peace and lack of crowds. We had arrived in a magical storybook village which was to be our home forever.

A few minutes later we reached the harbor. Except for a couple of bars, everything was closed. The wide, paved waterfront, dense with tables and chairs in the summer, was an empty expanse of stone.

The one open restaurant was a stark, white, neon-irradiated box of a place. We'd noted it in the summer as the old fishermen's' haunt. No plush seats or foofy drinks here, just creaky wooden chairs and tables made for an older, smaller generation of islanders to eat simple food at while washing it down with *oúzo* or *retsína*. It would do.

The food was simple and honest. We quaffed our *retsína* while a group of well-oiled old salts in the corner debated and declaimed at the top of their voices. There was only one other couple in the place, and a few young men sitting quietly, listening to the oldsters. We were definitely not in Kansas anymore.

Glowing from drink and warm food, we set off for Spýros and Mára's house, a fifteen-minute walk, mostly uphill, through the quiet village streets.

From the Aegean Dream blog:

Linda speaks

We arrive to the most unbelievable display of flowers and plants. I mean TOTALLY unbelievable. Every available surface, not to mention the floor and outdoor patio area, is covered in plant life. We are concerned. Is this some bizarre form of winter decoration? Have our landlords gone mad? Through repeated questioning we finally understand that their daughter, Anna, has become engaged, and it seems it is a tradition in Skópelos to completely bury a house in flora when a daughter becomes engaged. Picture this: Alfred Hitchcock is given one type of prop to use in a movie and it is greenery. This is no exaggeration.

We visit and have a lovely time. We sip Mára's home-made cherry liquor and eat dainties that have been prepared for the engagement party. We are severely underdressed. We take our leave, thanking our hosts profusely for the sheets they have loaned us. Sleep is much needed as the *teknítis* comes early in the morning to fix the heating.

Linda

WE SLEPT POORLY. The *teknítis*es, two young men, arrived just before eight a.m.. The name patches on their shirts read *Nikoláos A. Káltzas*. I later discovered that Nikoláos A. Káltzas—commonly known as 'Níkos'—was the owner of what we soon came to think of as the Home Depot of Skópelos, a big appliance and hardware store a few hundred yards up the ring road from our house.

They got the furnace lit but quickly determined that the thermostat was dead, victim of the wall-mounted air conditioner/heater, which we'd run all night. Expertly installed so as to drip water directly onto the thermostat's electrical junction box on the balcony, it had shorted out the system.

The *teknítis*es went off and returned with a replacement thermostat and a bucket, which they balanced carefully on the corner of the furnace to catch the drips from the air conditioner. Problem solved. We now had heat.

But overnight another problem had become apparent: the toilet was leaking from the bottom of the plastic tank, causing water to pool around the base. Linda fixed this problem by sequestering a towel from our very limited supply to place on the floor as an absorbent mat.

Simple teething troubles. Spýros would fix things, I was sure.

I trotted down to the village and brought back a couple of croissants and cappuccinos. We compiled a to-do list: buy a stove and fridge, get our tax numbers, get a phone line, buy food; borrow plates, spoons, and knives, and perhaps a pot or two to see us through until our belongings arrived.

An hour or so later we strolled down to the Internet café to check email and post a blog entry only to find it had just closed for a week's holiday.

Well, we had plenty of other things to do, such as getting our *afimís*, or tax numbers. Back along the *paralía*, I managed to locate Chrýsa the accountant's office, but the door was locked. We tried to call from a nearby phone booth; no recording, no reply.

We went off to find OTÉ, the public phone company.

The OTÉ office in the center of the village was undoubtedly the most neglected building in Skópelos not actually in ruins or housing goats. The cramped interior was cluttered with stacks of phone directories; along one wall were three ancient *cabines*, leftovers from the days when home phones were a rarity.

The bleached blonde behind the counter was clearly annoyed at having to deal with customers. We smiled and did our best to outline our needs, a simple phone and a DSL Internet connection.

I didn't understand most of the reply, except that the phone line would 'only' take a week or ten days. The DSL was another issue; they were all out of modems and lines, and it would take at least five weeks. *Maybe.* And there seemed to be some complicated procedure to actually qualify for DSL, but our Greek was insufficient to illuminate details. I whined and grumbled.

We signed several forms we couldn't read a word of, and promised to supply our *afimí* as soon as we had one. The blonde clerk scowled, took down my passport number, and proceeded to stamp and countersign both sides of every single form.

After a little shopping for essentials, we located the appliance store. The owner, Sotíris Manólis (every third person in Skópelos seemed to be a Manólis), was a short, grizzled balloon of a man so round you'd think he'd been hooked up to an air hose for an hour or so. Picture the Michelin Man without his glasses but with plenty of excited hand gestures and a perennial gray stubble.

Sotíris showed us a number of stoves and fridges. Nothing was priced. Could he deliver today? Certainly. Great! We opted for a low-end Greek fridge and a high-quality stove with ceramic cooktop and convection oven complete with rotisserie. We added an electric teakettle, and Sotíris gleefully rang up a thousand Euros even. Ouch! We'd only budgeted for a kettle.

SINCE WE'D DETERMINED to make a solid effort to speak Greek, I seized every opportunity to greet passing strangers with a smile and a *yássas!* (hello) or *kaliméra!* (good day).

"You know," said Linda, after I'd greeted an old woman as we walked by her house, "people are going to think you're weird."

"Why? I'm just being friendly and polite."

"Actually, you're confirming what everyone says about the British: that you're excessively, even intrusively, polite."

I was taken aback. "How can you be excessively polite?"

"Well, peering through open windows and saying hello to people in their houses is carrying it a little far, don't you think?"

Umm. The old woman I'd just *kaliméra*-ed inside her house did seem a little startled. "Okay, you may have a point. But given that we'll always be considered foreigners here, I think we should at least try for the title of 'Least Disliked Foreigners'. Besides, it's good language practice."

At six p.m., Michelin Man's tiny van pulled up and a couple of skinny Albanians manhandled our new fridge and stove into the tiny kitchen, scurrying off before I had a chance to even tip them.

A fridge! A stove! We thought we were in heaven but quickly discovered we were in Greece: the fridge didn't work, and the stove needed wiring directly into a wall outlet. I could do this. But when I removed the plastic cover in the wall, I discovered that the three wires within were colored entirely differently to the wires hanging from the back of the stove.

Reluctant to die and/or plunge the village into darkness on our first day, I trudged down the hill again in the freezing cold to the appliance store. Sotíris wasn't around, but his wife Eléni promised to get a *teknítis* there first thing in the morning to look at the fridge, as well as an electrician to connect the stove.

I called Spýros from the phone box to let him know that our toilet *káni neró* (makes water), the best Greek I could manage for a leak. Not to worry: he would get an *idravlikós* (plumber) to come in the morning.

At this rate, we were going to have quite a crowd for breakfast.

The good news was that we had a working teakettle. For dinner, Linda—inspired as ever—poured boiling water from the teakettle over some eggs, then sliced cheese and salami and several hunks of bread. We drank a bottle of wine. We were happy! Life was good! We laughed aloud and repeated the well-known Greek mantra, *sigá, sigá*—slowly, slowly.

Even in those first days on Skópelos, all of the elements that would later turn our dream into a nightmare were, in hindsight, discernible. But Greece's Medusa of institutionalized inefficiency and corruption was still far from touching on critical areas. It was, in those first weeks just taking our measure, toying with us.

A Fridge too Far

JET LAG IS a terrible ill.

Even after breaking our journey with a couple of days in London and Athens, we woke at three a.m., wide-eyed as movie vampires in their coffins. We chatted, we read… and sleep eventually arrived around dawn. But no lying around, as the appliance-*teknítis*, as well as the plumber and electrician, would be coming early. I dressed and crept from the bedroom, hoping Linda would be able to sleep through it.

The first fellow to arrive spoke some sort of dialect. I could hardly understand a word he said, so I showed him the leaky toilet. He looked offended, but brightened up when I introduced him to the broken refrigerator.

After a few moments squeezed between the back of the fridge and the wall—our kitchen really was very small—he pronounced the fridge irrevocably dead; apparently problems were common with new appliances on the islands, as they suffered many hardships en route from the parent factories in Munich or Milan.

But the appliance-*teknítis* was not done yet: he seemed to have heard about the dripping air-conditioner, and asked to be taken to it. One truly lavish application of silicone sealant to the air conditioner slobber pipe, and our drip bucket was freed up for other duties.

Shortly thereafter, the electrician arrived to hook up the stove. Sávas was clearly a professional, and quickly connected the three wires to the three other wires with skill and dexterity. He was also full of questions—where were we from? Why had we come to Skópelos? I had lots of answers, but language was a problem for both of us.

Cut to an hour later.

The electrician is gone. Linda emerges from the bedroom, looking worried. "Oooh," she moans. "Jesus Christ! I'm dreaming in flippin' French now. Seriously, I just dreamed a whole conversation in French!"

"Um, yeah. I was talking to the electrician—"

"No, no! I swear I just dreamed a whole conversation in *French!*"

"Sávas speaks French."

"Who's Sávas?"

"The electrician. He was just here. It was easier than speaking Greek."

Linda stared at me.

"*Lingua Franca,*" I explained. "He asked me if I spoke French, and since he did…" I spread my palms.

She slumped back against the wall. "Oh, is that all? Thank God! I thought I'd slipped into another universe, or maybe a Neil Gaiman story."

I switched on the kettle. "Let me make you coffee, dear, and all will be well."

The plumber didn't show and the toilet kept leaking. But it was a gorgeous, sun-drenched day, and the biting wind had dropped to a whisper. We cooked breakfast on our new stove and enjoyed our first proper meal sitting on the cold marble tile in our empty dining room.

Bath time proved a trial: there were only about three or four gallons of hot water before it turned lukewarm. It took ten minutes or so to heat the next few gallons, and so on. Aided by boiling water dumps from our electric kettle, we both managed to bathe in less than three hours. I grumbled; Linda was philosophical.

I could see another *teknítis* in our future.

At the appliance store, we received a promise that the Albanian delivery men would be by this evening with a new fridge. Good news. But Chrýsa, with whom we needed to meet to obtain the all-important *afimí*, was still away, her office mysteriously closed. Plague, perhaps, or a mer-people abduction case. We would ask Spýros if he could recommend someone else.

THE SUPERIORITY OF Greek civilization is perhaps most evident in the custom of the afternoon break. Shops and businesses close at two or two-thirty and don't reopen until six. The intervening hours are considered private or family time, and even if you don't nap you can relax in the knowledge that nobody will call or come to your door. Since Linda and I are partial to naps, we decided to immediately adopt this civilized custom[3].

At six p.m. the two Albanians arrived, cheerfully greeting me as "Italiano, Italiano!" Nodding and smiling, they carted off the ailing fridge, manhandled in a new one in its factory packing, and melted back into the night.

A few moments later I removed the packing only to discover that fridge number two had a badly crushed upper corner. I stormed down to the appliance store, where I found more than enough Greek to express my displeasure to a pained-looking Michelin Man. He promised to order a new one from Vólos on the mainland, and we would certainly have it within a day or two.

A moment after I got home the two Albanians returned, chanting "Italiano, Italiano!" They removed fridge number two, leaving me with a profound sense of *dejá vu*. Our groceries would have to spend another night on the cold kitchen balcony.

ANOTHER NIGHT OF waking at 3 a.m. Besides the jet lag, we were working so intensely at the language in the daytime that our minds were keeping us awake with an endless stream of internal Greek practice chatter. And when we did sleep, we dreamt we were speaking in Greek. "In my head," said Linda over coffee, "my Greek is really good!"

---

[3] Recent research has proved that taking afternoon naps significantly lowers your risk of heart disease, and I highly recommend them to all readers. Your employer will understand.

The heating *teknítis*/bucket brigade pair from Nikoláos A. Káltzas arrived far too early, accompanied by Spýros, our landlord. He explained the hot water problem to them. He also showed them the leaky toilet, but they couldn't seem to work up any enthusiasm for so humble a task.

The repairmen went out onto the balcony to look at the furnace. Spýros excused himself. *"Douliá, douliá, Dario. Katálava?"* Work, work, Dario. Do you understand? I did. Spýros, I was soon to discover, was a very busy man. By day, he worked for the *dimarhío*, or town hall, as foreman of a road repair and public works crew. We'd see him several times a day zooming back and forth from work to his house on his Honda moped, or passing extended periods in his gloomy little storeroom next door to us. In the evenings, he'd work late on the building adjacent to ours, where he was deep into the demolition phase of what was to be a remodel of the upper flat. In addition, he and Mára had the rental cottages, and, on the other side of the island, their *kalívi* (country cottage) with its little menagerie of farm animals to take care of.

On my previous trip, when Spýros was explaining how busy his life was, I'd asked if he had a hobby. He thought for a moment, then broke into a dreamy smile. "Seeps," he said.

"*Seeps?*" I got out the dictionary, and we squinted at the tiny print until he found the Greek word—*próvata*.

"Oh," I said, "sheep!"

Spýros beamed. "Seeps," he agreed.

The *teknítis*es had bad news. The furnace couldn't supply continuous hot water. If, however, they hooked up the tank to the electric supply, that would give us enough for a good bath.

They did, and it didn't—once they'd left and we tried to draw a bath, we discovered it was just as bad as before. I gnashed my teeth. Linda laughed and put the kettle on.

I called the shipping agency in Piraéus, the port of Athens, to find out when our belongings were due to arrive. The date they had been given, November 25th, was a week after the original estimate. The timing was going to be tricky, and I'd probably have to spend a couple of days in Piraéus so as to oversee clearance and pickup as soon as the container arrived. Port storage charges, they cautioned me, were a hundred Euros a day.

Time, then, to call Andréas the trucker and put him on standby. Coordinating all this worried me: while you can't rush customs officials, I would have to let Andréas know in advance when the container would be available for offloading.

We still needed to get our *afimís*. Mára referred us to another accountant, Kléa, and later that day we met her and her husband, Pávlos. Their office was directly below the Doctor's, whom I had met on a previous trip, and above the little Próton supermarket, which we judged the best in town. This building was destined to become a nexus of operations for us over the coming months.

Pávlos and Kléa were sweet and young and charming, and Pávlos spoke moderately good English. In between chat about the many, many words Greek has contributed to the English language, Pávlos took down all our details and promised they'd have our *afimís* in twenty-four hours. Fantastic!

We walked to the post office to inquire about the airmail package we'd mailed on our last day in the US, items we couldn't fit into our suitcases. There were also four boxes coming by surface mail, but we knew not to expect them until early January.

As is so often the case in Greece, the clerk sitting under the 'no smoking' sign was puffing away at a cigarette as he scowled at customers. You had to love the spirit of these people.

There was no package. When I explained we'd mailed it nine days ago, he shook his head impatiently. Greek customs, he assured me, typically held packages up to a month. *Sigá, sigá:* slowly, slowly.

At the cellphone shop on the next corner we bought a basic cellphone, the prepaid kind which you charge up with a card. It would do fine. The young woman who sold it to us explained the basics, and I thought we had the hang of it.

We strolled along the harbor enjoying the unseasonably warm day, and Linda called her daughter and grandson in Albuquerque from a payphone. I took pictures.

Despite the beautiful weather and having little to worry about, I managed to do exactly that—worry. We'd already had so many hassles with appliances and basic set-up that I was finding it hard to relax. I was impatient, anxious. We had no phone or email. I aired my anxieties to Linda as we sat cross-legged that afternoon on our cold dining room floor.

"We've only been here three days," she reminded me, "and we have heat, hot water, and a stove. Our tax number is on its way. I think that's pretty good."

"I know, but there's so much to do!"

She was quiet a moment. "One of the reasons we came was because time moves at a different rate here. Maybe we should not stress so much, and just enjoy the process instead?"

She was, of course, right. I made a silent little mantra of this truth and hoped it would percolate into my subconscious.

As we were preparing dinner, Pávlos, the accountant's husband, called with good news: our tax numbers ready to collect. Now we'd *really* be able to do stuff, like get phone service, and open a bank account. I even dared to hope we might have a working fridge soon.

OUR AIRMAIL PACKAGE arrived the next day. At the post office, the perpetually irritable clerk who smoked under the 'no smoking' sign made me sign a form and rubber-stamped it. Greek clerks and officials love their rubber stamps, and stamp everything they can, often several times and on both sides of the paper, before further validating every stamp by signing or at least initialing it.

He handed me the parcel with a scowl. "*Írthe grígora*," he grumbled: it came quickly. It seemed rapid arrival of packages was something to be frowned upon, the breaking of a tradition. I thanked him profusely; he scowled.

"What a misery-guts," I said to Linda. "I'm going to name him 'Doom'."

Back home, we rejoiced as we unpacked the box. Inside were Linda's new running shoes and our portable workout equipment, consisting of a jump rope, a stretch band with handles, and the star piece which Linda had found online, a pair of plastic dumbbells with removable weights which could be filled with water.

We were rapidly running out of clean clothes, and we didn't have a washing machine. We knew we'd have to buy one, but were in shock from having to shell out a thousand Euros for the stove and fridge. As a firm believer in the health and psychological benefits of physical labor, I therefore decided to do laundry the old-fashioned way, in the bathtub. There were clotheslines on our balcony and up on the roof terrace. A good breeze was a fact of life on these islands, and the *mílos's* location had been chosen for its exposure. Drying clothes would be no problem.

It took a half-hour or so of kneeling on the marble floor to get the wash done. Wringing out jeans and sheets by hand proved particularly wretched, and each session of linen- or denim-wrassling left me with stiff, claw-like hands, bruised knees, and a spine deeply reluctant to return to its natural shape. But I wasn't about to shirk a task which women the world over had stoically endured since the dawn of civilization. It would be character-building.

NOW WE'D GOT the basics sorted out and begun to sleep properly, we decided to take an afternoon hike and explore a bit. Our house was right on the edge of town, and once past the furniture store on the corner and left up the narrow, cobbled road that passed the cemetery, we were in open country. Olive, fig and plum trees lined the winding lane and wild oregano sprouted from hedges and rock walls. Donkeys flicked their ears at us as we passed; chickens clucked and hurried away; shaggy goats the size of ponies stared balefully from stinky pens.

Skópelos has a lot of topography—i.e., hills—and the day was warm. Cobbles yielded to a rutted, stony track, and the way grew winding and steep. We were soon breathless and sweating, and wished we'd thought to bring water.

But the views! From every bend the panorama of hills, village, and harbor, with the island of Alónissos beyond, grew more dramatic, a serene harmony of white, green, and diamond-flecked blue to the horizon.

"My God!" said Linda, as we stopped to catch our breath. "It's so incredibly beautiful! I can't believe we get to live here."

My heart felt suddenly full. It had been worth everything. "We made it. We're so fortunate."

She gazed out to sea, drinking in the view, the feeling, the moment. "We are. We really are."

After about an hour we reached a level, paved road and a tiny, one-roomed church, its walls inset with decorative white and blue dishes, the low-walled garden immaculate. We paused to rest and soak in the calm.

Our tiny island boasted over three hundred and fifty assorted places of worship, ranging from good-sized monasteries to tiny chapels as small as our kitchen. Each of these was dedicated to a particular saint and many, on their saint's day, were opened to the public, with an orthodox priest conducting a ceremony. Saints' days were very important in Greek

Orthodoxy, with every saint assigned his or her own day of the year. As a consequence, several saints had to share, since there were more of them than days on the calendar.

Back at home that evening, I heard the now-familiar cry of "Italiano, Italiano!" from down in the street. The Albanians, delivering another new fridge. To our great relief, this one worked, and we took delight in transferring our food from the balcony into its cool, humming belly.

This was an occasion to celebrate! In a dizzy transport of joy, I bounded up to the roof terrace and liberated one of the little plastic tables I'd seen tucked away in a covered alcove. Some years previously, Spýros had briefly operated a cafeteria on the terrace, and all the old equipment was still cached in little nooks and corners of the building. He would not mind.

An hour or so later, we enjoyed our first meal at a table in our new home. Sitting at a table was something we'd always taken for granted, but just a few days of eating on the floor made this simple event seem a major step forward. The first caveman to explore the arresting notion of eating his woolly mammoth steak sitting on a conveniently-sized rock rather than on a dirty cave floor must have felt a similar sense of revelation.

After dinner we took a walk into town. The night air was biting, the narrow streets mostly empty. About three-quarters of the way to the *paralía*, Linda lost her footing on the slick paving stones, landing hard, but upright, on one knee.

I helped her up. "Are you okay?"

She leaned on me, rubbing her knee. "Hurts. Slipped on the stone."

"Do you want to go back? Ah, shit. We don't even have an icepack in the freezer yet."

Linda flexed the knee, lowered her foot to the ground. I held her elbow while she took a few steps. "No, it'll be okay. Probably better to move it a little."

"We can get some liquid anesthesia at the Karávia bar."

"That'll help," she said, with a strained little smile, and I held her hand as we carried on down the street. I could tell she was in a lot of pain. We'd only been here a couple of days, and an injured knee in a place where we'd be walking everywhere was the last thing either of us needed.

Our Social Début

SATURDAY MORNING I went grocery shopping. Linda and I have many complementary qualities: she hates shopping and enjoys cleaning, whereas I am the exact opposite.

We were still building up our stock of basic necessities, and I'd taken to shopping daily, and sometimes more if there were heavy items like wine or fruit to carry. I enjoyed the walks, and these trips also provided extra opportunities for meeting the locals.

Fruit and produce availablility on the islands is strictly seasonal and much of the food is grown, if not locally, at least regionally. So although we missed tomatoes throughout the winter, the reward came in the form of winter greens, fresh and bursting with flavor. Yes, the produce required substantial cleaning, as I discovered on rinsing half a cup of sand from a bunch of spinach; but I'd settle for fresh over tasteless anytime.

A little later, we walked down into town together. Linda's knee was stiff and sore, and we took it slowly. We were surprised at just how many shops and tavernas were open year round; the village in the winter was less sleepy than we'd expected.

The darn Internet café was still closed, but we saw one of the owners inside, and she assured us they would reopen on Monday.

We crossed the street to the cellphone store to ask for help with enabling the English-language menu on our phone. Behind the counter was a solidly-built, friendly-looking man wreathed in cigarette smoke. "*Miláte Angliká?*" I said. Do you speak English?

He nodded, and I breathed a sigh of relief. I explained, in slow, precise tones, what we needed.

"No problem." He held out his hand for the phone. "It's very simple. Let me show you how to do it."

I handed it over. "Oh! Your English is very good."

"So is yours," he said, with a straight face. Linda and I cracked up.

We had met Vasílis. Both Linda and I liked him straight away, and he was the best English speaker we'd met so far on the island. I had a feeling we'd be seeing him again.

THAT EVENING, A week after our arrival, we had our first social engagement.

I had gotten to know the local doctor (the *private* doctor, as distinct from the doctor who worked at the Kéntro Igeías, or public health center) during our previous visit to the island, when I'd developed an excruciating sore throat and had taken myself to his office for treatment. Doctor Yiánnis, a trim, clean-cut young Athenian, had studied in Belgium and spoke good English. He couldn't do anything for my throat, but did, in the process of clearing a build-up of ear wax, manage to render me entirely deaf in one ear for 48 hours. In spite of this, I liked the fellow, so I contacted him a few days after we arrived.

We met for drinks and *mezés* (snacks) at 10 p.m.[4] at the *Ouzería Gorgónes* (Mermaid Bar), a cozy backstreet bar which, along with one or two other places, was staying open through the winter on an experimental basis.

Mina, Yiánnis's petite German wife, was a true sweetheart. They'd met at university in Liège and had fallen in love. They had two boys aged six and eight. After Yiánnis completed his internship at an Athens hospital, the family moved first to Alónissos, and then to Skópelos, where they decided to put down roots. "I have no stress here," Yiánnis told me. "It is a good life."

Mina and Linda ordered *tsípouro*, a fiery, 100-proof distillate with only a faint anise flavor; Yiánnis and I drank *retsína*. Two friends of Yiánnis's occupied a nearby table, and we traded rounds.

The traditional Greek *tsipourádikos* and *ouzerías* (*tsípouro* and *oúzo* joints, though the terms are somewhat interchangeable) serve their shots in sealed 50ml. miniatures, which makes billing easy for the server—at the end of the evening they just count the bottles on the table; it also gives the customers a growing array of decorative little empties to play with. *Retsína*, on the other hand, is sold by weight rather than volume, and served chilled in a cheap aluminum jug. After a little while, ordering wine by the half-kilo seems normal.

Greeks, like other southern Europeans, are wiser in their drinking habits than the English-speaking nations, in that drink is never served without food. With every round of drinks we were brought a selection of different, strongly-flavored *mezés*: vegetable and *kalamári* dishes, spicy sausage stews, or small broiled fish. Linda, who will try just about

---

[4] Greeks dine late year round, which takes some getting used to for anyone accustomed to American hours.

anything once, later admitted to not having been thrilled by the little carbonized fish which are eaten whole, head and all.

"So, Dario," said Yiánnis, "I googled you and I see you are a writer."

I smiled. My stories and even some reviews come up on web searches. "Yes. I write science fiction."

His eyebrows went up, but whether in pity or awe, I couldn't tell. "My uncle was a writer. He was quite famous in Greece."

"Do you read a lot?"

Yiánnis's chin went up in the traditional 'no' gesture.

Mina laughed. "Greeks listen to the television. It is never quiet in a Greek house. But Yiánnis… um… he *admires* writers, perhaps because of his uncle."

Yiánnis's cellphone rang. I heard the words *sto kreváti*—to bed—and guessed the children were calling to ask if they could stay up a little later.

"Do you have a babysitter?" asked Linda.

"Ehh, no." Yiánnis shrugged, a mannerism which was to become very familiar to us. "Skópelos is a safe place, there is no crime. We have our cellphone if there is a problem, but they are good boys. They will stay up a little later than we tell them, and then go to bed."

All Greeks are intensely political, especially the younger ones raised in the days of the dictatorship. So after the third drink, the talk turned inevitably to politics. Yiánnis explained he'd stood for the city council in the election a month previously and lost by just four votes. "I was so upset I did not sleep for a week!"

"His father was worse," Mina added. "He was so depressed he did not get out of bed for a month!"

I shook my head in wonder. I couldn't fathom caring so much about something so trivial. I'm a cynic where politics is concerned.

Yiánnis upped the ante, launching into a tirade against George Bush, American foreign policy, and (Linda and I had by now adopted 'brace position') the ongoing war in Iraq in particular. To underscore his point, he declared, "I am happy when I read that another American soldier has been killed," wagging a finger for emphasis. "I am *happy!*"

We'd been prepared for strong anti-war feelings in Europe, but here was a clear case of cognitive dissonance: a medical doctor—and a good man, to all appearances—rejoicing at the death of someone's son or husband. What he really meant was that the US deserved what it got for starting the conflict, but the passion behind his words took me aback.

"You know," said Linda, with admirable poise, "barely a third of the American electorate voted for Bush; I didn't, and most people I know didn't. But when only sixty percent of those eligible actually go to the polls, thirty percent of the electorate can swing an election. There are tens of millions of Americans who'd agree with you, and who oppose this war."

Yiánnis—who'd been hoping for some pushback and a more robust political exchange—looked puzzled, even deflated. I raised my glass and we toasted the downfall of Bush and his cronies.

I once read a very good bit of advice about drinking: that you should stop when you're absolutely certain you can handle one more drink, but aren't sure what the second might do. We were right on that line when we stepped out into the freezing night, a little after one a.m. Yiánnis and Mina were talking about going to a club, but we didn't have the steam left. We hugged our new friends, tottered up the hill, and fell into bed.

ON SUNDAY WE didn't do much of anything. The stores were all closed, and the custom of the afternoon nap seemed even more sensible after a night out. Bed called, and we listened.

That evening, we strolled down to one of the two pizzerias at the bottom of the ring road. The quiet in the air on a winter Sunday night was palpable.

"So," said Linda, as we dug into the indifferent, but comforting, pizza, "how are we going to stop the rumors?"

"The rumors?"

"About you shopping."

"Oh!" Last night at the *ouzería*, Yiánnis, with a mischievous twinkle in his eyes, had revealed there was already talk in town about 'the new American woman who sends her husband shopping two or three times every day'. Our faces must have been comical; Yiánnis looked delighted. "It is a very small village," he said, wagging a finger in triumph, "and I know *everything*!"

This wasn't at all the reputation we wanted, so over dinner we hatched a plan: for the whole of the next week, Linda would be the one to do all the shopping, at least once a day, and I would keep a low profile in town. If people were determined to talk, we might as well have a little fun with them.

WE WERE ENJOYING a few days without the endless stream of *teknítises*, but the toilet still leaked. And the bathing situation had not improved: taking a hot bath involved advance planning and much sophisticated manipulation of switches and faucets. Now we'd discovered that while heating bathwater we couldn't turn on the electric kettle or the stove without popping a breaker.

All the same, we loved our little house. But not having furniture beyond a bed, a plastic table, and two chairs was getting old. We longed for our things to arrive. We took walks, explored, and read a lot. We practiced our Greek on one another. Sometimes we sang, just to fill the silence. Linda tried to learn to whistle.

I CALLED THE shipping agent at Piraéus to get an update on our shipment, due to arrive any day now. She informed me that the stevedores had gone on strike at the port, and that nobody knew when any goods might be unloaded.

Fortunately I have low blood pressure, but this news, on top of the already tricky logistics of coordinating things with Andréas, made me want to strangle chickens. To make things worse, we discovered that storage charges incurred by delays or strikes at the docks are always billed to the customer. Aris Export, our shippers, confirmed this was an international rule.

Linda remained sanguine as ever; I was stressing out. With my adrenal glands pouring fight-or-flight hormones into my system by the quart, I was getting a bare couple of hours' sleep a night. And the location of our house didn't help my insomnia. It took weeks to become inured to the type and level of street noise that made its way through the single-glazed windows of our cozy apartment.

But, noise? In a small Greek village? Well, yes, especially living on a sharp bend in the ring road. Not 24/7, or even 8 to 5, noise, not in winter—in fact, throughout much of the day it was very quiet, with only light traffic. But early mornings were accompanied by a predictable sequence of hard-to-ignore sounds.

First on the daily cacophony rota was the crowing rooster a block or so distant (the notion that roosters crow at dawn is a fiction: these pea-brained and ridiculous-looking bags of feathers start their horrid screeching two or three hours before any glimmer of light).

Around six a.m. a few Albanian laborers would congregate on the corner opposite our bedroom, smoking and talking in loud voices while they waited to be picked up for work.

Next, a horse or two would clippety-clop past, stately and loud in the twilight, a charming, old-world prelude to the headline act, the unique and extraordinary *Psária Fréska* Man.

This star attraction came between seven-thirty and eight each morning. A pickup truck laden with crates of fish fresh from the night's catch would stop right below our window; and the driver's words, "*PSÁRIA FRÉSKA! PSÁRIA FRÉSKA!!*" (FRESH FISH! FRESH FISH!!), would blare loud and tinny from the loudspeaker mounted on top, over and over, in tones of dire, caffeine-fuelled urgency which would better have been reserved for a warning of spreading fire, or Turkish invasion. It was even worse on days when this crazed and malevolent disturber of the peace was inspired to fuller descriptions of his piscine product. On such occasions, he would shout entire sentences: "Red snapper! Squid! Crab! I have many different fish! All kinds of different fish for soup!!" for whole minutes at a time.

Then there were the motorcycles—if these shrieking, kiddie two-strokes from hell could be called that—which, doubtless in keeping with historic tradition, appeared to not be allowed to use mufflers. Their riders, all apprentice delinquents, would drop a gear on the bend just under our window and then accelerate up the hill, pulling wheelies whenever the road was dry enough.

Amazingly, we soon became accustomed to all this: after our first few nights, Linda often slept right through it all, and—if I could ever stop worrying about our shipment—I didn't doubt I would, too. The body and mind would eventually adapt to our new environment, striking stevedores and deranged mobile fishmongers notwithstanding.

Outside, the weather remained dry, although the gorgeous sunshine of our first week had given way to clouds and overcast. The toilet still leaked, and I began to feel nostalgia for those first, dizzy days when a new *teknítis* would rouse us every morning.

LINDA WAS GETTING the hang of our new stove and decided to roast a chicken for Thanksgiving, especially since we now had use of a tinfoil container left over from Sunday night's pizza as well as two small

Tupperware bowls, all extremely welcome additions to our kitchen equipment[5].

From the Aegean Dream blog:

Turkey Day
Monday, November 27th, 2006

Linda speaks

Today is Thanksgiving...my favorite holiday. There are no presents to buy, no Christmas angst. Just good food, time with family and friends, two days off in a row and an opportunity to give thanks. I LOVE this holiday. Only a few minor snags this year. It is quite possible that I am the only *Amerikanída* on the island. Even my husband, being a Brit, is not of my people. Family and friends are a bit out of reach. I don't NEED a day off. I have two plates, two forks, two spoons and two pots. A bit of a Noah's Ark type of kitchen.

But in true American fashion we WILL have Thanksgiving dinner.

We shop for food. We buy a chicken. The butcher, in Greek, asks if I want the whole chicken. Yes, I say. He appears a bit perplexed by my answer and asks again. Yes, I repeat, and I have the chicken. I am anxious to try out my new rotisserie, which came with my fabulously working new oven! What I haven't quite understood is how WHOLE the chicken is. At least it has been plucked.

My menu is complete. Roasted chicken, Oúzo, stuffing, Oúzo, mashed potatoes, Oúzo, fruit salad, Oúzo. *Oréo!* (Great!) I cook... (cut to the Roger Miller tunes playing in my head) ...'I ain't got no...' (insert everything here)

---

[5] Anyone who essays living with two cups, two plates, two sets of cutlery, and two saucepans for ten days is welcome to write in and tell us how many Cordon Bleu meals they can whip together.

As most of you know, I love to cook and pride myself on setting a good table. Now for my secret recipe tips!

Chicken. Always ask the butcher to clean chicken.

Stuffing. Take days old bread, add an egg, minced onion, whatever seasoning you find in the store (even if you can't decipher the label), and mix together in the used, flimsy, aluminum pan that you have been saving for just this type of occasion since your take-away pizza last week.

Mashed Potatoes. Put potatoes in water, boil. Take one of your two forks and mash them. An arduous task to be sure, but just imagine…what did we do before there were forks? Note: Wash fork for use at plastic dinner table, borrowed without permission, at meal time.

Fruit Salad. Get three oranges grown by your landlady, peel and cut up with other fruits you have found in the store. In the past I have whipped cream with nutmeg, cinnamon, etc. but found that a can of spray whipping cream works just as well and provides levity in trying circumstances.

Pray. That the power doesn't go out during the enormous thunder and lightning storm that has encompassed the island.

I LOVE my rotisserie oven!!

Cut to dinner. It actually tastes wonderful. We are well and happy, and anyway we wanted less stuff in our lives. We just didn't know how literally the Greek gods would take our pleas.

Trot down to the Internet café. Call loved ones. Call it a good day. A day to be thankful.

Linda

ON FRIDAY I made some calls and found that the ship carrying our belongings had just docked at Piraéus. Nobody had a clue when it would be unloaded.

I called the customs broker recommended by the shipping agent. Incredibly, considering he specialized in clearing shipments of personal effects, Mr. Economídes didn't speak a single word of English. I spent a couple of hours on the phone, alternately calling Mr. Economídes and the shipping agent and trying to make preliminary arrangements.

The shipping agent warned me the strike was getting worse, with other trades joining in. In the last week some ships hadn't been unloaded at all. It was possible the port would soon be at a complete standstill, and was I aware that storage fees are always the responsibility of the customer? I began to sweat.

Nor could I get a hard number on the cost of customs clearance. Figures varied wildly, creeping up with each call. Four hundred Euros. Six hundred. Perhaps seven hundred. You will bring cash, yes?

In the US, customs clearance of personal belongings is something of a formality. Customs broker's fees run in the region of two hundred dollars in most cases, and the broker doesn't need the customer to be present: forms can be signed and just mailed or couriered to the broker. Not so in Greece. I would need to travel to Piraéus and be present when the container was unsealed by customs.

I made a call to Andréas, the trucker. He was clearly regretting the deal and started trying to weasel out of it. With December approaching, he was slammed. He wouldn't make any promises about when he could get to Piraéus, especially if we couldn't supply a firm date.

This was making me crazy. Everything was vague, language was a huge obstacle, and nobody seemed to be on our side. We had no option but to wait until we got word the container would be unloaded, and then hope Andréas would cooperate.

With the mounting stress, an empty house, and no supportive group of friends in a strange town, Linda and I found new and creative ways to stay sane. The weather was warming again, allowing us to explore both the village and the nearby countryside. We walked miles every day, and worked out with weights and our stretch bands. We bought two decks of cards and played Canasta in the evenings.

I began writing again, polishing up some old, stuck stories. I fretted about our shipment. Linda started keeping an occasional journal.

That weekend we rented a car. It was time to explore, and the activity would provide a welcome distraction.

On the Saturday we packed a picnic, put on warm clothes, and drove across the island to visit the small harbor at Agnóndas. The tavernas lining the narrow pebble beach were closed for the winter, their windows covered with blue plastic sheeting against the winter storms. Fishing nets were draped over poles to air in the breeze.

We strolled along the quay where the ferry docks in times of rough weather, and marveled at the clarity of the water, even in winter. You could see every rock and pebble through fifteen feet of water, the vivid aqua dotted with the crisp black of sea urchins, the sharp-edged shadow of each boat rippling along the bottom.

We drove to Miliá, our favorite beach. A long crescent of sand surrounded by steep, pine-covered hills, with a small, green island a quarter of a mile out to sea, Miliá looks like a postcard from the Caribbean.

We hadn't reckoned on the cats.

Skópelos is overrun by thousands of feral cats. Through the winter, members of the British expat community drive around to various spots on the island where the strays hang out and put out food for them. They also run an animal charity on the island, and regularly have a vet visit to treat sick animals and spay or neuter as many of the rest as possible. The task is a hopeless one.

We noticed a couple of cats lolling by a dumpster as we arrived. The moment we got out of the car a dozen more appeared, adults and kittens of every color. They fanned out and advanced upon us.

There is something both creepy and a little intimidating about even the cutest domestic animals when a large number of them exhibit clear intent and purpose, and you happen to be their focus.

Linda eyed them nervously. "They want food."

"Yeah, we should have brought something. They're used to being fed." I pointed to the shiny steel bowl near the dumpster.

The cats had reached us. Some sat on their haunches and yowled, others circled us. They looked well-fed: the Brits were clearly doing a good job.

"We don't have anything for them," said Linda.

"Let's just walk down the beach. Maybe they'll give up."

But the cats followed us all the way to the far end of the beach, a good quarter of a mile, where we sat and picnicked, and we eventually left feeling a bit cheated of the relaxed outing we'd looked forward to.

That night we again went out with Yiánnis and Mina. We were joined this time by Yiánnis's friend, Láli Páppas, *aka* Lalíka, the real estate agent with whom I'd been in contact.

Lalíka was a restless bundle of enthusiasm. Owlish behind thick glasses, she talked nonstop and enthusiastically from the depths of her companion cloud of cigarette smoke. She was on the Skópelos city council, and politics were her passion. She and Yiánnis were the unlikeliest of allies: Yiánnis was a Conservative, Lalíka a Communist.

"We are of opposite parties, but we support the same man for mayor," Yiánnis explained. "And Lalíka is the only one on the council who does any work. All the others are very lazy."

One of Lalíka's current projects was choosing a new color with which to repaint all the wrought iron lampposts on the *paralía*; and Yiánnis—who I could see was trying to help me get started with my business—had suggested she solicit my input as a professional colorist. "I say to make them a dark green," said Yiánnis. "What do you think?"

I thought about it. Lalíka sipped her *retsína*, eyeing me intently across the table.

"Bronze," said Linda.

I liked the idea. "A *dark* bronze, not greenish. If we can get a metallic paint, all the better. They'll be unusual, and very attractive."

Lalíka nodded. "Very interesting," she said, puffing at her cigarette. "I think this will be very interesting. Yiánnis, what do you think? This is a good idea, I think. Yes, I think I will suggest this at the council."

I smiled. I'd gone from doing special finishes in fifteen million-dollar homes in Pebble Beach to assisting the Communist councilor of a tiny island with color selection for civic ironwork. I was clearly going places.

Lalíka left after an hour or so, and we adjourned to Ánemos, a hip little bar on the *paralía*. The place was busy and the music—mostly classic rock—was good, though loud enough that you could only talk to the person right next to you. Linda chatted with Yiánnis and I with Mina.

Mina talked of her experience adjusting to life on a small island. "Yiánnis changed when we came here. He has very strong ideas about how the wife of the private doctor should behave: 'you must do this, you must not do that.' We had many fights! But when I see how everybody talks, I see that he was right." She paused, then nodded, as though still trying to convince herself.

By two a.m., we were ready to go. Home was less than a ten-minute walk, but Yiánnis insisted on driving us back through the narrow, winding village streets, because he really, really, wanted to drive his new Audi. If you had a new Audi, or even an old one, you would *not* want to drive it through those mediaeval streets, trust me. There were spots so narrow he had to fold back the side mirrors.

Although we stayed clear of politics that evening, Linda wasn't sure whether she liked Yiánnis, and was becoming convinced he didn't like her. It wasn't just the anti-Americanism: our doctor friend was an intense and complicated man.

I believed Yiánnis had a more gentle and compassionate side, but I was forced to admit that pride and arrogance were part of the package with our young Athenian friend. I remembered a saying I'd heard Linda use more than once, that 'you should love your friends *because* of their faults, not *in spite* of them'. Yiánnis was going to prove a sore test of this one.

Satanic Practices

ON SUNDAY WE drove to the small monastery of Taxiárhes, near Glóssa, at the far end of the island. The monastery, set in a serene wood near the road, was small, well-kept, and empty. We finished up our picnic under the cypresses in the monastery garden and Linda rose to explore further. I stretched out on the bench, soaking in the peace and perfect composure of the place.

A few moments later, I heard a small scream, abruptly cut off. I leapt up and hurried around the building in the direction Linda had gone, shouting, "Linda! Are you okay?"

I found her in the deep shadows near the back corner of the church, standing utterly still.

"What is it?" I said, as I ran up to her. 'A snake?" Vipers are common on the islands.

Linda just pointed.

In front of us, a rusty metal gate hung half-open before a small, ivy-covered niche, almost a crypt, in the stonework. Inside, barely visible in the gloom, was a pile of long bones with three or four human skulls scattered among them. No bleached-white storybook or desert island remains these, but a crusty brown and very, very real.

Linda recovered her voice. "They have frickin' *skulls* in there!"

Despite the distinct chill crawling along my spine, I was fascinated. Whose remains were these? Monks who'd tended the church in the past? Why weren't they buried?

Where a moment ago this shaded corner of the garden had seemed a place of pastoral repose, the gloom was now charged with a palpable aura of disquiet. The bright Aegean day was gone, replaced by the shadow of the unquiet grave. Linda had already edged away; I turned and followed, seeking the sunlight. Let the dead rest.

Across a valley and over the hills we drove, to a place I'd seen in postcards and on the map, Ághios Yiánnis to Kastro (St. John's Castle), a small monastery perched high on a rocky crag overlooking the north coast[6].

We in the developed world are so removed from the reality of death that even so minor a thing as the sight of unburied human remains lingered in our psyches. But this was a day for sinister sightings. As we rounded a bend of the road by a ravine, we were startled to see three macabre figures in dramatic poses on the opposite hillside, standing beside a large, wooden cross—the moment in a horror movie when the pipe organ strikes a sudden, jangling discord!

"What the hell are *those?*" I said.

We both stared. After a moment, I realized I'd stopped dead in the middle of the road, and pulled over to the shoulder.

"What *are* they doing?" said Linda. "They're not moving."

The figures remained still, arms variously outstretched in attitudes of threat or power—it was hard to tell. One looked like a woman; another held something dark and blockish at its side.

"Scarecrows?" I ventured.

"Pretty weird scarecrows. They scared *me* though!"

I put the car in gear and drove slowly around the bend until we were below the figures. They *were* scarecrows, or perhaps just macabre effigies crafted in the same way. Two were dressed as men, one as a woman.

---

[6] Though we didn't know it then, Ághios Yiánnis would be the location of the wedding scene in the movie 'Mamma Mia!'

One of the male figures had a boombox balanced in the crook of its left arm, which only made it more disturbing.

What kind of place had we come to? Was our Aegean paradise a nexus of unwholesome, Satanic practices? Were our friendly island neighbors churchgoers by day and grave-robbers by night? I remembered the early 'seventies cult film, 'The Wicker Man', and shuddered.

THE HUGE ROCK under *Ághios Yiánnis to Kástro* leaned over the sea, connected to the beach by a short causeway. A winding stair flanked by a welded steel rail snaked up the crag to the monastery some hundred and fifty feet above, promising dizzy views of the crashing waves below.

Linda, who is less than comfortable with heights and steep drops, stood on the causeway, assessing the climb.

"What do you think?" I asked. "Are you going to be okay?"

She made a 'maybe' face. "I want to see it. Go ahead, let me follow you."

We took the climb slowly, and before long emerged onto the edge of the monastery's terrace through a narrow doorway in the wall. Ancient olive trees grew in the small, immaculately-kept yard. We walked the low perimeter wall, drinking in the views up and down the island's north coast and away to Alónissos in the east.

The monastery itself was closed, its door scarred by deep-carved and painted-over graffiti ranging back half a century. One, from an unlikely American traveler to this remote place in the days before mass tourism, read, CHAS A DENNERY—GEORGIA—1956.

I felt for Linda on the descent. There was no way to avoid the dizzying view down to the churning waters: everything was in motion except the rock wall to our right. But she kept going, one hand against the rock wall and the other on the steel rail, until we reached the bottom. I was proud of her.

AFTER THREE WEEKS of washing clothes by hand we broke down and bought a *plintírio*, (washing machine). It would be an early—and major—Christmas present to ourselves.

The *plintírio* was an immediate hit with us, and not just for laundry. It provided us with a new and exciting leisure activity: we could now choose between watching clothes go round in the *plintírio* or chickens roasting in the rotisserie oven. It was better than television.

The weather had set fair and mild. There was a good breeze most days, and our washing dried quickly on the line, with an interesting, crunchy texture. We walked, napped, played cards, visited the Internet café.

After the rains at Thanksgiving, the tavernas had now stored all their outside seating and awnings, so we would occasionally repair to the warmth of Karávia, a cozy, modern café, for a cappuccino or an *oúzo*. We started to feel as though we belonged here, rather than just being visitors who dreamed of living in a Greek village. Skópelos was our home, and we fell deeper under its spell every day.

Wednesday began with our phone being finally installed, a milestone on the way to becoming real people again. We rejoiced, and tried it out by using our cellphone to call ourselves.

Yiánnis stopped by to say hello and pass judgment on our abode. In immaculate jeans, brown loafers, and a powder-blue cashmere cardigan, he looked tidy and oh-so-preppy. He glanced around, noting the French doors in the kitchen and the way the marble sill had been installed on the inside rather than the outside. "This is not right," he announced. "You will have water in your house when it rains."

We knew the house wasn't particularly well-built, but this comment irritated Linda. "He's so critical," she said after Yiánnis left. "He never has anything positive to say."

Don't rain on my parade is one of Linda's trademark sentiments, and I could see trouble brewing between these two.

In the Snake Pit

ON THE LAST Monday of November, the shipping agent warned us that the situation at the port was deteriorating. There were no guarantees the ship would be unloaded before the port came to a complete standstill. I prayed Andréas the trucker would come through, especially given the need for precise timing at short notice.

On Wednesday we heard the ship was being unloaded. I must come to the container port and meet Mr. Economídes for customs clearance at 8:30 Friday morning, and bring seven hundred Euros in cash. We should arrange to have everything picked up as soon as possible after that, on Monday, or at the very latest Tuesday, since a complete shutdown of the port now seemed certain.

I called Andréas; he was evasive. He would have to see, he would call back tomorrow. Terrific. Was he just positioning himself for a fee hike beyond the agreed one thousand Euros in return for a last-minute rescue?

And then out of the blue came a lucky break.

We'd met a sweet young woman, Rita, who worked in the furniture shop on the corner. She had a terrific personality and a fine command of English, and had told us to come to her if we needed help with anything.

At Linda's brilliant suggestion we took our woes to her and asked if she would act as our translator and go-between with Andréas. Should we offer him a hundred-Euro bonus? This pickup *had* to happen on time.

On a tiny island, coincidences occur with surprising frequency. When I gave Rita the trucker's name and phone number, her face lit up. "Oh, *that* Andréas! His wife is my best friend. I'll talk to her and explain your situation."

"Brilliant idea, sweetie," I said to Linda, as we left. "If the wife pressures him, I'm sure our pickup will become a priority."

"I hope so. The last thing we need is our stuff stuck in the port racking up fines of a hundred Euros a day."

Frayed from all these uncertainties, we took ourselves to the Karávia bar for an *oúzo*, followed a short while later by another. We don't usually drink in the mid-afternoon, and Greek shots can be generous. An hour later we left feeling considerably relaxed and rather more at peace with the world.

That evening, Andréas's wife called. She assured me Andréas would be at the docks on Monday to collect our shipment, having apparently bumped another client in our favor. This was fantastic news. I thanked her profusely and called Mr. Economídes, the customs broker, to confirm I would leave tomorrow and meet him at the port on Friday morning.

IT TAKES A minimum of six hours to cover the hundred miles from Skópelos to Athens, and that's the short way, via the port of Ághios Kostantínos. In the winter, the ferries alternate between that port and the more northerly mainland port of Vólos. The Thursday ferry was going to Vólos, which meant an eight-hour trip starting at four p.m.

I was travelling alone; there seemed little point in spending an extra hundred Euros just so that Linda could share what I suspected would be a fairly tedious ordeal. But I had my ebook reader with a fully-charged battery and plenty of reading material loaded on it, and the ferry was my favorite, the plush, roomy Skiáthos Express, with all of a couple of dozen people on board. I bought a coffee at the bar, made myself comfortable on one of the big, curved sectionals in the main lounge, and settled in for a long, peaceful read.

From the Aegean Dream blog:

The last 48 hours have been trying, the sheer amount of travelling and conveyances itself daunting: 2 four-hour bus rides, 2 four-hour ferry trips, 4 taxi journeys, and several miles on foot. That was the easy part.

So I meet the customs broker at Customs Area 5 at 8:30 am on Friday—this after arriving in nearby Piraéus at 2:30 a.m. and rising at 6. The port entry is jammed by a three-quarter mile column of trucks trying to get in to load. The stevedores have stepped up their strike and are only working a couple of hours a day.

I'm led into a dingy building and thence into a dingier hall. In the center is an oval table piled with satchels and briefcases, the still hub around which the customs brokers perform their dervish-like gyrations. The customs brokers are a shabby lot, some of them looking more like street people than businessmen; Linda and I are clearly lucky, as our man, Mr. Economídes, is both civil and presentable.

The perimeter of the room is made up of several counters—I later came to think of them as stations of the cross—where various stages of the arcane process of clearing goods through customs may be attempted. Large amounts of cash are being counted, bills exchanged. There are several 'no smoking' signs, which everybody—especially the staff—cheerfully ignores. We review my paperwork, I sign something. Mr. Economídes takes off at a brisk pace, beckoning me to follow. Ten minutes later we're in the vast, cathedral-like customs shed 5, which deals with US shipments. We meet several women, whom I quickly realize are customs agents. Mr. Economídes knows them all and is wholly at ease. He introduces me and they enthuse about Skópelos.

The customs agents' offices huddle miserably at one corner of the cathedral. We enter one, following one of the women. Her office is a six-by-eight windowless box with a steel desk and file cabinet. It's cold. I begin to understand why all the business is conducted in cash. We review the written inventory of our goods, which neither the customs agent or broker can understand a word of except for 'TV', 'DVD', and 'stereo'. I assure them we are not transporting any guns, alcohol, or cigarettes.

After some difficulty locating the container, we emerge into sparkling sunlight and stand before the big red box. The customs seal is broken and I open the padlock. Although I have a good idea this will be just a perfunctory inspection, I am a little uneasy as the customs lady enters the container and asks the greasy-haired, hulking brute she has summoned to open the first box she sees, which contains our mattress. When no illegal immigrants or bags of white powder are apparent, she pokes at the mattress and points to another box. Mongo slits it open to reveal packing chips. *"Plastikós,"* he grunts. They open another, and see lumpy things wrapped in paper inside. Satisfied, the customs woman says we can close up the container and go back to her office.

Around us, all movement has ceased as the stevedores return to their strike. Cranes are idle, ships loll at anchor. Mr. Economídes points to a nearby vessel and tells me it's been there more than a week waiting to be unloaded: we are very lucky.

We move to a shoddy table outside the customs office and fill forms. Someone makes us coffee. I sign more papers. We return to the oval table where the brokers hang out and Mr. Economídes tells me to wait. After a while he returns with more forms to sign. He takes off again. This process repeats several times, with Mr. Economídes being gone the best part of an hour at one point. Eventually, everything is done. I hand over a truly outrageous amount of cash, for which I'm shown a number of official-looking forms and scribbled figures. Of course, it's impossible to determine which amounts are actually going where, and I suspect a good half of our money is lubricating the innumerable gears behind the bureaucracy which could so easily grind to a halt, stranding us in the hell of port storage fees.

Four hours have passed, and Mr. Economídes still has an hour of filing to do, but I am free to leave. He offers to drive me out of the container terminal, but we find that the gates have been blockaded by two big rigs operated by port union workers sympathetic to the stevedores. I set out on foot and walk perhaps three miles before finding a taxi that will take me back to Athens and the start of the journey home.

Dario

I'D ARRIVED AT the customs shed with a thousand Euros in cash, thinking it would be good to have a little more than the seven hundred I'd been asked to bring, and that this would save me from having to hit an ATM for the expenses back to Athens and Skópelos. Imagine my surprise when, at the end of all the form-filling-nonsense, Mr. Economídes informed me that the total came to one thousand Euros.

With the benefit of hindsight and a hard-learned understanding of the Greek way of doing things, I realized later that I should have shown my outrage, refused, and haggled. But I was new to the game; I was tired; and most of all, this man had me well and truly over a barrel, and we both knew it. The bastard's business instinct couldn't have been sharper if he'd had x-ray vision and counted the notes in my wallet right through my clothing.

Sick to my stomach, I handed over the whole sum. Mr. Economídes beamed. I left the place feeling used and disgusted.

Careful What You Wish For

LINDA MET ME off the ferry late that afternoon. It felt good to walk back up the sleepy streets of our little village after the mad rush of the last forty-eight hours.

In a few days we would have all our belongings. I'd asked Mr. Economídes to call Andréas directly to get our goods picked up on Monday morning, and he'd made the call right there and then, arranging everything to the last detail before I left. The man was a crook, but at least he was an efficient and affable one. I was confident our belongings would be collected Monday.

In the meantime, after four weeks in an empty house with no music, furniture, Internet, or anything, we were starting to become decidedly strange. Every little sound we made echoed off the bare walls and marble tile floors, and this must have infiltrated our psyche to the point that we found ourselves talking to walls. Singing to them, too.

Our odd practices began innocently enough. After dinner, Linda would sing a tone and listen. I would follow by calling out 'ECHO-echo-echo-echo', softer and softer, in imitation of the real thing.

All harmless enough, until we discovered that standing in a corner provided the best echo effect. We took to standing in opposite corners of our dining room and amusing one another with snatches of song, quickly graduating to full verses and entire arias. Linda favored Roger Miller classics, while I gravitated toward the eerie cowboy number, *Ghost Riders in the Sky*.

We stopped by the furniture store on Saturday morning to thank Rita for interceding for us with Andréas, and to see if we could hire the two Albanian lads who worked for Tákis, the owner, to help us unload the truck when our belongings arrived. Rita assured us it would be no problem and she would make the arrangements. We promised to have her around for dinner as soon as we got a little sorted out.

ON MONDAY AFTERNOON we got a call from Andréas's wife. He'd collected our goods and would be delivering everything on Tuesday afternoon. I thanked her and assured her we'd be ready.

Tuesday was another fine day. We waited excitedly for our belongings to arrive. About 3:30 they did, in a rapid-fire sequence of four dump trucks piled high with roped-in boxes and furniture.

A thousand cubic feet of packed goods decanted into an eight hundred square foot house is something to see: by the end of the day, the dining room was full to a depth of six feet, the living room half-full, and there was plenty of stuff in the bedroom too. As the saying goes, *be careful what you wish for…*

Over the next few days we seesawed from delight to despair: delight at finally having our things, despair at not being able to make a dent in the piles. We unpacked and organized, unpacked and organized, and still could barely move about the house.

With the bedroom, living room, and kitchen up and running, we desperately needed more storage. We went to Tákis's store and spent another thousand Euros on a glass/china cabinet that took up an entire wall of the dining room. We unwrapped chests and drawers. There was nowhere for the desk but in the hallway facing the dining room, about the only place it wouldn't impede passage; alongside that we placed two big bookcases, which we quickly filled with less than half of the books we owned. And still the dining room was absolutely unusable, still three-quarters full with boxes.

Of course, we'd known from the beginning that we wouldn't be able to get everything in the house. Our plan had always been to rent a workshop big enough to also store things which wouldn't fit in the house, until such a time as we were able to move into a larger house.

We'd mentioned the need for a workshop to Spýros, and asked him to keep an ear to the ground. There was a lot of empty property in and around the village, and I was sure that we'd be able to find something. But now everything had arrived, the need for storage had become critical.

The question of belongings had been a vexed one for some years. Linda always traveled light; she purged regularly and was ruthlessly efficient in filing and disposing of paper. She never sentimentalized over possessions.

I, on the other hand, came with stuff. *Lots* of it.

One of the consequences of being an only child of only children was that as folks died, everything—antique furniture, bric-a-brac, old diaries, love letters, ornate dinner services, delicate Venetian stemware, vintage cookie tins filled with buttons, embroidered and monogrammed ninety-year old linen—funneled down to me. And I already had my own extensive collection of belongings, chiefly in the form of books, photographs and paper, as well as old screwdrivers, age-darkened wooden rulers scratchily inscribed with the names of forgotten primary school friends, and irreplaceable bits of string for which I'd developed deep emotional attachments.

And then there were the eggs.

My mother loved to color Easter eggs. She was quite expert at it, dipping them in a vinegar and dye solution that resulted in the most exquisite marbling on the shells. Back around 1985, she'd given me three of these, assuring me that if I set them aside in a dark place for seven years, the yolks would turn into—she groped a moment for words—"a... a sort of *jewel*".

I was hooked, and it would be a long wait.

Cut to 2003, when Linda and I moved in together. As we began unpacking, Linda noticed that I still had a good many boxes of belongings that I'd not opened since moving to the US in 1989, and set about the task of helping me rediscover some of my lost treasures.

We were taking a lunch break, but Linda had the bit between her teeth. She loves to discover old family possessions and hear their histories. Still munching a sandwich, she picked up a small box. "What's in this one?" she said, reaching for the snap-off knife to slice open the top.

"Ah, wait. I have to explain that one first. You might not want to open it right now. I mean, you're having lunch."

So I told the story of my mother's Easter Egg painting hobby, and her assurance that—given sufficient time and some mysterious, but entirely reliable, alchemical process—the yolks would metamorphose into, uh, jewels.

Linda, who has serious issues with food spoilage, looked at me as though I'd grown an extra eye.

"No, no," I insisted, "they really are jewels! Look." I took the box from her and sliced it open.

There, carefully wrapped all these years in tissue paper and hidden from the alchemy-denying light of day, as per my late mother's instructions, lay the three colored eggs. Carefully, reverently, I picked up the red one, ignoring the miasma of long-imprisoned decay spreading over the dining area. Inside the fragile, bright-colored shell, something small and hard rattled ominously. Linda, one hand over her nose, was staring at me with horrified fascination.

I gently returned the egg to its tissue-paper sarcophagus. "Um. I think I should probably throw them away, after all, huh?"

Two Very Different Meals

THE FIRST TO call us on our new phone was my dear friend and fellow Science Fiction writer, Juliette.

Writing is a solitary business, and contact with other writers is a must, even if only to compare rejections. Undeterred by our move to the other side of the world, Juliette, who likes to talk through story and plot issues on the phone, quickly proved to be our most frequent caller. As well as discussing plot problems and writing issues with me, she and Linda came to be good phone buddies if I happened to be absent when Juliette called.

But we were missing friends in the US and dinner parties with other *bon vivants*. We needed to socialize. So the day before our belongings arrived, I'd called Yiánnis to see if he and Mina wanted to go out at the weekend.

He hesitated. "Eh, I cannot plan now for Saturday. Today it is Monday. How can I know if I will want to eat on Saturday night? We must talk on Friday or perhaps Thursday for this."

This was our first exposure to a very common quirk of the Greek character, the knee-jerk reluctance to schedule anything more than a day or two in advance. Linda and I are both planners by nature, and in the Bay Area people were so busy they often scheduled dinner dates five or six weeks ahead. Spontaneity is good, but this Greek custom reminded me of the maddening way teenagers like to keep their options open until the last minute in case they miss out on something really cool. Weren't we cool enough?

A few days later I was in the cellphone shop talking to Vasílis, the owner. It turned out he lived on the ring road less than a hundred yards from our house.

"Well, come and join us for dinner," I said. "We keep a fine table."

Vasílis explained they'd love to, but they had family staying that week. "But you know what," he said, in his South African-accented English, "I know this great couple, Matt and Carole. Matt's s'Efrican, but Carole's American, like your wife. And they live just up the hill from you."

Before I could say a word, Vasílis had picked up the phone and dialed a number. "Hallo, Matt? Listen, my friend Dario and his wife have just moved here from the 'States." He winked at me. "Anyway, they don't know anyone here and I know you and Carole would love them, so I'm going to pass you Dario right now, okay? Here he is."

There was no getting out of that one, so Matt and Carole came to be our first dinner guests that Saturday night.

With the dining room still full of boxes, we served dinner in the living room, balancing plates on our laps and wine glasses on a linen-draped box. Matt proved an affable fellow, Carole somewhat reserved. She played with her food and wine; he ate heartily.

They asked why we'd moved here, and how we liked it. They appeared stunned when we told them we'd spent a year learning the language. In five years, they'd hardly picked up a word.

Carole's eyes widened when we enthused about the Skópelites. "You find these people *friendly*? I don't think they're friendly at all! Or nice. We tried inviting someone to dinner one night and they turned us down, saying we didn't speak enough Greek to talk to them."

I bit my tongue.

"So besides Vasilis, who have you met here?" said Matt.

We ran down our short list. "And then there's Doom at the post office," said Linda.

"Doom?"

"The grumpy one at the counter who's always snapping at people."

Matt laughed. "Oh! You mean Leftéris! He's actually a really sweet guy. He just can't multi-task, so anything going on while he's trying to work sends him off the deep end."

"You mean like having people at the counter who need to mail things?" I said.

" Exactly! Now, how about Margaret Rodgers, have you met her yet?"

Linda and I glanced at one another. "No. But we know her little book," I said, pointedly.

During our first holiday on Skópelos we'd picked up Ms. Rodgers's 'Skópelos Rambles', a small volume with murky black and white photos, which claimed to be the definitive guide to the many nature hikes on Skópelos.

"We tried to use it when we were here on holiday," said Linda, "and got hopelessly lost. The directions are awful! None of her descriptions correspond to anything."

Carole came suddenly alive. "That's what happens to everyone!"

"She gets hate mail, can you believe it?" said Matt. "A guidebook author! People have sent her threats by email after getting lost with that book!"

We told them of the creepy scarecrow-figures we'd discovered near Ághios Yiánnis and asked if they'd seen them.

Matt turned suddenly serious. "They're not scarecrows."

"No," said Carol, "there's a story about them. How this woman killed her child near that spot. I don't know if it was illegitimate or not, just that there was a murder."

"And then she killed herself," added Matt, "and the figures are there as a kind of memorial."

"A gruesome one."

Linda and I made appropriate noises. It sounded like a tall tale to me, but the figures were definitely creepy. I made a mental note to inquire further.

The conversation moved on to the topics of owning land and dealing with Greek bureaucracy. Matt and Carole had built a big stone house high on the shoulder of a hill some distance above where we lived. From the description, I rather thought we'd passed it on our walks. But since neither of them was of Greek descent or even an EU citizen, residency was proving extremely difficult to obtain. Despite having engaged a lawyer, they had to leave the country frequently and had more than once been fined twelve hundred Euros ($1,500 US) each for overstaying their ninety-day permits. They were, in short, illegal aliens, albeit illegal aliens with a very healthy bank balance.

The evening drew to an early close and we bade our guests goodnight. We were lukewarm about them; pleasant enough, but we hadn't moved to Greece to hang out with expats. Just a few days later, on Saint Spýros's day, we discovered again how much we enjoyed the company of our Greek friends.

From the Aegean Dream blog:

Linda speaks

Saint Spýros's Day
December 12, 2006

FÍLIS MAS STIN ELLÁDA (Our friends in Greece)

Tonight we were invited to stop by our friends' house. Spýros and Mára have been kind and welcoming and have included us in their large circle of friends. It is St. Spýros day, and the day one is named for is quite a holiday. I bake cookies in the shape of angels to take. I attempt to decorate them using a packaged frosting. I have great confidence. Converting metric to US—no problem. Reading the directions—a slight problem. But I make the frosting, only to find out that I have made imitation whipped cream, not frosting. I send Dario to the store to buy a bottle of wine instead.

We arrive thinking we will have snacks and drinks. People have been stopping by the Balabánises' house all day. We chat with the guests in our still-pathetic Greek, visit for an hour, and then attempt to leave. We are met with emphatic OHIs ('no' in Greek). Absolutely no leaving for us; the only people left are family and we have been included in the family guest list for dinner.

The food is wonderful, the family kind and patient with our limited Greek. The food keeps coming, along with large tumblers of homemade wine. ORÉO! (beautiful!) We eat and drink and eat and drink, and pretty soon Greek songs about Skópelos are being sung at the table. It is wild! These people are real characters, making the actors in 'My Big Fat Greek Wedding' look rather wussy.

They begin singing a song which has many verses; they will pick someone at the table and sing it, modified to suit that person. Dario and I are both honored. The singing gets louder and more raucous and there is much laughter, directed, I believe, at us, when we can't quite interpret what we think might be naughty lyrics. We laugh, smile, and generally have a terrific time.

One thing is bothering us. We can't think of a single song to sing back to them. We must know a thousand songs but, as usual, my brain defaults to good old Roger Miller and I break out in my lousy rendition of 'King of the Road'.....Dario does a half-assed back up and—*Oréo!* Applause. They have confirmed what they suspected in the beginning; Dario is a crazy Britaliano and I am a nutcase Amerikanída.

A good portion of the family is there. Spýros's two sisters and brothers-in-law, Anna and her fiancée, his brother, the future in-laws, and us! More drinks, more food, and the dancing begins. We learn to dance Greek in the living room. We gather in a circle... three steps, kick right, kick left. We got it! This is IT! This is Greece! This is exactly like the story books. We live in a Greek village, on a Greek island. Wow oh wow!

Linda

A Plague of Licenses

ONE OF THE first things we'd unpacked when our boxes arrived were our acupuncture cupping set and our chiropractic activator tool.

I have persistent neck issues from being rear-ended in minor traffic accidents no less than five times in a seven-year period, a perfect example of what statisticians call 'random clustering'. These neck problems, and occasional flare-ups of low back pain when I sit too long at the computer, are handily managed by acupuncture and chiropractic, and the lack of access to these treatments on our small island had been one of my few concerns about moving here.

Well, neither of us was about to try wielding needles, but we'd always had good results with cupping, the suction technique practiced by acupuncturists which purportedly moves stagnant blood or *chi* from an inflamed or problem area. So a couple of months before we left California, following our practitioner's assurances that cupping, used with a little care, was unlikely to do harm, we got some instruction and bought a nifty little cupping set complete with hand pump.

Chiropractic was a trickier issue.

The research I'd done online revealed that although chiropractic was a known therapy in Greece—the very word was Greek, from *hiéro* (hand)—there was no licensing system or requirement, and hence no register of chiropractors. How would we find one, especially one of the activator persuasion? Over the years, I'd found that the 'activator' technique, whereby a precise adjustment to the joint is delivered by a smart tap from a small, spring-loaded tool that looks like a miniaturized, high-tech jackhammer, was both more effective and less unnerving then the brute-force skeletal manipulation more commonly practiced. The

---

[7] Be grateful: by attracting these events, I was lowering the probabilty of everyone else getting rear-ended by bad drivers.

only problem was that because it's illegal to practice chiropractic without a license in the US, activators aren't even supposed to be sold to the general public.

Well, nuts to that. A visit to eBay quickly secured an activator for a modest sum, and further research turned up a book on activator and diagnostic techniques similar to those used by our own chiropractor. After a little practice on one another, and careful observation and innocent-seeming questions during my last few chiropractic sessions before leaving the States, Linda and I found that we were able to effectively diagnose misalignments and perform basic neck and spine adjustments on one another without doing any harm. Linda seemed especially gifted, which was fortunate, since I am the one whose back and neck 'go out' most often. These new tools and skills were to prove a lifesaver during the coming months.

WE HAD ANOTHER meeting with our accountants, Kléa and Pávlos, to see what would be necessary to start our businesses.

Nothing to do with work is simple in Greece. The authorities arrange businesses into a bewildering number of categories, each requiring a different type or level of permit.

I explained to Pávlos that as a decorative painter I expected to work both in people's homes and in my workshop; and in addition to refinishing or painting clients' furniture, I intended to occasionally buy a piece, apply a decorative finish, and sell it.

By now, Pávlos was looking at me as though I'd proposed something truly ambitious, like setting up a passenger airline. He steepled his hands and took a deep breath.

"Well. For this, there are different licenses you must have," he began. "First is the service. To work in people's homes you must have the service license. This is not difficult to get, it is the most common. But if you want to take things from the client to your workshop, there is the problem of transport: how will you transport these furnitures?"

I shrugged. "We'll probably have a car by then. If it's a big piece, I'll get somebody else to transport it."

"To do this you must have another license. And if you want to buy things to paint, this is more complicated."

"Why?"

Pávlos smiled, warming to his subject. "Well. To buy things and sell them, you must have papers for the buying and for the selling. And also for the transporting."

I didn't see the problem. "So I keep receipts for everything. Bills. It's the same in America."

"It is not enough. You must have a different license to do these things. It is another category."

I opened my mouth to protest, but Pávlos held up a hand. "First, we will apply for the service license. Then when you have this you can apply for the other things. And to get the service license you must first register for the TEBE."

Greece, it turned out, had a mind-boggling 155 social security organizations, overseen by five different ministries. Of these agencies, IKA was the largest; TEBE, the one that collected contributions from the self-employed; TAXI, the agency for hotel workers; OGA for farmers; and so on. A veritable hell of TLAs and FLAs[8]

You could only register for TEBE at their offices on the mainland, and registration appointments had to be booked weeks ahead, but Pávlos had an old college friend who worked at the TEBE office in Vólos and could probably get me an appointment within two or three days. No, it couldn't be done by mail or fax, you had to go in person. With the restricted winter ferry schedule, that meant an overnight stay.

I sighed and thanked him. "Okay," I said, "that takes care of me for the moment. Now let's talk about Linda's business."

Linda outlined her plans to make luxury soaps using Skópelos olive oil and locally produced ingredients. She explained her desire to promote the island and support the local economy. Initially she would be the only employee.

Pávlos took a deep breath. "Well," he said, "this is more difficult." He conferred briefly in Greek with Kléa, who was actually the certified accountant: Pávlos was the bookkeeper and assistant. He went on, "We must find what are the laws about making these products. This will take some time."

This sent a chill down my back. Getting Linda's business up and running quickly was important so as to have adequate stock for the busy summer tourist season, when we expected to make most of the sales.

"Can't you just make some phone calls and get the details?" I asked. "At least to have some idea what is necessary?"

---

[8] Three-Letter Acronyms and Four-Letter Acronyms

Pávlos looked doubtful. He picked up the phone and dialed a number. A quick discussion in Greek during which I picked up the word *sapoúni* (soap). He scribbled a number and made another call.

Eventually, "They can not tell me," he said. "But certainly there will be laws and licenses about this. This will take time."

"In the US," said Linda, "there aren't any licenses needed for soap. In fact, you don't even have to list the ingredients." She was, unlike me, quite calm.

Pávlos gaped. "No license? This is not possible!"

"Soap, shampoo, and cosmetic products are mostly unregulated," she replied. "Generally, only foods and things taken internally need testing and ingredients lists."

Some more discussion among Pávlos and Kléa. Pávlos was starting to look harassed. He looked up a number, dialed again. A longer conversation ensued, with many glances at us. Pávlos thanked the person and hung up.

"Well," he said, "this was someone in the office for the manufacturing in Vólos. Also he does not know, but he says that you will need at least these things." He counted them off on his fingers:

"One, a list of all the ingredients."

Linda nodded. "No problem."

"Two, you must have a… I don't know the word. A *skédio*."

Linda thumbed through our pocket dictionary. We carried it everywhere. "A drawing?"

"Exactly, a drawing. So. You will need a drawing of the place where you will make this soap. Then the number three: to write and explain exactly how this soap will be made. And for the last, number four, you must show what system you have to take away what is left after you make the soap."

Linda and I stared at one another. "The waste?" said Linda.

"Exactly, the waste."

"But there isn't any. The only waste from soapmaking is the little soap that sticks to the moulds, and that just washes away in the sink."

"Like when you wash your hands," I added.

Pávlos was undeterred. "Eh, you cannot just do this. You must have a system to take away this soap that is left, and a special drawing of the system. There is a man here in Skópelos who can make you this drawing."

I threw up my hands. "This is crazy! We're not trying to start Max Factor here, this is just a small business with one person!"

Linda was patting my arm to calm me down. "No, look," I went on, angrier than I'd have liked, "I can't believe we need plans of the workshop and technical drawings for a waste management system just to make soap! The next thing will be an environmental impact report! At that point we might as well give up and go home."

"Calm down," said Linda. "Pávlos is just trying to help."

"I know, but this is ridiculous! I can't believe there are all these rules for something so simple."

Pávlos's smooth brow had developed furrows. "Ehh, we must have rules for this. We are not Afghanistan!"

I was incredulous. After seventeen years in the US I had developed a distaste for the excesses of the free market and had begun to think government really ought to exercise more control over industry. Now I was getting a taste of what it was like to be on the receiving end.

The truth was that neither system worked. Socialism was a crock, but so was an unregulated free market. Why were we so enamored of failed ideologies, instead of just legislating on a basis of pragmatism and common sense? God! but we humans were a pathetic species which never got anything right. We were surely doomed.

On the walk home I vented some more. Linda listened patiently; though we expressed ourselves differently, with her being the tactful one and I the hothead, we were philosophically aligned on the issue of excessive bureaucracy.

"You know what I wanted to tell them?" she said. "I wanted to say, 'do you know why the United States has the strongest economy in the world? It's because *they let people make soap!*"

I nodded glumly. "Yeah. And I bet they do in Afghanistan, too."

Slouching toward Christmas

WE'D INVITED SPÝROS and Mára for dinner on Friday night. The dining room was still piled high with boxes, but we'd unpacked an elderly gate-leg table which we could set up in the living room after cocktails.

We didn't know that when you invited someone to dinner on

Skópelos, you invited the whole family. Along with Spýros and Mára came their daughter Anna and her brother Rígas, home on a week's leave from national service. In traditional Greek fashion, everyone brought gifts. And Strátos, Anna's boyfriend, would be along in a short while, when he finished teaching a class in basic computer skills at a local tutoring center.

Fortunately, Linda had cooked a lot of food.

Greeks in general, and islanders in particular, seemed unadventurous in their food choices. But the cocktails—modified Cosmopolitans—were a hit, and Linda followed up with a Southwestern-style soup and chicken enchiladas, none of which our friends had experienced before, and all of which was devoured with gusto.

Despite the cramped conditions and the monstrous language barrier, the evening was joyous and filled with laughter. Mára and Spýros were becoming like family to us; or, rather—given that family often tends to be difficult—like what family *ought* to be.

What conversation we were able to manage proved interesting. We learned that Yiánnis, our doctor friend, was held in very high esteem; the Balabánises seemed very impressed that we socialized with him. And we discovered Greek employers could be quite lax about paying their staff: Anna hadn't been paid by her boss in almost two months and, despite grumbling over it, seemed to accept this as normal.

Since Strátos understood a little English, I would occasionally lapse into it and beg him to translate. But Linda was determined to speak only in Greek. She and Mára were especially good at finding workarounds: their ability to communicate was nothing short of remarkable, whereas Spýros and I often hit a wall. This was frustrating, as there was so much we both wanted to say.

I was also very aware that when a person speaks a language poorly, and, like pirates, uses only the present tense of those few verbs they *do* know… arr, well, it be natural to assume they's not very bright, eh, matey?

And pirate-speak was *way* better than our Greek.

From Linda's Journal, December 12th, 2006:

Things still seem incredibly strange and surreal, but surroundings are beginning to feel comfortable. I don't fear my daily trek into the village quite so much. I have learned that at the very least, if approached by a Greek I can say, "den katalavéno" … I don't understand … and play dumb.

I have had a few language successes. On a recent shopping expedition I was looking for several small items: pantyhose, for the rare dress-up occasions, food coloring for decorating cakes and cookies, and tissues to blow my nose! In the US, we refer to them as Kleenex, using a brand name to encompass all. I wander around the small market, endlessly looking for tissues—why on earth is this so hard?

My worst fears are realized. The shopkeeper makes her way over to me and asks what it is that I am looking for. Damn, I will have to respond! I point to my nose, sniff, and ask for Kleenex. Her startled look tells me she thinks I'm crazy, and she quickly leads me to a large display of Kleenex brand household products—but not a tissue in sight. I look at her and try to convey that no, I don't want cleaning products.

How can I get around this with the words I know? I want…hmm…I want … uh … napkins! Napkins … For my nose! It's the best workaround I can find, but she gets it! She leads me to a top shelf where little packets of tissues reside. Here in Greece Kleenex are CLEANING products!

Purchasing pantyhose only takes another half hour and by the end of my shop, I have made a friend. We manage some conversation, and I am gifted with a bottle of wine and a box of cookies. She extends a warm welcome to Skópelos, making me promise to bring by some soap for her store.

My confidence soars. Wow!

I STOPPED BY the furniture store one morning to say hello to Rita. As I was getting ready to leave, Rita reached over her shoulder and made rubbing movements, wincing a bit in the process.

"Stiff muscles?" I asked.

"It's my back. I've had this pain under my shoulder blade for two days and it's driving me crazy!"

"Oh, like here?" I said, turning and indicating the spot on my own back. "I know that one, it's maddening. Why don't you stop by when you close the shop this afternoon? I'm sure Linda could fix you. She's really good at chiropractic adjustments."

"*You told her what?*" said Linda, when I got home. "Are you *crazy?* I'm not a chiropractor! What if I make her worse?"

"You won't make her worse," I said. You always fix *me* just fine."

"Yes, but I know your back! Rita could have anything wrong with her!"

"No, look—it's just that little thing under the shoulder blade that goes out all the time, you know the one. Drives you crazy. I've had the chiropractor tap it lots of times, and it goes away at once. Just here," I said, indicating the spot.

"If you know it so well, *you* do it," she said.

"I can't start touching her! I barely know her!"

Linda shook her head in disbelief. "I am not—"

"Please," I begged. Look, Rita's been so helpful. And you have this *gift*! Just a little tap? Please?"

A little later, Rita arrived. She seemed a touch uneasy as Linda led her past the sinister stacks of boxes toward the bedroom. But a few moments later she emerged smiling, and thanking Linda.

"Better?" I asked.

"Yes! It's amazing! I haven't had a chiropractic adjustment in so long." She gave Linda a hug. "I'm so glad you came here!"

Linda hugged her back. Over Rita's shoulder, she mouthed a silent but unmistakable '*Bastard!*' in my direction.

WE'D PLANNED TO take a trip to Vólos before Christmas to apply at the regional prefecture for Linda's residency. But a visit to the Skópelos *dimarhío* (town hall) revealed that, contrary to what we'd been told at the consulate in San Francisco, the initial application had to be made here, on Skópelos. The functionary that dealt with these matters was on holiday, but would be back at work after the New Year. Since we had until the tenth of February before Linda's ninety-day permit expired, that would be no problem.

This assumption would later be proved wrong in every possible regard.

In the meantime, I continued to try to find an *ergastírio* (workshop) to rent. I asked Yiánnis, Vasílis, Kóstas the diesel supplier, and the man who owned the newsstand to keep their ears open.

Every time I walked past the island co-operative, where the olive press had been working 24/7 since our arrival on turning the island's olives into oil and in the process creating a growing mountain of steaming brown olive mush in the parking lot, I eyed the dilapidated industrial building next door. It was far too big for us, and all the windows had been knocked out, but I was becoming deeply anxious. Besides getting Linda's residency and permits, our future depended on us having a place to work.

We'd also mentioned our needs to Spýros. Spýros owned most of the block our building stood in, including what used to be a large restaurant kitchen next door, from which he had run a taverna on our roof terrace several years previously. The space, perhaps a thousand square feet, consisted of a fully-equipped restaurant kitchen and a big, open area now cluttered with old beds, armoires, and fridges from the Balabánises' rental properties. Spýros had hinted at the possibility of renting us this space, but he'd have to talk to Mára about it. We were excited at the chance of having a workshop right next door.

We were also excited that we might have an Internet connection soon. The rude peroxide lady at the OTÉ office had given me a disc with which to set up a 56k phone modem connection, insisting this was an essential step to getting full DSL. It seemed there were a number of bizarre hoops you had to jump through to get DSL service in Greece, though we were never able to understand why.

First, OTÉ converted our line from SNTP to ISDN, sold us their branded software, and insisted we enable a 56k dialup connection through a clunky modem box that looked as though it had been designed in North Korea, or some similar high-tech hub.

Next, they upgraded—or at least told us they had upgraded—our ISDN dialup line to a full DSL line, and sold us a DSL modem which had to connect through the aforementioned clunky box; we also needed a splitter in order for our phone to work along with the DSL service.

The eventual result was an ungainly mess of wiring and plastic boxes that clunked around gathering dust bunnies in the corner of the hallway where the phone hook-up was, but which entirely failed to provide any connectivity at all. Linda and I have many years of experience with computers and have set up a lot of connections, but even after several phone calls to OTÉ tech support people—who all spoke good English—we were getting nowhere.

I called Anna's boyfriend Strátos, who worked as an IT professional at the Skópelos tax office. But several hours and numerous calls to tech support later, he too had to admit defeat.

I returned to the OTÉ office and expressed my frustrations to the bleached Medusa as best my limited Greek would allow. She frowned, tapped at her keyboard, made phone calls to Engineering, and concluded by telling us we actually now *had* a full DSL line but were trying to enable a 56k dialup modem, and that would never work—what *were* we thinking?

My brain was starting to melt. If we had a DSL line, then could we just please have the DSL modem to go with it? No. She was sorry, but she had run out of them again and wouldn't be getting any more until January.

Greek public servants—I use the term 'servants' very loosely here—are filled with a festering, sulky malice that beggars description. They manage to bring a monumental ignorance and lack of professionalism to an already inefficient system, and are breathtakingly rude to boot. The American IRS at its worst is a beacon of friendly efficiency by comparison.

I left the OTÉ office ready to tear the heads off chickens, and my poor, patient wife had to listen to me whine and grumble for the next several hours.

From the Aegean Dream blog:

Happy Christmas! Now stop that shaking!!
December 22, 2006

So the weather finally turned cold yesterday, right on the solstice, with heavy cloud and strong winds. That said, the wind isn't what many of the locals were forecasting, which was force 8 or 9 gales.

It would have been more useful if they had forecast the 5.0 earthquake which occurred at 8:30 last night while Linda and I were playing cards. Right under us, 6 miles deep, according to the USGS website (which I checked just now, here at the Internet Café). It was a good, rolling shake: we stared at one another over the table, each of us wondering if it was going to get bad enough to head for cover. Weirdly, we had just a few hours earlier been talking about the possibility of earthquakes, and I saying how they weren't unusual in the Med and Aegean, and thinking about the half-acre of concrete roof terrace over our heads, and that we'd unpacked all our beautiful Venetian glassware! Glad it wasn't worse.

Dario

MÁRA CALLED EARLY in the week to ask us to join the Balabánis family for Christmas dinner on Monday. Delighted, I asked what time. "We will call you," she said. But by Saturday afternoon we still hadn't heard anything. So with everything closing for at least three days, we decided to buy a leg of lamb, vegetables, and various trimmings in case we had somehow misunderstood, and not been invited for dinner at all.

We enjoyed a pleasant Christmas morning watching our *plintírio* spin around. By early afternoon, with no news from the Balabánises, our mood was turning glum. Could we really have misunderstood so badly? Had they extended an invitation and then changed their minds, or forgotten us entirely? We discussed calling them, but decided that would be bad form—if we had misunderstood, it might be perceived as inviting ourselves to dinner. Our Greek wasn't up to any degree of precision in clarifying details and handling subtleties.

We were clearly going to spend Christmas alone.

So be it, then, we agreed; and with the decision made, we rallied: Christmas alone would be just fine!

Linda started to prepare the roast; I sliced and chopped vegetables. We opened a bottle of wine.

At 8:30 we were just about to put dinner on the table when the phone rang. It was Spýros. They were getting ready to leave for the restaurant and would stop by and pick us up as soon as Strátos arrived. Groaning inwardly, I thanked him and explained we were actually just about to have dinner and weren't even dressed to go out. Undaunted, Spýros said to come anyway just for *mezés* (snacks) and *glýka* (sweets).

Linda was standing close by. "They want to come by and pick us up in an hour," I said. "Can we do it?"

There ensued a mad scramble, in which dinner was unassembled and refrigerated, hair put up and makeup applied, suits and ties and evening attire donned; and we were ready five minutes before we heard the car horn honking outside the door.

There was an amplified bouzoúki band playing, and the restaurant, O Nástas, was packed. Looking around, I recognized a few faces, but was pretty sure that Linda and I were the only *xéni* (foreigners) among the two hundred or so people in the place.

A corner table had been reserved for us and an extra place was hurriedly set for Strátos's younger brother Kósmos, a moody, startle-haired, blue-eyed twenty-something who'd just split up with his girlfriend. They sat me to Spýros's right, Linda between Mára and Anna.

Linda, overcoming the difficulties of language with her trademark creativity, told our hosts about the eerie figures we'd seen on the hillside and asked about the story of the murdered child. For a moment, everyone looked puzzled. Then Strátos got it, and explained to the others.

There was a burst of laughter around the table. Spýros positively shook with mirth.

"No baby die," said Anna. "It is a, ehh, history only."

Strátos elaborated. "We know these people who make this. Some young people, they like to make joke. Only to make afraid. It is funny, no?"

"We met some *xéni* who believe this story," said Linda. Another gale of laughter.

I turned to Linda. "Still doesn't explain the skulls, though."

"I don't think my Greek is up to that one."

Wine came, and course upon course of lamb, sausage, potatoes, féta, olives, *kalamári*, and on and on. The assembly grew merry and loud, the band louder. I kept expecting an intermission, but Greek bands didn't seem to take breaks. Spýros began calling me his brother, and Linda became Mára's sister.

As the evening wound on, Spýros kept darting glances at Anna, then turning to me and shaking his head with expressions of confusion, amusement, disapproval—and most of all, disbelief. No wonder: his daughter, elaborately coiffed and dressed to kill in a bronze satin dress and strappy, high-heeled shoes of the most provocative sort, had publicly abandoned the realm of innocent girlhood for that of voluptuous temptress, and the looks she was getting every few seconds from Strátos, along with much thigh-touching and frequent kisses, underscored the fact.

The band played on, the food and wine kept coming.

At a nearby table, his back turned to us, a thin, dark-suited man sat alone, the only single person in the whole place. About one a.m. he half-turned, and I noticed with a shock that he was missing not one but both hands. In their place were shiny prosthetic manipulators. I froze a moment, the perception striking a sudden, discordant note in the middle of the night's joyous ballad, just as our discovery of the uninterred remains at the monastery had thrown shadows across a bright day.

Later, I asked Spýros—who knew everyone on the island—who the stranger was. To my surprise, he had no idea.

Around two, the dancing began. The mysterious stranger had left, and the band still hadn't stopped. Nor had the flow of *rétsina*: Spýros, clasping my hand, kept calling me his brother, and by now I felt I really was. Mára led Linda off to join the women's circle dance, and in no time Linda had the steps worked out and was dancing like a native Greek. Wine, she later assured me, helped the process no end.

The band had still not taken a break when we left at three a.m. This early departure was occasioned by Spýros's needing to be at the church at eight that morning—why, we weren't quite able to discern. How did these people do it? Linda wished him luck; he laughed, understanding her wry humor.

Strátos drove Anna home in his car. We piled into Anna's brand new Eurocar, Spýros at the wheel. Spýros used to drive trucks for a living and had more than once boasted to me of his driving skill. He didn't *appear* terribly drunk. He started the car and put it into gear without turning the steering wheel, so that we began to move toward the car parked in front of us. Spýros was chattering happily, either unsure what to do with the steering wheel or unaware the engine was even running.

When I realized what was happening, I had about one second to find the right Greek words, and what came out—in a surprisingly calm tone—was *"lígo aristerá, Spýro, lígo aristerá:"* a little to the left, Spýros. The effect was immediate. Spýros burst out laughing and wrenched the steering to the left, missing the car in front by a hand's breadth. There was fortunately no traffic on the road, and old reflexes seemed to kick in once he'd rejoined the world. We made it home without further incident and stumbled into bed.

Intermezzo

BRIGITTE RETURNED FROM Germany just before Christmas, with her fourteen year-old grandson Alexis in tow, and she invited us to visit. So on the 27th, Linda and I packed a couple of bags and took the Flying Dolphin to Alónissos.

After being greeted by Brigitte's three cats, we were led across the courtyard to the guest rooms on the far terrace. It was freezing cold. But the bed was piled high with blankets and quilts, and—despite the curious lack of doors anywhere in the guest apartment—there was a small heater in the bedroom. Brigitte assured us we would not freeze.

We had cocktails and chatted in front of the fire while Alexis slaughtered rampaging aliens in the bedroom. He'd brought an X-Box with him, and was deeply impressed when I told him one of my best friends was a game producer at Microsoft.

We shared laughs and memories of Mános over dinner. After, Alexis and I played a few games of chess. Alexis proved both aggressive and resourceful, but I am old and wily. I thought about letting him win a game, but decided that at fourteen he was a little old for that—he could take his lumps.

We woke to blue skies, breakfasted, and set out together for a hike through the pines. Brigitte had been having some issues with her knees, but held that exercise was good for them.

She was happy to have us close. Islanders can be very slow to accept strangers, and even after twenty-eight years on Alónissos, it appeared they had not accepted Brigitte. Immediately after Mános's death, people had begun to ask her when she would be going back to Germany.

"Do you ever think of leaving?" asked Linda.

Brigitte held up both palms, her wait-and-see gesture. "First, I will mark the three years after Manos's death with ceremonies, for the Greek tradition. Then I will decide. Also there will be papers to do with the death and the property which will be a lot of work. And of course the situation in Greece is not good."

"How do you mean?" I said.

"Eh, the economy. There will be big problems. The Greeks now they have credit cards and bank loans, and they are like crazy people. They buy new cars, they build houses, they take holidays… But they cannot afford any of this. Everyone spends, spends, spends, and they think they do not have to pay back the money. "

I was doubtful. "Really?"

"Eh. Of course. They are like their government with the money from the EU. This will be a catastrophe, believe me."

I left it at that, putting her statements down to simple pessimism and exaggeration. Four years later, the Greek debt crisis would send shockwaves throughout the global economy.

After lunch Brigitte drove us halfway up the island and up the narrow dirt road to the ridge where Mános had built his *kástro* (castle), which he sometimes called his farm. And with good reason: Mános, like Spýros, had such a fondness for *seeps* that Brigitte had once brought him a trio of German Heidschnucke sheep—an extraordinarily difficult business, considering all the import and customs restrictions involved— all the way from Germany for his birthday. Before long he had a small flock of sheep, some goats, and several chickens: a real little menagerie.

The *kástro* itself was both whimsical and eclectic, as was always Mános's way. To the basic whitewashed *kalívi* design, he'd added a small tower and crenellated stucco walls, giving the place the appearance of a blue-and-white castle in miniature. The rooflines were designed to catch and channel all the water into a room which had been purpose-built to conceal a giant water tank.

He'd sited the *kástro* on the rocky central ridge of the island, and the views were unparalleled. As well as broad swathes of the surrounding hills, both roof and back terrace offered almost one-eighty vistas over the sea to north and south, so that by turning in place you could take in the entire central portion of this long, narrow island. Bleached white rocks, verdant woods, and indigo seas stretched away on all sides, an overpowering surfeit of nature that commanded silence. We took photos[9] and remembered Mános before returning to the harbor and the five p.m. Dolphin back to Skópelos.

THERE WAS NOTHING we could do about moving Linda's residency forward until the town hall clerk returned in January, but there was still plenty to do to advance our work plans.

Linda had begun to unpack her soapmaking equipment and was eager to start experimenting with pure olive oil. For test purposes, she'd bought a five-liter can at retail. When she was ready to start production, we would find a bulk supplier of Skópelos olive oil. The only thing she needed now was sodium hydroxide, commonly known as lye.

Lye, typically sold as a drain cleaner, is one of the most common industrial reagents. Until a few years ago, it was universally available. But by the time we left the US, lye, along with Sudafed (an over-the-counter cold medicine) was becoming increasingly difficult to obtain. Why? Because it was an important ingredient in methamphetamine manufacture. As usual, our enlightened legislators—who have never cared where the road to hell begins as long as it gets them a good sound bite—were making life difficult for the innocent.

A little research revealed the Greek name for lye was *kavstikós* (caustic), and that it was sold in supermarkets. When I returned home with a couple of packets, Linda was delighted. She set up her moulds, weighed her oil, and mixed up the lye and water. She would just make a half-batch, enough for about fifteen bars, to ensure I'd found the right stuff.

Lye mixed with cold water will very quickly produce a solution close to boiling, but on this occasion it barely got warm. Still, she mixed the oil and lye solution, stirred and heated the mix, and waited for the telltale lingering traces that appear when saponification occurs and the mixture is ready for the moulds.

She stirred and stirred. "Pure olive oil soap can take up to an hour to trace," she said. Around the forty-five minute mark, I took over for a while.

Half an hour later the batch still hadn't reached trace. Linda plugged in the stick blender, which usually works magic on a reluctant batch. But after several minutes, the mix was no thicker.

Soapmaking is a relatively straightforward business, and though

---

[9] One of these, featuring Brigitte and Alexis, is on the front cover of this book

colors and oils can be difficult, Linda had never had a batch fail to reach trace at all.

"I think it's the lye," she said. "It never got real hot, and it looks more powdery than the lye at home. Most of this oil in the pan hasn't saponified."

We tried reading the fine Greek print on the label, but between the type size and the font, we couldn't make head or tail of it. Eventually, the entire pan of oily sludge went down the toilet. I vowed that if there was pure lye to be found on Skópelos, I would find it. Otherwise we'd certainly be able to get it in Vólos.

Frustrated at having wasted several hours and a few pints of good olive oil, Linda decided to refocus her creativity. We'd been craving Mexican food for weeks; but although the rest could be improvised, we didn't have that most basic requirement of all, tortillas. So, armed with a favorite Mexican cookbook and the bag of fine maize flour I'd bought for this very purpose some days earlier, Linda set to with a will.

A couple of hours later, the kitchen was plastered with scraps of dough and Linda was close to tears.

"I can't even make tortillas," she complained. "Look at this mess! It just won't hold together!"

"Um, don't you need actual *masa harina?*" I said.

She frowned. "It's just maize flour, like this. But a tortilla press would probably help. I've been in the kitchen all fucking day and I haven't managed to make anything except a mess!" she concluded, in a voice close to breaking.

I gave her a hug. "Maybe we could ask your sister Barbara to send us some. Tortillas keep well in the freezer."

"And some Thai curry paste," she said, with a sniff. "I want Thai food."

I agreed. "I think we need a care package from home."

DOCTOR YIÁNNIS AND his family spent Christmas in Athens with his parents. He returned to Skópelos, leaving Mina and the children in Athens until the New Year. Knowing he'd be on his own, Linda and I invited him to dinner, but he insisted on taking us out to a restaurant.

Angelós's taverna on the *paralía* was located just next to the town hall. The place was busy. Andréas the trucker and his whole family were there, and he greeted us warmly. Yiánnis excused himself for a moment while we got seated, and went to have a few words with the newly-elected mayor of Skópelos. Despite not having won a seat on the council, Yiánnis was a councilman and was on a number of boards and committees. We were starting to realize just how important and well-respected the private doctor in a small village was.

Yiánnis was cranky that night, and even more dogmatic than usual. With the island in the middle of the bi-annual olive harvest at the time, he complained about the scores of people arriving at his office with back pain and injuries from harvesting olives.

"They spend many days to pick the olives for oil that costs only five Euros a kilo," he said. "Then they have pain and can not work for a month. It is not necessary. They make a lot of money from tourism, and they can buy oil. It is a stupidity, and I hate stupidity."

"But it's their tradition," I argued. "It doesn't matter if it's economically justifiable."

Yiánnis was more interested in practicality than in custom. "Yes, but if it gives them pain and they can not move, it is a stupid tradition!"

Linda took another tack. What did he do in his leisure time? Did he have hobbies? No. Did he read? No. He had no time or interest. What did he think of such-and-such? It was stupid, or a waste of time. It was getting difficult to make any conversation at all, and I could see Linda biting her tongue.

Towards the end of the meal, I leaned back from the table and folded my arms. "Yiánnis, I can't believe your arrogance sometimes." I said it with a puzzled smile: I liked the man, but had to know what made him tick. "You're so sure of yourself. You have strong opinions on everything, and most of them are negative. Is there anything that doesn't annoy you?"

He met my eyes, level and serious. His reply held no rancor—he'd understood the thrust of my question. "Ehh, this is exactly what Mina said to me the first time she met me."

Interesting reply. Did he mean that was just his superficial persona, or that he felt had a right to his arrogance? I nodded and left it at that. Sometimes it takes time to get to know a person.

WE WERE NO closer to having a workshop. Very conscious of the need to start earning a living, or at least get into a position to do so, I was becoming more panicky by the day. Without a workshop, I couldn't even unpack my tools and materials.

Linda also needed room to spread out. Once we solved her lye problem she could make test batches of soap at home, but full-scale production and curing required serious space.

We also needed storage, as the box-filled dining room was starting to wear on us.

Finally, two days before New Year, Spýros invited us to come and have a look at his next-door restaurant space to see if we were interested in renting it.

The open area, perhaps three hundred and fifty square feet plus toilets off to one side, would suit our needs very well. Spýros offered to build a wall to separate it from the kitchen area; water and power could be separately metered. I was delighted: having a workspace right next door to our house, yet entirely separate, would be fantastic.

"This will work very well," I said. "How much would the monthly rent be?"

Spýros shrugged. "I don't know. How much do you want to pay?"

I smiled. The ploy was a classic, and clever, one. Some people will begin with an impossibly high number and let themselves be talked down; others prefer to make you name a figure.

Linda and I had discussed at length what we might be willing to pay for a workspace. The three hundred and fifty Euros a month we paid in rent on our house was probably more than most Greeks would have agreed to pay, and we reasoned that commercial space should cost a little less than residential. So we'd budgeted somewhere between a hundred and a maximum of two hundred Euros a month. When we'd asked Brigitte's advice, she insisted a hundred a month, tops.

"A hundred Euros?" I suggested.

Spýros looked uncomfortable. "Íne lígo." It is little.

"I'm sorry. We could pay a hundred and fifty. Would that be alright?"

Spýros hesitated. "It is little, Dario," he repeated.

Linda looked as surprised as I was. I said, "Spýros, I'm sorry. I don't know how much is rent for a workshop in Greece. It's difficult for me to know what the good rent is."

"Me too," said Spýros, "I also don't know. I must talk to Mára about this. Maybe it will be okay, maybe not. I don't know."

It wasn't an act. I turned to Linda, and could see she was embarrassed, thinking we might have offended our friend.

"Spýros, we are sorry," she said. "We are not Greek, and don't know what these things cost in Greece."

Now Spýros was looking embarrassed too. *"Katálava,* Linda, *katálava."* I got it, I understand. "But I must speak to Mára. Perhaps it will be okay, I don't know. I don't know."

I joined the circle of embarrassed apologies and we managed to disentangle, agreeing to speak again once Spýros consulted Mára on the matter. Preserving a good relationship with our dearest friend—who also happened to be our landlord—was crucial to us both. But we also weren't prepared to throw money away, and I was fairly sure that the space in question wasn't worth more than a hundred and fifty Euros.

NEW YEAR'S EVE found us with nowhere to go. There were undoubtedly local traditions, but damned if we knew what they were. It was a Sunday, and all the shops were closed; the spell of clear weather brought deepening cold as the evening drew in. Our phone remained silent.

We prepared and ate dinner, still half-hoping the phone might ring with an invitation. It didn't. We considered just going to bed, but our first New Year in Greece seemed an occasion to be celebrated. In the end we decided to walk down to the *paralía* and see what was going on. Even if there weren't major celebrations, we'd surely find a bar or taverna open where we could raise a toast and a cheer with the locals.

We left home around eleven and set off through the darkened village. The streets were quieter than we'd ever known them, with not a soul abroad. From time to time we caught the sound of voices or a television as we passed a shuttered window, but that was it. The town had closed.

That impression was reinforced when we reached the *paralía.* All along the waterfront, from the breakwater to the harbor beach, nothing appeared to be open. Even the ever-present cats had deserted us.

We strolled toward the harbor beach, the only sound the eternal kiss of water along the stone wharf. Overhead, the stars shone brilliant and hard. A single car slid past, heading towards the pier.

Following the curve of the bay out of the village toward the Ánesis cottage, we found ourselves a few moments later level with the Karávi bar, a realistic wooden mock-up of a sailing ship set right on the harbor beach road. It was 11:35.

"What do you think?" I said.

Linda shrugged. "There's a bench," she said. "We could just sit down right there."

Our breath smoking in the cold air, we considered the dark water lapping at the pebbles; the tranquil village to our left; the vast, star-pierced blackness above. As the moments passed, my earlier small melancholy gave way to feelings of peace and belonging. This was our home. We *owned* this beach, this moment, this night.

A couple of minutes before twelve, Linda reached into her purse and brought out a packet of sparklers. She handed me one by its wire end, lit it, and touched the tip of hers to mine until it caught. We wove patterns of hissing golden sparks, lighting fresh sticks as each burned down.

We were wishing one another Happy New Year when we heard a loud explosion from somewhere in town, more like a stick of dynamite than a firecracker. It was quickly followed by several smaller bangs. No cheering voices came from the village. No fireworks lit the sky, and there was still nobody to be seen. But in their homes the people of Skópelos were celebrating.

I want it Strong!

MY IMMEDIATE NEW Year's goals were to obtain some lye that would work, and to find us a workshop; we hadn't heard from Spýros and decided to let that idea go.

After a little time with dictionary and laptop (I had by now also unpacked our printer), I had a dozen or so little leaflets which read, *We need to rent a space for a workshop in or near the town. We are looking for about 30 sq. mt. with power and water. Please call, etc.*

On January 2nd I went out into the cold, bright day armed with my little leaflets. My first stop was Tákis's furniture shop. Tákis wasn't there, but I gave one to Rita, who said she'd ask around. We chatted a while, and penciled in a dinner at our house that weekend.

During our conversation I discovered that the islanders typically see in the New Year by dining at home with their families, going out later on in the night. "Some of the bars were open by one in the morning," said Rita, "but at midnight everyone is still at home." At least we'd know for next year.

I descended into the village, leaving a leaflet at Michelin Man's appliance shop, expanding in my halting Greek on the printed information. I left more at the news-stand, at the Internet café, and at Vasílis's store, wishing him a happy New Year in the process.

Back home, I called Yiánnis to extend greetings, and mentioned my quest. He suggested I talk to the Tsoúmas family, owners of the large Próton supermarket beneath his and the accountant's office.

"They have many properties," he said, "and it is possible they will have something."

"I knew they owned the big Élios hotel," I said.

"Ehh, not only Élios, but also another supermarket, some houses and many rooms for tourists... Their business is in the millions of Euros, you cannot imagine. They are so big they must use a class C accountant in Vólos, because there is nobody in Skópelos with the license to do their accounts."

I smiled. Categories and permits again. Nothing was simple in Greece. I thanked Yiánnis and said I'd stop by and talk to them when I went shopping tomorrow.

Later that afternoon, I went to Nikoláos A. Káltzas's store, the hardware palace, to see if they either had or could order lye.

Nikoláos A. Káltzas—Níkos, as I was later to know him—was a likeable, youngish man with piercing blue eyes[10]. He was always to be found behind the counter, and his staff were so friendly and well-trained you almost expected them to recommend you 'have a nice day'.

I explained my wife made soap, and that although I'd found some *kavstikós*, it was weak. Did they know where I could obtain some of the pure product? *Thélo dynatós!* I added—I want it strong!

He and the staff conferred for a few moments, discussing how old so-and-so used to make soap before he died, and such-and-such store used to stock *kavstikós* back in the day. Finally Níkos directed me to a small market in a quiet neighborhood nearby. "The owner has many old products. Perhaps you can find it there."

Níkos was right. In a large back storeroom away from the tubs of féta and olives, the owner, a slight gentleman with chiseled features and glorious silver hair, reached into a plastic sack and handed me a kilo bag of white crystals. He assured me this was the pure product, and that the

---

[10] Many Greeks have Slavic ancestry, and blue eyes are not at all uncommon

other stuff was for cleaning washing machines. I knew it was the real thing because my hands began to prickle from just holding the bag. This lye was *dynatós*! And, at two Euros, about one-fifth the cost of lye in the US, ridiculously cheap. The manufactured cost of Linda's soap had just dropped substantially.

Linda started a test half-batch as soon as I got home. When she poured and stirred the measured lye into the water jug, it began quickly to steam. "Yes! This is it!" she cried.

She added the solution to the warmed olive oil and I stirred while she set out her moulds and chose and measured dyes and essential oils. After about forty minutes the mixture reached trace. Linda added color and scent, and ten minutes later her first test run of Greek Island Soap sat cooling in its moulds on our kitchen counter.

It was a good day.

The next morning, a fresh-faced young engineer from OTÉ, the same who'd hooked up our telephone a few weeks ago, arrived to install our DSL modem.

Unlike the awful OTÉ counter staff, Pávlos actually knew what he was doing. He connected the modem via a splitter, tested the line, tested the telephone, and declared that everything was working. He also warned us that the OTENET DSL modems were of very poor quality and prone to failure, and that we should consider buying a better one soon. But all we had to do now was configure the connection in our computer and we'd be online. He gave us a number for OTÉ's DSL tech support in case of any problems.

As I mentioned earlier, neither Linda nor I are computer novices. We configured the connection exactly as instructed and attempted to use the user ID and password supplied. It wouldn't work: we couldn't get past the dialup login screen.

I called tech support, marveled at their politeness and perfect English, and was told that I had to go to the OTÉ office and have them switch the line on, whatever that meant. I explained the engineer had done that.

"They also need to do it in the office," said the young lady.

I whimpered. "You know, I'm sorry to say this, but the counter person at the OTÉ office here in Skópelos is an idiot, and very rude. Can't you do this from your office?"

"I understand. They are always like this." I couldn't believe my ears.

She went on, "I am very sorry. But I am afraid that you must go there. The government has made OTENET a separate company now, and we do not have control over the OTÉ telephone lines."

I was up and down the steep streets to the OTÉ office no less than four times in the course of the morning, and made three more calls to tech support. The peroxide floozy at the OTÉ office kept blaming OTENET, and OTENET insisted it was an OTÉ line problem. I was given different phone numbers for the dialup login, different user IDs, and different passwords. Nothing worked.

As the clock ticked towards OTÉ's closing-time, I returned to their office and allowed myself to get seriously angry at the creature behind the counter. Scowling, she went into the OTÉ system, tapping awkwardly at the keyboard with the palps of her fingers so as to spare her nail polish. She called OTENET tech support.

Some ten minutes later she declared that she had now switched the DSL line on (something we'd been told had been done over a week ago) and that I could now set up a connection.

"No," I said. I pointed to the clock. "Your office closes in ten minutes, and I'm not waiting another day if it doesn't work. You get your engineer Pávlos to my house right now or I'll make big trouble for you all the way to the top in Athens." This was a stretch for my Greek, and what came out was probably much closer to, *If engineer Pávlos not come, I will make very evil things with big people in Athens, understand??*

To my astonishment, the woman became conciliatory. I had, without realizing it, behaved like a Greek instead of a foreigner. She didn't argue, but actually apologized! Pávlos had gone home, but it would certainly work now. She went over everything again, called OTENET tech support to double-check, and insisted I'd be able to connect.

I didn't believe her for a moment.

A breathless stomp back up the hill, quick debrief with Linda, and a final try. Everything… *worked*! I was stunned. We were online, and flying! Screen after screen opened with surprising speed: OTENET; Google; Gmail; the BBC; The New York Times Online; MSNBC; Amazon; eBay.

Our lives had just undergone a radical change for the better. We were back in touch with the world!

Acropolis by night from Le Grand Balcon

...and by day

Flying Cat at Loutraki
Flying Dolphin entering Alonissos harbor

Tavernas at Agnondas closed for the winter

'Anesis' cottage

Panormos beach in the off season

Skopelos harbor and bay

The hóra with dimarhío (town hall) at center left

Cemetery at the Alonissos hóra

View across the Skopelos straits to Alonissos
with the islet of Ághios Giórghos inbetween

Artemis - the main house

The 'million-dollar view' from the terrace at Artemis,
looking towards the Dio Adelfi ('Two Brothers')

Manos's kástro (castle) on Alonissos

View from the battlements, looking North

Alonissos - the harbor at Steni Vala

Snow on Alonissos

The old kástro with its small church dominates the Skopelos hóra

Traditional kaíki (caique) in the harbor

Customs agent preparing to inspect our container at Piraeus

The first of four dump trucks delivers our belongings to the mílos.

Horse with traditional saddle

Brigitte's cats enjoy the winter sunshine

Country road on Skopelos

The 'Evagelistria,' Skopelos's workhorse, at dock.
Most of the island's supplies and heavy goods arrive on this ship.

Skiathos Express, one of the two ferries that serves the island, docked at Agnondas

Skopelos's cooperative olive press going flat out at harvest time,
with sacks of olives piled all around

The old and the new coexist everywhere in Greece

Our dining room in the first weeks

Hearth oven in an old ruin

The scary figures on the haunted hill

It's a balcony life

Ághios Yiánnis to Kástro, scene of the wedding in 'Mamma Mia!'
Above right, entry to monastery at top of stair.

Linda negotiates the vertiginous climb back down.

Assorted soaps, with clove scrub bars at left

Skopelos island bars, with loofah slice soaps at right

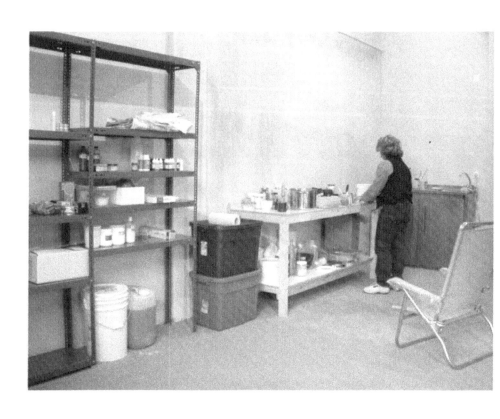

Linda at work

From the Aegean Dream blog:

January 6, 2007
Linda Speaks:

I have left behind the Roger Miller songs and entered into a Clint Eastwood film. Call it a Souvláki Western if you will.
THE GOOD.

A package arrives from the States. We have NOT been forgotten! A dear friend and former colleague has seen fit to send us a few things I have ordered from across the pond and decides to include….GOLDFISH! A NAIL CARE KIT! POPCORN! ALMOND ROCA! FRUIT FLAVORED TEA BAGS! ANDES MINTS! You cannot possibly understand how excited we are receiving this. It is heaven-sent after a rough week and I nearly have a meltdown. Thank you Shari!

DSL—SKYPE—Yee Haw! We finally have an Internet connection at home! We are in touch with the world and we find a key ingredient for my soap making, here on the island. A truly good week. These two things have only taken two months to accomplish. Let's see….accomplish one thing per month….at this rate…

THE BAD

Food preparation can be difficult. Although Dario and I are not fans of fast food, I find myself dreaming of Taco Bell.

Try grocery shopping to find items you need in a language that is still very foreign. I, of course, only ask for help as a last resort. I prefer to practice my Greek by reading the labels. However, this can be quite time consuming, as each label can take hours for me to decipher and also requires a dictionary. The owner of one little store hears me reading a label out loud in my painfully slow Greek. I am unaware that he is listening. He trots over and says in broken English, "This one is with onions, this one is without." I laugh hysterically.

Amusing things about food shopping on a small Greek island:

They do not have peanut butter, celery, or food coloring.

They do not have vanilla extract. They DO have white vanilla powder which comes in tiny little vials. Each time I purchase it I fear I will be arrested.

THE UGLY

We have not yet found a hairdresser on the island. Dario cuts my hair. He has never cut hair before in his entire life. He will not listen to instructions. I now have a mullet.

We still have a box museum. One day we hope it will become a dining room.

The toilet still leaks.

Linda

ANOTHER BRIGHT, COLD morning. *Psária Fréska* man was particularly loud and insistent, and impossible to ignore. While the kettle boiled, I trotted across the road to the dumpster which served our block and glanced inside before hefting my bag into it. I'd learned to look first after almost dying of fright the first time as startled cats erupted from the bin in a scramble of fur and claws after having a bag of garbage tossed on top of them.

Of all the public services on Skópelos, the trash collection was not only the best but was efficient to a degree the rest of the world could learn from. The dumpsters were emptied six days a week, occasionally seven. And unlike most municipalities, nothing was ignored: no need to tie and flatten cardboard boxes, stockpile coupons for extra pickups, or—unfortunately—separate out recyclables. These guys were heroes. They would have picked up spent nuclear fuel rods without missing a beat.

Our knowledge of the island and its society increased daily. When I remarked to Yiánnis that every other person on Skópelos was named either Manólis or Tsoúmas, he confirmed these were the two largest families on Skópelos. Between them they probably owned half of the island. But each was split into warring clans, effectively diluting their wealth and power.

The Tsoúmases, owners of the Próton supermarket, were all instantly likeable. The elder brother, Lázaros (*he is the CEO*, Yiánnis had told me) was thirty-something, a big, quiet, teddy-bear of a man; he worked mostly at Próton's deli counter and ran accounts in the back office. The skinny younger brother, Giórgos, olive-skinned and Levantine, with a habitual wry smile, spent his time either in the store or picking up goods from the warehouse. *He is the junior partner*, said Yiánnis. The middle brother, Spýros, ran the family's construction arm. And their sister Alexándra—tall, attractive, and twenty-something, with long black hair and a bit more English than her brothers, who spoke none—was generally to be found behind the cash register.

I had come in to shop and drop off my little 'Workshop Wanted' slip with Alexándra, whom I was on chatting terms with, but none of the family were around. I finished my shopping and called at the post office. There was nobody in line and Doom was shouting at someone on the phone when I arrived. This was not unusual. I waited patiently until he was done. He glanced at the grimy shelving behind him where they often put our mail.

"*Típota,*" he said. Nothing.

"No packages?"

That backward tilt of the head, the slight raising of the eyebrows. No.

"We mailed them three months ago," I said.

His scowl turned puzzled. "Three months?"

"Yes, the beginning of October."

"They should be here. Do you have the mailing receipts?"

I did, and showed them to him, a little stunned to see him taking an interest in a postal matter.

"Probably they are in customs," he said. "Usually things are one month in customs. Wait another week or two. If they still haven't arrived, we can try to ask."

On the way back past Próton I saw Alexándra at the register. I greeted her, chatted a little, and pulled out my 'Workshop Wanted' slip. "*Alexándra, kriazómaste na vrískome éna ergastírio yá ta érga mas,*" I began. We need to find a workshop for our businesses. I handed her the slip, and began to explain.

To my surprise, she was ahead of me. "Oh yes! Spýros Balabánis has spoken to us about this. Wait, I will get Giórgos."

She returned with Giórgos. He was all smiles. They had a place that might work for us, and would I like to see it?

A three-minute drive later we pulled into an alley just off the ring road, half a mile down the hill from our house. Giórgos unlocked a pair of green wooden doors and led me into a large, gloomy storeroom. Arches divided the place into two big bays, and stout concrete columns supported a beam that ran along the centerline of the ceiling.

Giórgos showed me into the second of the two bays, the one they were offering to rent us. Discarded doors, windows, and mattresses were piled against the walls. Tidy stacks of used furniture and odd timber covered the floor. Things from their hotel and guest rooms, Giórgos explained. They could clear everything out of one bay and build us a dividing wall.

I looked around and tried to imagine the space empty.

It was big, perhaps twenty-five by twenty-five, with a high ceiling and a good-sized window, as well as its own double doors, which would admit a lot of light. Cleaned up, it would be perfect.

"I like it very much," I said, "but it's very large. We are just starting our businesses in Skópelos, and we must go slowly. Can we rent just half of it?"

That little sideways nod. "Yes. We can build the wall here instead," he said, indicating the line of the columns.

"And we'll need a sink and water. Also electricity." There were no wall outlets visible, just a single dim bulb hanging from the ceiling.

The sideways nod again. "No problem. But a toilet would be difficult." He pointed to the concrete floor.

Inconvenient, but… "*Entáxi,*" I said. Okay. There was a little pizzeria on the corner and I imagined we could reach an accommodation with the owner.

Now to the crunch. "How much do you want for the place?"

The corners of his mouth twitched, and I saw it coming: "How much do you want to pay?"

These people were going to drive me crazy.

"No more than one hundred and fifty a month."

The bland smile gave nothing away. "I will talk to my father tonight. Call me tomorrow and I will know."

"If he says yes, how soon could we have it?" I was salivating. I could already see where our workbenches and storage racks would go.

"We must take everything out and make a big fire. Build a wall, put in water and electricity. A week, ten days, no more. *Entáxi?*"

"*Entáxi*," I agreed. We shook hands and I fairly ran back up the hill.

Linda was thrilled by the news. After two months of idling, worrying about belongings not arriving, worrying about too many belongings having arrived, and worrying about not having a place to work, we would finally be able to unleash our creativity and start working toward earning our keep here before our funds ran out. Now we just had to hope that the Tsoúmas patriarch agreed.

We busied ourselves with catching up on email and calling friends in the US on Skype; at less than two Euro-cents a minute, we could talk as long as we wanted, although long-distance calling on our computer wasn't terribly comfortable, and not at all private; the monitor and keyboard sat on the little plastic patio table in the entry to the dining room with a rug covering the Ethernet cord emerging from the huddle of cheap OTENET boxes hidden under our antique, slant-top desk in the hallway. It was a sight.

The next morning brought wonderful news: Tsoúmas the Elder had agreed: we could have half the space for a hundred and fifty Euros a month. *Or* we could rent the entire space for just two hundred. I took Linda to see it before committing ourselves, and we decided to take the whole place. I could have screamed with joy; we would have plenty of room to grow, and we could store all the stuff we didn't have room for at home.

We shook hands with Giórgos, sealing the deal. They would get the place cleared out for us on Sunday, then install the sink and the power outlets. We could move in ten days.

A COUPLE OF days later, I stopped by Yiánnis's office to tell him our news. It was ten a.m. Yiánnis had just arrived, and was eating ice cream for breakfast.

Yiánnis lived just a couple of hundred yards from his work, enjoyed plenty of family time, and didn't have to dicker with insurance companies and shyster lawyers. No receptionist, no admin staff, no billing specialists. Once inside the lobby of Yiánnis's immaculate little suite, if the examination room door was open, you simply knocked and stuck your head in. Yiánnis would glance up from his laptop, at which he was likely either downloading rock music or surfing the web, and tell you to come in.

The examination over and your problem diagnosed, Yiánnis wrote your prescription and handed you your bill. His rate was thirty-five Euros, (about $50 US) an hour, and he had a sliding scale for the island's poor. House calls were never a problem, unless you were the octogenarian nun at the big convent high on the mountain overlooking Alónissos.

"They always call in the middle of the night because she is having a panic attack," he told me once. "It takes half an hour to drive up there. Last time they called me at four in the morning for a panic attack. I told them, 'I will not come now, I will come at ten.' Ah, this was too much!"

The mention of panic attacks led me to air my growing anxiety over the complexity of getting Linda's business license. We hadn't heard anything from Pávlos, the accountant, and I was worried.

"Do not worry too much about the license ," said Yiánnis. "Even without this she can sell them. The only problem is if she gives her soaps to one shop, and another shop that sells soaps loses some business. Then they will make trouble for her."

"They'd report her?"

"Eh, yes, they will try. Even if she has a license they will try to make trouble with the tax authority. Sometimes people do this just because they are bored." He chuckled. "Even me: yesterday I was writing a letter to the newspapers to complain about the condition of the OTÉ building. You have seen it?"

"Yes. It's in a terrible state."

"Yes. And maybe I only did this because work is slow. Only of these people she must be careful. But she must not worry too much. No business in Greece is completely legal. Not one."

LINDA HAD DECIDED on the name 'Greek Island Soap' for her products, and we'd already registered the web domain. Her signature soap was to be a 3.5-oz bar stamped with the outline of the island. If this proved successful, we hoped to expand the range to include other islands. Between the quality of the product and Linda's skill at packaging and presentation, her Skópelos soaps would be the perfect take-away souvenir for the summer hordes. My biggest concern was whether she'd be able to keep up with demand.

Linda's small test batch was curing nicely. She'd removed it from the molds and was ready to try stamping it. After the first couple of attempts she got the knack: position the stamp carefully, deliver a couple of sharp taps just *so* with the rubber mallet, and the wrinkly brass lip would leave a perfect impression in the fresh soap.

She decided to try adding some color. A fine, OO artist's brush dipped in a blue/violet dye mix and drawn carefully through the stamped indent resulted in a precise blue outline of the island floating on a ground of pale ivory. The effect was both delicate and striking.

With a lifetime of decorative painting experience behind me, I was awed at the task she was setting herself. "Sweetheart, coloring that in must have taken you almost two minutes. To do that on a production basis…"

"I'll get faster," she said. "I really like the way it looks. Don't you?"

I kissed her. "It looks fantastic. People are going to *love* your soap."

Time slowed to a crawl as we waited for the workshop to be ready. A good time to be social.

On a freezing cold Saturday night Rita and her mother Sofía came to dinner. They lived less than half a mile away, just near the appliance store, but both were a bit breathless from the steep uphill climb through the village.

Sofía's English wasn't up to Rita's, but both were good conversationalists with ready laughs and a good sense of humor. Rita loved art and books. At one point she asked if we played chess. I told her I did, though I didn't play often these days.

"Will you teach me?" she asked.

"Sure. Anytime."

"Tákis, my boss, is a very good player, and I want to be able to beat him!" She balled her fists and grinned with fierce anticipation. "Well, at least I want to be able to give him a good game."

"He's a good player, then?" Always a vague and relative question. I thought of myself as a good intermediate player.

"Oh, he's a fanatic! He plays online every night, but he loves to play face-to-face. I will tell him you play, I'm sure he'll want to have a game with you."

By the end of the meal we were hearing a lot more about Tákis. I'd seen him once or twice: a fit, good-looking thirty-something with smoldering blue eyes, obligatory cigarette in his mouth, cellphone glued to his ear. He was always moving.

It seemed Tákis was a champion swimmer—he certainly had the build—and something of a local Casanova. It was also clear that Rita, who'd known him since childhood, had a serious crush on him. I decided to pass by the shop on Monday evening and see if he wanted a game. It would be nice to hang out with another guy once in a while, and would give Linda some much-needed space.

As they were donning their coats to leave, Sofía turned to Linda. "Rita tells me you can do chiropractic," she began. "I have very bad back pain for months, and there is nobody in Skópelos for this. Please will you come and adjust me soon?"

Linda's mouth flapped open. Before she could speak, Rita said, "I told Sofía you're very good."

I beamed. "She really is. She has a gift!"

THE WEATHER REMAINED stubbornly beautiful. By day, the skies were so clear that we could often make out Mount Athos, the center of the Greek Orthodox church, seventy miles away to the northeast; in the distant south, the mountains of Évia were white with snow. Night brought diamond-sharp stars, and the moonlight falling over the still, dark sea startled the soul.

I hiked most afternoons. As Linda's knee improved she would occasionally join me on shorter hikes. The only time we ever missed having a car was when we had a lot of heavy shopping to carry, and even that was something that I looked on as an opportunity to soak up my new environment. I would happily trot into the village at any excuse, and never tired of the sheer, simple beauty of sea and sky, land and village. I was hopelessly in love.

We explored the *hóra* as much as we did the countryside, climbing the steep stone stairs from the harbor to the old *kástro* (castle) which dominates the town. It was here, on a steep-sided crag overlooking the harbor, that the Venetians built a fort following the conquest of Constantinople in 1204. The steep, winding lanes around the fortress provided further protection for the stronghold, and Skópelos remained solidly under the sway of Venice for some three centuries.

When the Barbary pirate Barbarossa (Redbeard) sacked the island in 1538 and destroyed the *kástro*, many of the surviving inhabitants fled. Later, as the Ottoman Empire strengthened its hold on the region, Skópelos remained autonomous but paid taxes to the Turks. History radiated at you from every wall and paving stone of the *hóra*.

Our walks often took us down the wide road that led from the *paralía* to the T-junction where the main road to the waterfront met the ring road. Along this stretch were several small markets, as well as the venerable Hotel Amália and most of the island's car rental firms.

On one side of the road were parked twenty or thirty shiny new rental cars, all the same model Fiat but in a variety of colors; and every one had four flat tires. They sat there, day after day, entirely neglected. There had to be a story here.

One day, after my regular stop at the Post Office to annoy Doom, I stopped to ask Vasílis what the deal was with the slashed tires.

He lit a cigarette. "Well, there's this guy," he began, in his percussive South African brogue, "that nobody likes. He made a ton of money and loves to show it off. He's got a load of flashy cars. You've probably seen him driving around the island in his Porsche lately."

"Is he a Skopelíte?"

"Yah, yah. Anyway, guy decided to open a car rental business. He bought a shitload of brand new cars and started undercutting everyone else. I mean, *really* undercutting them: he advertised his cars at twelve Euros a day when everyone else was renting at thirty Euros. Bragged he was going to put everyone else out of business."

Vasílis blew out a cloud of smoke.

"So one night a couple of months ago, somebody slashed the tires of every single one of his cars. Of course, they never found out who did it."

I chuckled. With my Italian genes and old-fashioned sense of justice, I had no problem with this sort of thing. "Sounds as if he deserved it. He's lucky he didn't find himself in the harbor with cement overshoes."

Vasílis snorted a laugh. "This isn't Sicily, you know! we don't have the Mafia here. This is a peaceful island!"

Peaceful it may have been, but these islands were not lacking shady entrepreneurial activity. A few days later, Brigitte called us with a delightful bit of scandal. "Did you hear what happened here on Alónissos?" she said.

I replied that, no, we hadn't.

"They found the body of a local man washed up on one of the beaches. After some inquiries, the police arrested a Russian prostitute."

My mouth fell open. "A… *Russian* prostitute? There, on Alónissos?"

She laughed. "Oh, yes. Of course. Actually, there are two of them. Anyway, the police asked their questions, and it turned out that the man had visited her and, well, he died on the job. Heart attack. So of course the girl panicked and called her pimp in Vólos. He came out on the Dolphin, and they dumped the body in the sea."

"Oh my God! That's unbelievable!"

"Eh, yes. Of course, the police let them go when they found it was not a murder. But you see, even on this little island of three thousand people, we have some excitement."

LINDA STARTED DESIGNING the graphics for her soap labels and writing a leaflet, which she would have someone translate into Greek, giving some insight into her soapmaking philosophy and stressing the purity and local sourcing of the key ingredients. We talked about the look and feel she wanted for her website.

I redesigned my own website with the Greek national colors, blue and white, for a background theme. But there was also quite a lot of explanatory text alongside the photos of my work, and I would need help translating these.

I thought I'd done a fair job of translating the photo titles and various button labels ('Home', 'Back', etc.) until I showed it to Katerína, an acquaintance of ours, and she almost fell off her chair with helpless laughter. The 'back' button apparently read, 'he returns', and the text which should have read 'Greek translation coming soon' translated as 'The Greek translation, he arrives.' You could sort of tell what was meant, but there was a certain lack of polish. It reminded me of early Japanese motorcycle maintenance manuals, or the Spanish guidebooks for English tourists of my childhood. It would be a long time before we mastered this language.

Chess , Drugs, Oil

I CALLED BY Tákis's shop on Monday evening to see if he wanted to play a game of chess. He seemed delighted, and asked if the next evening would work for me as he had a delivery to make tonight.

"About six-thirty or seven," he said, in English light-years ahead of my Greek. "We will have a beer and play chess, and it will be very nice time."

The next morning I went by our new workshop to see if anything was happening and found Giórgos there loading the last of the junk onto his van. "I make big fire," he explained, with a grin.

I went to Tákis's shop around six-thirty, figuring we'd chat, play a game, and I'd be home for dinner by eight or so. Tákis greeted me warmly and poured us a couple of beers. Business was very slow at this time of year, he explained, and he was at the breakup end of a difficult relationship, the kind that are all work and no fun. I'd been there and I sympathized.

After a while, he fetched out the chessboard and a satin sack of handsome wooden pieces. He asked me whether I recognized the *en passant* protocol for pawn capture. "Of course," I said. Tákis smiled. I got the black side.

After a standard Double Queen's Pawn opening, I saw I faced a strong player. As we probed and poked at one another, I found Tákis's pawns always in my way. Once his defense was solid, he mounted an attack that culminated in my resignation.

We turned the board around.

"You play the black side quite differently," I commented, after a few moves.

"Eh, of course." He moved a knight and lit a cigarette. "You have the start. It is more difficult to play the black."

This surprised me. "Really? I thought that only really mattered in high-level or championship play."

"No, even for this. The white has the, eh, *pos to léme?* What is the word?"

"Advantage?"

"Advantage, yes. White has big advantage."

You wouldn't have known it from my game. I tried for an aggressive attack, only to find it deftly neutralized and myself on the defensive within a few more moves. I called Linda to let her know I probably wouldn't be back till nine, when the shop closed.

"How's it going?" She sounded glad that I was having fun and making friends.

"He's a killer," I said, "but I'm giving him a good fight." Tákis grinned.

He beat me again, but at least I made him work for the victory. We agreed to play again later in the week.

I WALKED PAST the workshop most days over the next week, usually just trying for a casual glance so as not to bug the workmen. They did appear to be working on the place most of the time: the old window had been taken out and replaced, and a cinderblock wall was being built to divide our space from the adjacent bay. Still, I chafed at the slow pace.

In the meantime, we worked on the house. We'd bought voltage transformers before leaving, and an all-region TV/VCR/DVD combo. I unpacked my guitars and set one on a stand in the living room. Music, and the ability to watch videos and DVDs, made a big difference to our lives. The local video store's DVD collection was mostly bootlegged[11], and we discovered a new dimension in entertainment when we tried to watch the animé classic, 'Howl's Moving Castle.' Despite the DVD package being printed in English, the movie had only Japanese audio and Greek subtitles.

After two months here, going everywhere on foot, we were starting to become known. Walking down the ring road to the little grocery store or the workshop, I would find myself honked at, as some acquaintance or other drove past[12]. Walking to the *paralía* or to Próton, a ten-minute walk at most, now often took half an hour or more because of the chats with friends or acquaintances on the way. We realized that the fact of our walking everywhere rather than driving, and our efforts to speak Greek and integrate, served to make us more popular than most foreigners. The Balabánises had welcomed us into their family, and I

---

[11] Although our island saw an influx of several itinerant African vendors during the tourist season, one lived on Skópelos year round, supplying the islanders, as well as the ferryboat officers and crew, with pirated CDs and DVDs. Small and rotund, one eye milky with cataracts, she spent much of the cold winter days hanging out in the ferry office and in one of the local bakeries, wholly accepted as an integral part of the community.

[12] This form of greeting grew extremely annoying in the warmer months, when we were forced to keep windows open; since people tended to congregate on the bend in the ring road outside our house, the honking, added to the normal traffic noise, made us climb the walls.

suspect that had got around. We also lived modestly in a rented house and wanted to work, unlike most of the expat community who came here as retirees with big chunks of money, bought land and built big homes, got blind drunk every night, and kept to their own community.

Yiánnis confirmed this impression.

"One time," he told us, "Mina and I were invited to a fundraiser by the English people who have the animal charity here. When we arrived for the dinner, they had made two big tables. One was for all the English people, and the other for the Greeks. Can you imagine?"

"Unbelievable!" I said. "Us and them. My God."

"Eh, yes. This is how they think."

But although we believed we were being accepted into the community (and I think we were), others had warned us not to fall into the trap of thinking that way. Brigitte on Alónissos was one: "These people are *not* your friends," she insisted. "Look at me. I have lived here for twenty-eight years and they still do not accept me. They will pretend to be your friends, but they are not." Yiánnis had cautioned us as well. After three years on Skópelos he was still thought of as an Athenian, an outsider. "They are very closed people," he said. "It will take them ten years to accept me."

I PLAYED CHESS again with Tákis later that week. He beat me again, but he seemed as interested in enjoying a good game as in winning. He made me take back one or two bad moves, and took time to point out my mistakes. He attached more importance than I did to pawns, or *péons*, as he called them.

"You must not lose your *péons*," he said. "In the second part of the game, they are very important. If the other player has more *péons* and he can use them, surely he will win."

I asked him how much he played. "Three or four hours every day," he said. "Sometimes more if I find a good player on the net."

I asked the obvious question. "Do you have a girlfriend?"

"Aaah." Tákis lit another cigarette. "We fight very much!"

As if on cue, a car stopped outside and a slim young beauty entered the shop. Tákis introduced us, and we exchanged politenesses. He told her he would see her after he closed the shop, and she went off.

Tákis's love life was convoluted. After a long relationship with a girl who'd ended up marrying his best friend, separated after a year or so, and then begged him to take her back, Tákis had started dating again.

He was thirty-five, financially secure, and had cool toys in the form of a Ducati 900 SS motorcycle and a Zodiac inflatable with a huge outboard. But he was lonely, and wanted nothing more than to settle down and have a family.

Takis's family owned half of the block we lived on (Spýros owning our half). His grandfather had founded the original *Épipla* Doúkas (Doúkas Furniture) in the northern city of Thessaloníki, and had done very well. In the early '80s Tákis's father, Vangélis, came to Skópelos and opened a branch of the *épipla* here. Tákis's parents' house was above and slightly behind the business; Tákis lived in a small cottage set further back at one corner of the garden, next door to a second cottage reserved for visiting family and friends. His father still worked in the store during the busy periods and whenever Tákis went to Thessaloníki to bring back a shipment of furniture.

"I am afraid I will be alone," Tákis concluded. "It is difficult to find the right person in so small an island. But I love the place and the sea, I do not want to live in the big town. Of course," he said, matter-of-factly, "I can always find girls for sex, this is not a problem. But for a family it is difficult. Many girls come in the summer, but their life is in Athens or another place. What they can do in the winter in Skópelos?"

He puffed on his cigarette. "So I play chess. If I can not find the right woman, perhaps I will become a big chess champion."

It's always been apparent to me that machismo and sensitivity aren't mutually exclusive. Tákis was the living proof of this: fiercely competitive and highly physical (he swam daily throughout the year in all but the worst weather), he also had a strongly intellectual and emotional side, and a wider frame of reference than most; and he was an excellent communicator, even with limited English. I liked the man a lot.

SKÓPELOS CONTINUED TO surprise us.

Linda was bringing in some laundry and I was preparing to go to the store when we heard a police siren. For a moment this seemed perfectly normal; then it struck me that we were on Skópelos, not back in the US, and that this was the first time in two months here that we'd heard an emergency vehicle. And it was getting louder.

The police SUV roared up the narrow street alongside the Hotel Denise opposite, paused for a heartbeat at the junction, then slewed across the ring road in a screech of tires, leaving rubber on the asphalt as it sped down the hill with lights flashing. Linda and I looked at one another. "What the hell was that about?" I said.

She shook her head. "Did you see them spin out?"

"No kidding! I'm going to run up to Tákis's shop and see if he or Rita has the scoop."

Rita had no information. But on my way back, I saw Spýros coming out of his workshop on one of his frequent rest breaks from *dimarhío* business. I asked if he knew what was going on.

"*Narkotikós, Dario, narkotikós! Íne Máfia, gang-ster! Bam! Bam!*" he added, making a pistol of his thumb and forefinger.

"On Skópelos? No!"

He nodded, his face serious. "Yes, Dario, on Skópelos."

"But it's so small a town," I protested. We'd seen young children out caroling alone at Christmas; storekeepers often left their keys in the shop door all day.

"Drugs are a big problem," he said, stubbing out his cigarette. He reached for his helmet, hung it on his wrist by the strap[13], and clambered onto his old moped, which he used as a runaround for his errands during work hours.

"*Duliá, Duliá, Dario. Ého duliá tóra.*" Work, work, Dario. I have work now. And he was off, leaving me to shake my head in disbelief.

WHILE OUR DAYS passed in maddening idleness, everyone else on the island was toiling in the olive groves.

The Balabánises owned a *lot* of olive trees. It had taken them a full month of effort, several hours a day, to harvest all their olives. I'd seen them and others at it, and it was brutal work.

Olives are harvested by hand. After spreading giant plastic tarps under the trees, the olive-pickers beat the branches with sticks until the ripe olives and some of the smaller branches fall to the ground. Next, all the leaves and woody matter have to be separated out until only olives remain. Finally, the tarps are gathered in and the olives transferred into heavy sacks.

Once the olives are bagged, each family delivers their crop to the co-

---

[13] Greeks use motorcycle helmets as talismans rather than skull protection; they are judged equally effective whether hung from the wrist, dangling from the handlebars, or, more rarely, bouncing around in a plastic crate attached to the seat behind the rider.

operative olive press near the post office. The sacks are counted, and the family allotted a slot in the pressing schedule and told when their oil will be ready for collection. By Greek standards, the process is a miracle of organization.

Between the overhead work and the bending over and heavy lifting, I understood why so many Skopelítes ended up in Yiánnis's office after harvest. It was a good thing the olives were only harvested every other year on these islands.

A COUPLE OF evenings ago I was taking the garbage out when Strátos and Spýros pulled up. In the bed of Spýros's pickup were eight large plastic drums of freshly-pressed olive oil. I offered them a hand to carry it into Spýros's little basement office/workshop space, and quickly regretted it: the drums, which probably contained fifteen gallons of oil apiece, were monstrously heavy.

Two or three days later Spýros arrived with a gift from Mára to Linda. It was a generous one: twenty liters (five gallons) of virgin olive oil. Mára, prior recipient of several gift bags of Linda's soap, was a true believer.

The oil came in a plastic container bearing the remnants of a label that looked for all the world as though it had previously held some industrial chemical. We decanted a couple of liters of the oil for culinary use. It was delicious, and we didn't fall ill. It would be fine for soapmaking.

WE KEPT UP our blog entries and spoke frequently to friends and family. Linda's sisters, with whom Linda's relations tended to be terse and episodic, seemed to like her much better now she lived on the other side of the world. They communicated often, and seemed to miss her.

From the Aegean Dream blog:

January 10, 2007
I Adelfés Mou (My Sisters)

Linda speaks:

A package from my sisters arrives. I knew it was coming and I have been watching the FedEx on-line tracking now for days. It leaves Pacheco, California, and heads for Oakland, California. It then takes off for Indianapolis, Indiana, stops in Memphis, Tennessee, and takes a long haul to Paris, France. When it departs Paris and arrives in Athens I begin to smile. When I notice it clears customs in Athens and is "In Transit" my smile grows larger. Only a truck and boat ride left to go. The package was estimated to arrive yesterday. I wait all day until at last I turn off the porch light and go to bed. Where is my package?

I awake. The island is beautiful, the sun is shining. It is almost balmy. My friend Mára's husband, Spýros, delivers a large container of olive oil for my soap making. I give him some home-made chicken noodle soup for his cold.

I throw in a load of washing, tidy the house and step outside to hang out the laundry. Walking down the street is Panayótis, a dear, sweet old man who always says a warm hello to Dario and me when we are out walking. He has a heartwarming, toothless grin, and has on occasion gifted us with oranges from his tree and a walking stick for me. He calls to me as I hang the laundry on the balcony, "Ella, Linda!" (come, Linda). I quickly grab the loaves of banana bread I have baked for him and dash outside. He presents me with a beautiful bouquet of greens from his garden. I give him the banana bread, a hug and kiss, and we exchange greetings and wishes for a good year. I am SO touched.

The phone rings. Dario answers..."*Embrós!*" It is Leftéris from the courier office announcing we have a package. We should have known! FedEx doesn't do door delivery and we are given directions to a harbor side location. I send Dario down to collect our package with a suggestion that he hurry. My sisters Barbie and Ali have sent the most wonderful package.

Dario and I savor the opening of each item. I get a little teary-eyed. Families have their difficulties but ain't no one like family that knowed where you been and where you done come from. They got all the dirt on you but they can also walk with you down memory lane.

Wonderful surprises are in the box. Does anyone remember Fuzzy Wuzzy Was A Bear? Yep, got one of those in a Saint Nicholas version in my box. Homemade caramels (we girls are all good cooks), Pop Rocks, Razzles, chocolate coins (Ali, please send real money next time), a book... IN ENGLISH... and all manner of good things. I melt.

One thing is puzzling, there is a pack of Beeman's gum, opened, with a stick missing. Wow, I think, my sisters haven't changed, they are still a bit bizarre.

Turns out, after inquiring, that customs took a piece of my Beeman's gum. Huh....go figure. And as a tribute to my sisters, I'm posting a couple of photos only they will understand. Love you two.

Linda

Omens

ON MONDAY JANUARY fifteenth, with almost a month to spare before Linda's ninety-day permit expired, we returned to the town hall to apply for her residency permit. The employee responsible would be back from leave by now.

We'd followed the consulate's instructions to the letter and had all the necessary paperwork. Our file was fat and good to go. All Linda had to do was fill in a form, pay four hundred Euros, and receive a five-year renewable residency permit. There should be no problems.

What the consulate in the US hadn't done was explain the skill that Greek bureaucrats have for deviating from the script and making your life difficult at every opportunity.

The woman at the town hall in charge of such matters, one Irène, met our politeness with savage hostility. After staring at our documents as though they were alien spores, she threw them back across the table at us.

"*You* cannot do this!" she snapped. "You must have a lawyer! I will give you his number." She scrawled a name and phone number on a scrap of paper and turned to talk to her clearly embarrassed young assistant. We had been dismissed.

We made an appointment for 7:30 on Tuesday evening to meet with the lawyer, Mr. Rígas Kákos. The problem, we thought, was a simple one: the harpy at the town hall couldn't verify that our papers were kosher, and perhaps the fact that our passports show different last names was also an issue for her. On the other hand, one would expect the person employed to deal with foreign residency permits to be able to deal with foreign documents.

The lawyer's office was a block from the Próton market, in a side street just off what Yiánnis called Souvláki Square, the little tree-shaded plaza encircled by gyro and Souvláki joints.

Vicky, the lawyer's young assistant, greeted us in excellent English: "Please have a seat. Mr. Kákos is running a little late but he will be here soon."

We looked around the office. A drab room, cheaply furnished. Mr. Kákos's desk was piled with papers. Vicky, dressed in jeans and wearing her coat, sat with her back to us, working at a desktop set at an awkward height on an antique side table. Linda and I looked at one another, both stirred by pity for the poor child. The ergonomics were even worse than our setup at home.

The minutes ticked by and Mr. Kákos didn't show. I had a heavy cold and was ready to chew on his neck if he gave us any crap. I could give him chapter and verse on the regulations, down to the waiver applying to spouses of non-Schengen agreement citizens ratified on January 1st, 2006. Just verify that our papers are the real thing, write a note to your stooge in the town hall, and we'll be on our way, pal.

Vicky tried to call him after ten minutes, and again ten minutes later. "Mr. Kákos is in a meeting with the mayor and his mobile is turned off," she said, in an apologetic tone. "But I think he will arrive soon."

After forty-five minutes of waiting, we decided to leave. Vicky promised to have her boss call us in the morning. He didn't. I called again that evening and we set up an appointment for Thursday morning.

Rigínos ('Rígas') Kákos is one of the few people I have ever met to whom one could justifiably apply the term 'lugubrious'. Tall, thin, and fortyish, he had all the animation of a corpse. His watery blue eyes rarely strayed from under their heavy lids. In his crisp jeans, open-necked blue shirt, and black bomber jacket, Mr. Kákos looked more like an undertaker about to go out clubbing than a lawyer. You would not hire this man as a babysitter.

He did speak excellent English, a big plus. We explained the situation in detail. We pointed to the November tenth entry stamp in Linda's passport and made it very clear we had to file the application before February tenth.

"As you see, we have everything we need," I said, handing over the papers one by one. "Our original marriage certificate; an apostille of the same; the document from the British Home Office stating that our marriage is registered in the UK; both our passports and *afimís*; and the original copy of our lease. There shouldn't be any problems."

Mr. Kákos looked over our papers. "Perhaps not," he said, with little conviction. "But those people in Vólos are unbelievable. You must leave me Linda's passport and all the papers to copy and make translations."

We offered a deposit; he declined. The accountant had done the same. Apparently Greek professionals only billed at the end of a service.

As we walked home, Linda said, "I don't like him having my passport. In the US that's not even legal."

"He could have just photocopied them, " I agreed. "I'll call Vicky tomorrow morning and pick them up."

In the morning, when I called, Vicky said, "Yes, I will take them to be photocopied now, and then you can pick them up."

"You don't have a photocopier in your office?" I said.

"No," she said. "But it will not take long, it is very near."

A lawyer's office without a photocopier, imagine that. As big a red flag as I ever missed in my life.

WE WERE SEVERAL days past the promised ten, and our workshop was nowhere near ready.

All the same, I was pleasantly surprised by the quality and thoroughness of the work being done; the Tsoúmas family's crew were doing a first-class job. After building the new wall, they had not just surface-mounted the new electrics onto the exposed cinderblock walls, but instead cut chases, buried the conduit, and installed outlets on each wall prior to recoating all the walls and ceiling with a fresh skim of cement render. We were going to have a beautiful workshop.

If it ever got finished.

I stopped by the Próton market and told Giórgos how impressed and grateful I was at the job being done. I asked if—since we'd overrun his original time estimate—he could give me a completion date.

A confident nod of the head. "Two days, maybe three," he said. "No problem."

I was skeptical. "*Vevéos?*" Really?

"*Sígouros.*" Certainly.

I smiled and thanked him. We shook hands.

Three Days? Double that, I thought.

The days dragged. The weather remained fine: where were the wild winter storms I'd been hoping for? Instead, there was talk of serious drought. "In the summer we will drink seawater!" one storekeeper told us.

Linda kept busy working on the house and on her soap packaging. She made another couple of test batches of soap, until we ran out of flat surfaces for them to cure on. I wrote, shopped, and took long hikes into the surrounding hills and valleys, going up to five or six miles and returning home with bunches of wild sage and oregano, both of which grew in abundance on the island; I wondered about *hórta*, the edible wild greens that apparently grew everywhere. I made a mental note to ask someone to show me what they looked like.

We'd begun to invite friends to dinner on a weekly basis. Since the arrival of Linda's care package, we had tortillas and Thai curry paste, as well as the spices needed for Indian food which we'd included in our shipment. Linda prepared Mexican meals for Rita and Sofía and for the Balabánises, who had never eaten Mexican food. We cooked fiery curries for ourselves. Linda spent the best part of a day making four dozen vegetable samosas, most of which we froze[14].

The only trouble with cooking elaborate meals and using a lot of fancy dinnerware was that it produced serious washing up. This wasn't such a problem in the 'States, but cleanup in a sixty square foot kitchen with no dishwasher and a single sink was a true pain. You couldn't turn around without knocking something over, and the marble floors were unforgiving. We were losing glass and china at an alarming rate.

---

[14] Fruit and produce availablility on the islands is strictly seasonal and much of the food is grown, if not locally, at least regionally. So although we missed tomatoes throughout the winter, the reward came in the form of winter greens fresh and bursting with flavor. Yes, the produce required substantial cleaning, as I discovered on rinsing half a cup of sand from a bunch of spinach; but I'd settle for seasonal over tasteless anytime.

POWERLESS TO PUSH progress on the workshop and Linda's residency, we decided to go and spend a day or two with Brigitte. Every time we spoke on the phone she would ask 'when are you coming?'

In spite of already living on a Greek island and not working, we thought of our visits to Alónissos as a vacation. And Brigitte was a fine host: from the moment we arrived at her house she wouldn't let us do anything. With her grandson Alexis now back in Germany, she would welcome the company.

But when you live on a small island, planning even a five-mile trip in winter is difficult. Although we could actually *see* the houses and beaches at the western end of Alónissos, getting there was another matter entirely. A persistent wind had kicked up, blowing a stiff breeze through the day and gusting to a fresh gale at night. The sea was stitched with whitecaps, and even the harbor grew choppy. The Flying Dolphins wouldn't risk winds over about 15mph, and the ferries became iffy around 20mph. Some days nothing came into the harbor.

One afternoon I watched a ferry leave for Alónissos and turn around when it hit the open water between the islands. But in the fifteen minutes it took to return, the harbor entrance had become rougher than the captain would have liked, so he turned the ferry again and steamed around the island to the tiny, sheltered harbor at Agnóndas. Anyone who'd been bound for Alónissos was just out of luck.

Within three days the shops started to run out of milk and produce. There were no mail deliveries. Even if the wind let up and we could get to Alónissos, we might not be able to get back for several days. Desperate as we were to get the damned boxes out of our dining room and start working the moment the workshop was ready, we decided to stay put.

A Cozy Evening

WITH THE ISLAND cut off from the world, we received an invitation to drop by Rita's house and join her and Sofía for drinks and *mezés*. Rita gave us directions. We thought we knew the house, since it was right on our usual route into the village, just before the appliance store and the OTÉ office.

Many streets in the *hóra* have name plaques, but Skopelítes appear not to know it. They never use addresses in the conventional sense. Location is by parish, and referenced to the nearest church. Thus the Balabánises' house might be 'the house with the big entry patio a little below St. Spýros's'. This system—heavily dependent on a number of variables, such as the distinctiveness of the house, the size of the parish, the speaker's powers of description, and so on—leaves much to be desired. We were more than once grateful for our cellphone.

The night was damp and the way slick. Not far from Rita's house, Linda lost her footing; fortunately we were holding hands and I caught her, but not in time to stop her giving her bad knee a pretty good twist, just when it had been improving, too. I fussed around, but she waved me off, promising to ice it when we got home.

Rita's house, three storeys and four bedrooms, dated from the late 1800s. Both Rita and Sofía were born here. From the geometric tiles in the hallway to the high ceilings and solid, paneled doors, everything about the Toúni house was authentic. Simply furnished with antiques handed down through the family, the place was comfortable as an old slipper.

After a brief tour we were shown into a spacious living/dining room. Rita fixed us Campari and sodas while Sofía brought *mezés*. Big iron radiators under the windows kept the room toasty warm.

We'd only known these people a few weeks. But sitting beside Linda on Sofía's comfy old sofa, I felt entirely at ease with the world, my habitual burden of floating anxiety set aside. It was like hanging out with old friends in a house I'd known all my life. I glanced at Linda, and saw she was equally happy.

After a little small talk, Rita asked if we'd seen Tákis. I told her I'd played chess with him just a couple of nights before.

"Did he say anything about me?" said Rita, a phase that was to become predictable as we came to know her better. A glance at Sofía told me the topic of Tákis was already a very familiar one to her: poor Rita was clearly in love with him, a love doomed to remain unrequited.

"I can't figure him out," said Rita, as she opened a bottle of wine. "I mean, sometimes he's so kind and sweet. And then he tells me all about his stupid girlfriends, and all the problems he has with them!"

"Shows he trusts you," I said. "You're his friend."

"I guess. I mean, we've known each other all our lives. But I don't want to know all this about his affairs!"

"Have you tried letting him know you're interested?" said Linda.

Rita's eyes widened. "I could never do that! He'd freak out."

"Why?" I asked. "A lot of guys like women to take the initiative."

"Not Tákis. He's too Greek." Rita sipped her wine. "Last Saturday night I was out with his best friend, Tímon. Nothing serious, just a few beers at Ánemos. I asked him if he thought Tákis liked me, and he said that he thought he did. Anyway, we had more drinks, and about three in the morning he walked me home."

I raised my eyebrows; Linda was smiling.

"No, it's not what you think!" said Rita, laughing. "Anyway, I was saying goodnight to him and I said something more about Tákis, and you know what he did? He bit my hand!"

My mouth fell open.

"He *what?*" said Linda.

"He bit my hand! Really! He just grabbed it and—" she raised her hand and mimed the action—"He bit me, hard! It hurt so much that I screamed and started shouting at him in the street. '*Are you crazy?*' I said, '*Why are you biting me?*' All the neighbors were opening their windows now and coming out on the street. It was so embarrassing!"

Sofía nodded vigorously. "Everyone they hear this."

"My God," I said, between laughs, "you lead a really exciting life!"

"Why did he bite you?" said Linda, sticking to the point with admirable focus.

"I don't know! *He* doesn't know! I asked him, and he said he just wanted me to stop talking about Tákis!"

I thought a moment about this. I'd met this young man, and seen him in Tákis's shop. Fine-featured, soft-spoken, there was an almost feminine delicacy to him. The pieces fell into place.

"I wonder if he's gay," I said. "He has a thing for Tákis, but of course Tákis is so hetero that Tímon can't tell him. He may not even know."

The doorbell rang, suspending further speculation on this topic.

"Ah, that is Léda," said Sofía, heading for the door.

"Léda is one of our best friends," explained Rita. "I've known her since I was born."

The woman who entered was arresting. In early middle age, with an intensely olive complexion and jet-black hair, Léda had the most alert and piercing gaze I've ever encountered. She was the human embodiment of a hawk.

She greeted us in perfect English. Her mouth smiled, but her eyes drilled into us as though their instructions didn't include cooperating with the rest of the face.

We returned the greeting in Greek; the eyes softened just a little.

Léda owned a travel agency on the *paralía* that catered mostly to British tourists. After the usual what-brought-you-here questions had been addressed, she asked us how we liked Skópelos.

"We love it," said Linda, "especially the people."

Léda looked incredulous. *"You like the people?"*

I wondered why everyone asked us that.

Linda replied, "Of course. People have been wonderful towards us." I added my endorsement.

Léda looked sideways at Rita. Sofía was beaming at us.

"We didn't come to just hang out with expats," Linda explained. We want to get to know people and become part of the community."

Léda's eyebrows went up.

"Which is why we spent a year studying the language before we moved," I added.

Léda turned at Sofía. Sofía smiled.

"Linda makes soap," said Rita. "She's going to start a business here."

As Linda outlined her plans, Léda's manner changed. It turned out that Léda was fiercely proud of Skópelos's agriculture—"this island fed ten thousand people during World War Two!"—and was also a committed environmentalist with a profound knowledge of native plants and herbs. Her father, who had once been mayor of the island, had also made soap.

When Linda explained that her soap would be made only with Skópelos olive oil, Léda offered to give her some leftover oil she had in storage; when she heard the soap was to be stamped with the outline of the island in blue, her hand shot up. "Can I sell it to my clients? I want to be your first customer."

I had the clear feeling we'd just passed some kind of test.

MOST OF SKÓPELOS was down with some bug or other. People blamed the unseasonably warm weather. The last few days we'd been buffeted by warm, moist winds from the south. When you considered that the only thing of any size between us and the north African coast was the island of Crete, you began to understand the humidity: the dry Saharan wind blowing north from Egypt and Libya was sucking moisture off the Aegean for 550 miles along the way.

A couple of days later, I passed by the workshop again. Three days had passed since Giórgos's last estimate and there was still work to do. "Tomorrow," he promised me; then, all sheepish, he added, "maybe the next day."

"*Vevéos?*"

"*Sígouros,*" he said, with his hand on his heart.

I grinned.

Pondering the mysteries of this culture, I began to understand why there were so many monasteries in Greece. It was because you couldn't plan anything. Uncertainty was in the very air these people breathed; heck, why narrow life's possibilities by actually completing anything? The Greek mind revolted at the thought! And when you truly, fully, realized that you had no control over anything, the idea of living a simple, ordered monastic life became curiously seductive.

Linda's knee was still giving trouble, so I took my long walks alone. Not only did exercise keep my mood up and stop me obsessing over the delays with the workshop and Linda's residency, but I couldn't get enough of the beauties of the island.

I had adopted a favorite hike, a two and-a-half mile loop that generally took me about forty-five minutes, which I did daily on top of my trips into the village.

From Tákis's store and up past the cemetery, the cobbled switchback led steeply up for perhaps half a mile, a real cardio workout which rewarded with fantastic views of the village and harbor. Fork right on to a rocky dirt path flanking a meadow where a white horse would occasionally graze. The way became level here; once in a while a car or pickup would jounce by in a cloud of dust, forcing me to stand aside as it scraped the bushes. A sharp right then, through ancient, terraced olive groves. A melancholy-looking donkey lived in a lean-to on the left of the bend; to the right, down the hillside, goats, sheep, and chickens munched and pecked happily away.

After about another half a mile, past another small farm with a noisy Cocker Spaniel for a guard dog (thankfully, we never saw a single Rottweiler or Pit Bull), the view opened out again. The path became a road, flanked by newish villas to both left and right. A left turn around the shoulder of the hill, and such a view of Glyfonéri beach and its limpid waters that I always stopped in my tracks to drink it in.

From there, the road wound steeply down around the coast until it met the far end of the Skópelos ring road; just seven or eight minutes more, past Nikoláos A. Káltzas's store and Tákis's shop, and I was home.

It was the perfect hike in every regard: length, accessibility, variety of terrain and views. And it was never the same twice. On this occasion, the first bright red poppies were appearing and the almond trees were in full blossom. If the wind was blowing, as it was today, a wide swath of water at the eastern point of the harbor would turn from its usual deep blue to a startling turquoise. On a cloudy day, the water turned the color of steel.

I had purposely not passed by the workshop for three days. When I next went there I met Tsoúmas the elder, Giórgos's father. He was smoothing over a hole while another fellow worked inside, installing power receptacles. The place looked terrific. The Tsoúmas patriarch and I shook hands, and he flashed a gold-toothed grin when I thanked him for doing such a good job. He explained that they only had to put in the electric meter and the sink, and they were done.

"When will the wiring be finished and the water connected?" I asked Giórgos ten minutes later. "Please be realistic."

"Yes, yes, tomorrow, no problem! I will call you tomorrow night."

"*Vevéos?*"

Giórgos inclined his head solemnly. "*Sígouros!*"

I didn't believe him for a moment, but I could see the end was in sight, three or four days at the most. I went home and gave Linda the good news.

"Finally! We can rent a car and get these damn boxes out of the house. Then I can do some deep cleaning," she added, frowning at the dim corners of the hallway.

"Yeah. But Giórgos's tomorrows can mean anything. I'm pretty sure it won't be more than three or four days, but I don't want to book one till we have the keys."

Linda was undeterred. "Today's Saturday. Let's rent a car for Monday through Friday. That way even if it's not all ready this weekend, we can do a bit of sightseeing and be ready to start moving things the moment you get the keys."

The rental agencies were all shut for the winter, but the owner of one had a couple of cars which he rented out by arrangement, and I'd gotten his cellphone number. Off-season rates were highly negotiable, well under half what they were in the summer season.

The car we got on this occasion, a five-year old Fiat Panda, was a beat-up piece of junk: one mirror was half hanging off, the pedals were crammed so close together as to make driving positively dangerous, and the interior smelled as though someone had cremated a rodent in the car. But it was transport, and how much car did we really need on a twelve-mile long island?

Predictably, the workshop wasn't ready on Monday, but the wind had calmed. I collected the car while Linda packed a picnic, and we drove to Pánormos beach, a long, beautiful crescent of sand. The tavernas were all closed and we had the most popular beach on Skópelos to ourselves. We ate, did a little beachcombing, and lazed in the sun.

The next morning I found the workshop clean and empty. A heavy coat of green oil enamel was still tacky on the doors and propped-open shutters. The electric meter had been installed, and instead of a simple sink the Tsoúmases had put in a compact all-in-one, stainless sink/stove and fridge/freezer, all of which were necessary for Linda's work: soap had to be cooked, and came out of the mold most easily after a brief spell in a freezer. And we'd be able to make coffee, and keep beer on ice during those hot summer days.

I called Giórgos. He confirmed everything was finished and the paint just needed to dry. We could pick up the keys anytime. I thanked him and said I'd stop by next morning—coincidentally the first of the month—and bring the first month's rent.

Tomorrow we'd start moving things, but we had the rest of today free. Linda and I had discussed visiting Sendoúkia, the site of three ancient tombs high in the center of the island, variously described as 'Pirate tombs', 'Roman tombs', and 'tombs of unknown origin'. Whatever they were, the grainy black-and-white pictures we'd seen looked intriguing. We decided this would be the perfect day to visit them.

We set off in the late morning, exploring first along the parts of Skópelos known as Péfkias (Pines) and Potámi (Rivers), a low-lying area that the island's main river—really little more than a stream—flows through. The dirt road was rutted and rocky, and we rattled along at five or ten miles an hour, grateful for the Fiat's generous ground clearance.

A few miles and another dirt road brought us to the bottom of the hill where the trail up to Sendoúkia began. It was about three, and the day was cooling. No ancient olives groves or smelly goat pens here, just a clean, needle-piled track through a pristine pine forest. The air felt bracing, alpine.

After a half-mile or so we reached a rocky crest. The path ran out, leaving us in a jumble of boulders and stones. We knew from the map that the graves were somewhere on the far side of the crest, but there was no clear summit, and the map was less than precise. After a little confusion, Linda found a red spot painted on a rock. A little further on, she found another, and then another.

"Those must be Margaret Rodgers's marks," I said, remembering what Matt and Carole had told us of the island's infamous tourmeister and authoress of 'Skópelos Rambles'.

"I hope they're more accurate than her guidebook," said Linda.

They were accurate enough: ten minutes later we spotted the graves.

The site was striking. Three big, rectangular cavities, each about seven feet long by three wide and four deep, cut into the island's limestone crown. The lids—huge sarcophagus-like slabs of rock—had been edged aside just enough to allow looting in some period past. The tombs were empty. Between two of them was a rectangular depression the same size as the adjacent tombs but only a few inches deep, showing wide, parallel tool marks—a fourth grave, begun but not completed.

"I can't believe how cleanly they cut into the stone," said Linda. "They're almost perfectly square."

"No kidding. But I don't buy the 'pirate tomb' theory for a minute. I think these are way older. Maybe even Pre-Roman or Neolithic." It was true that these islands had been fought over and changed hands many times in the course of history; one of the most famous pirates of all time, Barbarossa, had sacked the island in 1538, murdering many of its inhabitants. But... "Why would pirates have sweated in the sun high up a hillside to carve tombs in solid rock with this sort of precision when a simple burial at sea or in soft soil would have been so much easier?"

Linda squatted down. She ran her hand along the rim of one of the tombs; her brow furrowed. "Pre-Roman? What kind of tools would they have used? Can bronze tools cut limestone as perfectly as this?"

"Maybe. It's a soft stone. And bronze tools have been around since about 3,000BC."

"For that matter, why cut graves into solid rock? They must have chosen this site for a reason."

She was right. We looked around us. From 1,800 feet above sea level, the view toward Alónissos and the nearby archipelago, where islands and islets seemed to float on the water, was unforgettable.

As though reading my mind, Linda went on, "It can't just be the view. I mean, the people buried here were dead—at least, I hope so!" she added, with a laugh.

I pointed towards the North, where a distant mountain lit by the late afternoon sun was just visible. "Mount Athos?"

Linda peered into the misty distance. "That would make sense. She glanced around again. "It's dead center of the view from here, and it *is* the holiest site for the Greek Orthodox church. Still, I wish there was more information on this place."

The problem with archaeology in Greece is similar to that with art in Italy: there's just too much of it to study, let alone maintain and care for. You could hardly dig a foundation or build a road in Greece without uncovering some ruin or relic, at which point the Ministry of Culture would stop the project. Consequently a great many of these unwanted finds went unreported, with smaller artifacts being spirited away, and larger ones—chunks of columns and the like—being re-interred as fast as they were dug up. So although this site was both striking and well-preserved, it had attracted little scholarly research and no preservation effort.

Though we wouldn't discover it for several weeks, another equally remarkable archaeological site on Skópelos went even more unnoticed by almost all visitors to the island.

Friends and Neighbors

NEXT MORNING I went to the Próton supermarket. The Great Day had arrived! Giórgos handed me the key and I handed him two hundred Euros in cash. No security or cleaning deposits required.

I paid cash, but we needed some kind of receipt for our taxes, and I mentioned this to Giórgos. Like everything in Greece, it wasn't simple; he would have to get their accountant to draw up a lease before he could give us receipts, but they would get it done. We shook hands and I sped off home to start loading boxes into the car.

The tiny Fiat was a three-door wagon. Stuffed with an average of five or six boxes per trip, it would take us at least a dozen trips to empty the dining room. Some of our boxes were mighty heavy, and awkward to maneuver in and out. We worked for a few hours, whizzing up and down the hill like crazy people. The pile in the dining room was shrinking, and the workshop big enough that even with all our overflow belongings in there we'd only lose ten or fifteen percent of our floor space.

Around three o'clock we'd just returned home for another load when Spýros and Mára showed up.

"We're going to the *kalívi*," said Spýros, "just for an hour of quiet. Would you like to come?"

"We'd love to," I said, "but we have many boxes to move."

"And we are dressed for work," Linda added, indicating the old clothes she was wearing.

Mára laughed. She pointed to Spýros, who'd just finished work and had splashes of cement on his jeans. "It doesn't matter, look at us!"

"Come," insisted Spýros. "we'll have an *oúzo*, some *mezés*. Just an hour or two."

I was sold: I'd had enough of moving boxes for a day. My eyes met Linda's and she smiled.

"Can I take five minutes?" she asked.

Spýros laughed. "Five, ten minutes, no problem, Linda! *Periménome.*" We will wait. "You like, I have *seeps*," he added, in English.

"I have *seeps* also," said Linda. "I will bring them!"

Spýros guffawed. "Ah, Linda! You do not have *seeps!*"

Linda put her hands on her hips. "Yes I do! I will bring them!"

"No, no! *I* have seeps! You have not seeps!"

I touched her arm. "Sweetheart, I think he means *sheep*, not chips."

Linda's mouth worked for a second. She burst out laughing. Mára got it now, and started me off.

Spýros was just about crying with laughter. "Ah, Linda! You have *seeps*, not seeps! *I* have seeps! *Beeeh! Beeehhh!*" he added, for emphasis.

The *kalívi* was across the island, not far from Pánormos beach. It was cold inside, and Mára built a fire while Spýros showed us his little menagerie of *seeps* and chickens. The sheep numbered eight or nine, with four darling lambs—soon to be three, I feared, with Easter not far off. Spýros gave us a grocery bag of bread scraps with which to feed the little flock while he collected a few eggs from the coop. A big rooster strutted about the yard, watchful, but too proud to beg crumbs.

A large, one-room cottage with a small kitchen and bathroom, the interior of the *kalívi* was a postcard. Everything that wasn't a wall was made of rich knotty pine: chests, hutches, doors, windows, tables, sofa, benches, chairs, bed—the traditional Greek sort, a wide, wooden platform on which a whole family might sleep—and the open-beamed ceiling itself, all sang with warm color. A handmade ladder led to a further sleeping platform overhead. Bright rugs filled the floor, and patterned woolen blankets, the bed. Fabrics in a myriad traditional designs covered chairs and pillows, and hung from walls. *Objets*—*tchótchkes*, if you asked Linda—stood in tidy files on every flat surface, like soldiers on parade. A big, rounded fireplace and bow-fronted chimneybreast softened one corner, and Mára's little fire was beginning to warm the room. On the far side, French doors opened on to a spacious, blue-railed balcony overlooking the lower acre or so of the property.

Spýros fetched the *oúzo* while Mára busied herself in the kitchen, emerging with a bowl of olives, and féta to accompany them; she set a few onions wrapped in tinfoil at the edge of the fire to cook.

Mára sipped a sweet liqueur—traditional Greek women shun hard liquor—while we chatted and munched and laughed until well after dark. The simplest pleasures are often the best.

To round off an already excellent day, I came back to an email informing me that my satirical/magic realist short story, 'America is Coming!'—in which the North American landmass literally loses its moorings and drifts around the globe smashing everything in its path—had been accepted for an upcoming anthology, and a contract was in the mail.

Sometimes life just doesn't get any better.

WE MOVED THE remainder of our boxes the next morning and I started on the workshop.

I began by applying a couple of coats of concrete paint to the floor to keep the dust down and make it easy to clean. With an extension pole and the fluffiest roller sleeve I could find—it looked like a Persian cat puffed up for a fight—I did a quarter of the floor first, then shunted all our boxes into that corner and proceeded to work the rest. It was a tedious task. The floor was uneven and the concrete mix soft and powdery, so that the first coat took forever. Three days and six gallons later, I was done.

Now we needed worktables and storage.

We had taken to stopping by Vasílis's shop and chatting when we passed by, which was almost daily, and had become friends. Since we'd sold our power tools before leaving, Vasílis lent me an electric drill and circular saw to make the job easier.

Two doors down from our workshop, just past the pizzeria and the little market, was a hardware store and lumber yard, where I bought several four-meter long two-by-twos and two-by-fours, walking them back to the workshop balanced precariously on my shoulder. In the process of all this to-ing and fro-ing, I discovered we had interesting neighbors.

On the corner of the main road was the O Níkos pizzeria. The owner was a gray-haired man built like a small industrial furnace, all muscle and energy. When we introduced ourselves in Greek, he answered in rough English, or something like it.

Níkos—"Call me Nick!"—had spent twenty-nine years in New Jersey until his return to his native Skópelos a few years previously. During that time he had not only managed to retain his Greek accent but had overlaid it with a heavy coat of Joysey. This, um, *coloratura* coupled with a gruff, rasping voice, made Nick more than a little difficult to understand. But he was kind, his pizzas were decent, and his prices were keen. He also agreed to let us use his toilet whenever we wanted.

The little market on the next corner, past the butcher's shop which we had already discovered to be the best in town, was owned by yet another Rígas. But the person who actually seemed to run the store was a cheeky English girl called Jilly.

Fit, overly boyish, with standard geek-issue, red-framed glasses which never sat straight, Jilly bantered with the locals in heavily Cockney-accented Greek, and addressed everyone as 'darling' or 'love'. Unfailingly upbeat and a hard worker with tremendous people skills, she was undoubtedly a major asset to Rígas.

Jilly was also well-informed. She knew everyone, and was immediately curious about us. In turn, we discovered that she and her female partner had lived on Skópelos some three years and built a house here. All they needed now was electricity, for which they'd been waiting over a year.

The last and final store on the block was the hardware store. I loved this place: it was dimly-lit and old-fashioned; pretty much everything was sold loose, and when they received a delivery you had to clamber over things to reach the shelving; they had things I'd never seen before, including great sacks of powdered pigment which you could buy by the kilo for tinting plaster or limewash.

The hardware store was owned by a father-and-son duo. We had briefly met the son, Páris, on our first night out with Yiánnis and Mina. Páris was in his early thirties, and looked more urban than islander. Wiry hair worn long enough to tie at the back framed his strong features; intelligent eyes weighed and measured you. "Páris is my best friend now," Yiánnis had told me once. "But he spends a lot of time online. He is always in a virtual reality game where you live in another world." I couldn't help but wonder why anyone living in this paradise would prefer to hang out in Second Life, or whatever it was.

I RETURNED HOME from prepping the workshop one afternoon to find the house gleaming and utterly spotless. Every surface shone, and the air was sweet and fresh.

"Wow. You've done a serious cleaning here," I said.

Linda grinned. "Yeah, now the boxes are gone. And it was so funny—Anna stopped by to say hello when I was on my knees scrubbing the floors. I had the front door open, and she just stood there open-mouthed. 'You wash the floor!' she said. 'Of course I wash the floors,' I told her."

I laughed. "They probably think foreigners consider themselves above cleaning their homes, and have to hire people for that."

"Or that we're just not very clean. You know how clean Mára keeps her house."

"Well done," I said. "I think you just won us another gold star with our Greek friends."

BY NOW, OUR social life was shifting into high gear. We'd been told this would change in the summer, as everyone became busy, but we were enjoying our developing social network. Every weekend we were either invited to someone's house or having them over to ours. Rita and Sofía were becoming close friends, and I thought that we'd enjoy Vasílis and Lítza's company if we could ever pin him down to a date.

I'd been getting to know Tákis better over our weekly chess games, and we had him over one evening. A city boy who'd traveled, he had refined table manners and a wider frame of reference than most; and he was an excellent communicator, even with limited English. Linda liked him a lot. His sheer life force was inspiring: exercise, food, drink, women… Tákis was someone who devoured life in great, lusty mouthfuls.

He was also interesting in his sensitivities. He'd read Carlos Castaneda, and had strong metaphysical leanings. "Every time before I swim, I make prayer to the sea," he said. "It is very strong, the sea. It can kill you. Always I know this."

THAT SATURDAY WE had Yiánnis and Mina to dinner. It had been some weeks since we'd seen them, time enough (I hoped) for any lingering tensions between Linda and Yiánnis to dissipate.

The table looked magnificent. It had been set for two days. Linda had pulled all the stops and brought out the Bavarian ivory-and-gold china, antique Venetian wineglasses, and gold-plated flatware, setting it all on a white linen tablecloth with deep red napkins for accent.

She'd prepared Thai food, which Yiánnis and Mina had told us they loved. They were a little stunned by the opulence of the table. "When you come to our house, it will not be like this," said Yiánnis.

"And I can not cook like you," Mina added. Until now, we had only eaten at our house, with them taking us out twice.

"We don't judge or keep score," Linda assured her. "We just enjoy your company."

The food came, complemented by a brace of splendid Greek white wines our guests had brought. We talked and laughed. Sometime around midnight, during a break before dessert, we asked Yiánnis—possibly the most well-informed person on the island—about the dramatic police action near our house a couple of weeks ago. I still couldn't believe Spýros's story about drug gangs on Skópelos.

"It was a suicide," said Yiánnis. "A young man. He was a gay man, and he had argued with his lover. So, late in the night, he drank a bottle of whisky and threw himself from the roof." He pointed to the window. "There, just one street down from here. They did not find him until ten the next morning."

"Oh, how terrible!" said Linda. I added similar comments.

Mina agreed. "Everybody always made fun of him. Just a few days before, they made fun of him at the big Christmas party."

We commiserated some more. Traditional society. Greeks tolerated gays, but expected discretion from them, especially on a small island.

"Yes, it is very sad." said Yiánnis, nodding gravely. After a moment, his eyebrows went up and a mischievous smile crept onto his face. "But you cannot imagine how gay this man was. I mean," he went on, rising from the table with napkin in hand, "he was *so* gay that he walked like this."

What followed would have befitted a burlesque drag queen. With pursed lips and a silly smirk on his face, Yiánnis minced to and fro, wiggling his bottom provocatively, the red napkin dangling from one limp-wristed hand. Our sober, serious friend, the private doctor, who had such strong ideas about how the wife of the private doctor on a small island should comport herself, queening around our dining room. After a moment of stunned surprise, we laughed until we hurt. His performance wasn't cruelly intended; but it was a vivid reminder that in societies untouched by the taint of political correctness, humor took no prisoners.

After they left, Linda and I were still chuckling at Yiánnis's hilarious posturing. "I didn't think he had a sense of humor," she said, as we cleared the table, "but he can be a clown. He was *so* funny!"

"He really was," I agreed.

She was thoughtful. "Maybe he and I will get on after all."

THE WINDS HAD finally calmed, and we'd made a good start on the workshop. It was time for a weekend trip to Alónissos.

Brigitte met us off the Dolphin in the late afternoon. We sat in front of the fire and got caught up over a drink and snacks. Brigitte was always thirsty for news.

I reflected on the parallels between Manos's and my father's situation. Whereas Mános had been laid low by a single, big stroke, my father had suffered a series of micro-strokes over a long period, resulting in severe neurological damage. Like Mános, he retained all his alertness despite losing his mobility; and, also like Mános, he'd been able to remain at home and engaged with life and family thanks to a strong German wife who flatly refused to listen to the nurses and social service workers who insisted he needed to be in a full-time nursing facility. "I am a Prussian," my stepmother once told me, "and duty is what we were taught."

The word 'duty' is uncommon currency these days, and to hear someone speak of themselves as Prussian rather than simply German was downright nineteenth-century; so the phrase had stuck with me. I related it to Brigitte.

She looked grave for a moment, then nodded. "Yes. That is correct," she said. Brought up in the same culture, these two women shared the same solid values in defiance of the modern world.

The next day Brigitte drove us along the spine of the island, past a few patches of snow left over from a brief shower the previous day, all the way to the Gerákas biological research station at the far end of Alónissos, about an hour's drive.

The deserted little harbor at Gerákas served only the research station and a few fishermen living at this lonely end of the island. One bright red fishing boat had been pulled up to winter on the shingle at the far end of the little bay. A smaller caïque was moored along the quayside, along with a pair of rowboats. The water in the harbor was clearer than any I could imagine. The silence was absolute.

The research station was built in 1985, after the EU declared the waters around Alónissos and a number of nearby islets a sanctuary for the protected European Monk Seal. The 'Core Zone', which contained the seals' breeding areas, was off limits to everyone except accredited researchers, but tour boats were permitted to cruise the less sensitive waters around it.

"Look at it now," said Brigitte, waving at the white complex of buildings which together comprised the research station. "Empty! All that money they took from the EU, and now it is closed!" She muttered a string of Greek curses under her breath.

"They closed it down? What about the seals?" said Linda.

Brigitte shrugged. "Ehh, the seals are in the water, as always. Only the research station is closed. The bloody *dimarhío* takes the money from the EU, and what they spend it on, nobody knows! But you see, there is no-one there. It is closed."

We returned home the next day. Coming into the harbor, seeing the familiar buildings come into view, stepping off the Dolphin and walking the narrow streets toward home… all this was very comforting. We felt we were really starting to belong, despite the occasional warnings and red flags.

From the Aegean Dream blog:

Linda speaks
February 15, 2007

Well, it's been an interesting beginning for a February. At times I wonder what the heck we've done and other days I believe we have done the best thing ever. I am continually amazed at the things we learn, the counsel we receive, and the people we meet.

Things are very black and white on a Greek Island, with an enormous amount of gray lurking in between. Some friends warn us that we will never be accepted by the locals and that people we believe we are beginning to make friends with will soon wash their hands of us. Others disagree: Láli Páppas assured us that yes, we can build a life and have friends; she too is a "foreigner" not born on the island and she was elected to the council! Yet we hear from others that they have made no strong friendships.

Warnings abound and I find myself being torn between believing people actually like us, and feeling that perhaps the comments of friends and acquaintances, and their cautions to beware, should be heeded more strongly. Perhaps I am naïve, perhaps I choose to believe better things about people and their motives. Does the little old man up the road really bring us oranges and greenery just to see what the foreigners are up to? Does the woman in the little market congratulate me on my attempts to communicate with her in Greek and gift me with a bottle of wine because of ulterior motives? Are we invited into the homes of locals for meals and family celebrations for reasons I don't understand? Do they accept invitations to our home, spend evenings with us and invite us out with the intent of severing ties in the future? I do not know. I am confused with the widely swinging opinions of people we talk to.

Enough of my confusion dear readers! And on to the Pagan Rites we have witnessed. Carnival has begun......

On Sunday, we stroll to the harbor to witness the beginning of the celebration. In a small village you can't help but meet several acquaintances while you are out and about. So on our way to take a look at the building of skeleton boats that will be paraded through the streets and later set fire to and sunk in the harbor, we are sidetracked by Láli Páppas, a local city official and real estate agent. She and her husband invite us for a coffee and we find ourselves sipping hot chocolate and discussing the look of the island. She knows of Dario's work and has convinced him to choose colors for various civic fixtures. Now she wants him to apply some sample paint to the iron lamp posts that line the harbor walkway. She then asks if he would be interested in assisting with the design of the kindergarten playground. She is full of life and possible offers of work. A good woman to know. We chat, discuss life on Skópelos, and her young daughter eventually shows us the way to the area by the island olive press where the boats are being built.

Imagine this in the US: A group of kids, in the range of 12-16, with their faces smeared black (why?) are building boats from wood, tin cans and whatever happens to be available, with NO adult supervision—none! They are in high spirits, toxic smoke is billowing all over the area from the burning of what smells like plastics and kerosene in the make-shift burners attached to their masterpieces. Generally, it is chaos.

We can't believe that kids are allowed the freedom and the creative space to play in this manner—it's fabulous. We can't wait to see them burning in the harbor. (The boats... not the kids!)

We trot home for a little relaxation prior to heading out with the Balabánis family for a meal. At 8:30 we are picked up and driven to the harbor restaurant. Upon entering, our jaws drop! There is a group of young men, dressed in all manner of wild apparel, one playing an accordion, several dressed to the nines (as women) and singing songs which I believe would have made me blush if I could have understood the words. The Balabánis family were shaking their heads (among chuckles and guffaws) and Mára was the brightest shade of red I have ever seen. We can understand a few of their words: *érotos... gynéka...* just enough to get the general jist of it.

But more importantly, should our interpretation of the language not suffice, the highly graphic simulated sexual activity most certainly clarifies our understanding. Including, but not limited to, a man, dressed as a woman with pink hosiery, hiking up her/his dress and bending over while the gentleman(?) with the accordion snuggled up close and made suggestive movements while playing discordant notes on the accordion. There was more, but the Balabánis family assured us this only took place once a year... at least in public.

Linda

Our Troubles Begin

WE STILL HADN'T heard from Kákos, our lawyer, and Linda's entry permit was about to expire. A day before the due date, I called his office to make certain he'd filed Linda's application.

"I'm sorry, Mr. Kákos is not in the office," said Vicky. He would be in on Monday (this was Friday) and would I like to leave a message. I did, and she said she'd make sure he called us on Monday.

I was mildly concerned, and wished I'd called a few days earlier; but he had all the documents, he knew the deadline, and it was a simple business. Greeks just weren't good at returning calls, and there was no reason to worry.

On Monday morning I called Kákos. To my dismay, he hadn't filed Linda's papers, and sounded shocked when I told him her permit had expired over the weekend. I reminded him that we'd clearly pointed out this deadline at our prior meeting.

"You must come to my office immediately," he said. "We have to go to the police station."

As we hurried together along the windy *paralía*, Mr. Kákos turned to me. "Do you have your passport?" I didn't. "You must get it," he said. "We will be at the police station." I turned and ran back towards home.

Fifteen minutes later, I arrived breathless at the police station to find Linda and our lawyer standing outside. Linda looked stressed. The air around them felt prickly.

Kákos turned on his heel."We must go to the town hall." Crisis or not, the man's manners left a lot to be desired. Besides which there would have been no crisis had the fool filed the application on time.

"What happened?" I asked Linda, as we hurried to keep up.

She kept her voice down. "He tried to get them to extend my permit. The police refused and there was a big argument."

"So what happens now?"

Her gesture said she hadn't a clue.

Mr. Kákos stopped at an ATM Machine near the town hall and made us wait while he withdrew some cash.

We followed him up the stairs to the office where Iréne, the official who'd referred us to him, worked. The door was open. She looked up as Kákos knocked on the door.

Kákos walked in, reached into his pocket, pulled out a handful of crisp Euro bills, and tossed them onto Iréne's desk. The notes fanned out as they slid across the surface: fifties, and a good few of them. My jaw dropped. Without turning, he put out his hand and pushed the door shut in our faces.

Linda and I stared at one another. "Did you just see what I saw?" she whispered.

I nodded.

"I don't believe this!"

"He's going to have her backdate the paperwork," I said.

Linda's voice was urgent. "I don't want to be a part of this. This is criminal!"

"I'm sure it's not the first time it's happened. Besides, I don't think there's much we can do about it right now."

Mr. Kákos emerged a few moments later. Avoiding our eyes, he made straight for the stairs.

"Well?"

He ignored me. A few dozen yards outside the town hall, he stopped. "Linda's application is dated the twenty-second of January," he declared in low tones.

Three weeks ago. Linda was dumbstruck. I said, "What's next?"

"We must file all the papers immediately. Do you have a certificate of family status?"

We'd never heard of such a thing, and said so.

"It is a paper to say that you are together as a married couple."

"I don't think we have those in the US," said Linda.

"Our marriage certificate is only a year and a half old," I said. "We gave you an apostille. And we registered our marriage in an EU country. Your consulate assured us that was more than sufficient."

"Yes, but you could have separated during this time. The certificate of family status is necessary to prove the marriage is current."

"I can call the US embassy in Athens," said Linda, "and see if there's something like it. Perhaps they can write a letter to say the marriage is current and there's been no divorce."

"Good." And he dropped his bombshell: "You must also deposit a thirteen thousand Euro bond."

For the second time in a few minutes, neither of us could speak.

"*Thirteen thousand* Euros? *Why?*" I said.

"Because Linda does not have insurance for illness. You are covered as an EU citizen, but she is not."

"The Greek consulate never once mentioned it."

"It is the law."

"So what do people do who don't have that sort of money lying around," said Linda. "All the Albanians and the poorer immigrants?"

"It is a requirement," he insisted, zipping up his bomber jacket. "Please bring the certificate to my office," he said, and began to walk away.

"Wait," I said. I pointed to the Ánemos café a few doors away. "Can we discuss this a little more over a coffee?"

"I must return to the office. We must start the papers." And he was gone.

Over a couple of cappuccinos, in a swirl of emotions, Linda and I discussed our predicament.

We had lost all confidence in our lawyer's integrity and competence. Our financial cushion was shrinking fast, and there was no way we could deposit thirteen thousand Euros (then about US $17,000); nor did we believe his assertion that this was a requirement which applied in Linda's case.

Linda went home to call the US Embassy in Athens and I went to get the day's groceries. I stopped by Vasílis's shop to say hello. I needed to debrief.

When I told him our lawyer had forgotten to file Linda's residency papers within the specified limit, Vasílis looked up sharply. "Who's your lawyer?"

"Rígas Kákos," I replied.

Vasílis's face contorted. "That bastard! He almost cost me my business a couple of years ago!"

I spread my hands. "We were told to go to him. I assumed he was the only one who handled residency permits here."

"Bullshit!" said Vasílis. "Who told you that?"

I explained the whole story. When I'd finished, he said, "Kákos is an idiot. I had a problem a couple of years ago with a supplier who said I owed him a load of money and threatened to sue me. I took the case to Kákos and you know what he said?" I shook my head.

Vasílis lit a cigarette. "He said to me, 'What do you want me to do about it? I don't know what to do.' Can you believe it! *He's* the bloody lawyer and he asks *me* what to do!"

"What *did* you do?"

"I took the case to another lawyer. He wrote one letter to the supplier and that was the end of it, case closed." He jabbed his cigarette in my direction. "And you know what? He didn't even charge me! You go to my lawyer friend Pétros and he'll sort it out. I'll give you his number." He picked up a pen and began to scribble it down.

"Well, we'd certainly like a second opinion," I said. Does he speak English?"

"Yes. Here. Pétros Haralámpos. You tell him I sent you." He handed me the slip of paper. "Better still, let me call him right now and you can make an appointment." Vasílis dialed a number, outlined the situation in a machine-gun exchange of Greek, and handed me the phone.

Mr. Haralámpos was deep-voiced and courteous. He would be delighted to see us at seven-thirty that same evening.

"Thanks, Vasíli," I said, after hanging up. "We owe you one."

He waved it away. "That bloody Kákos," he went on, the subject evidently irresistible. "He's such a moron! Do you know he ran for mayor last year? Can you believe it? Of course he lost."

I tried to imagine our lugubrious, shifty-looking lawyer running our island paradise, and quickly pushed the idea aside.

Vasílis looked pensive. Then he smiled. "Hey, I've got an idea. What's your home number?"

I gave it to him. "Why?"

Grinning, he gestured me to silence and dialed. I heard Linda's faint answer. Vasílis angled the earpiece slightly so that I could hear. I leaned closer.

"Hallo, is this miss Linda Whitaker?" he said, suppressing his broad South African accent in favor of a bizarre mid-Atlantic affectation.

"Yes, I'm calling from the US embassy in Athens." He winked at me. "Miss Whitaker, I'm afraid there's a problem with your residency. Yes, I'm afraid we must ask you to leave Greece at once."

There was stunned silence from the other end. He was very good. I was trying not to laugh, though a part of me felt terrible for Linda, upset as she already was; but she had a pretty wicked sense of humor herself. She could handle it.

"I—" she began; then, "*Vasílis!*"

He burst out laughing and owned up. After a moment he handed me the phone. "He totally had me!" said Linda, laughing. "I just got off the phone with the embassy, so I fell for it completely."

"Vasílis had better look out," I said, grinning at him. "He doesn't know you yet, does he?"

I arrived home a short while later. "So what did the embassy say?" I asked, as I unpacked the groceries.

"As I thought, there's no equivalent of this 'certificate of family status' in the US. The man I spoke to says it only exists in Greece and Italy, and they've run into this problem before."

"So can they at least confirm that we're not divorced?" I said.

"What they can do is to write a letter stating that no equivalent document exists in the US. In fact, they offered to fax a copy to Kákos right away so he has something to work with, and they'll put the original in the mail to us. He said we'll have it within a week."

"A document saying there's no such document. God help us."

Out of the Frying Pan

PÉTROS HARALÁMPOS WAS the perfect white hat to Kákos's black. A big man with a neatly trimmed beard and rich brown eyes, the new attorney could have passed for a young tenor. He greeted us warmly and showed us into his private office.

Mr. Haralámpos's English, though less polished than Kákos's, was adequate. After a short exchange of niceties, Linda asked if we had attorney-client privilege.

"Of course."

"Okay," said Linda, and went on to relate our experience. When she reached the part about the cash thrown on Iréne's table, the lawyer's brows knitted. He held up a hand.

"Wait, can you repeat this? He gave her money?"

Linda repeated the facts of the incident, qualifying it as she did so: "I'm just telling you what we saw."

"And it didn't look very good," I added. "When we left the office, Mr. Kákos told us our application had been backdated by three weeks."

Mr. Haralámpos's face darkened. He looked from one to the other of us, frowning.

"You are saying Iréne took money to make a false application?"

"It certainly looked like that," I said, "although we don't know what was said after the door was closed."

His temper shattered like a bomb casing: "You cannot understand what this is you are saying!" he shouted, throwing up his hands. "I am responsible for this department of the town hall. And it is not the first problem with Iréne! And now this! Do you know what this means? Now I must involve the Minister of the Interior! Because you are foreign nationals, I must make copies to your embassies, the American and the British. This will become an international problem!"

I was speechless for the third time that day. Victims of professional incompetence and witnesses to apparent corruption, we'd come in good faith to seek a second opinion. Now this man, who was supposed to be on our side, was bellowing at us.

The lawyer's glare had not softened. Linda laced her palms together and leaned forward, elbows on his desk. Her voice was steady and calm. "Mr. Haralámpos, we're not trying to make trouble for anyone. All I'm interested in is getting my residency. We came to you for a second opinion, and you assured us we have attorney-client privilege. What do you advise us to do?"

He snorted and grumbled a bit before replying. "Well, your permit is expired. The best is for you to leave the country and return after a week or two with a new permit. Then you can make a new application."

Linda asked about the thirteen-thousand Euro bond. Mr. Haralámpos, calming by degrees, asked me if I intended to work here; I replied that I did, and soon.

He spread his hands. "Then you do not need this bond. You will get TEBE insurance and this can also cover your wife. I do not think there can be any problems."

"If I did leave the country and return, would you be willing to handle the application?" said Linda.

"Of course. This is a simple thing. I have an office in Vólos also, I can get this done. Bring all your papers in to me tomorrow and I will look at them, but I think it is a simple case."

Since this man had some direct responsibility over the department concerned, we aired our feelings about the rudeness and lack of professionalism we had encountered, not to mention being directed to one lawyer in particular. He agreed. "I will talk to Iréne about this, and also to the mayor. Foreigners should not be treated this way."

That evening Linda and I discussed our options. Leaving the country and returning with a new permit was certainly feasible, but she would probably have to leave the entire Schengen area of the EU, which was most of it. London was an option, but a week or two in London was an expensive proposition. With the possibility of unplanned legal bills, we didn't want to further deplete our already marginal finances further. But our viability on this island depended on getting Linda's business going, which in turn depended on her being a legal resident. And even if we did leave and return, what if the Greeks didn't re-admit her after a week because she'd overstayed her first permit?

The accountant had suggested we might start her business up in my name to begin with, but Linda was leery of playing games with a system we barely understood. She always does things on the up-an-up: where I tend to be lax in these matters, she always pays bills and taxes on time and keeps everything squeaky-clean and above-board. The outlaw life was not for her.

Besides which, we had complied with all the rules. There shouldn't have *been* any problem. But thanks to Mr. Kákos's incompetence, Linda was now party to a falsified application at a minimum, and possibly bribery of a public official.

We still couldn't believe the second lawyer's outburst. "The first thing I asked him was whether we had attorney-client privilege," said Linda, "and a moment later he's yelling about reporting it to the Minister of the Interior and making an international incident of it. All I'm asking is for them to process my damned residency!"

THE NEXT MORNING I went to Mr. Kákos's office to retrieve our papers so I could show them to the other lawyer. Expecting trouble, I'd prepared my pitch, though I hoped Kákos would be out.

Vicky showed me in with a smile. Annoyingly, our lawyer was in the office, alone at his desk, carefully ignoring me.

I thanked Vicky, pulled out the chair opposite Kákos, and sat without being asked.

"So Linda called the American Embassy," I began. "They're faxing you a letter confirming that the certificate you wanted doesn't exist in the US."

A slight nod: there was something about the man that went beyond a simple lack of people skills. His eyes were red-rimmed, and he had the reactions of a fresh corpse. I wondered if he was on drugs.

I went on. "The gentleman she spoke to said they could probably help us expedite things if we went to the embassy in person. I made an appointment for the day after tomorrow. They asked me to bring all our papers, so I've come to collect them."

"This is not a good idea," he said, instantly suspicious.

I made a dismissive gesture. "We'll be back the next day. I can return everything then."

There was a long pause. "I don't know who you have been talking to, but…"

Interesting. I imagined people did talk about him, and often not kindly. I let my exasperation show. "Look, what's the problem? These are *our* papers. The embassy offered to help, and I want to get Linda's residency moving. And I'm *really* not happy about the fact that you forgot to file the application on time."

"I made a mistake, and I have fixed it."

"I appreciate that, Mr. Kákos. Thank you. Now if you'll give me the papers, I'll let you get on with your work and I'll drop them back by at the end of the week."

Another long pause. The man was creepy.

"If you are stopped by the police on the way, they will see from her passport that her permit has expired and there will be problems. She is in the country illegally now, and we have an application filed after the date of her permit."

I chuckled. "Oh, that's not a concern. We're not driving. Actually, we don't even have a car. I don't think it's very likely that the police will stop the ferry or the bus."

I'd won, and he knew it. He reached into a pile on his desk and eased out a folder. Vicky, not eight feet away at her desk, typed away purposefully. See no evil, hear no evil.

He handed me the papers and watched as I slid them into my briefcase.

"Be careful," he said.

"I DO NOT see any problem with Linda's residency," said Mr. Haralámpos, after reviewing our paperwork. "You are an EU citizen, you are legally married, and you will have TEBE insurance. This is easy."

"Thank you." I took a deep breath. "Look, we really don't want to make a big deal of this and get anyone into trouble; we came to you for a second opinion, and you've been very helpful."

Mr. Haralámpos smiled. He'd regained his composure since the previous evening.

"So here's our question: since we have an application already filed, we'd prefer not to have Linda begin all over again: do you advise us to proceed with Mr. Kákos, or should we start again with you?"

He gave a small shrug. He said, "I think Rígas can do this. It is not a difficult thing."

I sat back. "You're saying we can trust Kákos to get this done? We should stay with him?"

"For this, yes. Why not?"

Mr. Haralámpos wouldn't take any money. I thanked him at length and went on my way, mostly relieved. I was troubled that he'd counseled us to stay with Kákos in the light of what had taken place: either he didn't want to open up a can of worms in the town hall, and/or he considered us a hot potato. But at least we'd taken a sounding and knew what we were dealing with.

On Friday morning, I dropped the papers back off with Kákos's secretary, Vicky. The lawyer wasn't in the office. "Vicky, please tell Mr. Kákos I would like an estimate of what this is likely to cost," I said.

"Of course, I will ask him."

"And as soon as possible, please, so we have no more surprises."

Tákis's Story

THAT EVENING, TÁKIS took us out to dinner. The restaurant was only a few minutes' walk, but he insisted on driving, threading the little beat-up Peugeot through the twisty and ever-narrowing lanes of the old village until we came to a place, just yards from the taverna, where no cars could fit.

It was our first time at Anna's. The place was bustling, and had an upscale feel, more bistro than taverna. A trio of young musicians—a guitarist, a bouzoúki player, and a fiddler—plucked and sawed happily at their instruments in a corner. The bouzoúki player was a youngish woman. The music was uptempo, and very good.

Tákis knew what I did for a living, but he was curious about Linda's plans to set up a natural soap and cosmetics business, which quickly led to a discussion of the regulatory environment in Greece.

"I can not believe that you are two foreigners who want to make business here in Greece," he said, shaking his head. Even for Greeks it is difficult." He poured wine, and began to relate the story of his own dream.

"Four years ago, I made a bar in the building and on the roof where my *épipla* is. I called it 'Bábalos'. I had live music every night, and musicians and bands came from Athens and Thessaloníki. I had all the licenses, everything. You can not imagine how busy it was. Every night of the summer, full, full, with sometimes six hundred people. It was fantastic, something incredible!

"But the other clubs, they lose business. So now I start to have problems with the police. Every night the police come to take me for breaking the laws about noise. I say, 'but look, here is the license you give to me for live music! Why you give me this if you do not let me play live music?' 'There are complaints,' they say.

"In this one summer I had one hundred and ten visits from the police, so many that I pay a man to go to the police station in my name every time they come. In the end they arrest me. You know what I write when they ask me to make a statement for the court?" He laughed. "I write, 'Fuck you! All I am trying to do is make a business, and you arrest me.' Ah, it was big story! In the end I could not continue. That was the end of my dream."

We were shocked and saddened, and said so. He drained his glass and refilled ours as well as his. "Yes," he agreed, "for many months I was sad. I lose three hundred thousand Euros with this. But then we make the *épipla* up there from the little shop in the village before, and now I have a good business.

"So when I hear what you want to do, I see that you are crazy people. For foreigners to make business in Greece…" He waggled his palm, as if threatening to scold someone. He was laughing, and so were we. "You are crazy, but you have much courage. And I will do anything I can to help you, to see you make your dream."

We told him about our meeting with the accountants, and all the things they said we needed (Pávlos had *still* not gotten back to us with hard information) in order to get a license for Linda's business.

"Ah, to get papers in Greece is like swimming in the open sea," said Tákis.

"There's just so much bureaucracy," I complained. "How does anyone do business here?"

"Yes, it is true. These people do not care if you do not make money even to eat."

"The accountant said they want me to have a special waste disposal system," said Linda. "And there *is* no waste from soap!"

Tákis almost choked on his wine from laughing. "Ah, Linda! You are in the *big* waves now! It was the same when I make Bábalos. Even with a bar they wanted this, it was a big problem. To make this system is expensive, but also stupid. So I do this: I find a picture in a book that shows exactly the pieces of this system, and I take this to a friend who makes me a drawing of it, and this I send to Vólos, and I say, 'this system I have.'"

"No!" said Linda.

"Did it work?" I said.

"Of course. They accept it. But then after one month they say 'we must send a man to see that you really have this system in the bar.' This was a problem."

"I can imagine."

"Eh, yes. So when he comes, I say, 'I am sorry. As you can see, I am still waiting for the *teknítis* to put this in.' We talk, and then I give him fifty Euros and—" he rubbed his palms together as if wiping dirt off them—"everything was okay."

Linda and I gasped. "Unbelievable!" we said in unison.

Tákis laughed. "Ehh. This is Greece."[15]

We got to talking about relationships somehow. Tákis reiterated his desire to have a family. "I am very close with my family, as you see. I would like to find a woman to make my own family now."

"Maybe we can find you an American girl," said Linda. "I know a few single girls."

"No. I do not like the American women," said Tákis. Then, grinning, "You know this song? *American womaaan... Stay away from me-eee!*"

Linda mimed outrage. She turned to me, then back to Tákis, who was laughing. "Tákis! So tell me, how many American women do you know?"

A sheepish look came across his face. "Ah, Linda," he said.

Engage brain before opening mouth, I thought.

"No, come on," she insisted, "how many? I want to know."

"Ah, Linda. Ehh. Only you."

When we got home, we debriefed on the incident. Linda was having trouble processing Tákis's statement. "If I'm the only American woman he knows, and he doesn't like American women, where does that leave me?"

I shook my head. "I think Tákis likes you a lot."

"I'm not so sure of that."

"Trust me. It's more of a knee-jerk reaction toward the culture, and the war in Iraq."

"Do you really think so?"

"I'm sure of it. I'm getting to know Tákis pretty well: he's a straight shooter."

---

[15] As Lao Tzu famously wrote, *when laws become too restrictive, the people will become devious and cunning.* Making criminals out of honest citizens is a really stupid way to run a country.

"Well, then I should take him at his word when he says he doesn't like American women."

"No. Look, it's like Yiánnis. Remember his blanket anti-American speech? It's the politics. It's that idiot, Bush. Unfortunately, you're going to find yourself faced with that prejudice sometimes. But I don't think America could have a better ambassador than you."

I watched her work through it, until a mischievous smile stole over her face. "I'm going to file what he said away for future reference," she said.

THE NEXT DAY Tákis showed up with a bowl of unusual-looking greens sparkling with olive oil. "It is *hórta*," he announced. I'd mentioned my interest in learning about the edible wild greens, and he'd remembered. "Very fresh. You will see if you like this."

I thanked him and took a taste. It was delicious, both sweet and a little bitter, with complex, nutty depths.

"O my God! Tákis, this is wonderful! Can you show me where to find it?"

"My father will take you," he said. "He knows all the *hórta*. There are many different kinds, and now until April you can find this. Then you clean it, cook it just a few minutes, and put olive oil with lemon and salt. It is good, eh?"

"Fantastic!" I said, around another mouthful.

"Also it is very good for you. You will talk to my father and he will take you. He will be very happy."

We Get to Work

I SET ABOUT the task of making the workshop fully functional. First, I built a solid, laminate-topped workbench for Linda, and a large cabinet with adjustable shelving for her soaps to cure in. Since the workshop got cold at night and the fresh cement on the walls made the air humid as it dried, I set a pair of lampholders with sixty-watt bulbs in the base of the curing cabinet. This simple arrangement worked nicely, and kept the inside temperature at a steady sixty-five degrees.

Vasílis's drill was mighty useful, but the circular saw wasn't great. I'd never liked the things anyway. But I had a couple of good hand saws, and it was no great hardship to cut all the lumber the old-fashioned way, and provided a good workout in the process. After so long a layoff, the hard work was deeply satisfying.

From Linda's Journal, February 13th, 2007:

Sapoúnia. Káno sapoúnia. I make soap. I keep trying to remind myself that I am now a soap maker—trying to transform my self-image from my formerly corporate life. It's not easy. And I have trouble fully embracing it. I worry about offending someone—it's easy to offend people on a small island. Then what? Be turned in to the authorities for my illegal business? My illegal status? Have the tax authorities come down on me?

I try to push these thoughts from my mind. But everyone comes at me from different angles. Don't worry unless you have a big business. Do worry, they will come after you because you are xéni. I'm willing to take all the legal steps, but no one seems to know what they are.

My husband moves forward with confidence. Putting final touches on our workshop, building workbenches, curing racks for my soap. He doesn't seem to feel the same doubt.

I sit on the marble floor of my living room and make pretty labels in Greek that slowly spit out of my little inkjet printer. I wonder if my translation is even partly correct. Heavy sigh.

IT WAS MID-FEBRUARY, and I thought it time to touch base with Warmboard and let them know I was available for CAD work. Framing on new homes typically stops during the cold months, so Warmboard generally gets busy around mid-April, when the construction season in the US emerges from the winter doldrums.

Accordingly, I sent the design director an email, expecting to be told things were still slow. To my great surprise, I received a reply within a couple of hours, with a project attached. Business was already picking up, and she was starting to send out jobs. This was tremendous news: income!

And suddenly, my days were full. I would put in a few hours at the computer, then take myself down to the workshop for a spell of physical activity. Being busy also kept me from obsessing over the problem of getting our licenses and Linda's residency.

I built myself a huge workbench, like a fabric cutting table, and started on my first commissioned piece.

In the course of our chess games, I'd told Tákis about my work and shown both him and his father my portfolio. Tákis was impressed, and offered to give me a few pieces to paint on spec. "You will paint them and I will sell them in my shop, and we can make business."

I was flattered. Tákis had good taste, and *Épipla* Doúkas was popular; most of the expat community, as well as the locals, bought from him. The shop's style tended to the European modern, with a few traditional pieces thrown in for the older locals. Large or custom orders were no problem, and several of Skópelos's bars and hotels furnished their premises through Tákis. If you could draw it, Tákis could get it built and deliver it on time.

The first pieces he gave me were an oak hat stand and a small pine chest, both raw and unfinished. I had an open brief: "You are the artist," he told me, grinning around a cigarette as I contemplated my first commission here. "They will be very nice work, I am sure."

I considered the hat stand and chest while I built shelving and unpacked my tools and materials. Both had to remain affordable—Skópelos was not San Francisco, and Tákis had to make a profit, too. So my challenge lay in finding a way to produce art pieces without getting too bogged down in the process, always a danger for a perfectionist.

I began to see what the hat stand wanted: bright colors in heavy enamel, like the local caïques, but deeply weathered. Yes.

A couple of days later, Linda and I stood back and considered the result. The thing looked as though someone had built a hat stand from the wreckage of an old fishing boat and then flown it through a space battle. It was a lot of fun, modern and traditional at once. The colors reminded me of Mexico as well as Greece. I called it 'Mexicaïki'.

I turned my attention to the pine chest Tákis had given me, a cheap footlocker with no ornamentation, really just a box with a lid. The pine used was very soft and the grain stood up in ridges almost the way it did on driftwood. This would really limit my technique, as whatever glaze color I applied would settle into the valleys of the grain. Since I couldn't fight this, I decided to make it work in my favor.

Over a white base, I applied a sky-blue glaze, scraping the wet color off the raised grain while leaving a film of it in the 'valleys'. The effect was striking: the wood grain jumped out in the Greek national colors, blue and white, with just the right degree of contrast and 'lift'.

I'd expected to have trouble finding materials, but was both surprised and impressed by the range and quality of paint and varnish products available in Greece. Whereas US manufacturers—who typically put price point before quality—had reacted to ever-tightening air quality regulations by reformulating their products to the point where they barely performed, European manufacturers, faced with rules every bit as stringent, had managed to maintain and even improve the quality of some of the products available. The oil enamels were a joy to use, the latex flowed off the brush like real paint rather than some weird plastic goop, and you could still get long-oil varnishes and primers. A proud, old-school craftsman, I was in heaven. So what if the products were expensive? Labor, not material, is always the biggest factor in any project. For me, it's always been about quality.

At least one of us had begun to work.

An Evening with My People

JUST A COUPLE of days after our nightmare with the lawyers, I ran into Matt and Carole at the hardware store. They apologized for not having been in touch, and invited us to dinner at their house that weekend. Carole's directions were a little confusing, but from her description, I thought I knew the house, not far up the hill from where we lived. I was sure I could find it, and we had a cellphone.

But although just a mile or so away, they were out in the country, up the steep, rugged path where I took my walks. Impossible in the dark: we would need transport.

Since the weather had gentled again, I suggested we rent a small motorcycle. Most of the locals got around on little 90cc Hondas, and although I'd been tempted to rent one of the big 500cc trail bikes, I thought the small Honda would be both adequate for a weekend and less intimidating to Linda—not a fan of motorcycles—than one of the big thumpers.

This proved a bad decision.

What I came home with was a worn-out, six-year old piece of junk that could barely get up the ring road with just me on board. As for the loaner crash helmets, they looked like something from a bad 1950's sci-fi film. Mine had a peak, and a sort of vestigial crest along the top, with the brand name, 'NOVA', splashed across the front in a bold, digital-style lettering clearly designed to appeal to teenagers back when Casio digital watches were all the rage.

"Since we've got transport, I think I'll dress up for a change," said Linda. We were both bored with jeans, and this seemed a good occasion to put on a little style. I wore pressed khakis and dress shoes, Linda black slacks and boots with heels.

I was sure Matt and Carole's house was up on the next paved road above the ring road on which we lived. This road was accessible either by hiking a mile up the rocky path behind our house, or via a long, looping route out past the end of town, along the high sea-cliff toward Glyfonéri beach, and then back inland. It couldn't be more than three miles at the most, perhaps ten minutes on the motorcycle. No problem.

The night was moonless and clear; as we left the few lights of the village, the sky filled with stars like splinters of ice. We started up the mild slope that would lead to the big hairpin, and the engine sagged. I dropped a gear, and then another. But even on full throttle it wouldn't make the hill with a passenger. I cursed and apologized. Linda chuckled and good-naturedly walked a few hundred feet while I nursed the gutless rustbucket up the steeper section of the slope. Even the mildest grades proved a problem, with me frequently having to paddle along with my feet while the engine tried to get its breath. Eventually, we reached level ground and drove the last mile or so without mishap.

There were lights on in the driveway, but none visible in the house. I frowned. "I'm sure it's this one," I said, removing the stupid sci-fi helmet and fumbling for the cellphone. We were only ten minutes late.

Matt answered. After some confusion, we discovered that we were at the wrong stone house, near the wrong little church. The house was actually directly below us, halfway back to our house along the now pitch-black rocky path I knew so well from my walks, and not on the paved road at all! I declined the offer of a rescue, insisting we could make our own way. Matt said he'd turn all the outside lights on.

Linda was horrified. "You're not going to try and drive down *that* on *this*, are you?"

"The local kids do, but that's in daylight, on real motorbikes, with brakes. This…" I wanted to kick the Honda, but not in my dress shoes. "Think you can walk it in those boots? I know the trail really well. We can probably make it in fifteen minutes or so, taking it slowly. It's that or call back and ask for a ride, and I'd feel a real fool."

"What about the motorcycle?"

"I'll pick it up in the morning. Though with a bit of luck, it'll fall to pieces before dawn."

"The one night I wear heels." In the starlight, I glimpsed a rueful smile. "Just let me hold on to your arm, okay?"

Our progress was slow. The path was water-gouged and potholed, with rocks the size of footballs in places. Even four-wheelers took it carefully, and that by day. Where branches blocked the starlight, the path became a vagueness distinguished only by the density of the black. As usual, Linda saw the humor in the situation, though her grip on my arm as we navigated these sections was excruciating.

Lateness, fortunately, is not considered an issue in Greece, even by *xéni*. We finally reached the house, an austere structure that I now realized I'd gazed at from our roof terrace. We were made welcome and introduced to the other guests, an older English couple and a single Englishwoman, who turned out to be none other than Margaret Rodgers, noted authoress of 'Skópelos Rambles'. A diffident, unhappy-looking woman; I felt an instant dislike for her.

The rest of the party was already merry. Our hosts fetched us drinks and retired to the kitchen, leaving us to mingle.

We all know our own culture best, and one look at the two English women, and the speed with which they engaged Linda, told me everything I needed to know: these were exactly the sort of expats we had made a point of avoiding. Even across the room I could hear the claws coming out. The man, Peter, had already latched on to me, and I had a moment's concern for Linda, before remembering that she was more than able to take care of herself. I relaxed.

Peter was intelligent and charming, and had me deep in conversation in a few moments. A glance at the women's corner confirmed my initial impression: all smiles on the surface, but I could already see Linda biting her tongue.

Carole had put out a beautiful spread. We served ourselves buffet-style and sat at two adjoining tables, the dinner table being a little tight for seven. Linda and I shared a table with Peter and his wife Jane, Margaret with Carole and Matt.

By this point, all three of the English people—as is the wont with my countrymen—were clearly deep in their cups. Peter was becoming increasingly animated and jocular; Jane, his wife, had developed a serious flutter of her eyelids and was having trouble seeing past them; Margaret was loud and obnoxious, with nothing good to say about anybody whose name came up in the course of conversation. Our hosts remained charming and convivial.

It was at about this point that Carole asked Linda if she'd begun her residency application. "Oh my God! You won't believe it," said Linda, and launched into the story. Aware of how things got around in this small community, she did her commendable best to avoid mentioning Kákos by name, but eventually caved to Carole's persistence.

"That's exactly what happened to me!" cried Carole. "Iréne sent us to Kákos, and he forgot to file my papers too!" She was laughing, amused rather than angry.

I didn't see the point in Carole's applying in the first place, since neither she nor Matt were entitled to residency; they traveled when they needed to renew permits and paid fines when caught out. But they could afford to.

Linda had the bit between her teeth now, and galloped on. When she reached the incident of the seeming bribe, Jane, the older woman, muscled into the fray. She didn't believe any of it. Mr. Kákos was a great friend of hers as well as her sponsor into the Greek Orthodox church, and he was honest as the day was long. Jane was Godmother to his daughter. "Rígas Kákos is a great friend to all the British community on Skópelos!" she drunkenly proclaimed, looking for all the world like the presiding witch at a black mass, eyelids a blur of motion.

In a moment, it was a free-for-all. Carole was all over the details, eager to know more; Linda repeated that she wasn't accusing Kákos of anything, but simply relating what we saw at the town hall; I voiced my doubts about our lawyer's competence; Jane launched into a litany of Kákos's many sterling qualities; Matt was laughing; Peter kept glancing from one speaker to another, repeating, "Really? Really?"; Margaret Rodgers drained her glass and reached for the bottle.

Carole, who clearly enjoyed watching her guests mix it up a little, managed to quiet everyone down so she could hear the rest of the story.

"Look," I said, once Linda had related our meeting with the second attorney, "there are two professions where mistakes can't be tolerated: medicine, and the law. If you have doubts about a doctor's competence or integrity, you get a second opinion. Same with a lawyer."

"And the other lawyer told us to carry on with Kákos," said Linda. She looked straight at Jane. "We decided to trust him. Backdated or not, the application was filed and hopefully it'll go forward without any more problems."

The conversation turned to other topics, and other locals. Láli Páppas's name came up: Margaret couldn't stand her. Sofía's friend Léda, the travel agent, was mentioned: Margaret couldn't stand her. Anyone you mentioned was on her hate list. The woman was poisonous.

Eventually, Linda, who had behaved with formidable restraint through a very trying evening, turned purposefully to Margaret. I held my breath, knowing from experience just how lethal my wife could be if she decided to take someone out. The others seemed to sense it too: the room went suddenly quiet.

"Margaret, is there *anybody* on Skópelos you like?" She was gentle, almost concerned. I breathed again: a simple, surgical strike; respect for our hosts.

It was enough. Margaret spluttered a bit, turned surly, and said very little for the rest of the evening.

Our hosts lent us a flashlight for the walk home.

"That was a good dinner," I said, as we rounded the curve of the hill across from the cemetery. "Carole did a great job, and she was a lot more relaxed than at our house. I really enjoyed both their company."

Linda agreed. "But what is it about English women? They're so catty!"

"I don't think it's just *English* women, more the *type* of women. Americans do it too, you've seen them. It's some kind of weird primate mate-hierarchy thing."

"Maybe. But, God, those two! They started on me the moment I walked through the door. *Mrraoww!*"

"Oh, sure. But isn't it funny how if someone's not going to get on, it's always the women? Every time. Sometimes I think it's because they're not traditionally the warriors. I mean, at some level, guys know they have to get on, because throughout most of human history if guys started to fight, someone would end up dead. So men developed a much higher tolerance for one another in social situations."

We reached the tiny church by the spring at the bottom of the hill and started down the lane that led past the cemetery to the corner by Tákis's shop.

"And what is it with the horsey faces?" said Linda. "Every Englishwoman I've ever met has that look."

I knew just what she meant—they *did* all look horsey! "The English as a whole are not a particularly handsome people. Unlike the Italians," I added.

It's always nice to have options as to your roots.

NEXT MORNING I walked back up the hill to collect the Honda, passing by Matt and Carole's to return the flashlight on the way. It was a cold, sunny day, and the ride back down the cliff road, with its views out to Glyfonéri and then Alónissos, was inspiring. I returned the motorcycle to the rental place, where the owner asked if I was interested in buying it from him. I assured him I preferred walking, paid him, and went home.

"Kákos called," said Linda, as I took off my jacket.

"Uh-oh."

"I was in the shower. He left a message saying he wants us to go to his office at six tonight."

"Why?"

"Haven't a clue. He was all mysterious about it." She put on a deep, dark voice: "This is Rígas Kákos. I want to see you both in my office at six o'clock tonight."

"You think Jane's spoken to him?" I said.

"I think that's exactly what's happened."

"Oh fuck."

"I know. I wish I hadn't opened my mouth last night."

I waved the concern aside. "Don't blame yourself, Carole really pushed you on it. How could you have known Kákos and Jane were buddies?"

"We could just call him and find out what it's about."

"Good idea. Besides, we can be busy this evening. He can't just command us to be there."

Linda reached for the phone. I hovered.

"Hallo Mr. Kákos," she began. "Yes, we got your message… No, unfortunately we're going to be out with friends this evening. Maybe you can just tell me what you need over the phone? If it's more papers, though, you're out of luck," she added, with a light laugh.

Listening, she winked at me. "Okay, thank you, Mr. Kákos. We'll be in touch with you when the paper from the US embassy arrives, then. Thanks. Mh-hm. Bye-bye."

"Well?" I said.

"He backed off. Said it wasn't important."

"Good."

WE WERE HAVING coffee next morning when the phone rang. Linda picked it up. "Oh, hallo, Jane," she said. I rolled my eyes.

Before long, Linda was patiently reiterating that we weren't accusing anybody of anything, but what were we supposed to think when we saw a large sum of cash thrown at a public official, and a document backdated in the same meeting? Yes, Jane. No, Jane. Three bags full, Jane. And on and on and on. The woman was trying hard to steer Linda around to the Official Version of events. Finally, Linda managed to get her off the phone.

"So what's the story?" I said. "Can we assume the old bat told Kákos all about the conversation at Matt and Carole's party?"

"Of course. And since we didn't go and talk to him last night, he had Jane call us to straighten it all out."

"Good God. And?"

"Well, according to Jane, he was paying his rent. Iréne owns the building, and Kákos rents the office from her."

"Do you believe it?" I said.

She shrugged. "She sounded sincere enough."

"It could be," I agreed. "Sort of makes one wonder about his intelligence, though, doing something so liable to misinterpretation. When this is over, I never want to see the bastard again."

IN AN IDEAL world, or even in America, we would have single-mindedly pursued Linda's residency problem to its conclusion as a tiger chases down its prey on the savanna. In Greece, this was utterly impossible: it was more like stalking something you think might be a deer through a forest at midnight in dense fog—now you see it, now you don't. So although our problems were always on our mind, there were swathes of days where we could do absolutely nothing to further our goals. You can't push in Greece—the system and the culture force their own leisurely pace on you. There were days when we chose to simply socialize or explore our new environment just to avoid going nuts with frustration.

At least Kákos had started the application process; we'd have to give him a chance. Pávlos, the accountant, said we could probably sell Linda's soaps under my business license to begin with, though he clearly didn't like the idea. In the meantime, she could at least start building her stock while we waited for the great gear-wheels of the bureaucracy to turn.

Clean Monday, Fat Tuesday

KATHÁRA DEFTÉRA, CLEAN Monday, the seventh before Easter, marks the beginning of the Greek Orthodox Lent. With an invitation to a Lenten feast at the Balabánises' *kalívi*, we felt like quite the social gadflies.

With flesh off the menu, we prepared a big bowl of orzo salad. We also bought a couple of bottles of a decent Syrah to take along, partly in the hope we might get to drink a little ourselves—the homemade wine that Mára generally served was very thin, with a marked vinegary flavor. The seemingly infinite supply of the stuff was no consolation. It was, in truth, ghastly.

Strátos and Anna stopped by to pick us up at about three-thirty. We squeezed into the back seat of Strátos's tiny Mercedes hatchback, a model we'd never seen in the US.

The guests hadn't yet arrived. Men in Greece aren't allowed to help in the serving of, or cleanup after, food—it's just not done, and no amount of insistence can alter this. So I watched as Linda helped Mára and Anna load and set out serving platters until the two big tables groaned with food: *gigantés* (giant beans in tomato sauce); the special *lagána* bread, eaten only on Clean Monday; *dolmádes*; faláfel balls; *hórta*; spicy cheese dip; a tubular variation on *spanakópita*; pickled green peppers; and of course, bowl after bowl of olives and big hunks of excellent féta.

The guests began to arrive. Strátos's parents and his angst-soaked brother, Kósmos; Dimítris, Anna's employer, with his son and daughter-in-law; Spýros's young cousin, Alexándra; and two couples whom we didn't know.

The meal proceeded amid merriment and clatter. Cigarettes were smoked, cellphones talked on. Linda was in fine form, chatting up a storm of Greek while I got into a long, muddled conversation with Strátos's brother Kósmos, trying and failing to find common ground, as both of us wrestled with the other's language in a half-assed attempt at discussing things like the benefits of different computer operating systems and third-generation cellphones.

Strátos and Kósmos's parents were an entertaining pair. Their dad wore a knowing smile much of the time but said very little: picture a very slight, beardless garden gnome—a gnome, in short, without the usual gnomish attributes of beard and gut. Now take the missing bulk and a hint of beard, and transfer it to his wife, a warm, likeable woman with an unpredictable tendency to dissolve shrieking in gales of laughter every time I addressed her in Greek.

Perhaps it was an excess of food, but I had further reason to question my language skills later that day. I'd been following a conversation between Spýros and another gentleman for some while, and rather well, I thought; in fact, I was quite pleased with myself. Even if I only understood about one word in five, I could recognize a verb ending and make up a lot of the missing data by context. I was getting good.

Until I clearly heard the guest say, "…so you see, I have always been able to speak the language of sheep," to which revelation Spýros gave an entirely serious reply.

I began to wonder just how much of this language I really did understand.

THE PLEASANT WEATHER broke, with cold winds from the north driving blustery showers. One afternoon, I'd just rounded a corner of the lane three minutes from home, carrying a load of shopping and leaning into the wind, when I saw an old woman emerge at the intersection of the street above me. She glanced in my direction, crossed herself, and moved on. What on earth was *that* about? Had I been deluding myself about our status in the village? Good grief!

A few days later, the same thing happened at the same spot, with a pair of women this time: They saw me coming, and crossed themselves!

My mind turned somersaults for a moment before the truth struck me: the lane I was on was the same one where the young man who'd killed himself had lived. I felt much relieved: as usual, I'd thought it was all about me.

I'D JUST POPPED into Rígas's little corner market near our workshop to buy a pot of fresh yogurt when Jilly spotted me. "'Allo love!" she said. "'Ere, come out a sec, there's someone I want you to meet!"

She led me outside, where a tall woman was loading some bags into the back of a car. The woman straightened and turned, a little unsteadily, as we came up to her. She had apple-red cheeks and a big smile.

"Sue, I want you to meet my friend Dario," said Jilly. "He and his wife Linda have just moved here from California. Dario's an artist and his wife makes soap."

Sue stuck out her hand. "Hal-lo!" she said. Very English, very proper. Omigod. The last thing I wanted was to meet other Brits. "Yes, pleased to meet you! I'm Sue," she concluded, shaking my hand at some length.

Despite the *Expat Alert!* siren blaring in my head, there was something I immediately liked about this woman. She was perhaps fifty, and attractive in a low-key sort of way. Very country. I returned the smile and said I was pleased to meet her.

"Sue's got a lovely 'ouse on the 'ill back there," chirped Jilly, pointing towards Pévkias. "She could probably use some of your lovely painting there."

"Oh yes," said Sue. "You must come and see it. Perhaps you and your wife would like to come up for drinks?"

"We'd love to," I said. Or at our house." I pointed up the road. "We live under the *mílos.*"

"Oh, yes! Lovely!" Sue spoke with a bubbly enthusiasm which I felt was not forced but the real thing. "Unfortunately, I'm a little indisposed today." She pointed to her ankle, and I caught a glimpse of bandage between jeans and tennis shoe. "I just sprained my ankle outside the post office. There's a nasty pothole out there, and I didn't see it."

I'd seen that very pothole, and commiserated. It was at least eight inches deep.

"Yes, well. I went to the doctor—Yiánnis, do you know him? I take Greek lessons with his wife, Mina."

"Yes," I said, "we know Yiánnis and Mina. Actually, they're our best friends here."

"Oh, really? Splendid! Anyway, he strapped me up and made me promise to stay off it for a few days." She laughed. "Which is going to be pretty difficult where I live. But I'd love to have you both up. Look, let me give you my phone number…"

We exchanged numbers, and I suggested she should ice the ankle. I promised we'd give her a call in the next day or two and set a date to get together.

Sue beamed. "Oh yes. Yes, that would be lovely!"

A few days later, Linda and I set off on foot one late afternoon for Sue's house, and cocktails. Sue had made earnest offers to pick us up—it was about three miles to her house—but the weather was dry and we were looking forward to a country walk. I assured her than we both loved walking and had a cellphone in case we got lost.

In fact, we did get a little lost; most of the directions were clear, but the final instruction to 'turn left at the big pine tree, and look out for the pine marten,' caused some minor confusion, since we were in a pine forest, and *surrounded* by pine trees. But there *was* a fork, and it seemed the correct point for a left turn.

We were also mildly uneasy about the pine marten, since neither of us was entirely clear what these were; but I had a vague notion they were something like a squirrel or ferret, and probably unlikely to try to take down an adult human.

The last half-mile was a solid uphill trek on a dirt road, with widening views to the harbor and the bay, and by the time we reached Sue's property we were quite ready for a cocktail.

Sue met us by the gate. The location was idyllic: six or seven acres of olive groves, sloping steeply up to the crown of the hill, with sweeping, scenic vistas in every direction. An airy place, and full of sky.

Her ankle was still giving her trouble. "I stayed off it as much as I could for a couple of days, but there's so much to do on the property. And as you can see, it's all hill and rocks. Would you like a tour?"

She led the way up the hill, pointing out favorite places as she went, and trees she particularly liked to sit under. She showed us the small structure she was planning to turn into a *kalívi* for guests, and the plantings around the house. I was impressed by her evident love of the land and respect for its past. She seemed unusually attuned to place, and I said so.

"Oh," she said, "yes, well, I suppose I do tend to *feel* things."

I cocked my head. Coming from someone else, I might have thought this a vacuous reply, but I felt there was a lot more to this woman. Later, we learned that in her youth Sue had been a professional flautist, and something of a prodigy. Just as her career began to take off, an accident to the mouth had robbed her of her ability to play. Linda and I listened with horror. "Yes, it took me a long time to come to terms with it," she said. "I had to look around and ask myself what I should do with my life. But you pick yourself up and you get on with it. And now here I am," she concluded, with a bright smile.

The house was tasteful and unpretentious, with tiled floors and simple furnishings. Outdoor patio areas afforded views down the property and across to the harbor. The sense of peace was palpable.

The day was cooling off, and Sue asked me to build a fire while she and Linda took care of drinks and snacks. As the windows filled with night, we gathered around a table filled with *mezés* and told our stories. The logs popped and crackled in the grate.

Sue's experience in building her home had been as harrowing as any hero's journey through the underworld. "You have to be very careful when you're a foreigner. Even if you can build a house, you can find yourself unable to sell it if your builder doesn't do everything by the book. And I had to fight dreadful battles over the rights of way."

"Didn't those come with the property?" said Linda. I refilled our glasses.

Sue chuckled. "Well, at the time, I thought they did. Then next thing I knew, my neighbor was refusing to let the builders onto the land. It all got rather unpleasant."

"How did you resolve it?" I asked.

"Yes, well, I hired a lawyer. Unfortunately, he only made things worse. It took me forever to get it sorted out. Not to mention what it cost."

This prompted Linda to detail our experiences with the town hall and the legal profession. Sue's eyebrows went up; her sympathetic expression turned to a knowing smile. "I think we might have the same lawyer," she said.

"Tall guy?" said Linda. "Hooded eyes?"

"Yes," said Sue.

"Looks like an undertaker?" I said.

Sue was giggling. "Yes! That's him."

Linda laughed. "Well, God forbid we should mention any names!"

"Do you know he wanted to be a DJ?" said Sue, her eyes sparkling with mischief.

"He *did*?" I said.

"Yes. He told me that was always his dream, but his father made him study for the bar instead."

"That explains a lot," said Linda.

Sue went on to detail her traumas over the house and land. The story was long, and awful. We were to hear many similar stories from foreigners in Greece.

"Anyway, after more than a year of this," Sue concluded, "I was so fed up that next time I met with him, I looked him in the eyes and said, 'It's all a game for you, isn't it, Rígas?' And, you know, he didn't have an answer. He wouldn't even look at me anymore."

"It *is* a game!" I cried. "That's *exactly* what it is!" I said. "They think we're all rich, and that they can just milk us!"

Linda said, "You're pumping your money into the local economy by building a house. We're trying to start a business and help promote local products. You'd think they'd try to make it a little easier for people, wouldn't you?"

"Yes," said Sue. "And of course, if you're a woman, that's even more jolly, isn't it?" Sue's husband lived in Vienna, where he worked for a major financial institution; she'd handled the entire project alone. "Anyway, I still don't really know if it's over. I won't know until August."

I asked what she meant.

"Well, after all the to-do, they eventually refunded some of my money. But the check's postdated until August, so I haven't a clue if it's valid or not. It might go through, it might bounce. I'll just have to see." She chuckled.

I was impressed by Sue's resilience and sense of humor in adversity. If only I were made of the same stuff.

TUESDAY, THE LAST day of Carnival, was known elsewhere as Mardi Gras. Rita had told us there would be processions in town and along the *paralía*, but we had no idea where or when.

In the mid-morning, I strolled into the village to see if there was anything going on. It was cold, and a strong northerly raked the streets.

As I neared the *paralía*, I met a growing number of people dressed in their Sunday best going back up toward their homes. I started walking faster, only to find the *paralía* deserted by the time I reached it. Damn! whatever had been going on, I'd missed it.

I trudged back up the hill. "We're just not in the loop yet," I told Linda. "Sorry. Next year I'll make sure we know what's going on in advance." I felt I'd let her down—I *should* have taken the trouble to find out what was going on—but Linda was perfectly content to let it go. She's good that way.

I took myself down to the workshop to build a second shelving unit for my side of the workshop. Everything had closed, and the streets were deserted. Perhaps they'd all been spirited away in some Orthodox rapture, or a similar supernatural event nobody had informed us about.

The wind strengthened, with squally showers and the occasional barrage of hail drumming against the workshop window. We had no heating, but four fat pipes carrying hot water to the apartments above kept the temperature tolerable. I drilled and sawed, and built up a good sweat.

Later that afternoon, I caught the lament of an oompah band not far off. I opened the door just in time to see the bedraggled end of a procession following the fading notes along the road—I'd missed it again! But for the foul weather, I might have hurried after them, but there seemed little point. Next year, I thought. Next year.

LINDA WAS UP and off early the next morning. She was going to make her first full batch of soap. I knew she was continuously stressed over the lack of progress with her residence, but had decided to stuff her fears and forge ahead. Good. It would all get resolved, and she needed to have soap to sell when the tourist season started.

I tried to go online to write a blog entry, only to find that the net was down. I picked up the phone to call Yiánnis, but the phone was dead as well.

Instead of the short way down the ring road, I took the longer, scenic way through the village to the workshop, in part to go by the post office to check our mail, but mostly because of the picturesque streets and sea views on the way. I had the best commute in the world.

The wind had died overnight, and the day was mild. Pávlos, our accountant, was chatting with Yiánnis in the sunshine outside the Próton supermarket. With both phone and Internet down, a leisurely day was clearly indicated.

What would Yiánnis think, I wondered, if he saw the fresh cupping marks on my back, or—worse—knew that Linda had started performing chiropractic adjustments without any formal training or experience other than what we had practiced on one another? Opinionated as Yiánnis was, it wasn't something I ever wanted to find out.

When I reached the workshop, Linda had already made one batch of soap and was heating a large pot of olive oil for her second batch. The scent of Peppermint was in the air, and bottles of essential oils and jars of dye were lined up on her bench. After years of working in garages and make-do situations, I was dizzy with joy that we'd found such great premises, with ample room for both of us to work.

We'd set up a folding camp armchair on Linda's side of the workshop. Besides providing a place to relax over lunch or a cup of coffee, it also proved handy for sitting in during the hour or so it took olive oil soap to trace. With the hot oil and lye mixture set on a low wooden platform by the side of the chair, she could stir the pot with one hand while holding a book in the other. Of course if I was in the workshop and had the time, like today, I would relieve her for a spell. I had plenty of experience from years of stirring polenta, one of my favorite dishes.

WHEN YOU LIVE in a place like Skópelos, it's impossible to become disconnected from the beauty and rhythms of the place, even if you work every day. The environment saturates you, especially when you don't wall yourself off in a car. The heartbeat of the island is your heartbeat, its breath, your breath: you feel every mood, every change, every cycle.

With carnival over and spring in sight, the pace of island life was picking up. It started quietly, almost imperceptibly: here a small pile of sand and cement outside a door, there some hammering and cabinet demolition. Work crews began to appear in town. The owners of the Hotel Denise across the road from us took up residence and started knocking holes in a side wall. Previously empty houses became construction sites, with cement-splashed wheelbarrows and little piles of brick or tile in the entry. Cement-mixer trucks began to rumble past our house on a regular basis.

Psária Fréska man was doing great business too. With four more weeks of Lent to go, the demand for squid and prawns (the truly devout eat no fish during Lent, only seafood) had risen considerably. A second *Psária Fréska* man appeared on the scene, this one with a proper van, in the back of which were piled trays of fish and seafood on ice, and a big vending scale. But although this second vendor—who did his rounds later in the morning—also had a PA system mounted on his van, he didn't push his product with the same demented enthusiasm that our old regular did.

We had become so used over the months to the original *Psária Fréska* man's amplified cries—*Fresh fish! Prawns! Squid! Various fish for soup!!*—that when one morning I heard his approaching voice calmer and less strident than usual, I ran to the balcony. Perhaps *Psária Fréska* man was sick, or the victim of a failed love affair. I recognized the tinny, amplified voice, but the calm, conversational tone was not like our man at all.

As I watched him drive slowly by, I understood: *Psária Fréska* man was actually talking on his cellphone. He had omitted to turn off the mike, and his conversation was being broadcast up and down the ring road as he drove. I hoped it was something worthy of spicy gossip.

WITH FEBRUARY GONE, the wildflowers which had been coming up for a couple of weeks were in full bloom, the woods and meadows a riot of color. I'd seen the first small poppies starting to unfurl, a slip of wrinkled crimson at the bud's edge, and now they were out in squadrons and battalions. Tall, bearded, white irises were suddenly everywhere; on the Glyfonéri walk, we found a stretch of hillside covered with several hundred of them, all in magnificent bloom, with buttercups and yellow daisies sprinkled among them for contrast. The meadows and groves were everywhere carpeted in white daisies so thick you could mistake them for clover.

There were many flowers and plants we didn't recognize. One of these—there was a patch of them on a bend of the Glyfonéri road—was a heavy-looking green pod the size of my thumb on the end of a drooping stalk.

This plant had an especially neat reproductive trick.

The pods looked so plump and ripe that you just *had* to touch them, so I reached out to palpate one between my thumb and forefinger. The moment my fingertip touched it, the pod exploded. It happened so fast I didn't even see it: one instant the pod was there, the next it was gone, accompanied by a small, soft *pop*! and a sense of tiny, tiny things— spores, perhaps, certainly not seeds—spraying over my face like microscopic meteors.

After recoiling in surprise, and not without a vague concern that the spores might have got inside me, I examined the pods closely, careful not to touch them. They were covered in tiny hairs, sensors to trigger the pod's explosion.

I popped another, this time with a stick, from a distance of a few feet. The outer pod matter, the shell, as it were, appeared to almost vaporize on explosion: I couldn't find a shred of pod shrapnel anywhere. I popped a good few more, until eventually I was left with a number of smaller, unripe pods that even a good poke wouldn't set off.

Linda's bad knee had improved to the point that she felt up to a serious hike. So that Sunday, a clear, windy day, we set off on a long, looping amble, into the hills and back among the ancient olive groves east of the Stáfilos road. We chatted, and Linda picked wildflowers for a nosegay as we walked. She looked really well, better than I'd seen her in a long time. Island life suited her. The stress had left her face, and her cheeks were rosy. She was strong and fit from walking. The sacrifices we'd made to get here, the risks we'd taken, the challenges we still faced—it was all worth it to see her looking like this.

THERE WAS A total lunar eclipse due on Saturday night, beginning at twelve-thirty, with totality around one a.m.

"Let's have an eclipse party!" said Linda. "We could have it up on the roof terrace."

"Hm," I said. "It's supposed to stay clear the next few days, but it's mighty cold at night."

"We'll serve hot cocoa and *mezés*!"

I laughed. "Go for it. Whom shall we invite?"

"Yiánnis and Mina, they'd enjoy it. We'll have a cocktails and *mezés* downstairs, and then go up and watch the eclipse with mugs of cocoa."

Our guests arrived a little before eleven. Of course, Linda's *mezés* turned out closer to an elegant selection of hors' d'oeuvres than informal snacks, and Mina commented on this. We'd still never been invited to their place for dinner, though we'd more than once expressed how easy we were, and how we loved simple food. This was true. Linda cooks gourmet meals not to impress others, but because cooking is her art, and because of the pleasure the serving and eating thereof brings others. Maybe we should just open a restaurant.

As we came to know Mina and Yiánnis better, I became more frustrated by my poor language skills. Yiánnis and Mina both had serviceable English—enough to hold a good general conversation—but we were in *their* country, or at least in Yiánnis's. It was we who should be making the effort. But despite the fact that I longed to communicate in greater depth with friends, I'd become lazy about actually studying since we arrived. We'd both improved through daily practice and listening, but had reached a plateau. I thought our friends sometimes felt similarly frustrated: deepening a friendship requires language sufficient to explore thoughts, feelings, and other abstractions. Language was the key, and we didn't have it, not by a long shot.

The full moon rose red-tinged from fine Saharan dust carried north across the sea. At twelve-thirty we went up to the terrace. The night was clear but not brilliant, with wraiths of thin, high vapor misting the stars. It was freezing, and though we were well wrapped-up, Mina, being the thinnest, wasn't sure how long she could take it. I had set up my camera and tripod. Linda brought hot cocoa, and we laughed and chatted as we watched the eclipse progress.

The moon darkened, turning coppery as it approached totality. The thin cloud stopped the event being the stunner it should have been: the earth's shadow was never crisp, and at times the lunar disc was so veiled that you couldn't make out much at all. But it was quite a show for all that, and a very primal pleasure to gaze at the heavens in the cold Aegean night. Such shared experiences also deepen friendships.

THE NEXT DAY I began work on another piece of furniture for Tákis.

He'd been delighted with the first two, and both were now in the *épipla*, an unusual splash of color, a new direction.

We had settled on a hundred Euros for my work on the hat stand, and a hundred and sixty for the chest, which worked out perhaps fifteen Euros an hour for me, a third of what I charged for my work in

California. By Skópelos standards I was being well paid, and Tákis insisted on paying me on delivery for both pieces.

The new item was another, larger chest, hand-carved in traditional designs. Priced at nine hundred Euros nude, this attractive piece clearly merited a truly striking and unusual finish.

Simple staining was out of the question: apart from being too obvious a finish, the chest, for all the beauty of the carving, was cheaply built. No seductively-grained marvel of the carpenter's art this, but a simple pine carcass with carved oak moldings on the corners and edges; the hand-carved panels at sides and top were plain fiberboard or MDF, a cheap, dense material commonly used on production furniture.

I had a lot of metal leaf in my kit, and Linda suggested copper leaf might be appropriate as a finish. I love the stuff, and it doesn't take much to persuade me to apply it to a surface; I once covered an entire wall of a client's living room in California with the stuff, followed by a toning glaze and varnish. The result was sensational.

I spent the day on the tedious but vital preparation work. Linda came down in the afternoon and made a fresh batch of soap, this time scenting it with cinnamon and clove. The result was dramatic and exciting: I couldn't wait to try this one once it had fully cured.

A Day in Vólos

I HAD CALLED Pávlos the previous week about getting my TEBE insurance as a priority, since Linda's residency was now contingent on medical insurance. He'd spoken to his buddy at the Vólos office and set up an appointment for me. Linda and I would go together, a micro-break on the mainland, and do a little shopping while we were about it. Linda hadn't been off the island in the entire four months since our arrival.

The Skiáthos Express was almost empty and the sea calm. My appointment at TEBE was at nine the following morning, and our return ferry was not until one p.m.

We arrived near dusk, booked into the Phílippos Hotel near the harbor, and went shopping. There were lots of things we'd been craving. Chief among these—Linda and I are serious coffee drinkers—was French Roast coffee. I'd always enjoyed the European Viennese-style roasts before I moved to the US, but now even the very best of these had a distinct background note of old socks which I just couldn't get used to.

"Maybe there'll be a Starbucks," said Linda.

"In Vólos?" I replied. "I doubt it. It's not that large a town."

But after just a few months on Skópelos, this port city of seventy thousand with its broad avenues, traffic signals, and just about every kind of shop you could imagine, felt like a teeming metropolis. Hardware and furniture stores dominated, especially near the port, and I guessed these catered heavily to the population of the islands, for whom trips to Vólos are a frequent necessity. Registering with TEBE ? A trip to Vólos. Renewing your auto license? A trip to Vólos. Gynecological visit? A trip to Vólos.

Seriously.

Our first stop was Sephora, a branch of the famous cosmetic store.

"I don't suppose there's a Starbucks in Vólos, is there?" Linda asked the young assistant who was ringing up her purchase.

The girl looked surprised. "Yes, it has just opened, I think, one month ago."

Linda's eyes lit up. "Do you know where it is?"

The girl made inquiries, and gave us directions. If we just walked to the end of Yásonos street—Jason, of Argonaut fame, was Vólos's most famous son—we would see it on our right.

Fifteen minutes later we were standing in front of a weirdly familiar building, though we had never seen it before. The enigmatic, wavy-haired, green angel of caffeine hovered over the doorway as we entered. Inside, the usual trendy graphics adorned the walls.

The young staff were eager, and happy to practice their English. We bought four pounds of French Roast and a couple of coffee drinks, and sat under the canopy at an outdoor table in the brisk evening air.

Walking back along Yásonos street, we were drawn by the lights of an enormous supermarket. At least, it was enormous to us, accustomed as we were to the tight confines and limited selection of our little island's Mom-and-Pop stores.

Inside we found heaven, almost everything we'd craved for weeks: tortillas; salsa; coconut milk for Thai dishes; Cheddar and Brie; fresh Italian Mozzarella; real Prosciutto di Parma, for goodness's sake! We were in there over an hour. We hadn't brought along an empty suitcase in vain.

Next morning I strolled to Starbucks and brought Linda back a coffee prior to my appointment at the TEBE office, just a half-mile from our hotel.

The TEBE office was busy, another bear pit of bureaucrats smoking under 'No Smoking' signs. I'd been told this particular agency was just beginning to computerize, and the evidence was clear: piles of paper everywhere, people writing longhand in oversized ledgers while others carried stacks of books about the place; files were stacked knee-high along the walls. In a small side office, like a private chapel, was a rack of half-installed, sparkling new IT equipment, with a pair of monitors on a nearby desk.

Pávlos's friend asked me a list of questions as we worked through a long form. Under the solemn gaze of the Christ (or his likeness, hanging on a nearby pillar), I signed, the official countersigned and stamped. I stood in one line, then another, and paid the hundred-Euro filing fee. The entire business took about ninety minutes.

I picked Linda up at the hotel—it was mid-morning by now—and we made one last trip to buy some colored card for Linda's soap labels, and raffia twine for securing the wrapping.

We checked out of the hotel with a couple of hours to go before our ferry left, and ensconced ourselves in a cozy wharfside *ouzería* for an early lunch.

"Isn't that Tákis's truck?" said Linda, as we were finishing up. Sure enough, there was the big box truck with its distinctive green and black 'Épipla Doúkas' logo, turning onto the quay towards the waiting ferry.

"He was in Thessaloníki," I said, "picking up a load of furniture. It has to be him. I don't think the ferries go from there in the winter, so he'd have to drive from Vólos."

Once aboard the ferry, we found it was indeed Tákis, looking more than a little dog-eared. He was a party animal, and all his old friends were in Thessaloníki. I didn't imagine he got much sleep on these trips.

Tákis's cellphone had a larger-than-usual screen, and a chess program. "The only reason I buy this mobile," he said. We played a game; I found it nearly impossible to play on the tiny screen, but would probably have lost just as fast on a full-size board. Even half-asleep, Tákis could hammer me.

We'd brought along a couple of decks of cards, and we played a few hands of poker for small change. Linda cleaned us both out.

The passage was rough, and I was starting to get a little queasy despite the Dramamine I'd taken. Annoyingly, both Tákis and Linda seemed impervious to motion sickness. Linda wove and stumbled along the aisle in an attempt to take the tray with our coffee and snack debris back to the bar. "Oosh! It's rough out there!" she declared, plopping back into her seat.

The next day, I dropped the TEBE forms off at the accountant's. We were pushing as fast as we could to get Linda's residency and—eventually—her business license. It felt like swimming in mud.

Cinnamon Rolls

WE FINALLY GOT a date on the calendar with Vasílis. He and Lítza and seven year-old Kóstas were coming for dinner on Sunday.

Linda decided on a simple chicken; the butcher's poultry was always fresh, and our rotisserie oven never failed to deliver mouthwatering results. Trussing the chicken up so that it remained tight on the skewer took some doing, but Linda had the technique dialed.

When we asked what Kóstas ate, Vasílis insisted that all his son would eat were chips (in the European sense of French fries) and cheese; I suspected he was exaggerating, but bought a jumbo pack of frozen fries and made sure we had plenty of féta in the fridge.

Vasílis and Lítza were both outgoing and appreciative. Lítza spoke some English, but we made an effort to speak Greek as much as possible so as to include both her and Kóstas, with Vasílis providing translation where necessary.

Little Kóstas—who, to our amazement, really did eat only chips and cheese—had trouble understanding my Greek. Nonetheless, he delighted in throwing his arms around my neck at every opportunity, and pulling himself up as though to kiss me.

I found this behavior both endearing and puzzling, especially as he insisted on calling me 'Raffaele' In the process. His parents explained they'd had an Italian acquaintance of that name for whom little Kóstas had developed an inordinate fondness, and that I looked a little like him. Kóstas was a sweet kid, but I feared the huggy-kissy stuff would quickly get old.

Vasílis's parents had emigrated to South Africa when he was three, taking their young son with them. When he reached majority, he discovered he could avoid the two-year mandatory national service by volunteering for duty in the Special Forces, where conscripts were only required to serve six months fighting rebels and guarding the frontier.

"I didn't know what I was getting into," said Vasílis. "The first night I was in the bush, the rebels cut the head off one of our patrol. They use a steel wire. Sneak up behind you, loop it over your head, and—" he crossed his wrists and made a fast, pulling motion with both fists— "*tzak*! It's a trick the Soviets taught them. We found his head there in the grass. I tell you, I was terrified to go to sleep for days after that."

I nodded my head, horrified, fascinated.

"We'd look for the rebel camps in the bush. Whenever we found one…" He made a machine-gunning motion, hands jolting as he swung the imaginary weapon from side to side. He shook his head and sighed. "I killed so many people."

Vasílis and Lítza had met after his return to Greece. A couple of years later, they moved to Germany, where Kóstas was born. They had a restaurant in Leipzig, and did well. But Vasílis worked long hours, returning home in the small hours and sleeping a good part of the day, and the strain on the family began to tell. In 2003, they moved back to Greece and settled on Skópelos. A quality of life decision, and a good one.

"I can leave the shop at two p.m. and be fishing ten minutes later," said Vasílis. "In the summer I go to the beach every afternoon with my family. It's a good life."

The only stress was financial. Vasílis had a monopoly on the cellphone business in Skópelos as well as a good location, but the winter trade was incredibly slow. "Business is shit for ten months of the year," he said.

"Why did you get rid of the clothes?" I asked. When we'd first arrived, his store was divided in two, with the cellphone shop occupying one half and the other stocked with cheap clothes.

"They were a legacy from the previous owner. They sold fairly well until the Chinaman opened his cut-price clothing store in a village."

"The Chinaman?"

"Yah, a whole family of them. I can't touch their prices. Which is why I'm bringing in all the gift items now—pens and lighters and trinkets—to supplement the cellphone business."

"How does a Chinese man get a residency and a business license in Greece?" said Linda.

"Ha!" barked Vasílis. "How do all the Albanians get work permits? An island of five thousand people, and there are seven or eight hundred Albanians working here! And of course, they don't spend any bloody money. And tourism's down since Greece adopted the Euro and all the prices skyrocketed. With all the self-catering rentals now, tourists who used to eat at the tavernas and bought things in the village shops now only come into town to buy food. They stay by their bloody pools all day and cook in their villas. The only people doing good business are the builders, food markets, and car rental agencies."

Kóstas had gone into the living room to amuse himself, away from the boring, grown-up conversation. We could hear him singing happily along to music he'd never heard. Once in a while he'd run in, call me Raffaele, and hang lovingly on my neck, lips pressed together in a smooch. He really was the sweetest child, if a little eccentric.

I commented to Lítza and Vasílis on their son's unusually loving disposition. They glanced at one another.

"He's had some problems," Vasílis admitted. "For a long time, he wouldn't speak."

"In Germany," said Lítza in English, "Vasílis always work late, then all day sleep. I tell Kóstas, *shhh*, you must be quiet, your father sleep. I think is why he not speak."

"In the end," said Vasílis, "we decided we just had to leave. It was too hard on all of us. We returned to Vólos and took him to a specialist. He said the boy was autistic—what a load of bullshit! He didn't even do tests, just looked at him. So we came to Skópelos, where we could live a more normal life. Now he speaks, and he's doing well in school. He has friends. Bloody specialist was talking out of his arse!"

"Autism's become a kind of blanket diagnosis," said Linda. "I think a lot of behaviors that fall into that category—Asperger's syndrome is a common one—have always been there, but today they've been given a name, which of course means more diagnoses. A lot of kids diagnosed as autistic wouldn't have been considered out of the ordinary when we were kids."

Next door, Kóstas was singing along to an album of Doo-Wop ballads. He had the voice of an angel.

For dessert, Linda had made Chocolate Chip Cinnamon Dessert

Rolls, which I'm certain was a first on Skópelos. They were warm. They smelled delicious.

Our guests were ecstatic. Lítza's eyes widened at the first bite; Vasílis was clearly in heaven. I smiled. This was a secret family recipe of Linda's, handed down from her mother, whose father had owned a chain of Danish bakeries on the East Coast before Wonderbread put them out of business. Linda sent our happy guests home with a tray of six or seven cinnamon rolls.

The next morning I stopped by Vasílis's shop on the way to the workshop. He enthused about the previous evening. "I got up in the night just to have another of Linda's cinnamon rolls. And you can't imagine the trouble they caused at the breakfast table this morning—we were all fighting over the last one!

"Lítza really enjoyed herself last night," he added. "When we were invited to Matt and Carole's, everybody just spoke English. She and Kóstas felt totally left out."

I smiled, glad we'd made at least *some* effort with the language.

Thirteen Views

LINDA MADE MORE soap and began to stamp and detail the first batches. Not for the first time, her creativity and freedom astonished me. There was a spontaneity, a playfulness, in her approach to her craft that I envied. She took risks, and most of the time they paid off. If a corner broke off a piece of soap, she'd break off the other corners and apply a little soap paint, turning it into a miniature, snow-capped mountain. If a bar stuck in the mould, so that the top tore a little, she would carve the top into a floral or abstract design and color it in. If there was a muse for soapmakers, Linda was on first-name terms with him or her.

I worked on the carved chest. I applied copper leaf to the top and panels. After smoothing and brushing off the excess—a process which inevitably results in thousands of minute fragments of leaf floating around the workshop—I brushed on a thin, greenish-brown glaze to tone and antique it. I painted all the corner moldings and trim in an antique bronze, weighty and sober against the brighter copper, and finished the whole thing with varnish.

The result was all I'd hoped for. The chest looked as though it belonged in a church; a sarcophagus, perhaps, for a very small monk.

"I want to keep it," said Linda.

"I wish we could afford to," I said.

I'd always considered myself more a technician than an artist, whatever my clients liked to call me. My clients liked to think they were employing an artist—if nothing else it made them feel better about the bill—but it always seemed to me a pretentious label. After all, I worked strictly to other people's design parameters, creating and applying finishes to work with the rest of their home. Whenever I'd set out to do an 'art' piece for myself, with no client and no brief, able to do anything I wanted, I always stalled—I was too afraid of failing, of screwing up. And when I took real chances the experience was stressful rather than enjoyable. Without boundaries, my creativity evaporated like dry ice.

Now, to my surprise, I realized that I was enjoying my work for the first time in years. I was excited to be playing with color and metal leaf again. And I was taking chances.

Whether it was the island, or our spacious workshop, I had no idea; perhaps it was watching Linda work so spontaneously, from the heart, like a child, and obtain fabulous results.

In a place like this, perhaps I could dare to call myself an artist.

THE BALABÁNISES CAME to dinner that weekend. This time we served them in the dining room. Linda showed them some of her first batch of Skópelos soap with the island's outline stamped on it in blue.

Spýros was particularly impressed. "You will do very well with this," he said. "In two years, everybody will buy it."

Linda smiled. We needed to hear this.

During the course of dinner, Spýros's cellphone rang. It was their son, Rígas, calling as he did every evening. He'd visited on leave from the army—where he worked in the kitchens—twice since our arrival, but was now back with his unit.

"He is in the mountains, on the Albanian border," said Spýros. "It's very far, and very cold. There is much snow."

Mára, who missed her son a great deal, nodded glumly. Then, chuckling, she announced, "But he's been promoted. He doesn't just clean vegetables now: they made him a cook!"

"When he finishes his service, perhaps we'll open another taverna on your roof," Spýros announced, to general laughter.

Linda asked when Rígas's next leave was, and Mára replied he would be back at the end of the month. His leaves were frequent, and I wondered how seriously Greeks took military service. During his last visit in January, I'd asked him, *what if the Turks invade while you're on Skópelos? Who will stop them?*

I was of course joking, but I suspect my Greek may have cracked him up more than my joke. Apart from being conjugationally challenged, I knew the root but not the actual noun for Turk, so what came out was likely along the lines of, "and if coming the Turkishes? Who make finish them?" Rígas put a hand on my shoulder and, between chuckles, reassured me that there were many others left, and they could handle the Turks without him.

In keeping with our philosophy of introducing new and fun things to our Greek friends, Linda made Pineapple Upside-Down Cake for dessert. This went down very well; but Mára had been especially delighted by the Banana Nut Bread Linda had given our friends a couple of weeks earlier, and would Linda write the recipe down for her? Linda promised she would. Wow. She was going to translate a whole recipe into Greek? I was impressed.

ON THE THIRD week of March, the weather turned a corner. The winter, though mild and far too dry, had still felt like winter, with its bare trees, cold northerly winds, and Orion locked high up there in night's black vault. But over the course of a few days, the great gear-wheel of the seasons had turned, and everyone felt it.

We hadn't imagined the noise that would come with warm weather. *Psária Fréska* man was nothing to what we were about to endure.

In the daytime, there was the Káltzas project. Nikoláos A. Káltzas, soft-spoken Hardware Emperor of Skópelos, had started work on an extra storey above his premises. The shop itself was already large, well upwards of five thousand square feet, an attractive two-story structure comprising a large central area with an angled wing on either side. The architecture was classical modern, with big, symmetrical picture windows and a wide, curving driveway sweeping up from the ring road. The views out over the harbor were even better than from our terrace.

Unfortunately, the scale of the project meant that prodigious amounts of concrete had to be trucked up the hill. Week after week, cement-mixer trucks rumbled past our house at all hours of day, rattling the floors, and our nerves with it.

There was also the Crying Baby from Hell.

This little horror started shrieking every day in mid-morning and went on, hour after hour, often into the late afternoon. The sound seemed to come from one of the houses across the street. You could easily imagine the creature's head spinning through 360 degrees on its shoulders, as soul-consuming fire lanced from red, lidless eyes.

"I can hear it from *my* house half a kilometer away!" said Mára, when she stopped by one day. It drove us so crazy that at one point I conceived the notion of striking that same note on my electric guitar and setting my amplifier, cranked up to eleven on full distortion, on the balcony. Let the neighborhood deal with *that*!

At night, there were the motorcycle races.

Every evening around ten, the local teenagers would start tearing along the ring road like a swarm of testosterone-crazed hornets, up and down, up and down, until two in the morning. Our location on the sharpest bend in the road demanded a gear change, sometimes two, whichever direction the racers were going in. With the windows closed, the noise was annoying; as the days warmed further, forcing us to keep windows open, it was so bad we had to shout to be heard across the table, or pause any video or DVD we happened to be watching. If we were on the phone, friends six thousand miles away would complain that the noise hurt their ears.

ONE SUNNY MONDAY morning, taking the longer, more scenic route to the workshop, I was surprised to see that the cafés and tavernas on the *paralía* were putting tables and chairs out on the sidewalk. The locals knew their weather: winter was over.

By noon, I was convinced they were right. I called Linda, who'd stayed at home to work on her soap label designs and take care of laundry. "It's gorgeous out here, and the tavernas have put tables out. What do you say to lunch outdoors on the *paralía*?"

Linda is nothing if not decisive. "God, yes! Give me thirty minutes. Meet at the bakery?"

We settled on a taverna by the small waterfront park. Most of the hotels, tavernas, and bars on the islands import staff from the mainland for the summer season. Sometimes these come on spec; the better ones are re-hired year after year.

Our waiter was one of the seasonal regulars, an older professional with oiled black hair and a pencil-thin moustache. We recognized him from previous years, and he recognized us. He unfolded the paper tablecloth with its fanciful map of Skópelos, smoothing it into place with a practiced motion, and slid on the four metal clips to keep it from lifting in the breeze.

We ordered simple dishes—*tzatzíki*, Greek salad (tomatoes were starting to come into season again), a few meatballs, and a half-kilo of *retsína*. The sun felt good.

We basked like lizards. Linda is an unrepentant sun-worshipper. She has a thing about the smell of Coppertone, and there's little in life she enjoys more than putting on flip-flops and sitting in the sun with a good book.

We people-watched: half the island seemed to be either strolling the *paralía* or sitting at the popular Ntókos bar nearby. On such a day, you would have to be dead to not understand that Life Is Good. My memory of that moment is diamond-bright.

"God, I hope we can make it work here," I said. "I just want us to be able to make a good living."

Linda nodded. There'd still been no word from Kákos, not even a reply to my request for an estimate, and both us were becoming uneasy. So much hinged on getting Linda's business launched for the summer.

Several people had told us to just go ahead and sell Linda's soap in a low-key way, assuring us that most businesses in Greece didn't have the correct licenses, and that if retailers wanted the product, they could easily cook up the paperwork to cover themselves. Others, though—not least Anna's boyfriend Strátos, who actually worked as an IT engineer at the tax office—had warned us of the consequences of getting caught. And with Linda's residency up in the air anyway, she was adamant about doing things on the up-an-up. Selling a half-dozen bars of soap to a friend here or there wasn't an issue, but she wasn't keen to have her products out in store displays until she was legal.

Given the suffocating bureaucracy, the fact that the country functioned at all was a miracle. The secret lay in ignoring laws: Greeks, in the main, just didn't give a shit[16]. One friend boasted to us that he'd never in his entire life paid a single Euro (or drachma) in taxes, adding, "also my father never paid tax in his life, and he was a very successful lawyer!" People went through all kinds of shenanigans to buy foreign cars and generate fake paper trails to evade the punitive hundred-percent duty on vehicle imports[17].

I wondered that the birthplace of democracy should be so lacking in civic-mindedness. Nobody *likes* paying taxes, but they are in a very real sense a commitment to and an expression of faith in a society's future. But Greeks, perhaps because of their terrible history of occupations, ethnic disruptions, civil war, and military dictatorships, which lasted through most of the twentieth century, have a commitment only to family, to blood. Distrust of the state and a (justifiable) contempt for the corrupt political establishment is hardwired in these people, and no number of laws will change that.

THE FOLLOWING SATURDAY we rented a car for the weekend. We took a picnic to Miliá beach, armed with a can of tuna to feed the feral cats so they wouldn't follow us. It worked.

The day was sunny and Spring-like. We had lunch and sunbathed for the first time since our arrival. We had the entire beach to ourselves.

Lying there, seduced by sun and gentle breezes, we began to feel the pull of the sparkling water that lapped at the pebbles just a few feet away. We dipped our feet in the water: it was cold, but tempting. I stripped down and waded in. The water was on the icy side of cool, mightily invigorating. I swam a few strokes and emerged feeling refreshed in spirit as well as body.

On the way home, we stopped at the newly-opened hypermarket on the Stáfilos road, part of a Spanish chain called Día. For weeks the island had been abuzz with talk of amazing discounts, and how this was the beginning of the end for the smaller merchants. I hoped not. I've

---

[16] The Italians are the same. They even have a popular term for the ability of a people to prosper despite their nation's incompetent and often corrupt government: 'Il Malgrado', or 'the in-spite-of'.

[17] The EU repeatedly warned and even fined Greece for imposing this duty on cars made in EU countries, whose import should have been duty-free. The Greek government ignored them and continued the policy because they generated more revenue by levying the duty than the nation was paying in fines.

never been a fan of shopping in aircraft hangars that you have to drive to, nor of worshiping the bottom line to the detriment of an entire community: cheapness, in my book, is *not* a value.

When we got there, my fears evaporated. Día did have keen prices if you wanted mega packs of toilet paper or pallets of mineral water, but everyday food items were generally no cheaper than at the local markets, and the ones that were tended to be off-brands of lesser quality. And the place was soulless. It didn't belong, and both the building and the depressed-looking employees knew it.

Sunday was wet and stormy, so we drove to the far end of the island with the intention of just sightseeing, and maybe walking a bit between showers. Linda had mentioned that she'd read something about some Roman ruins at Loutráki, the harbor of Glóssa village, but I wasn't expecting much.

Skópelos was really not good at advertising its archaeological heritage. We were in for a surprise.

We strolled along the harbor beach, walking atop a long, shoulder-high bank of dried, compacted seaweed, the accumulation from past winter storms. As was so often the case on our winter rambles, we might have been the last humans on Earth (a possibility which, I freely admit, I never found disturbing. But I digress).

All the caïques had been pulled up onto the shore for the winter. The only thing afloat in the harbor was a rusting dredge. But on its side in the parking area lay what looked for all the world like a dragon trap: an enormous scoop, consisting of a pair of great steel jaws with rusting fangs clenched tight. The jaws, along with various pulleys and shafts, were attached to a mounting frame. The thing was easily big enough to pick up a family minivan.

Further on we found a series of illustrated signs detailing Skópelos's turbulent history and piratical past. On one blue sign was a large block of Greek text followed by its hallucinatory English translation, the fantastical word choices and unlikely syntax of which must, if nothing else, serve as a warning against the perils of attempting to translate mythopoetic language.

Another sign boasted that Loutráki had fully seven unexcavated Roman baths; it carried line drawings illustrating their workings, but neglected to mention precisely where the baths were. A signpost marked 'Roman Baths' pointed vaguely toward the water.

Vagueness in Greece is not a question of imprecision, but rather a well-developed art form. We walked down the harbor and along a bramble-bordered path past a row of fishermen's houses until we came to another sign that simply announced the Roman baths without pointing anywhere at all. No ruins, Roman or otherwise, were visible.

After some fruitless clambering about, Linda, who has an uncanny knack for finding antiquities, suggested we just walk along the shore to where a row of large boulders a couple of yards into the water formed something of a tide pool. A few yards along, to my amazement, was an intact slab of well-preserved Roman mosaic floor the size of a single bed, with another piece evident just at the waterline, covered by gravel and pebbles. Above this, unmistakable in the eroded cliff of the headland, were the baths themselves, with layers of different materials—stones, flat clay tile, and mortar—clearly visible.

Most archaeological sites require the visitor to exercise their imagination somewhat in order to visualize the ruins as they once were; an unexcavated site requires even more work, since we were effectively looking at a two-dimensional cross-section of the baths. But the mortar and tile bed of the tubs themselves, with the supporting subfloor, were clear, and, below that, the floor of the crawl space within which were set the fires to heat the tubs above.

The baths were anchored onto solid stone by a remarkably tough, pinkish mortar: here and there, fragments of construction material were still firmly attached to the rocks. One lump of material larger than a brick remained solidly cemented to a boulder three feet from the baths.

Extraordinarily, we had the place to ourselves. In most countries, a site such as this would have been cordoned off to the public. But we could feel, touch, and sit on the mosaic floor (probably once a patio or walkway) and contemplate the enclosed tidewater pool exactly as those first guests had contemplated it two thousand years earlier.

We Do Not Use This in Greece

From the Aegean Dream blog:

What's Going On?
March 26, 2007

Linda Speaks

I cut and colored my own hair. I like it. Sorta cute and bouncy and a change from the mullet style Dario gave me last time. Dario of course doesn't want to admit that I did a better job than he did so his comments were, "Hmmm…..a bit retro….it will take some getting used to…." Stuff like that… even though he decided to dye his hair himself today and wound up with black ears, extended sideburns, and an interesting swoop of black stain on the back of his neck. I am hopeful this will fade away in two or three months.

Hair stuff aside, I have had other challenges. My dear friend Mára, who speaks NO English asked me for my banana bread recipe. Of course I promised her she could have it. It took me FOREVER to write it out. First everything had to be translated from English to Greek and then I had to convert volumes in ounces to volumes in milliliters, as well as converting Fahrenheit to Celsius! Argh!

Saturday I planted seeds. Must grow a few things to ward off the cravings we have for cilantro, regular parsley, cherry tomatoes, hot peppers, and basil! I impatiently await the sprouting and check them every hour. Photo on this one soon!

Linda

THERE WERE INDEED a number of essentials we persistently couldn't obtain on Skópelos. Cilantro, or coriander leaves, was one of these items. Although everyone we asked knew what coriander was and occasionally used coriander seed in cooking, we always met with a 'we do not use this in Greece' statement when we asked for the fresh herb. In the end, we tried planting some of the coriander seeds from our spice box, and—to Linda's lasting delight—they soon began to sprout.

Limes were another essential. Infuriatingly, these were readily available on Alónissos. Why the least-visited, farthest island of the Spórades should have limes when we couldn't get them was a mystery.

I asked Giórgos at Próton if he could get them for us.

"We do not use these in Greece."

"They use them on Alónissos," I said. "If they can get them, can't you?"

Giórgos looked dubious. "Perhaps the bars use them for drinks?"

My rejoinder about there also being bars on Skópelos met with a shrug.

Linda thought we could just use bottled lime juice, and tried to explain the concept to Giórgos.

He gave the sideways nod of assent. "Yes, I can order that," he said. "I'll have it next week."

"Not the sweet," I said, concerned he might order lime cordial.

"No, no, unsweetened. I understand".

A few days later Giórgos told us our lime juice had come in. Great! We would buy several bottles. Giórgos showed us to the shelf. "Here," he said, pointing to a number of neatly-arranged bottles with bright yellow labels.

"*Ine limóni*," said Linda. It's lemon.

Giórgos's smile faded. "This isn't what you want?"

"No, we wanted lime juice. We can get lemons," she said, pointing to the display outside. "Lime is green."

Giórgos picked up a bottle and inspected it closely. The lemon pictured on the bottle remained stubbornly yellow, the words 'Lemon Juice' unchanged. He looked crestfallen.

The third essential was ginger ('*dzíndzer*'), also strangely available on Alónissos but not on Skópelos. We decided not to even try to order that.

Fortunately, Brigitte came to our rescue.

We'd been trying to get her to visit for several weeks, but couldn't pin her down, though she had business to transact with the land surveyor. After twenty-eight years in Greece, she had gone quite native, and plans—for no reason I could understand—could only be made a day ahead.

"I'm starting to think it's a control thing," I told Linda one day. "Because everything's so haphazard here, people like to assert control in weird ways, like not making dinner dates until a day before."

In my more creative moments, I began to wonder if one might not derive some profound insight from this irritating habit. Maybe it wasn't just cussedness but a fundamental cosmic rule, like Heisenberg's Uncertainty Principle. In the same way that you could never know both the location and the speed of a subatomic particle, perhaps it was impossible to know both the location in space and the time of arrival of a Greek.

Finally, Brigitte called us. "I will arrive on the dolphin at six fifty-five tomorrow morning," she announced. "Only for the day. I can not come longer because who will feed my cats?"

Since we'd got used to getting up around eight or nine a.m., meeting the early dolphin was quite a challenge. But the day was fine, and walking through the still-quiet village in the crisp hour after dawn, a joy.

One of only three people arriving on the Dolphin, Brigitte marched down the gangplank, full of Teutonic energy and purpose. "Where is Linda?" she demanded, after we hugged. "Is she sleeping?".

I assured her that Linda was up preparing breakfast, and offered to carry her bag.

"It is heavy," she said, with a smile; "It is full of limes and ginger."

I laughed. "Bless you, Brigitte! You have no idea how this will improve our lives!"

Brigitte had been having knee problems, and we took the ascent slowly. "I cannot tell you how happy I am that you are here," she said. "Before, if I had business in Skópelos, I always had to sit for hours in the café, because the Dolphin comes at seven and nobody will see you before nine or ten. And in the winter with the rain, this was so depressing!"

Linda had cooked a full breakfast, a kind of egg soufflé with sausage in it, and set out toast, juice, and a big pot of coffee. After a brief protest about going to such much trouble, Brigitte ate with relish.

She wanted to know all about our meeting with the lawyers, and Linda's residency issues.

"Ach!" she said, when we'd debriefed. "You see, you are in Greece! Nothing is ever simple."

If anyone had learnt this lesson, it was Brigitte. Since Mános's death, she'd been forced to deal with land and tax and car registration issues, and every one of these was a nightmare. Even getting bills transferred to her name involved major difficulties. Now, with the one-year anniversary of Mános's death approaching, and with it the deadline by which relatives could lay claim to part of his estate, she was sparing no trouble to ensure that she had everything in order and on paper. And since Alónissos didn't even have an OTÉ or tax office, everything entailed a trip to Skópelos or Vólos.

Before she left for her appointment, we showed her around the house. She made positive comments and admired the view from the roof terrace.

"Beautiful! But you pay three hundred and fifty for this?" she said. "It is far too much. You should not be paying this!"

That was Brigitte: kind and thoughtful, abrasive and dogmatic, all at once. Like Yiánnis, she had strong opinions about everything. In the same way Linda found Yiánnis's pronouncements annoying, she found herself at a loss for how to politely deal with Brigitte's directness.

As a European who'd lived in America, I thought I had a window on the problem. In the US—and particularly in California—social conversations tend to be boneless and non-confrontational. Europeans, on the other hand are far more argumentative, and, to my mind, socially honest. They get in your face with opinions and advice and question your own, and you had better learn to argue with them if you want to get along.

But in the US, to directly challenge someone's ideas or beliefs, however ludicrous, is considered a breach of etiquette, and very un-PC. Which may be one reason the place is such fertile ground for right-wing religious nuts and loony-left conspiracy theorists. In California I'd more than once been at a dinner table where the women considered it their duty to kick their husband under the table whenever he expressed a remotely contentious opinion, or tried to engage someone who had just voiced one.

I suppose the fear is that once you get into a heated discussion with a friend (or, heaven forbid, a business colleague), that's the end of the relationship. So don't rock the boat. If the Smiths want to believe the US government developed the HIV virus in secret labs to kill blacks and gays, or that the CIA masterminded the 9/11 destruction of the Twin Towers to start a war, just smile and nod. If the Joneses swear the Antichrist is walking the Earth and the rapture is imminent, well, that's all right, isn't it?

But to challenge anyone's beliefs, however wacky, is the ultimate *faux pas*.

AFTER OUR RETURN from Vólos, I dropped off the stamped forms and receipt from the TEBE office at the accountants. Now they could perform whatever arcane ritual was necessary (sacrificing a lawyer would have appealed to me) to get me set up with medical benefits so that

Linda could apply for her residency, which would in turn allow her to begin the application process for a business license. The whole affair was becoming so tortuous, the requirements so interdependent, that I could barely understand it anymore. For all I knew, it really might require a human sacrifice. I didn't care. I just wanted it done.

Imagine my relief when, a few days later, Pávlos called to tell me that he'd sent off the TEBE papers and that I could pick up my receipt books at his office.

At the office, he explained they had filed everything and I was good to go. The cost of the TEBE insurance was about a hundred and fifty Euros a month, billed two months at a time. It was the end of March, and I would receive my first bill in a few weeks.

He had three receipt books for me, and instructed me on their use. One was for commercial clients, another for private clients. "And this one?" I said, pointing to the third, smaller format book.

"This is for the transport."

"The transport?"

"Eh, yes. Let us say somebody wants you to paint a thing for them in your workshop. Well, you must take this thing there somehow. So for this you must give them a receipt for the transport."

My mouth opened, then closed. Don't ask. The answer would only irritate me.

I opened the 'private client' receipt book. At the top righthand corner of the first page was a bold number 1 in blue ballpoint. I turned the page; yup, number 2. I flipped more pages.

"You number these *by hand?*" I asked, unable to hide my incredulity.

Pávlos looked embarrassed. "Eh, yes. We must do it this way, the books do not come with numbers."

I nodded. Amazing.

The format of each page—two different-colored carbons were attached to each—was recognizable, a standard heading/item cost/total format, with lines for subtotal, tax, and total at bottom. But there were various boxes with small initials and words I didn't understand running along the top and bottom of the page. Pávlos photocopied the first page of the book and walked me through it, filling in the copy as an example for me.

Apart from the things one would expect—my name, my client's name, the date—the boxes were for my *afimí*, the number of the tax district, the location of the tax district, and the percentage of tax to be charged (these varied). Pávlos filled in the sample with some imaginary figures, added the tax, wrote in the numeric total. In the long box to the left of the total sum he wrote out the total in text, as on a check.

"Numbers aren't enough?" I said.

"Well, numbers can be changed."

"Of course. Thank you so much." I folded the sample receipt into the book with a growing sense of unreality, as though I were slipping into another plane of existence. "This helps a lot."

"Good, good!" Pávlos beamed. Something special was coming. "Now, the last thing: you must have a stamp."

"A stamp?"

The *yes* nod.

"You mean from the post office? To put on the books?" Official documents in many European countries still required a postage stamp, which was then countersigned and rubber-stamped, to validate the document.

Pávlos looked amused. "No, a *stamp*." He made a fist and pounded his palm a couple of times. "With your name and *afimí*, and what work you do. Without a stamp you can not make the bill."

"Oh, I *see!*" I did. Without a rubber stamp, you were a nobody. This was the Greek equivalent of a membership to the country club. And I could get it made in a day or so, he assured me, for about forty Euros at the stationery store on the *paralía*. Fifty-five bucks for a rubber stamp!

I wasn't remotely happy or grateful for any of this, but it wasn't Pávlos's fault. I thanked him, and promised to go to the stationery store directly. "But first, do you have the TEBE book for me?"

"No. This you will get after four months."

"*Four months?*" He flinched. I must have said it more sharply than I'd intended. "*Why?*"

"Ehh, this is the normal. Probably they want to make sure that you are paying into the TEBE system."

Another delay! I felt the heat rising to my face. *It's not his fault. It's not his fault.* "Pávlos, I *must* have it sooner. Linda can't get her residency until I have the TEBE book!"

Pávlos's normally serene expression had vanished. He ran a hand through his hair. "Eh, it can not be quicker."

"What if we pay the whole four months in advance?"

He looked dubious. ""Well. I can call them, but I do not think it is possible. I will try."

"Thank you, Pávlos. *Please* do your best for us, it's really important we have that book! Do you need to give us a bill, by the way? I'd be happy to pay what we owe you."

He held up a hand. It wasn't necessary. They would bill us in September for the entire year. I shook his hand and thanked him, asking that he call me immediately after he spoke to TEBE.

"Of course," he said, "of course."

AS I BECAME angrier at the endless delays and roadblocks, Linda grew more fatalistic. In unguarded moments, the mounting dejection in her manner was evident. It tore at my soul. We could both see that matters were sliding out of our control, but where I was still in active fight mode, I feared she was beginning to give up. With every added complication I felt her enthusiasm wane.

I'd read that the two greatest sources of stress for primates come from a lack of predictability, and the feeling they have no control over their lives. And here we were, facing both those circumstances, in spades.

We came across yet another example of how Greece treated enterprising foreigners when Sue introduced us to her friends Alice and Joe, who had moved to Greece from Boston a few years ago.

Alice was a painter and a potter. Back in the 'eighties, as her pottery grew, Joe sold his business—he'd owned a hair salon—and went to work with his wife, helping to run the pottery, mixing the clay, and leaving Alice free for the creative work.

Over the following decades their business flourished, until the pottery was well-known. Alice's painted replicas of historical pieces became collectible, with pieces offered for sale in the Smithsonian museum catalog. They had a huge old home in Boston, two grown daughters, and a good life. Then they came to Skópelos and succumbed to its magic, exactly as we had.

Soon after, they bought a plot of land on Skópelos, sold everything they owned, including the name of the pottery, and moved themselves and two shipping containers full of their belongings to Skópelos. They began to build a house.

Alice's mother was Syrian but her father Greek, making her fully entitled to Greek citizenship. She had all the necessary paperwork and—as in our case—the Greek consulate in the US had assured her that getting her residency would be simple, a mere formality.

Three years and two lawyers later, she was still waiting. Every now and then the lawyer would assure them that there was no problem and she would have her residency 'by the end of the month'.

It was an interminable month.

We sat by the pool of their beautiful, just-completed home overlooking the harbor, listening as their sad story concluded.

"We're broke," Alice told us, over a delicious plate of Baba Ganoush. "Like Linda, I can't start my business until I have my residency. We used to take a trip every three months just to renew our permits. The one time we overstayed, they fined us."

"We're over our permits right now," said Joe. "But we're not going anywhere this time, not even to Turkey. We can't afford it."

Our hearts hurt for them. They'd spent close to half a million dollars on their home, and had had no income for more than three years. They were in their early sixties, and not in the best health. The years of stress showed in every tired smile.

"How do you keep your spirits up?" I asked.

Alice shrugged. "What else can we do?"

"They got us by the balls," said Joe.

AS THE PRACTICAL obstacles to our business enterprises grew, the local awareness of our work was expanding, creating a kind of schizoid tension in our lives and psyches. Even as we struggled against the faceless bureaucracy grinding away at our dreams, we saw tangible, daily proof that both we and our efforts were well-liked and that there might be a good market for our work.

People had begun to drop by the workshop semi-regularly, curious to see what we were up to. With the water department office and the municipal materials yard just a few doors down from our workshop, we'd see Spýros whizz by on his little Honda two or three times a day. One day he stopped by with one of his laborers, Kóstas, a scarred, rough-looking character who lived on the corner by Nick's Pizzeria.

Linda had arranged a few dozen bars of her soap—some loose, others in gift assortment bags—in a display basket on a shelf. I showed our guests the display. Spýros and Mára had been recipients of gifts of Linda's soap for some time, and Spýros knew enough about Linda's craft to explain to Kóstas what he was looking at. I caught the words *fisikós* (natural), *elaiólado,* (olive oil), and *votanikós* (herb). Kóstas nodded. Despite his broken nose and mud-spattered overalls, he was shy and soft-voiced. He peered at the Skópelos bars with their indented blue outline of the island.

"May I touch it?" he asked.

I smiled. "Of course."

He picked up a bar, held it delicately to his nose. "*Kanéla,*" he said. Cinnamon. He worked his way through the clove scrub bars and the lavender loofah slices, coming eventually to the final grouping.

"Goat milk and honey," I said. "The honey, like the olive oil, is from Skópelos."

Kóstas said something to Spýros; I caught the words *polí oréo*—very beautiful. I gave him a couple of bars to take home to his wife.

Spýros glanced around "And you, what are you working on?" .

I pointed to the copper leaf chest up on the workbench, which I had just completed. "It is Tákis's. For the *épipla.*"

They moved to the workbench, and I opened the shutters wide. The copper surfaces came alive in the afternoon sun.

Both men were quiet for several seconds. I explained that the chest was made of wood, and what my process had been. I gestured at the box nearby where I'd collected the sweepings of copper leaf fragments.

Spýros asked if he could touch the chest. Both of them ran their fingers over the leafed panels and lid. The impulse to touch something says more than words ever can.

They looked at the chest from different angles. Spýros turned to me. "*Ísse* pollí *kaló kallitéhnis,*" he said, with the utmost gravity. You are a *very* good craftsman. Kóstas nodded. "*Pollí kaló.*"

I murmured my thanks. Whereas it's not difficult for a competent artist or craftsman to impress a rich client, the opinions of people who work with their hands have always meant a great deal to me. I had put my heart into this piece. These men *felt* it, and their compliments moved me deeply.

Tákis came by the next morning to pick up his chest. Linda was also there, and he asked to see her soap.

"Ohhh! Linda!" he exclaimed. "It is very beautiful. I can buy this, yes?"

Linda laughed. "Tákis, you don't have to buy it—I'll give you some!"

But our friend was adamant. "No, I am going to Thessaloníki and I will buy them as gifts for my friends, also for my mother. Now, this one I will take three pieces. And this one… and this one…"

Linda had made her first sale in Greece.

THE NEXT EVENING, I stopped by Tákis's shop with my brand new books and rubber stamp, ready to issue my first official receipts for the items I'd painted for him, and for which he'd paid in cash. Tákis looked surprised.

"Yes. It is not necessary, but you can make one receipt if you like," he said.

I opened my 'commercial client' book on the desk and picked up a pen. Tákis came around the desk and glanced at the book.

"Dario, this is not, ah, *pos se léme*,"—what is the word—"it is not valid."

I looked up. "It's not?"

Tákis chuckled. "No, it is just a book." His father had come into the store, and he came over to look. Tákis filled him in and Vangélis laughed.

Tákis went on, "The tax office must make special numbers on the top." He went to the other side of the desk, opened a drawer, and pulled out a similar book. "Like this."

The receipts in the book were identical to mine, except for one thing: the entire book, from front to back, including carbons, was perforated right across the top with a series of numbers about an inch high. "You see? Only with this it is valid." He pulled out a cigarette and stuck it between his lips.

Back to the accountant's with the books. "Yes," Pávlos agreed, "they must put the books in a very big machine, and—" he raised both hands and made a mighty, pulling-down motion—"KA-CHONGG!"

"KA-CHONGG?"

"Eh, yes. Exactly. KA-CHONGG! Only at the tax office they can do this. I will take them tomorrow."

I put my palms on my cheeks and shook my head. Why hadn't he just taken care of it in the first place? I would never understand these people.

When I returned a couple of days later to pick up my freshly-perforated books, I met Yiánnis in the street. We chatted and made small talk. After a time, he lowered his voice and said, grave-faced, "Ehh, you must know that Pávlos is offended because you laughed at the numbering of the pages on the tax books, and you say that Greece is like Afghanistan. It is not good to say these things."

Gods. "Yiánnis, I'm *so* sorry! I never meant to hurt his feelings! I'll try to be more careful. But Pávlos was the one who brought up Afghanistan," I added.

It was a poor simile. One of the more moribund African nations would have been a better comparison.

It is a Dog

THAT SAME WEEK, I met the young couple above our workshop. I'd seen them before with their two small girls and new baby. The wife, Iréne, was very attractive in a statuesque, post-partum kind of way, with a poise that somehow didn't quite belong. Apostólos, her husband, had enviably raffish good looks. A perpetual five-o'clock shadow framed a ready smile and warm brown eyes.

Apostólos drove a beat-up blue VW bus, signwritten with his name and the word *Homatogríkes*, which as far as I could make out meant he did earthworks or grading of some sort. He had a small steamroller which he kept in front of the little derelict house opposite our workshop. After work he would ride or tinker with his 500cc KTM single, about the toughest dirt bike you can get. An ex-rider myself, I loved the beast's thumping exhaust note, and the way it made the workshop windows rattle.

One morning, I saw Apostólos bottle-feeding a puppy so tiny it kept falling over its feet. I took the opportunity to introduce myself. Apostólos spoke no English.

"What is its name?" I asked.

Apostólos smiled. "*Íne Zoí.*"

Ah. *Zóa* meant animals, plural. He was telling me it was an animal. He had misunderstood me. Try again: "Yes, but what's its name?"

"*Zoí,*" he repeated.

I looked at the puppy, tried another tack. "It is a dog," I observed.

"Yes, it is a dog. It is Zoí!"

We looked at one another a little warily. The conversation seemed to have reached an impasse. He thought I was nuts, and I would only dig a deeper hole for myself if I pursued the issue. I smiled and nodded. I petted the puppy. "*Zoí*," I agreed.

Back home, I consulted the dictionary. *Zoá* was indeed the plural of animal; the singular, however, was *zóo*. So… Oh.

Zoë? Who'd call a dog Zoë? Not for the first time, I reminded myself I was in Greece: *Trapézi, trápeza*—table, bank.

Next time I saw Apostólos with the puppy, I asked him, "Is it a boy or a girl?"

"A girl."

"Zoë is the name?"

Apostólos grinned. "Yes, yes! The dog is Zoë!" The dumb *xénos* had finally got it.

I was deeply relieved.

AFTER FIVE MONTHS of waiting for DEÍ—the state electricity board—to connect up a separate meter for our apartment, they finally came and did the job, leaving a hideous, two-inch thick black cable draped above the ring road to a steel pole on our roof terrace in the process.

I went with Spýros to the DEÍ office to set up our account, but discovered that my passport and tax number weren't enough; they also needed thirty Euros in cash for a deposit, and to see our lease.

When I returned half an hour later with our lease, the rules had changed. The DEÍ clerk—a fat and violently unkempt fellow—took the thirty Euros and started filling in a form. Did I have a photocopy of the lease? No. Well, I had to get one made: the office had no copy machine

The next day was Saturday, so it was Monday before I returned to the DEÍ office. After forty-five minutes in line, I handed over the photocopy of our lease. The fool didn't remember me, but eventually found our papers. He made some notes on a form.

"Good," he said, looking up. "Thirty Euros for the deposit please."

"I paid this on Friday," I said.

He gave me a blank stare, then looked at the form, running his finger down it as if checking a list. The office had filled behind me, and people shifted restlessly.

"You have not paid the thirty Euros." He said it matter-of-factly, and pointed to the form, as though there should have been a check mark where there was none. Someone behind me muttered something.

I knew I'd paid the fee, but with no proof or receipt, my poor language skills, and a line of impatient Greeks behind me, I could see I wasn't going to win this one. Thirty Euros wasn't worth the trouble of a big scene, and he knew it. I shook my head and slapped down the money. He gave me a thin smile, scribbled something on the form, and handed me my copy. I cursed him silently.

At least there was good news at the post office. The first of the four boxes we'd sent surface mail back in November had finally arrived. In fact, all four boxes with those last-minute things we'd packed arrived within a week of one another.

Sometimes, as I trudged along the street with boxes of belongings or multiple bags of shopping, I wondered what Skopelítes thought of us. Not that they didn't carry shopping around from time to time, but everyone else seemed to have at least a scooter, and often a car as well.

We'd spoken to Vasílis at one point about looking for a car, and he'd been keeping his eyes open for any bargains that might come along. One day, I went on an errand with him to the mechanic who worked on his little Fiat.

The man's workshop was a big, well-kept shed out in the country off the Stáfilos road. You can tell a lot about a person's work from the way they keep their workspace and tools, and I was impressed. Not only were things tidy, but there were potted plants peeking out from behind the hydraulic lifts and workbenches. I'd never seen such a thing.

An odd noise in the gloom beyond the office cubicle caught my attention, and I turned to look. A bird, scratching and pecking at the floor of an attractive wire cage hanging from a rafter. As I watched, it hopped up on its perch and began to preen. "A canary!" I said.

"He is beautiful, yes?" said the proud owner.

I nodded. I wondered how the poor thing managed with all the noise and exhaust fumes. I grinned. "So when he falls over, you know it's time to open the garage doors, eh?"

The man's English wasn't that good and he looked at me blankly, but Vasílis roared with laughter. "Like the coal mines!" he said. A quick translation followed, and I was rewarded with general mirth and a friendly slap on the back.

There were a number of cars in the yard, including an elderly Mercedes. All were for sale. One in particular—another of the ubiquitous Fiats—seemed a great bargain at two thousand Euros. "Why don't we go halvesies on it?" said Vasílis. You and Linda put in a thousand and we'll do the same. We could use an extra car sometimes, and you'll have something to drive whenever you need it."

It was a good offer, but even a thousand Euros now was an expense I was reluctant to face, given the difficulties and delays on the business front. We really were managing very well without a car. I hemmed and hawed, and said I'd talk to Linda about it. It was as good a deal as we were likely to get, but I knew we weren't going to be buying.

Truly He is Risen!

EASTER WAS RAPIDLY approaching. Church steps were scrubbed and cleaned, and fresh coats of limewash applied. Bells pealed. Masses were crowded. The larger churches had been holding daily services during the week leading up to Good Friday. There was such a sense of excitement and anticipation in the air that at times both of us wished we were believers, so as to more directly experience the joy in the air.

Not wanting to miss the Easter celebrations as we had Carnival, we asked Sofía and Rita what the schedule was.

On the Thursday evening, they explained, each parish's ceremonial bier would be garlanded with flowers by the girls and women of that parish, in preparation for Good Friday, when the Christ-effigy was taken down from the cross and placed within the coffin before being paraded through the streets.

Good Friday was a day of mourning. The very devout ate only sour foods, in memory of Christ's being given vinegar to drink. The evening procession was the big event of the day.

"The next evening," said Sofía, "at the Saturday night Mass, all the lights except one candle on the altar are put out. Then, one by one, everybody lights their candle from this one. It is incredible to see this. They carry the lit candle home, and make a cross with the smoke over their front door, to bring them blessings for the rest of the year."

Linda asked if it was all right for foreigners to participate. "Yes, Yes!" said Sofía. "Come at seven-thirty. We will have aperitifs together, and then we go."

Katerína, the Frenchwoman who worked at Gorgónes and who had hooted with laughter at my attempts to translate my website into Greek, had warned us about a language pitfall specific to the season. In Greece you grow used to replying to greetings with the word *epísis*, meaning 'you too', or 'and you also'. But on Easter Sunday, and for days afterward, it was traditional to greet everyone with the words, *Chrístos anésti*, Christ has risen.

"So in my first year," she said, "when somebody said to me, '*Chrístos anésti!*', I would reply, '*epísis*,' the normal answer to a greeting in Greece. People were shocked, even angry, because I was saying 'You also are risen!'"

"So what's the correct form?" said Linda, when we'd stopped laughing.

"You must say, '*Álithos anésti*', which means, 'truly He is risen'. Telling someone they too have risen from the dead is not considered polite!"

WE ARRIVED AT Sofía's house a little before seven-thirty on Good Friday, had a Campari and soda, and strolled together to the church. The night was cool and clear.

Several dozen people were already gathered in small groups on the large terrace outside the building. Inside was a press of people, beyond which we glimpsed a mass of flowers covering the top of the bier. The moody owner of the pharmacy on the *paralía* was on the steps; Alexándra Tsoúmas was coming out as we entered the church.

Once inside, we discerned a distinct current among the crowd, a circulation toward the bier and then back toward the entrance. As we approached, I saw first Sofía, and then Rita, dip forward. They were kissing the brow of the Christ-effigy in the coffin.

Linda, who was ahead of me, didn't miss a beat; I followed her example. I leaned into the cave of flowers, and for a second entered another world, a place of bright, sweet-scented blooms and the warm candlelight dancing on the olive-skinned face of the Savior.

We lit our candles and joined the growing crowd outside. The candles came with little plastic guards to keep the flame from blowing out in the breeze. Rita and Sofía met friends, some of whom they'd not seen in years. We chatted and watched the crowd.

A little before ten, the bier was brought out from our church as the head of the procession arrived. The procession had started at the parish farthest from the *paralía*. As the first bier and the priest of that church arrived, he was greeted by the priest from our church, litanies were exchanged, and the procession moved on. Ten minutes later, the next bloom-bedecked bier arrived, and the process was repeated.

The flowers, the incense, the liturgical chants by the light of hundreds of candles, the faces recognized as the entire village flowed steadily past like a great, slow river, the knowledge that we were witnessing a ritual unchanged over centuries: these were the invisible cables that bound this community together. Witnessing it, I felt a great peace, a comforting sense of security and permanence. It was beautiful.

When the final group had paused and moved on, the bearers of the bier from our church followed and we all folded in behind. An hour had passed since the first bier's arrival. The night had become crisp, and we were glad of our leather jackets.

We flowed down the narrow streets toward the *paralía*, borne by the current of villagers carrying candles. Nearby was Lázaros Tsoúmas, CEO of the Próton grocery, walking solemn-faced with his children. The procession was hushed. It was, I remembered, a day of mourning.

As we arrived at the last small church before the *paralía*, the procession ahead began to dissolve as if by unspoken command, breaking into small groups that trickled away without fuss. "We can leave our candles here," said Sofía, pointing to the interior of the little church. Other people were doing the same: the small space pulsed by the light of hundreds upon hundreds of half-consumed candles, its saints staring out of their icons among a sea of rich wood and glinting gold.

"Shall we go to Ánemos and get a drink?" said Rita. We were more than willing; it was eleven-thirty, and there was a general movement toward the *paralía* and its bars just one street down. Both of the big ferries that served the island—the G&A Lines Jet Ferry and the Hellenic Seaways Skiáthos Express—were moored alongside one another in the harbor, something I'd never seen in the off-season: the sons and daughters of the Spórades had returned to spend this most important of all holidays with their families. Above the giant, dark opening of the loading bays, the red digital banners that usually displayed the ferries' sailing time and destination glowed with Easter greetings.

The bars were doing a roaring trade. Ánemos was packed, so we settled ourselves at a small outdoor table. I saw the owner of Omorfiá, one of two high-end craft stores on the island, a place where we both hoped to place our products, sitting with a group of friends. A few minutes later Kákos, our lawyer, walked by. Rita greeted him by his first name; he acknowledged her without stopping.

We sipped our drinks and took in the atmosphere. People kept stopping by to greet Rita and Sofía. There was merriment as friends and relatives who hadn't seen one another since the previous year became reacquainted. The day may have been one of mourning but, as after any funeral, celebrations were now appropriate.

By one-thirty we'd begun to feel the cold. Rita, with her twenty-year advantage over her Mom and ourselves, was just starting to liven up and was ready to party. There were men out there, and the night was young. We gave her a farewell hug and accompanied Sofía to her door on our way home.

Greek Orthodoxy, Linda and I agreed, was a religion we could live with: big on ritual and eye candy, party- and alcohol-friendly: a faith wherein both Saturday night and Sunday morning could coexist.

WE'D ARRANGED TO join Rita and Sofía again the next evening for the Saturday night mass; but Linda, who is somewhat allergic to pollens, had broken out in an alarming rash and was feeling awful. We called to apologize and spent a quiet evening at home.

Next day, Easter Sunday, found Linda on the mend. This was fortunate, since Spýros and Mára had booked us several weeks earlier for the big Easter feast at the *kalívi*. We'd had several other invitations—from Tákis, Vasílis, and Apostólos, the neighbor above our workshop—all of whom were grilling lamb and hosting large gatherings. We assured them we'd at least stop by late in the day if we had the steam left.

But how to dress? It was sunny, and there was a good chance we'd be outdoors. But in the past we'd more than once found ourselves underdressed for an event, so clueless were we about the social protocols of this land. Given the importance of the day, we decided that casual-smart—slacks and dress shoes for me, a crisp dress for Linda—would be appropriate. Best to err on the side of elegance.

Strátos and Anna picked us little before noon. We arrived to find several people already seated outdoors in the small meadow by the chicken coop. A long wooden table had been set out, flanked by two long benches and an assortment of chairs. A little distance away, Spýros was turning a spitted lamb over a fire, while Dimítris, Anna's employer, likewise attended to a goat; on the same spit, a dark, sausage-like mass three feet long was sizzling away. Spýros had started the cooking a couple of hours earlier, and the meat was about halfway done.

We were hugged by all those we knew, and greeted with expressions of *Chrístos anésti,* which we countered with the requisite and traditional password *álithos anésti.* We were grateful we'd been coached in this beforehand.

Everyone, except for a small old gentleman and two black-garbed, elderly women we'd never met, was wearing jeans. We were seriously overdressed. And it was warm here on the southerly side of the island. Shorts would not have been inappropriate.

We were introduced to the older guests, who turned out to be Dimítris's parents and aunt, and to his two sons. The sons could not have been more different. One was round and flabby, with long, frizzy hair tied back in a ponytail, and owlish eyes behind alarmingly thick glasses; the other was a small bull of a man, with hard, close-set eyes and a distinct aura of menace about him. Father and sons owned a car hire business as well as the ACS courier agency where Anna worked. Another couple, friends of Strátos's, had come from Alónissos for the day.

Linda had baked chocolate chip cinnamon rolls for the occasion, and these, along with our bottle of premium red wine, were whisked off to the kitchen. I was handed a glass of the usual thin homebrew, and took a turn cranking Mr. Goat's spit. Between the greasy smoke and the occasional spritz of goat fat, the smart clothing was a wasted nicety. But it was pleasant to sit in the spring sunshine, smelling wood smoke and crisping meat. Spýros and Mára had once more made us feel like family. We were very blessed.

The sausage-thing was first off the spit. By now everyone was hungry, and lightheaded from the wine and sun. "*Koukourétsi,*" announced Mára, with her usual enthusiasm, sliding three thick slices of the stuff onto our plates. A casual question confirmed my suspicions: we were being served the organs and innards of at least one of the spitted beasts, and were left in no doubt that this was considered a great delicacy by everyone present.

With the notable exception of foie gras, I'm not a fan of organ meats: haggis, brains, tripe, kidneys, tongue, blood pudding—all deserve a polite but firm *no, thank you* in my book. And now—oh God!—how was I going to get out of eating this stuff?

But with our dear hosts sitting so close, and Mára clearly eager to see our faces light up as we sampled this treat; and Linda encouraging me to 'just try a bit;' and the admittedly mouthwatering smell coming from my plate as, fork poised, I tried and failed to find a graceful exit from my predicament; and the undeniable fact that it looked pretty much like a dark and lumpy version of *cotechíno*, a variety of cooked salami served in northern Italy which was, face it, one of my favorite foods on Earth…

I cut off a piece and popped it in my mouth.

Bit down on it, ready for a quick swallow if the taste proved unmanageable.

To my great relief, it *was* rather like a salami of some sort, albeit a very complex, nuanced, and distinctly liver-flavored member of the family. But it wasn't bad, and I was able to muster appropriate sighs and moans of delight without feeling too false about it. Mára and Spýros beamed.

Salads came, along with beans, slabs of féta, olives, and more sour, wine-flavored liquid. Before long, the lamb arrived. Spýros and Strátos set it down at the end of the table in front of Mára, and slid out the skewer. Mára made a couple of big incisions, plunged both hands into the steaming carcass, and began to tear off big hunks, piling them onto our plates as we handed them down the table to her. She was chuckling. We'd never seen meat served this way at a dinner party, but at least it must be tender.

They set the half-emptied lamb on the table not far from Linda, the ghastly remains of its face, complete with pointy teeth and cooked, milky eyeballs, facing us. We tried not to look that way.

The meat was excellent, at once more fatty and gamey than any lamb we'd eaten in the past, with the spiciness you'd expect from a flock whose diet included wild sage and oregano. Happily, Mr. Goat never even made it to table, so stuffed was everyone by the time it was even mentioned. This was a good thing, since neither Linda nor I are fond of goat.

The sun grew hot. Dimítris sat to our right, one of his sons beside him, one facing. He spoke some English, but insisted on making us work hard at our Greek. I liked the man: he was charismatic, with a gentleness that belied his dark, weather-beaten exterior. He liked to laugh, and it was clear he thought Linda a good sport as they bantered in Greek. I was proud of her: my wife had proved herself courageous, adaptable, and wonderfully crazy. Not for the first time, I could hardly believe we lived among these extraordinary people.

The chocolate chip cinnamon rolls came and went, along with coffee, and the party began to break up. The remaining few of us adjourned to sit at a table in the shade of the house. Linda and I excused ourselves and took a stroll up the lane and back, admiring the nearby *kalívis* and olive groves. Many of the houses still had working wells complete with iron bucket and crank, and I was unable to resist lifting the lid on one of these and peering in to see my head silhouetted against a perfect disk of deep blue in the blackness some twenty feet below.

We returned to find a neighbor had arrived, a loud, fat man who'd clearly drunk more than was good for him. In an aside, Mára let us know she wasn't pleased at the man's arrival, and it was easy to see why: he'd monopolized the conversation and showed every sign of going on for hours. Spýros saw me watching and did a surreptitious eye-roll to indicate his own feelings, but our hosts were too polite to interrupt their new guest.

By now it was evening, and when, a short while later, I asked Strátos if he could give us a ride home sometime soon, he and Anna seemed happy for an excuse to leave.

Mr. Goat, all wrapped up in yards of tinfoil but still on his spit, stood propped against the front door frame, ready to ride back to the Balabánises' in the back of the pickup, where I imagined he would end up in the freezer.

Into the Fire

WITH EASTER OVER, I called the lawyer's office on Tuesday morning to see if there was any progress on Linda's residency. Mr. Kákos wasn't in the office yet, but Vicky expected him any moment and would tell him to call. The next morning we still hadn't heard back from him.

Exasperated, I stopped by Yiánnis's office to get his perspective. Not wanting to impose or use up too many favors, we'd refrained from asking him to intercede with the town hall on our behalf, though he'd more than once offered to do so. "I have direct access to the Mayor," he had boasted, "and I can help you."

I explained what had happened with Kákos at the town hall, and the apparent bribe. Yiánnis steepled his hands and listened.

After a brief pause he said, "A year ago, Rígas Kákos was my best friend on Skópelos. But when he was standing for Mayor, I voted for the other party. From that day, he has not spoken to me. Still, I know him, and I do not think that he is so dishonest. Probably there is another explanation for this money."

"Someone told us that he was paying rent on his office to Iréne," I said.

"Yes, this is possible. Also you must know that this Iréne is the most stupid person on Skópelos. You cannot believe how stupid! She is one of the Tsoúmas family, but even they will tell how stupid she is."

"As well as rude. After that experience, we decided to get a second opinion. We went to another lawyer, and somehow it got back to Kákos."

Yiánnis's eyebrows went up. "How do you know this?"

"Because an Englishwoman who is a friend of his called us and told us it wasn't a bribe, that he was just paying his rent. I think he asked her to."

"Who was the other lawyer?"

"Pétros Haralámpos."

A smile flickered on Yiánnis's lips. "Ehh, you must know that he and Kákos are enemies. They hate each other. Now you are a *traitor* to him!"

I threw up my hands, exasperated. "How was I supposed to know? All we want is to get Linda's residency processed. It's a simple business. Kákos has all the papers but he won't even return my calls!"

"He will not do anything for you now. You must go to the KEP."

"What's the KEP?"

"The citizen's advice office. It is free, and the Mayor's daughter works there. If you come back at one, I will take you there."

I stopped by the workshop, where Linda was painting and wrapping soap, gave her an update, and putzed about unpacking a few more things and getting my supplies in order. A couple of hours later, I returned to Yiánnis's office.

"What did Haralámpos say when you went to him?" asked Yiánnis, as we walked along the *paralía* toward the KEP office.

"Well, he got pretty annoyed." I explained how the second lawyer had spontaneously combusted on hearing about the cash thrown on Iréne's desk, and gone into a rant about this becoming an international incident. "And this after he assured us we had attorney-client privilege! In the US we could sue him for that."

Yiánnis quickened his pace. "We must go to the police station."

I hesitated. "Look, Yiánnis, I don't want to make things worse."

"Ehh, this is not possible," he said, grim-faced. "It is already so bad that you can not make it worse."

THE YOUNG POLICEMAN looked up from the pile of papers on his desk as we entered the clerical office. Yiánnis introduced me and briefly explained what we'd come about.

I caught snatches of the conversation. Yiánnis was asking the police clerk, whose name was Stávros, what we needed to do in order for Linda to get her residency papers.

"You are EU citizen?" said Stávros.

"Yes."

"You have Greek residency?"

"No. Do I need it?"

A burst of Greek; I turned to Yiánnis. "Eh, he says that for Linda to apply for residency you must have this first."

The surprises never ceased.

I asked what I had to do to get Greek residency. It couldn't be difficult for an EU citizen, could it?

Stávros began to recite a list of requirements; Yiánnis made him write them down on a slip of paper. Later, he told me this was a must in dealings with public officials if you didn't want to fall prey to endless delaying requests for further papers and documents.

Stávros asked me a couple of questions, which I answered in Greek. The third I couldn't understand. He looked me straight in the eye and said, in English, "You are condemned of any crime?"

His melodramatic delivery and the unexpected question brought an unintended chuckle. "No," I said.

Stávros was not amused. "*Tha doúme*," he said, his tone ominous: we will see. Then something about the computer, and Schengen.

"How long will it take?" asked Yiánnis.

"For his permit, only one or two days after he brings us everything."

Yiánnis thanked him and I did likewise, extending my hand for the officer to shake. After a visible hesitation he stuck out his own, limp palm.

Outside, Yiánnis glanced down the list. "Passport… five copies of a photograph… for the criminal record, they will check the Schengen computer, but it is not working today… marriage proof… Ah. Do you have a chest X-ray?"

"A *what?*"

"You must get a chest x-ray to show you do not have tuberculosis. You can do it at the Kéntro Igeías, the public health center. It is free."

"Kákos never even mentioned it!"

"Eh. You must have this."

I gave up arguing. Resistance was useless. We walked the few steps to the KEP office. A big, open-faced young man was behind the counter. His name was Stélios, and he spoke good English. I shook his hand.

Once more, Yiánnis explained our predicament. Stélios grinned and gave a derisive little snort when our lawyer's name came up. He assured me they could help us, and that we didn't need a lawyer. "Here is my business card. Please call me when you have all the papers."

"Thank you," I said. "Part of the problem is that I don't even know if Kákos has filed Linda's papers yet."

Yiánnis nodded. "We will go to the town hall now, and see if the application has been made."

On our way down the long stair to the *paralía* and the town hall, Yiánnis said, "Dario, you must not shake hands with these people you meet." He looked annoyed. "It is not correct."

I stopped, taken aback. "Not shake hands? Why?"

"It is not something we do. You saw how Stávros was surprised when you did this in the police station."

"Well, in most countries it's a sign of courtesy and appreciation. What's wrong with that?"

"Not in Greece," said Yiánnis, starting down again. "It makes people uncomfortable, especially when you do not know them. It is not done."

We arrived in the town hall to find Iréne—whom I had come to picture with warts on her nose and a pointed black hat—absent from her office, her broomstick gone. Yiánnis spoke to another woman. She knew nothing about it, and could we return the next day?

"I will call the KEP office this evening," Yiánnis told me, "and ask Stélios to go with you tomorrow to check this application. Call him first thing in the morning."

As we walked out of the door, the Mayor—whom I recognized from the evening at the restaurant—appeared from another office and greeted Yiánnis. They chatted a few moments, and I caught the words for 'American woman' and 'very beautiful soap,' as Yiánnis introduced me. The mayor proffered his hand without hesitation, and I took it. The man had a warm, solid handshake. He'd done this before.

They spoke for a minute or two longer during which I heard our lawyer's name yet again, and we took our leave.

"So, Yiánnis," I said, once we were outside, "the Mayor doesn't seem to have a problem shaking hands,".

"Ehh, yes." A goofy smile. "But he is the Mayor. It is different."

I WENT TO the KEP office next morning. Stélios introduced me to Iliána, the mayor's daughter, a bright, personable young woman, with terrific English skills. We ran through the background of the case again, and both she and Stélios shook their heads in wonder at our lawyer's behavior. "And this man wanted to be the Mayor," said Stélios, laughing.

I returned with Iliána to the witch's lair. To my surprise, a slim, alert young woman greeted us. Iréne, it turned out, no longer worked in that office. I expressed my joy at this news. The slim woman who had replaced the witch-queen smiled.

They located Linda's file, discussing the contents as they pulled out papers one at a time. The slim woman's body language put me on alert.

Iliána turned to me. "There is an application," she began, "but Mr. Kákos has not filed all the papers."

My heart skipped a beat. "But… but we submitted all the papers to him at the time of the application, weeks ago."

"Yes, but there are only copies of some papers here. Many are missing, and the application can not be filed unless it is complete."

"Ah, shit." I couldn't help myself. "Tell me what we need, and I'll get it to you."

There was some discussion. Iliána looked uncomfortable. "She says you must file a new application. It is too late to proceed with this one. The papers must all be filed at the time of the application."

I wanted to scream. I forced myself to take a deep breath instead.

"Iliána, we gave Mr. Kákos all the documents he requested in plenty of time. Now Linda's permit has expired. To file a new application she'd have to leave the country, re-enter on a new permit, and start all over again. This isn't our fault!"

Iliána explained this to the other woman, who appeared to have followed most of it anyway. There was some urging from Iliána, which met with spread-palm gestures of impotence from Maria's replacement.

Iliána was apologetic. "I am sorry, it is not possible. Mr. Kákos did not do things properly. Linda must make a new application, and you must also have your Greek residency permit."

"And if we start a new application, how long will it take to process?"

"I can not tell you," said the slim woman. "Some months, certainly; perhaps more."

I couldn't believe what I was hearing. "And if we need to travel in the meantime? What if there's a family illness or something? Can we at least get a temporary document saying there's an application in process, so that Linda can leave the country without having to pay a fine for overstaying her permit?"

Iliána translated. The woman frowned. "I do not know. I do not think so."

By the time we left the office, I was ready to kill. My jaws were clamped shut, my body taut as a bowstring. If I saw Kákos walk in, I would do violence to him. I didn't give a shit anymore. Let them throw me in their fucking jail, nobody liked the son of a bitch anyway.

Iliána looked flustered and concerned. "Please wait a moment. I must talk to the mayor."

I paced, fantasizing about what I'd do to our lawyer should he happen to appear on the stair. Had Iliána gone in to her father's office to plead our case? I hoped so. The mayor was the highest official on Skópelos, and our only chance at this point. But when she finally emerged, there was no reprieve.

She led me to the police station, where she spent some time talking to Stávros, seeing if there was any way we could get an extension on Linda's expired entry permit. No dice.

"I'm sorry we could not do more," said Iliána, as we emerged onto the sunny *paralía*. Twenty feet away a fisherman sitting on the gunwale of his little caïque was mending his nets. "When you are ready to start the new application, we will do everything for you."

I thanked her for her efforts, struggling to keep my composure in the grip of an emotional hurricane.

Fade to Black

"THESE BASTARDS!" I told Linda a little later, "they play with people's fucking *lives*! At least in the US civil servants give you the right information, and the lawyers are generally competent."

She was grim. "It doesn't seem I have much choice, does it? I'm going to have to leave the country and re-enter. And now I've overstayed my permit, are they going to fine me on the way out?"

"Do you think they'd do that? You're only a few weeks over the expiry."

"Two months. They fined Carole and Matt twelve hundred Euros each."

"This isn't your fault, though. You thought your application had been filed."

Linda shrugged. It hurt to see my normally upbeat wife so fatalistic. "Maybe. How long would I have to be out of the country?"

"I think a week or so is enough."

"But do I have to leave the Schengen countries?"

"Oh. Damn, I see what you mean." The Schengen treaty—intended to facilitate travel between borders—included all the EU nations except England and Ireland.

"Exactly. Since they don't stamp passports, or keep records of travel between Schengen countries, I'm not sure it would be considered leaving unless I travel to a non-Schengen nation."

The blood felt hot in my veins. Christ! That meant that if we had to leave, it would have to be London. We had friends in London, but with travel and a week in the most expensive city in Europe… fifteen hundred Euros, easy. And if they fined her on the way out…

"There's Turkey, of course," Linda went on, "but I don't know what that would cost us. And what if they don't let me back in after such a short time? There's no guarantee they will now I've overstayed my first permit."

I cursed. What a mess! The worst of it was that—unlike the US or UK—we couldn't just ask someone official, since no civil servant could be relied on to provide a correct answer. And in matters of entry permits, as at any border, the attitude of the immigration officer on duty was certain to be a big factor. They typically have a lot of discretion.

But the core problem was that our money was hemorrhaging away at a terrifying rate. Add to that the fear that Linda wouldn't be able to get a business license in time for the summer tourist season, and our situation was beginning to look very chancy.

That night we had our first real crisis. Always at night. Fears feed on the dark, and this was no exception.

Lying in bed, we'd not long turned out the light when I realized Linda was crying. I moved to comfort her. In the glimmer of light that came through the shutters, I could see her cheeks were wet with tears.

"I've ruined my life." Her voice was a ragged whisper. "I gave up a ninety thousand dollar a year job for *this*."

"Look—" I began.

"We sold two perfectly good cars," she went on. "We sold our beautiful dining table and chairs, and all the patio furniture. And what for? So we could come and live in a country where they don't want me and they won't even let me fucking *work*!"

Her pain filled me, overwhelming, uncontrollable. I felt a riptide of cold fear at what was certainly coming as the hurt turned to anger, building like a wave.

I have little memory of the precise words that came after that, except that it was a litany of hard, honest truths, crushing in the dark, to which I offered little defense. In fact there was more grief than blame, but blame was unnecessary: I could supply myself that, and in spades. It was I who, in the face of Linda's better instincts, had pushed hard for an early move. We'd done the cashflows, hadn't we, and if I could sell a little of my work and we just made moderate sales of her soaps through the busy summer season, we would be all right. The first year would be tight, but we'd make it.

How wrong I'd been. From the first day, things had gone awry. Fifteen hundred Euros spent on appliances; then the trip to Piraéus and back; accountant's bills and TEBE expenses were coming, with the TEBE a fixed monthly cost regardless of income; and now the cost of a trip and possible fine to reset Linda's permit so she could reapply for a residency which might well not be granted until fall at the earliest, given the glacial rate at which these things moved in Greece; and of course there would be unforeseen hiccups and extra expenses on *that* road; beyond which, our dollar funds were declining in value every week: in the five months we'd been here the dollar's value had declined by ten percent and there was every indication it was headed lower still.

All my fault. I'd been a complete, overbearing idiot, and the person I loved most was paying the price. Linda had always run her life prudently; now, between years of helping me through the lean times muse-driven artists are so famously doomed to cycle through, and seeing her daughter through *her* numerous crises, Linda had hit bottom. Without her residency she couldn't even get a job waiting tables.

I hated myself. I wished she had never met me, she'd have been better off. I cursed the system, and—not for the first time—the whole miserable human race. This Earth could be a paradise, but between our mindless reproduction and our insistence on creating suffocating structures of stupid rules that only serve to crush honest people, we had turned it into a hell.

I wished myself dead.

Linda had turned her face away from me, and eventually I heard her breath settle into the rhythms of sleep. Eventually that same blessing, less final than death but sometimes as peaceful, stole over me also.

Eye of the Storm

WE WERE WOKEN next morning by the doorbell. I looked at my watch: it was almost ten. I pulled on a pair of jeans and stumbled to the door, on which someone was banging with purpose and enthusiasm.

It was Dimítris, Anna's employer. He was agitated. "We went to your workshop! There is nobody there!"

I fumbled for my Greek. "Uh, no. My wife is, uh. We'll be there in an hour. About eleven, eleven-thirty."

"But we want to buy Linda's soaps for gifts! We're going to Athens, and the Dolphin leaves at eleven!"

I blinked in the sunlight. After the despair of a few hours ago, the magnetic poles of our world had inexplicably flipped again. "Oh. I understand. I, um, I can be there in fifteen minutes, okay?"

I ran back into the bedroom and pulled on socks and shoes and a sweatshirt while quizzing Linda on what to charge for each type of soap. Splash water on face, comb through hair: good enough. Hell, I was an artist, and these were men I was meeting. Besides which, Linda's business wasn't even legal. Who cared what I looked like?

I loped down the hill, a suddenly elated fool, and had barely opened the doors when Dimítris and his elderly father arrived. The notion of these tough, grizzled men buying foofy soaps was extraordinary. But these were men on a mission: they looked, sniffed, and selected without even asking prices, and in less than five minutes had fourteen or fifteen bars picked out.

Linda had told me to give them wholesale, and the total came to around fifty Euros. Smiles all around: I put their purchases in a bag, took the money, wished them a good trip to Athens, and off they went.

I put the pot on for a much-needed cup of coffee and reflected on the crazy rollercoaster of our lives. The unexpected soap sale would have been cheering at any time, but after last night's excursion into hell it seemed downright auspicious, one of those events where even the most hard-headed rationalist might dare to think that perhaps the universe has a decent plan for him after all. I called Linda: she was happy.

If we could just survive Greece's nightmare bureaucracy, maybe everything would turn out all right after all.

LATER THAT MORNING I called our lawyer's office. He was in Vólos.

"That's fine," I told Vicky. "Actually I was just calling to say we've decided to do without Mr. Kákos's services from this point. I'll come by in a short while to collect all our documents, and of course we'll be happy to pay for the work Mr. Kákos has actually done."

Vicky was nonplussed as ever. It'll be interesting to see what he tries to charge us, I thought. If it was over a hundred Euros, just let him try to sue us for it!

After collecting our papers, I went to the Kéntro Igeías to get my lung x-ray taken. The large, single-story building was next door to the fire station, kitty-corner from the lane where we had our workshop.

The receptionist spoke wobbly English. I explained what I'd come for and showed her the written note from the police station. She said it wouldn't be long and asked me to take a seat.

A medical visit in Europe is an experience almost unimaginable to the average American. Nobody ever asks you for money, a credit card, or even ID. The healthcare system is exactly that, not a conveyor belt for the transfer of sick people's money to insurance company and hospital shareholders, supporting armies of bean-counting parasites in the process. And while Americans will doggedly insist theirs is the best healthcare in the world, WHO studies actually show it to rank somewhere around number forty. It's amazing how you can brainwash a whole nation just by repeating the same myths over to them.

I waited on a chair, people-watching. The Kéntro Igeías employed two of the three doctors on the island—the third being Yiánnis—and met all the general medical needs of the community. Specialist treatments invariably required a trip to Vólos, with accident or emergency cases getting helicoptered out, weather permitting. A helicopter from Vólos could be in Skópelos in under twenty minutes, and anybody who needed one damn well got it, without being billed.

I didn't wait long. The receptionist led me down the hall a few yards to the radiology room. I suppressed a chuckle when she knocked on the door; it was an ordinary, hollow-core door with a small window pane, but the window and most of the door had been covered in a patchwork of thin lead sheet, attached with an assortment of nails and screws. I've always been a fan of appropriate technology, and it was probably adequate shielding anyway, certainly better than a crucifix or a bulb of garlic.

The radiologist, a young woman, spoke excellent English. This was fortunate, as I suddenly remembered that my back was embossed with red and purple sucker-marks another recent cupping. She laughed when I told her, and commented on the symmetry of the marks. I told her we had a Chinese cupping set.

"I have only seen it with the glasses before," she said. "Many of the older people do this. It is a very good treatment for some problems."

Fifteen minutes later I left the building with a crisp, life-size x-ray picture of my lungs rolled inside a sheet of paper. In the workshop, I held it up to the light and examined it carefully for scary lumps. It looked okay to my untrained eye, but I decided I'd ask Yiánnis to take a look at it, since pulmonology was his specialty. It was good that I did.

"Your lungs are okay," he said. "You have no problems. But what do you think of the Kéntro Igeías?"

"I was impressed. They took the x-ray, clipped my photo to it, and I was in and out in half an hour. Very efficient."

His eyebrows went up and he broke into a toothy grin. "You think they are efficient? Why do you think this?"

I shrugged. "Well, they were polite, they were fast. Okay, so they have lead sheets nailed to the door of the x-ray room, but the radiologist was very professional. They were good."

"The doctor looked at your x-ray?"

"No. Why?"

He was chuckling now. "Ehh, the police, they do not know how to read an x-ray. The Kéntro Igeías must attach a declaration from the doctor to say that you have not had TB. It is written on the paper Stávros gave you."

I started laughing. "Okay, so maybe they're not quite as efficient as I thought."

"As I told you. Now you must go back to see the doctor." Yiánnis leaned back in his chair with a satisfied smile. He loved being right. And he was the island's only *private* doctor.

I'd wanted to give Yiánnis something for all his help, and had remembered him saying how much he liked Tequila. Próton had a surprisingly good selection, and I'd stopped in there on my way.

"I brought you a gift," I said, reaching down into my pack, "just to say 'thanks' for everything you've done for us." I set the bottle of Reposado on his desk.

He smiled, faintly embarrassed . "Dario, you did not need to do this. Not for this I help you."

"You've done so much for us, Yiánnis. It's nothing."

He lifted and admired the bottle, thanking me again. He turned to his bookcase and slid open the lower cabinet door, then another. The cabinets were filled with immaculately ordered papers and files; everything had its place, but there were no bottle-sized gaps. Anywhere. He slid open a desk drawer, peered inside, and closed it. "The problem is, where shall I put it? I cannot have this out because what will my patients say? And my furniture is all full!"

Sometimes it pays to be untidy.

I returned to the Kéntro Igeías and got my letter from the doctor. It didn't take long, and the doc was friendly and helpful. I still thought the place provided a good service.

On my way home along the narrow lanes, I saw the familiar figure of Mr. Kákos, our lawyer, gentling a shiny new motor scooter down the slick stones in my direction. Lanky and helmetless in his leather jacket and shades, he looked like a poster boy for Vespa. As he approached, he lowered his sunglasses along his nose and gave me a pointed stare over the frames. A pathetic attempt at intimidation? A plea for recognition? The man was nuts. I returned a disinterested look and let him pass.

The next morning, I took everything along to Stávros at the police station. He looked over all my paperwork, asked a few questions, and filled in a form. By the time we were finished I was able to get a smile out of him. "Come back in a week," he said, "and your permit will be ready."

And, fool that I was, I believed him.

THAT SATURDAY MORNING, Spring was a certainty that could no longer be ignored. We took our coffee up to the terrace and looked out over the harbor and across the straits to where Alónissos floated serenely on the shining waters. The sea was calm, the light breeze warm on our bare arms.

We'd scouted out Tákis's shop for outdoor furniture, a set of four chairs and a small round table. All were of teak; the chairs were collapsible, director-style, with cobalt blue fabric backs and seats. We'd put off the purchase for as long as we could.

We strolled into the shop to find Rita in charge. Tákis was in Thessaloníki picking up furniture. The price for the set—the *épipla* offered a ten percent discount for cash—was three hundred Euros, which seemed pretty good. We handed over the cash, and an hour later were breakfasting on our roof, feeling like royalty. From the day we'd decided to rent this place, Linda had said she would be living on our roof when the summer came, and I needed no convincing that this was one of The Great Ideas of Our Time. The summer evenings were long, the nights warm. I foresaw a lot of good times up here, especially since we would have visitors before too long. Over the last weeks, several friends from the US and the UK had booked trips to visit us, including two of our very closest friends, Robert and Lucy.

Adjacent to the opposite end of the terrace from the harbor view was Anna and Strátos's future apartment, where Spýros had been working hard for weeks. With an assortment of ratty old planks, he'd erected a precarious, L-shaped ramp connecting the second-story work site to the courtyard below. Up and down this rickety structure he would go, bouncing load after load of rubble in a dented old wheelbarrow until all the debris from the demolition was gone. He did everything himself, working from three every afternoon until dark. The only job he contracted out was the new tile roof, which was installed by three workers in a single day. If he'd worked as hard at his day job as he did on Anna's apartment, the island could have had a six-lane freeway by now.

Village kids testing their ship's boiler at Carnival time

Spyros's little flock at the kalívi

Easter procession leaving the church

One of several funeral biers is carried through the streets

Psária Fréska Man on his morning round

Our sparkling new workshop is ready to go

Our roof terrace at the mílos

View from roof terrace to the harbor, with Alonissos visible at left

The Balabánis family's kalívi
near Panormos. Ample family
sleeping space is provided
in both the living area
and the platform above.

The corner fireplace
in the living area
is both functional and
traditional in design.

The waters around the Northern Sporades are some of the world's clearest

Worn marble steps to the water along Skopelos's paralía

Tractor by Lamborghini

Skopelos's 'ship' bar

On Skopelos, you don't need a Stairmaster

The dimarhío (town hall), on the paralía

Skopelos boasts some 360 churches and chapels,
most of them quite tiny.

The monastery of Saint Barbara, now deserted

The nearby nunnery of St. John the Baptist (Prodrómos)

The 'copper chest' in Takis's épipla

One of the so-called 'pirate graves' at Sendoúkia

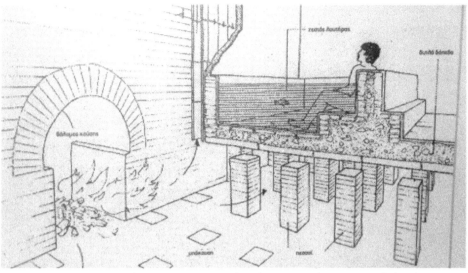

Artist's impression of Roman Bath technology on informational display

A portion of Loutraki's Roman Baths

Mosaic terrace on thick bed of Roman mortar between the baths and the sea

Olive grove on Skopelos

Ancient olive trees with Spring wildflowers

Springtime on Skopelos - hundreds of wild Irises in the woods

Greek creativity is second to none. Town or country, rain or shine, this custom rod does it all.

Garage full of clutter? Truck won't fit? No Problem!

Billionaire Spyros Latzis's yacht leaving Skopelos
with President G.H.W. Bush and family on board

Linda's handpainted signs are all over Skopelos

The Temple of Poseidon at Soúnion

Ancient graffiti on the base of a column at Soúnion

Wet street in the hóra on a winter's night

I would bring Spýros a *frappé* once in a while, and we'd sit and chat as best we could. Some days he looked gray from fatigue and smoking, and I could tell his back was killing him. I admired the man, and his single-minded devotion to his family moved me.

"You are a good man, Spýros," I told him one day. "You are good to your family."

He was quiet a moment; then, "My father was a good man," he said.

I smiled. What a wonderful reply.

The building project involved cantilevering the concrete floor of the apartment out over the interior courtyard at the rear of the house by some five feet and reconfiguring the interior to a new floor plan. With the interior and rear walls demolished, Spýros drilled rebar into the outer edge of the floor. He built a sturdy wooden form, supported on long jacks from the courtyard below, into which was poured the concrete for the floor extension. Once the new floor had cured, he started work on the interior.

As soon as I saw him building a cinderblock wall, I knew his true trade: he was a mason. You can always tell a person's core skill by watching them work, and Spýros handled the trowel with an ease and economy of motion that spoke of mastery.

"This is your work," I said, pointing at the rising wall, "making walls. This I see in your hands."

"Yes, Dario. I learned from my father. He was a builder. He built many houses in Skópelos."

Spýros was, however, no architect.

Linda and I went over one afternoon to say hello and see how the work was going. The interior walls were up, and Spýros showed us around proudly.

"This will be the bathroom," he said, leading us to a dark room along the new rear wall. "It will have a big bath and two sinks."

We admired the size of it. "But there is no window," said Linda.

"I don't know where I will put it. It depends how the bath and sinks fit. I don't know how big they'll be."

I was puzzled. "You must break the new wall for the window?"

"Yes." He slapped the cinderblock. "It's not a problem."

Classic. From the corner of my eye, I caught Linda's smile.

He led us into a small room along the rear wall, opposite the bathroom. "This will be a small bedroom," he said.

Linda's face lit up. "*Yá to pedí?*" For the child?

Spýros grinned. "Yes. And here—" he indicated a doorway to the right "—is the big bedroom for Anna and Strátos."

It was indeed a good-sized bedroom, filled with light from a big opening clearly intended for a French window opening onto the front balcony. We commented on the size and light. Spýros looked happy.

"But there is no door," said Linda. "You must walk through the child's bedroom?"

"It is a problem," admitted Spýros, removing his baseball cap to scratch his head. "I do not know where to make the door."

"How about along here?" I said, indicating the long right-hand wall.

Spýros hesitated. "There will be a fireplace somewhere on this wall. And I don't think it will look right, opening from the living room. It is a problem."

I nodded. I could see Linda was trying hard not to laugh. "You must make a drawing," I said.

He frowned. "Perhaps. It is a big problem."

Hórta!

WHILE THE POLICE station was processing my residency, I made a date to go *hórta*-picking with Vangélis, Tákis's father. Since tasting the wild greens Tákis had brought over, I'd been fairly obsessed with procuring more. I'd done a little research and discovered there were some 30 varieties of the stuff, and that it was among the healthiest food on Earth, bursting with antioxidants and disease-fighting mojo. The inhabitants of Crete, who ate *hórta* daily, ascribed their unusual health and longevity to this practice.

Vangélis didn't speak a word of English, but he was good at getting his meaning across. His mainland Greek was also easier for me to understand than the Skopelítes' dialect. We'd arranged to meet at eleven a.m. on Sunday. "We'll be gone three or four hours," he'd told me. "I'll bring snacks. All you need to bring is some water, and a knife to cut the *hórta*."

I was ready at eleven sharp. Eleven-thirty came, and then twelve, and Vangélis didn't show. "I wonder if he's forgotten," I told Linda. "His wife's in Thessaloníki, and I think he hits the bottle pretty hard."

I didn't have a home phone number, only the shop, and (it being Sunday) that was closed. Linda suggested I just go and knock on his door. I shook my head. "The arrangement was clear, he was going to stop by at eleven."

"Maybe you misunderstood him. Maybe he's waiting for you."

The thought had occurred to me, but... "I don't feel comfortable going and knocking on his door. What if he's with another woman, or unconscious with drink? It would be too embarrassing."

By one o'clock I'd given up on the excursion. Linda and I had lunch and walked down into the village to stretch our legs.

Next morning I went into the *épipla* to find out what happened. Vangélis and Rita were going through a pile of papers; Tákis was on the phone. All three looked up as I approached.

"Where *were* you?" said Vangélis, arms outstretched in a despairing gesture. Oh shit.

"We said eleven o'clock. I waited until one o'clock, then we went out."

He seemed more hurt than angry. "I was waiting for *you!*"

Facepalm. "I thought you were coming to our house!"

"And I thought you were coming to mine!"

We went back and forth a bit, agreed it was a language issue, and expressed our mutual regrets. With Rita's help, we made a clear arrangement that I would meet Vangélis at the store at two-thirty on Wednesday, which was the *épipla*'s half-day. I felt a fool. Sure, the language issue was real, but why hadn't I just walked the fifty yards and knocked on his door? Why, for that matter, hadn't he? Was it an excess of politeness on both our parts, or an excess of pride? I wondered if Vangélis and I were not cut from similar cloth.

From the Aegean Dream blog:

You Want me to Eat That??
April 30, 2007

If you wander coastal Greece or the islands in winter or early spring, you will see Greeks behaving oddly in the fields. Young and old alike, they pace the hills and fields, armed with kitchen knives and plastic bags. They are going after Hórta.

Hórta—of which there are at least 30 varieties—are essentially edible shoots and weeds. The Greeks love to eat them, and praise their health-giving properties. Hórta is more or less divided up into two main groupings, sweet and bitter. Some hórta, like dandelion, are eaten in the west also; others are utterly unrecognizable.

Knowing I was curious about the stuff, our friend Tákis gave us a bowl of cooked and dressed hórta a few weeks ago: the mixed greens are first cleaned, then boiled or steamed a few minutes, drained, and finally tossed in olive oil, lemon juice, and salt. Linda was lukewarm about the stuff; I loved it.

So last week I took an afternoon off and went hórta-picking with Tákis's father, Mr. Vangélis. Vangélis doesn't speak a word of English, so it was—among other things—good Greek practice. We drove off into the countryside, up hill and down dale, pausing whenever Vangélis spotted a likely-looking hórta patch.

The hórta picking part was fun—I came home with a huge bag of free, nutritious (or at least non-toxic) food. The remarkable part was Vangélis's driving. The fact that an elderly Greek will destroy a clutch and risk his—and my—life for a bag of weeds shows just how highly Greeks value their hórta. Okay, the car only got stuck twice, once on a deeply overgrown, weedy path, and later on a steep dirt road, but I had warned him on the second occasion, and he'd ignored me! Now he couldn't get the car back up the track.

Eventually, I persuaded him to let me get behind the wheel. I reversed way back down to a level spot, wound the car up and screamed the little Peugeot uphill. It slid and slewed at full bore up the track, overcoming poor traction by sheer upslope momentum and causing Mr. Vangélis—I'd made him get out of the car—to stagger back into the bushes to avoid being hit: there was no way I could slow down without getting stuck again, and I had minimal steering control, with the front driving wheels fighting for traction. I barely made it up the hill, leaving Vangélis to walk the 300 yards back up the road to the level spot where I stopped.

What does hórta taste like? Well, I thought it delicious: some is woody, some nutty, some anise-y, some quite bitter, some sweet and delicate—but then again, I'd risked my life with a crazy man to collect this bounty of the field and hill. I'd better like the stuff.

There is also the fact that most anything drenched in olive oil and lemon juice, and lightly salted, won't taste too bad. Linda.... was less enthusiastic, though she munched her way stoically through the stuff for a couple of evenings to humor me. What a trooper.

Dario

Linda's note: I like the hórta, I just wish he'd clean it better. The pine needles keep stabbing my palate!

"WHAT ARE YOU doing on Sunday?" said Vasílis. "The taverna at Pánormos beach has opened. Want to join us for lunch and a few hours on the beach?"

We didn't need to be asked twice. It was the last weekend of April and the weather was getting nicer by the day. Our weekdays had been full: I'd been dividing my time between CAD work and working in the studio, and Linda had been making, wrapping, and labeling soaps. We were both frayed from worrying about our situation, and a day at the beach sounded like the perfect antidote.

"The taverna owner is my friend," said Vasílis, as he parked the car. Everybody was Vasílis's friend.

It was a little before twelve. I peered into the shade of the newly-unshuttered taverna as we threaded through a score of empty tables set right on the beach; it looked as though we were the first clients of the year.

We ordered *tsípouro* and *mezés*. The sun felt wonderful, and my ray-worshiping wife was in heaven. We kept the sun umbrella folded and spoke of cabbages and kings.

I'd put on my swim shorts under my jeans, and headed for the water after the first drink. The others laughed: even young Kóstas couldn't be persuaded to join me out in the cool blueness, though he did come in to his ankles. Vasílis was adamant. "I don't go in the water until the first of June," he said.

I'm always amazed by the delight of slipping into the sea, or even a lake. No matter how cold the water, this primal imperative is unmistakable, irresistible: deep inside, we are still aquatic creatures, and if we have any sense we return to this element at every opportunity. On this day, the water was cold, but no worse than the central California coast in summer, perhaps sixty degrees. It felt sublime.

One way to stay young is to behave as though you *are* still young— in a word, attitude. People surrender their youth in tiny increments, giving up things they formerly enjoyed, *thinking* themselves prematurely into old age. Just because something (plunging into cold water, say, or backpacking and sleeping on hard ground) isn't as easy at fifty as at thirty, that's not—to my way of thinking—a reason to stop doing it, but a reason to *keep on* doing it.

As a result, I'm far more adventurous now than I was as a youth. I like to push my body and my mind because it keeps me youthful and feels good, an affirmation of life and vitality[18]. So the body hurts a little more than it once did: big deal. *That* should stop us? Why? As the poet said, *do not go gently into that long good night*. Age and death are inevitable, but we don't have to go like sheep. Get into that cold water!

Oh, remember to drink a little, too[19].

We ordered more food and *tsípouro*. Neighboring tables started to fill up. Nikoláos A. Káltzas, hardware baron of the ice-blue eyes, sat at a nearby table with his family. A little later, Alexándra Tsoúmas arrived with a friend.

Vasílis spoke to the owner, and they set up sun loungers for us next to an umbrella by the water. Kóstas played with his bucket and spade, chattering happily to himself without the need for adult input. Linda and Lítza were deep in Greeko-Anglish conversation. Dímitris suggested he and I go for a stroll over to the adjoining cove and have a look at Michael Carroll's house. Michael Carroll is an English yachtsman who sailed to the Spórades in the 1950s, fell in love with

---

[18] This is probably what Keith Richards was thinking until he fell out of the coconut palm he was climbing in Fiji.

[19] This is probably also what Keith Richards was thinking.

Skópelos, and never left. His book, *Gates of the Wind*, is still in print and sells steadily to English-speaking visitors to the islands.

"These bloody guys," complained Vasílis, as we strolled the road that led to the next cove. "They write one book and make a shitload of money. Hell, *I* could write a bestseller. I ought to do that."

"Mm," I said. Every author is familiar with the amusing notion that writing is an easy way to riches and that anyone can write a book. There's a saying I like to quote at such times: 'writing is easy—you just stare at a piece of paper until your forehead bleeds'.

And I very much doubted that *Gates of the Wind* had made its author a shitload of money.

We came around the bluff to the Carroll house. An older, rambling villa with mature gardens enclosed by a whitewashed stone wall, it absolutely *belonged*. Concrete steps led down to a small stretch of shingle and a wooden jetty, to which were moored two caïques and an inflatable. A few small sailboats lolled at anchor in the sheltered cove.

The first bit of the path back along the bluff was steep, and Vasílis was puffing by the time we reached level ground. We stopped on the edge of the woods for a breather. "Bloody smoking" he said. "I've got to quit."

"If you really want to, you will," I said.

"I did stop once, for three years."

I cocked my head. "That's a long time. What got you started again?"

"Ha!" he barked. He fumbled for a cigarette and lit it, gazing down at the long crescent of Pánormos. We could just see the deck chairs where we'd left Kóstas and the girls.

"I was on a visit from S'Efrica, and they stopped me at Athens airport. Some bloke with the exact same name as me had skipped out on his national service, and they arrested me. By the time they discovered the dates of birth didn't match, they said they couldn't stop the court process. But because it was to do with national service, it was a case for a military rather than a civil court. They threw me in jail."

He pulled hard on his cigarette so that the tip glowed fiercely. "You know how long I was in there?"

"Huh-uh."

"Three months. *Three fucking months!*" He shook his head. "That's when I started smoking again. Eventually, when my case came to court, the judge threw it out. He was furious. "Why is this man here?" he shouted at the cops. "You knew it was the wrong man! He hasn't bloody well done anything!" The Judge apologized to me, and ordered them to pay me compensation. You know how much that came to?"

The question was rhetorical, and he answered it before I could ask. "Thirty cents! Thirty fucking cents a day! That was the pay rate in the army, and that's what they gave me." He threw his cigarette on the stony ground and stomped on it.

We started walking back down to the beach. "In the 'States you could have probably retired on the lawsuit," I said.

"Hah! You try suing the bloody government here!"

"I'm surprised you still came back after that. I don't think I could have."

We were nearing the beach. He made a gesture that included the sand, the water, the pine forest, the hills, the perfect sky. "Look at this country, Dario. It's beautiful. It's just the bloody government."

I nodded. "And the bureaucracy—it's impossible to get *anything* done. Why do people put up with it, Vasíli? The country's a basket case. Take away the tourism, and the economy would fall through the floor."

"Ha! Try changing it. Did you know Greece has more than half a million civil servants out of a total population of ten million? And that's nothing—fifteen years ago, a third of the workforce was employed in the public sector! So you've got these huge voting blocks of civil servants. Every time there's an election, the politicians promise their favorite block more money and more jobs if they vote for him. So what happens? It gets worse instead of better."

Political as the Greeks were, they could be damned fatalistic. With the single exception of Yiánnis and Láli Páppas, who actually worked hard to change things on a local level, everybody seemed resigned to their lot. What sheep we all are! Keep people's bellies full and dull their brains with TV, and you can lead them to slaughter without a backward glance.

On the drive back from the beach that afternoon, Vasílis slotted a tape into the cassette player, and Kóstas sang along to *Men at Work's* classic 'Land Down Under'. "Doodadada Dada dunda? Deh-de-do, dedidunda!" The kid had a great voice.

Linda squeezed my hand; I smiled back at her. These were good, dear people, *real* people. We were fortunate to have them for friends.

"I CAN'T BELIEVE they did that to Vasílis," said Linda.

I nodded. "Horrifying, isn't it?"

"And they only compensated him *thirty cents a day?*"

"Apparently. What I find amazing is how Greece treats *its own citizens*, never mind foreigners. You create a system so bloody complicated nobody understands it, you make it hard for anyone to work legally, you fine them when you catch them out, and people have bugger-all right to sue their own government when it screws up." I had the bit between my teeth now. "Christ, they take shots at America for beating up on other countries, but at least the US treats its own citizens fairly, and makes it easy to earn a living.

"But Greece, this proud birthplace of democracy, utterly brutalizes its people. It denies them the dignity of work and the chance to make a good life for themselves without looking over their shoulder all the time! It's a bloody human rights issue, and next someone bitches to me about America I'm going to point it out to them!"

The next morning I returned to the police station. It was well over a week since I'd given Stávros all my documents, and I really believed my residency papers would be ready. After waiting in line an hour and a half, I discovered they weren't. "They are coming," he said. "Two or three days. Give me your telephone number, I will call you."

I gave him my number and left. What had Joe said? *They got us by the balls.*

A COUPLE OF days later, there was a welcome break in the gathering psychic cloud cover:

From Linda's Journal, May 20th, 2007:

I love Greece, I love the Greek people, their celebrations, the facial expressions used in place of the word 'yes' (the head tilts sidewise and the chin dips down to the collarbone), in place of the word 'no' (raised eyebrows, eyelids half closed and a slight raise of the chin... intuitively close to opposite on my home side of the pond).

But today, I'm simply tired of trying to absorb the culture, study and learn the nuances, and am chronically afraid of sending insults in a boorish American way. I fear I'm developing a tick from practicing the facial contortions in front of my bathroom mirror while my toilet methodically leaks pools of water around my feet.

I'm homesick.

But the Greek gods, in spite of their reputation for wreaking havoc, have heard me.

Rita and her mother Sofía have family in town: Sofía's brother Léo and his American wife Jacqui. I trot down into the village to keep my appointment with Sofía, whose back has been troubling her. Yes, though many don't realize the true extent of my talents, I have become the island chiropractor and cupping practitioner. I'm actually not bad. I adjust Dario regularly, Sofía frequently, and Vasílis has outrageous purple cupping bruises on his back that may never go away. The irony in Greece is that no license is required to be a chiropractor. Ah, but making soap..... this is a legislative impossibility! Argh.

I arrive at Sofía's and there, standing in the kitchen, is a home-grown, blonde, frickin' totally American Woman! I give Sofía her chiropractic adjustment, and Dario and I are kindly invited to join the family for dinner at Agnóndas. I try to decline, thinking it's a family get-together but am pushed until I am convinced the invitation is sincere and heartfelt.

We head to Agnóndas, our favorite place for an evening meal, the extended Greek family, Dario and me and JAQUI! Léo's wife is a true delight. I use every American cultural language reference I can think of and she gets them all.

I am saved!

Cold Calling

WE WERE APPROACHING our six-month anniversary on Skópelos.
Over the last few weeks, our little village had undergone a

remarkable transformation. The construction work which had begun all over town after carnival was proceeding apace in hotels, bars and restaurants. What had seemed a modest side entrance remodel at the Hotel Denise had turned into a major teardown, with the Albanian crew working from dawn till dusk seven days a week. Great holes were cut into the lobby's flat roof, and fancy pyramidal skylights installed. Work everywhere intensified as the weeks passed, the *sturm und drang* of construction work gradually giving way to the smell of fresh paint and varnish.

And suddenly, just a week ago, the first tourists arrived, owlish and startled. Mostly Brits, some French. A gaggle of pale, gangling teens from Sweden or Denmark. It was odd to see a lot of new faces here, and we began to worry that we might be confused for tourists ourselves.

And you had to watch the buggers. One day I caught a party of French tourists up on our terrace, who swore they thought the *milos* tower upstairs was a museum. I made a mental note to put a sign up.

We bought two bags of soil and some pots, and Linda began to plant things on the roof. She'd already weeded and tidied up the neglected planters all along the balustrade, and her cuttings were taking hold, so that we had a flush of strong new Geraniums nodding in the breeze. Our tomatoes and hot peppers were thriving in the sun. On the kitchen balcony we had pots of basil, cilantro, and mint. With mint, you could make Mojitos!

The unglazed clay pots gave me an idea, and I bought some extras. Back at the workshop, suddenly muse-possessed, I let fly with the copper leaf, followed by glazes of viridian and black. I knew the results were good when Linda begged me to take them home for our own use.

I went back to the garden store and bought several more small pots and one tall, amphora-type clay vessel embossed with leaf patterns. The smaller ones got the copper leaf treatment; the larger one became a song of silver leaf and bright, vibrant acrylics. The pots were quick and fun to do, and at the least would make good gifts. Perhaps I could sell some.

One of the things I'd been intending to sell to the Greek market were floorcloths. Floorcloths are painted and varnished canvas rugs, the precursor of linoleum, and were much used in the nineteenth century. A well-made floorcloth is both decorative and nigh indestructible; they can be rolled in a tube and transported easily.

I'd brought dozens of yards of canvas from the US and I set about the business of stretching and priming the material prior to painting. I couldn't wait to lay the biggest one—a full six and a half feet by four feet—out on my big workbench and start decorating it. I had a vision of something splendidly rich and oriental for this one, perhaps incorporating designs in gold leaf against a background of Chinese reds.

I also had an another piece of furniture to work on for Tákis, a rustic hutch with glass-fronted uppers. It was another cheaply-built piece, and he wanted a traditional look, so I had to keep the designs simple and the cost down.

After the obligatory period of head-scratching while waiting for inspiration, I went for a pale buff base color with an aged, scrubbed look, accented with decorative sprays of shiny black Kalamáta olives on the twig.

Linda now had a stock of perhaps two hundred bars of soap wrapped and ready to go. These first batches were made with store-bought olive oil. Now, following an introduction from Jilly at Rígas's corner market, Linda invested six hundred Euros in a whopping 119 kilos—about 22 gallons—of extra-virgin olive oil, enough to make perhaps two thousand bars of soap. The oil came from the groves of one of the local firemen, and tasted delicious. The soap business would not miss the occasional liter that found its way to our kitchen.

And the buzz on Linda's business seemed to spreading. Every few days, someone new would drop by the workshop to buy some. One day the local butcher stopped by. He wanted a gift for his wife, and somebody had told him about Linda's soap. He bought six assorted bars and went away a happy man. Despite our growing concerns, I was encouraged.

ON THE TENTH of May we took our courage in both hands and went out to try marketing our work. Our first stop was Argo Travel, the business owned by Sofía and Rita's friend Léda, who had begged to be our first customer.

Argo's office was on the ground floor of one of the older buildings on the paralía, not far from the town hall. The right half of the stately three-story was in excellent repair and bright with new paint; the left half, where Léda's business was located, was decrepit and poorly-maintained, its paint peeling, its ornamentation crumbling, so that you wanted to hurry inside before you got brained by a chunk of masonry.

The office interior, however, was a complete surprise: minimalist design, modern lighting, and stylish use of color all combined to create a sense of cool efficiency.

Léda greeted us cordially and apologized for the state of the building. "I can't get the landlord to take care of it," she complained. "I'm afraid someone's going to get killed one day." She turned to Linda. "Anyway, show me what you have,"

Linda took a basket containing various kinds of wrapped soaps from her bag, and proceeded to explain what each was made from. Léda listened attentively, examining each and holding them up to her nose.

"I'm thinking the Skópelos soaps would work best for you," said Linda. "I'd be happy to make up one or two display baskets like this one with an assortment of soaps for you to try out."

Léda was enthusiastic. "That, or maybe even a wall display," she said. "And I could put a bar of the Skópelos soap in the villas as a welcome gift for guests. These are really excellent!" She turned suddenly serious. "Now, do you have an *afimí* and a license? Because if you don't, I absolutely can't work with you. I do everything above board."

We were ready for the question. "We both have our *afimí*," said Linda, "and Dario has his business license, and is registered with TEBE and the tax authorities."

"I have a service license," I explained, determined to be upfront. I showed her my receipt book and stamp. "You'll have a tax receipt for the full amount."

Léda turned an intense gaze on me. "Are you sure?" she said.

"Sure, I said. "I can bill you as a service: we made guest products for your business. Our accountant said we should do it that way until Linda gets her manufacturing license, which is more complicated."

Léda looked dubious. She asked who our accountant was. "I'm going to have to check it with my own accountant," she said. "I'm very honest, and I pay for things the moment I receive them, but I do everything by the book. This office is right on the *paralía*, in full view. In the summer the tax inspectors watch all the *paralía* businesses, and God help you if they decide you're up to something."

She went on to tell us how, a couple of years previously, the tax authorities had raided her business. The whole thing had been a misunderstanding, a detail missing on her printed invoice forms because she hadn't been notified of a required minor change. "They burst into my office, accusing me of 'economic crimes' and threatening me with prison. Unbelievable. They were all over the place, five of them. It was like having the SS come and tear your house apart—terrifying!"

Fortunately, her accountant was able to clear up the matter in short order, but the experience had left an indelible impression on her. "That was when I started smoking again," she added.

Léda promised she'd call us just as soon as she'd spoken to her accountant. She was crazy about Linda's soap and really wanted to sell it.

Our next stop was Omorfiá. Also on the *paralía*, Omorfiá was probably the best artisan/craft store on Skópelos. We'd bought gifts from Omorfiá on previous trips and chatted at length with the owners, Pláton and Thékla, both good English speakers and very personable. And they had excellent taste: the store was resplendent with blown glass, ceramics, objets d'art, jewelry, and richly-patterned textiles.

Thékla was there, and she remembered us. We told her of our move to Skópelos, and asked after her husband, and how had their winter been. She was cordial and charming. Now we were living here, she suggested we get together one evening for dinner.

"Linda and I," I began, "are starting our craft businesses on Skópelos, and we'd like to show you some of the things we're making."

Thékla's smile chilled instantly. The reversal of buyer-seller roles had caught her off guard. Undeterred, I swung my bag off my shoulder. I'd brought my tall, silver-leafed and painted pot along, since I thought it was a good match for the Omorfiá look.

She considered the piece for all of about three seconds, scowled, and turned to Linda. I was dismayed by the abrupt change in her personality.

"And you?" she snapped. "What do you have?"

I was already repacking my pot, and Linda set her basket of soaps on the counter in its place. I feared for her.

"I make soap." Linda took a bar from the basket and handed it to Thékla. "This is a vanilla and cinnamon bar." Thékla lifted the bar to her nose and raised an eyebrow, tilting her head slightly; the scowl melted away.

"Lavender loofah soap," said Linda, handing her another. Another still: "Goat milk and honey. All my soaps are made with only pure

Skópelos olive oil. And this—" she'd saved the stamped bar for last—"is my Skópelos island soap."

A broad smile had settled on Thékla's lips. She nodded her appreciation. "These are very beautiful," she said. "*Very* beautiful." She turned the bar over and read the label securing the wrapping. "And you do everything yourself, even the wrapping?"

"Everything," said Linda.

Thékla chuckled. "You must find a faster way, because I think these could sell very well. Is anybody else selling them already here?"

"Not yet. I've spoken to some other people who are interested, but I've not made any agreements."

"Good. If we buy them, it must be exclusive to us. I will talk to Pláton, but I like these very much. *Very* much." She nodded, agreeing with herself.

We'd worked out a simple price structure based on size and ingredients, the wholesale prices ranging from two Euros for the Skópelos island bars to three for the large goat milk and honey soap. Inevitably, Thékla asked if we had our *afimís*, and marveled that I actually had a registered business with invoice pads and rubber stamps.

"You are very organized," she said. "We will have no problems at all." She gave Linda her card and asked for our phone number. "As soon as I have spoken to Pláton, I will call you. And I want to buy some of your soaps right now; tonight is my friend's birthday, and they will make a very nice present for her. I will take two of these, two of these, and two of these."

She took out cash there and then, and Linda thanked her. Linda took out another half-dozen bars and placed them in a small bowl on the counter.

"I'll leave these here," said Linda, "and you can see how people react to them."

Big smiles all around. Thékla said, "My friend will be very happy with her present. I will call you tomorrow."

"That's so cool she bought your soap for her friend as a gift," I told Linda, on the way home. "Especially with a shop like that to choose from. She was really impressed! But how do you feel about her wanting them exclusively? You've already promised them to Léda, and I'm not sure one outlet in Skópelos is going to give you enough sales."

"Let's see how many she wants to order," said Linda. "If you want exclusive rights, then you have to guarantee a certain sales volume."

"True. But it's a great beginning, isn't it? Omorfiá does huge business in the season. Now if I can just start interesting people in *my* work, we'll be on our way."

WE MADE A couple more calls the next day. We took Linda's Skópelos island soap into one of the little gift stores at the far end of the *paralía*. The owner expressed interest, but of course he'd have to show it to his wife, and would call us tomorrow. Very well. The next one, a gift shop near Vasílis's, garnered an identical reaction.

Back at home, I loaded up my pack with pots and took them to one of the upscale florists in the village. The owner admired my work but insisted my already tight wholesale price was the maximum she could sell them for at retail, leaving no room for a markup. She expressed regrets, and bought one for herself.

It was a hot day. I felt like a pack mule climbing back up the hill, and not a happy one, at that. "Did you hear back from Thékla or Léda?" I asked Linda, after I'd downed two big glasses of iced water.

Linda did that Greek backward head-tilt with the eyebrow twitch. No.

"I can understand the issue with *my* prices," I said. "After all, I'm trying to sell hand-painted artisan pots and competing with cheap junk from China and the Philippines. But after Léda's insistence on selling your soap, and Thékla blathering about wanting exclusive rights, you'd think they'd at least have the courtesy to call back."

"We were only there yesterday," she said. "Give them a day or two."

But a day or two passed, and then a few more, without either Léda, Thékla, or the other two storekeepers calling back.

The Hinge

CAREFUL WHAT YOU *wish for*, the saying goes.

Beware of Greeks bearing gifts, goes another, older, one.

Yiánnis called me to ask if I wanted to paint some signs for the Folklore Museum. I'd been wishing for work, right enough, but signwriting is a highly specialized craft; the first time I'd done any had been the last as well, and I'd sworn that in the future I'd sub out any lettering work I got to a professional.

Now my friend was asking me to paint signs in both Latin and Greek characters.

This posed a dilemma. Although signwriting was the last thing I wanted to do, we needed the money, and this was high-visibility work: the signs would be mounted on street corners all over the village. Yiánnis was clearly trying to help us out. He was on the board of the museum, and the woman who used to do the island's sign-painting had recently closed her shop, so the monopoly was up for grabs. That woman, curiously enough, was none other than Mrs. Kákos, our lawyer's wife.

Any freelancer who survives the brutal early years develops an instinct for jobs. This one would be a royal pain in the butt, but there was no turning it down: if nothing else, I'd have done it for Yiánnis.

We discussed the size and style of the signs. There would be ten of them, half pointing left, half right. Yiánnis wanted the words ΛΑΟΓΡΑΦΙΚΟ ΜΟΥΣΕΙΟ above the directional arrow, with the English translation, FOLKLORE MUSEUM, below the arrow.

Yiánnis hesitated. "Of course, they can not pay you in cash, because this is the museum and everything must be done correctly. But the payment is guaranteed."

I laughed. That would be fine. I had my *afimí* and TEBE number and I could give them an official invoice. No problem. I promised I'd email him a bid by the next morning.

I set about breaking the job down. I could get the ten signs out of a single sheet of plywood. The lettering would be most efficiently done by cutting a stencil and then using it to pencil in guidelines, which I'd then paint in: unlike arty shapes, the requirements for lettering were too exact to use the stencils for direct painting, and the letters many, and fiddly. This was going to be damned difficult.

Eventually, I figured on about two and a half or three days' work plus the cost of the plywood. Cut stencils, prime, paint, two full coats of varnish to stand up to sun and weather… Pricing my time at a bare minimum, I came up with a total of 285 Euros; about thirty-eight dollars for each hand-made, hand-painted sign. The price sounded very fair to me. If I was very lucky, I might make eighty Euros ($110) a day.

Two days later, Yiánnis stopped by the workshop, where I was working on the big floorcloth. Of course, they'd choked on the price for the signs. The previous signpainter had been charging between five and ten Euros for a small sign; I'd seen her work, and even though it wasn't that good, I wasn't surprised she'd gone out of business.

Yiánnis asked if the price would go down if he supplied the wood ready cut; one of the other men on the museum board had offered to do so. This suited me fine. In the end, we settled on two hundred even.

"Ehh, I must tell you this is still very expensive," said Yiánnis. "But I will see what they say." I chuckled to myself. I didn't really see that they had much choice unless they went to the mainland; I certainly wasn't going to drop my price any further.

"Also, I must tell you that you can not ask to be paid on delivery as you say on this estimate," said Yiánnis. "Nobody in Greece will do this."

I shrugged. "Those are my standard terms. Yiánnis. Actually, in the 'States I used to insist on fifty percent deposit with order—that's fairly normal practice there."

Yiánnis peered at me as though I'd begun sprouting hair from my eyeballs. "Ehh, Dario, you are in Greece now. It will take perhaps three or four months before you get your money. But I guarantee—"

"*Three months?* No way. I can't take a job on those terms!"

"Ehh, why not?"

"Oh, come on!" I protested. "It's hard enough doing a difficult job, but worrying about how long it's going to be before I get paid is something I don't need."

"Dario, you must know the payment is guaranteed. It is from the museum funds, and I am on the board. You will certainly be paid."

"That's not the point," I said. "Look, I really appreciate you offering me the job, Yiánnis, but I'm not prepared to work on those terms. No way."

Yiánnis spread out his hands. "Dario, you must understand, Greece is a poor country. Ten million people work like this. Even I work like this. I have some bills for TEBE that they still have not paid after a year—but I know that in the end they *will* pay me. Actually, it is quite good, because even when I retire I will have money coming in for a year or two. Only at the beginning it is a problem for the cashflow."

He still didn't get it. "Look, Yiánnis, I'm not a loan company. If ten million Greeks do this, it's no wonder the economy is such a mess. Sorry, but it's just not worth my peace of mind."

Yiánnis was insistent. "Dario, you can not have a business here and expect to be paid right away. Nobody will do this. Nobody. Páris at the hardware shop was telling me he is owed seventy thousand Euros. You have seen, everyone has a small book by the cash machine to write down what people owe. In the winter, especially on the islands, the people do not have money. They take things on credit, and then in the summer they pay their bills. Even me, and I *have* the money, I do not pay the bills right away. Yes, if an electrician comes and does a job in my house for thirty Euros, I will pay him then. But if the job is for three hundred Euros, I will tell him, 'I will pay you when I am ready.'"

I clasped my hands on my head. This was madness.

I knew Yiánnis was trying to help me understand how to do business here, but everything he was telling ran counter to my own business ethic. I'd always believed in honesty and transparency in my billing, and expected my clients to pay me on time and according to my terms. In return, I put one hundred percent of myself into the job. I didn't play games, and I expected the same of others.

"I will try," said Yiánnis, "to make the payment come faster. I can ask for this, and maybe it will be in one or two months. But I promise you that the payment is guaranteed."

I sighed. "Look. Of course I'll do the job, Yiánnis, but I'll do it for *you*. And it's not that I'm worried about not getting paid, it's the principle. If this is really the way people generally do business—"

"Ehh, it *is* the way. If Linda takes her soaps to sell in one of the shops, she must not imagine that they will pay her. Now, the shopkeepers have no money. They will pay her later, in September, when they have sold the soaps."

And what were we supposed to live on in the meantime? In my mind's eye I saw a chain of debt, ten million people with their hands out waiting to be paid. No wonder serious Lázaros at Próton always smiled when we walked in on the first of the month with our rent; Spýros looked downright startled when we paid him, always punctually.

"How long will the job take?" said Yiánnis.

"Um. We're going to Alónissos for the weekend, so realistically, two weeks. I'll have them ready by the first of June."

From the Aegean Dream blog:

Trials, Tribulations, and Celebrations
May 26, 2007

Linda Speaks:

Part I

A visit to the neighboring island of Alónissos brings a much-needed respite from the trials of trying to survive the ordeals of Skópelos. Dear Brigitte has read the blog and knows of our 6 month anniversary.

Our weekend away begins with a warm welcome at her beautiful home, and champagne and hors' d'oeuvres on the patio overlooking the harbor. We laugh as evening comes, looking at the pier at night, which I have mistaken in the past for a big yacht mooring in the harbor. I will be teased about this forever I believe.

The weekend weather is glorious and we spend an afternoon at the beach, have a lovely dinner out, and sleep in peace and quiet in her fabulous guest cottage. We are pampered and spoiled. Bless you Brigitte.

We return home to begin again the battle of trying to decipher how life works in Greece. Immediately we are thrown into another challenge. Shortly after our return from our idyllic weekend at Brigitte's, our phone no longer works. It appears to be disconnected. As we try to sort out what happened we find out that in Greece, you simply must be aware of when your phone bill is due because the actual paper statement may arrive, as it did in our case, two weeks after the final date for payment. (Note to self: stop by electric office.)

Dario tries to argue our case with the phone company over the reconnection fee, with no success: OTÉ blames the post office and of course the post office blames OTÉ for mailing out the statements after they are due. No win here for us. We pay the reconnection fee and wonder how OTÉ and the post office split the reconnection fee between them. Yes, we are cynical, this is Greece. Sigh...

My sisters have sent me another care package, and as usual, I anxiously track the FedEx package daily. They have sent me $124 worth of US goodies. Peet's coffee, chocolate chips, guitar strings, a $20 pair of drapes ...

Customs must know how badly I want my coffee, as they hold up the package. The customs broker (translation: rip-off artist) indicates that I must pay duties and fees to get my package delivered. I inquire as to how much??? They want 195 Euro to clear my package. They don't take credit cards: I must print out a release form and deposit money into one of their chosen banks. Of course we don't have any of their three designated banks on Skópelos. Their response is to wire transfer to their bank in Athens. This will cost another 30 Euros. I argue and whine, we go back and forth via e-mail because I want to understand why this is going to cost me $263 US dollars... WTF?

I finally get a breakdown of costs... only $80 is customs and duties....the rest???? Why of course, it is to pay the Greek bureaucrats for stamping the forms.

To cut to the chase, my package takes 20 days to arrive, involves my whole family to get it out of customs, and costs a boatload of money. But finally, we have our package. By this time we are just a bit wacko as evidenced by the maniacal gleam in Dario's eyes as he holds up the curtains my sisters have sent.

I, on the other hand plop down on the floor, like a kid at Christmas greedily opening my package. I immediately start eating the Jelly Bellies from my box and tomorrow I will have Peet's coffee. Jelly Bellies! A New Book! Peet's Coffee! Hair Conditioner! I will be ok.

Part II

Trash Duty

Skópelos has a trash problem. Skopelítes tend to throw their garbage wherever. Our friend, the good Dr. Yiánnis, organizes a clean up Skópelos day and we are commanded to volunteer. No problem, of course we will spend a day picking up trash.

We arrive at the appointed time on Sunday. The weather is wet and drizzly and with the exception of two people, all volunteers are xéni—foreigners.

We don our gloves and grab our bags and start cleaning up the paralía (road and parking lot along the harbor). At one point I find myself in the harbor parking area, alone, dirty, grubby, picking up garbage, when a Skopelíte stops by to observe me. There are rows of filled garbage bags near where I am working. The man looks into the bags, finds a rusted light pole top which has at some point fallen off the post and lain in the parking lot corroding away. He pulls it out of the bag and starts yelling at me.

I am so taken aback that I forget all my Greek and can't defend myself. I am in this man's village cleaning up trash and he is yelling at me. I refrain from walking over to him and throwing my foul bag of garbage in his face. I will never volunteer for trash duty again. Asshole!

Greece is a beautiful place. Skópelos one of the most fabulous sights I've ever seen. But we fear that we will never understand the rules. Even the Greeks don't.

Heaven help us, as at the moment I feel we are two human pawns in Dan Simmons's novel, 'Olympos'.

The toilet still leaks.

Linda

TRASH DUTY DAY was the turning point for me: the day on which, in hindsight, the door to our dreams began to swing shut.

The day had turned out cold and wet. I was peeved at having been dragooned into this garbage collection job when not a single Skopelíte other than Ilías, husband to Léda from the travel agency, was to be seen. To make things worse, I felt I was coming down with a cold.

Yiánnis was perplexed at my unusual whininess about the weather. "Eh, you are so delicate?" he kidded.

I grunted, the best I could do.

The truth was that my anxiety was turning into an angry depression. The more I heard about the way things were done in Greece, the less I liked it. Yiánnis's lecture on Greek bill-paying traditions had been bad enough; immediately on the heels of that had come the business of the gift package, with the customs broker demanding the equivalent of a month's rent on our workshop to clear half that value in goods. And then our phone getting cut off because of OTÉ's quaint tradition of sending bills out after the due date.

And beneath everything, the deepening mess of Linda's residency.

What had Sue said to the lawyer? *It's just a game, isn't it*, Rígas?

It *was* a game, all of it. A cruel game that kept the ordinary, good people of Greece down. But, oh! how much more fun when *xéni* were involved; then the game became *Screw The Foreigner*. They want to live here? Milk them for everything they have! They're rich anyway, they can afford it. And if they give up and want go home after being fools enough to build a house and give local people work, well, maybe we'll get to keep their house as well. Almost certainly, they made some mistakes and didn't follow the rules to the letter.

This is Greece. This is how things are done in Greece. This you can not change. And so on.

Bull.

How did these people put up with it? More to the point, how could such a good-hearted, generous people have developed these gangrenous institutions which existed only to crush people's dreams? This was Europe in the twenty-first century. How the heck had Greece even been *admitted?*

Between Nigeria and Malawi

IN THE COURSE of trying to understand all this, I happened on a World Bank website which rated 175 nations according to the ease of doing business there. Greece, with a ranking of 95, was nicely sandwiched between Nigeria and Malawi. The only other European member nations with worse rankings (Bosnia-Herzegovina and Ukraine) at least had the excuse of recent bloody wars or of having just lately been freed from decades under the Soviet yoke. Even Greece's near-Eastern neighbor, Turkey, managed to come in comparatively healthy in 65th place.

"I'm so sorry I got us into this," I told Linda that evening as we were finishing dinner. "If only—"

"Honey," she interrupted, laying a hand on my arm, "don't take all the blame. It was a joint decision."

I took her hand. "I pushed for it. I just had no idea…"

"There's only so much research you can do at a distance. How could you know what the town hall would be like? Or that it's impossible to get a straight answer out of a civil servant about the requirements for a workshop, or what's needed to get a license to make soap!"

I finished my *retsína* and refilled our glasses. I wanted to turn back time, to unmake the choices I'd so stupidly made. I could see the woman at the Greek consulate assuring us that Linda's residency would present no problem.

"If I'd had any idea it would be so hard," I said, "I wouldn't have pushed for moving when we did. I should have listened to you. It's just… hell, we'd already put it off a year, and we still weren't getting ahead. And how much of a cushion is ever enough? I was afraid if we waited any longer we'd lose our nerve and never do it."

I know," said Linda. The sadness in her eyes was terrible to see.

We stared at the table, at our joined hands. I cleared my throat. "We're real close to the point of no turning back. Another couple of months and going back might not be an option."

There, it was out. The fear clawing at my heart.

"I know," she murmured again. "The terrible thing is the uncertainty. If we just had some idea how long my residency papers would take, we could at least evaluate and plan. I can't do anything without those papers. I can't even get a job waiting tables!"

"You shouldn't *need* to get a job waiting tables. I hate that nobody ever even returns a damned call. Not the lawyers, not the accountants, not the people who *ooh* and *ahh* over the soap they insisted they were so hot on buying. As far as I can tell, the only businesses on this fucking island that deserve to make any money are Tákis's *épipla* and Nikoláos A. Káltzas." I took a swig of *retsína*. "On the other hand, I suppose if everyone here were efficient go-getters it'd be just like the US, and we wouldn't want to live here."

I snorted in irony; Linda broke into a smile and met my eyes.

I saw it coming, the first line of a three-line formula we had, a mantra for when things got really ugly, a spit in the face of an unfriendly universe. The three parts could be used in any sequence, but they must all be there. If there's one thing Linda and I share it's resilience in the face of bad odds, and contempt for those who would test us. Back to back, locked and loaded.

"Bastards," she said.

"Fuck 'em," I replied.

"*Whatever!*" we said in unison.

AND NOW I had these stupid signs to paint.

Lettering, as I said, is an art. Until a decade or so ago, a professional signwriter would draw a couple of lines, quickly pencil in the letters in rough, and then paint them freehand in long, flowing strokes, getting each letter right first time. Today, the preferred technique for most applications is to set the job up on a computer, color-print it directly onto transfer material, and apply the plastic transfer to the surface in question. This can then be strapped down with varnish if further protection is necessary.

I had neither the signwriter's training nor the transfer technology, but I did have some sheets of stencil card and a number of scalpel blades in my kit.

I wrote out the Greek and English wording on my laptop and played around with size and spacing, printing it on sheets of paper and sticking them on the wall until, at 56pt type, it looked about right for the size of the sign.

But I was getting slammed with Warmboard design jobs with tight deadlines. I could see I was going to get into a time crunch. Delivering jobs on time has always been a point of pride for me, and I'd made Yiánnis a promise.

Linda could see me starting to stress. "Why don't you let me help? I think I could probably cut the stencils, and help with the painting too, if you tell me what to do."

I gave her a hug. "I'd love some help," I said.

I'd already primed the boards, sealed the edges and back against weather, applied an antiqued basecoat in pale cream, and run a thin coat of varnish over them to enable mistakes to be wiped off. Linda had some painting experience, and she was every bit as meticulous as I.

She ended up doing eighty percent of the work, and, God! was it tedious: the stencil-cutting was tricky enough, the painting was even more so.

I'd been having trouble settling on a color palette for the signs. She came up with a subtle, unusual combination on muted greens for the letters and a rich, bronze-tinged russet for the central arrow, with a light gold for the border. They looked great.

Unfortunately, I'd got rid of my 'One-Shot' enamels—heavily-pigmented oil paints made exactly for this sort of job—because I hadn't wanted to ship anything so flammable. The artist's acrylics provided fine color, but just didn't cover well enough to do the job in a single coat, which meant my poor, dear wife had to go over the whole thing not once but twice: thirty-one letters, ten times, twice…

I would drop by the workshop to give advice and moral support from time to time, and to stretch my legs after sitting at the computer hour after hour. I felt bad inflicting such a job from hell on her, but she actually welcomed the change; besides which, the work helped distract her.

After five days of working on the signs as long as she could bear to, they were finally complete. I sealed them with two coats of varnish and recited the decorative painter's secret incantation, a closely guarded secret known only to adepts.

THE HOURS WE worked that week were a mercy, a release from the hell of fear and uncertainty. Warmboard was sending me as much work as I could handle, and the ride would likely last through September.

But what then?

We'd kept our deepest doubts to ourselves, but people weren't stupid. The strain must have shown.

I met Spýros in the street one morning. After the usual greeting, he cocked his head and looked serious. "All is well? Are Linda's soaps selling?"

"Íne dískolo," I replied: it's difficult.

"Why, Dario? The shops?"

"We have problems with permits, and with Linda's residency."

Spýros's eyes narrowed. "Ah. Problems?"

"*Ólos íne dískolo stin Elláda*," I replied. Everything is difficult in Greece. These words would become a catchphrase for us. I could see them carved on my headstone.

"Yes, Dario," he agreed, "it *is* difficult. For us, also." He gestured at the electricity meters outside the house. "It's taken me five months to get the meters, and I am a Skopelíte! This is Greece." He scratched his head a moment. "Ah, I wanted to let you know, there will be people renting the *mílos* next month and during July. The Ánesis cottages are booked, and so is the *kalívi*."

"I'm happy for you. That's great!" I said, and meant it, not knowing that in another few weeks I would feel quite differently about having visitors staying in the *mílos*, located as it was right in the middle of our beloved roof terrace.

YIÁNNIS WAS FULL of helpful suggestions for us. Since Mina had bought some of Linda's soaps and he'd begun using it, Yiánnis had become a convert. For the last couple of weeks he'd been badgering Linda to hawk them round the better hotels on the island. "For this, she does not need a license," he said. "She does not have a shop on the *paralía*. If the hotels want to buy, they will find the way."

Linda had already made a couple of hundred tiny hand bars with the idea of giving them away as promotional items. The hotels could commission more, and could offer her larger bars for sale in the lobby, or—better still—advertise them on the welcome card in the rooms. The sales would be cash over the counter, and the hotel would make a hundred percent markup. The ideal, last-minute, souvenir purchase. But it was the end of May, and she would have to move fast: in four more weeks it would be full season. And soap took a month to cure.

But Linda wouldn't budge on bending the rules. "It's okay for Yiánnis to say just go ahead and try to sell soap, but he's Greek. I'm three months over my permit. I'm an American here illegally. What if I get caught? I could be thrown out of the country and never allowed back in. And *then* where are we?"

I understood her. It was one thing to take risks at home, because you knew how the system worked—governments are a lot more tolerant of their own citizens bending the rules than they are of foreigners doing so. Brigitte and Tákis, on the other hand, insisted the Greek state was 'afraid' of America, in the sense of needing to retain its goodwill, and that they would never come down hard on a US citizen. But Linda had felt the bias toward Americans at first hand and wasn't willing to take chances.

To people who weren't in our shoes we must have looked like a couple of airheads who didn't understand that product didn't sell itself, you had to *market* it. But the truth was that the snafu of Linda's residency and the tangled mess of even understanding the business license requirements had us trying to scramble through a minefield, increasingly dejected and frustrated. And nobody had any idea how thin our financial cushion was.

Now, after everything we'd been through, after committing all our resources, we were facing the possibility of turning our back on the dream. We passed days and nights of misery, a promenade through the outer circles of hell without a compass, as we tried to get clarity on an equation in which most of the values were unknown variables.

The Door Swings Shut

"WHEN I COME to collect the signs tomorrow," said Yiánnis, "make sure you bring your tax bill and the stamp. I will give the museum board the bill immediately, and push them to pay it. Perhaps it will only take one or two months."

I was ragged from worry, but this made me smile. Here was our friend trying his damnedest for us over a sum that wouldn't make the slightest bit of difference to the mess we were in. "Yiánnis, thanks, but it's not a problem. It's only two hundred Euros. I'll see you in the morning."

Then it struck me.

I turned to Linda. "What the fuck do I do now?" I said.

"What do you mean?"

Sometimes I wished I still smoked. "Well. Right now I'm registered with the tax authorities but I've done no business. If we decide to leave, there's no record of any income. But if I give him a receipt and then we leave…"

She got it right away. "Yes. If they have a record of earned income and you never filed, you could be in trouble if we ever wanted to come back and visit."

"Exactly. I'm thinking that for two hundred Euros, it isn't worth it. I'm just going to have to stall him while we figure out what the hell we're doing."

"THEY ARE VERY nice," said Yiánnis, examining the signs. "Thank you, Dario. Now, do you have a bill for me?"

My tax receipt books and rubber stamp were on the corner of the workbench. I wasn't sure why I'd brought them. In case of a miracle, I suppose, or at least a sign from the God I so didn't believe in. I'd had a lot of such signs in my life, and most of them led to bad places. Every Eden came with snakes.

"You know, I'm not going to give you the tax receipt just now," I said. "I need to think about it a few days."

"Ehh, why?" Yiánnis's honest surprise set me back on my heels. Something in the moment, either our closeness as friends or the doctor's gut instinct for secrets, made it impossible for me to hedge. I was emotionally drained. I hadn't slept. I couldn't keep it in any more.

I hopped up on the corner of the workbench and sat on my hands. "We are... There's a possibility we might not stay. That we might return to the US."

Yiánnis's dark eyes widened; his posture changed, softening as if to absorb an impact. The concern in his voice cut like a knife. "Dario, what are you saying?"

I nodded, ready to burst. "I don't know if we can make it work here, Yiánnis. It's just too hard. Everything we try to do. The bureaucratic shit, the crazy license requirements, Linda's residency—"

"Ehh, Dario, you are emotional now. It is not so difficult. You must not feel like this. I can help you with these things."

A huge lump had crawled up into my throat, and I felt my chin start to quiver. I turned away. "You *have* helped us, Yiánnis. You've done so much already. And we love this place and its people with all our hearts. But it's too hard. I don't think we can do it."

I took a shuddering breath, trying to keep the trickle of tears from turning into a flood. I could feel the pain radiating from me like gamma rays. Even six feet away, Yiánnis's eyes were shining.

"It's not just those things," I went on. "Even if we do get a business going here, it's always going to be difficult. How can you work in a country where people don't pay their bills, where everybody is owed money all the time? Nothing works here, Yiánnis, *nothing*. The lawyers don't do their jobs. The accountants don't know the rules. The police can't be bothered. The civil servants are lazy, corrupt imbeciles. When you think you have everything covered, they tell you need another piece of paper. You bring that one and they tell you need another. It's just not worth it, Yiánnis! This isn't how we want to spend our lives."

Yiánnis was silent for a long time. Somewhere nearby, a baby began to cry.

"Dario, what I can say? You can not expect to come to a new place and make money right away."

"Why not, Yiánnis? Why not? Both Linda and I have moved many times. When I came to California from England, I had work—*good* work—in three months. When I moved from California to North Carolina, in six months I had more work than I could manage. Linda—"

"Eh, Dario, you are in Skópelos. This is not California."

"That's not the point! The point is that the system here is so fucked up that it makes it impossible for honest people to work. Look at the businesses on Skópelos, Yiánnis: every one of them is breaking some law or another. The only reason they get away with it is because they're Greeks! And it's not just us. Talk to Sue Miles, or Joe and Alice, about the problems they've had trying to do things legally, and what it's cost them. Jilly who works at the supermarket has been promised electricity for the last year and a half! Even the Skopelítes: Spýros waited five months to get electricity meters installed; his daughter, Anna, hasn't been paid by her employer for three months—they just keep promising they'll pay her next week."

Yiánnis shook his head as if to clear it. "And after six months here you will just give up? You must not give up! You must *fight* for what you want!"

I took a huge breath and tried to compose myself. "Yiánnis, you lived in Belgium as a student. You've seen how things work in other countries. Linda and I are more than capable of fighting, believe me. The point is we don't want to spend our whole damned lives fighting. We're both willing to work like dogs to get our products on the market and make a living, but what's the point in a country where the whole system conspires to make your life hell? For all America's problems—and God knows it has a lot of them—at least they let you work, and people pay you on time."

Yiánnis looked dazed. "You have thought all this in such detail. You must have been thinking about this for a long time. I never knew." He made a helpless gesture. "Why you did not come to me earlier? I could have helped you more."

"Yiánnis, I know you would have. It's a question of pride—we're not the kind of people to ask for help all the time. And this isn't just about Linda's residency. It's about the long-term realities of living here, of trying to get the simplest things done." I hopped off the workbench—I felt steady enough that I could trust my knees to hold me up—and went on.

"Our friend Brigitte, for instance. She's lived on Alónissos twenty-eight years. She was married to a Greek. The car was registered and insured in his name. Well, the insurance company said that now her husband had died, she had to insure the car in her name, and she couldn't drive it anymore until she did. Which meant she first had to register the vehicle in her name. In the US, this would take a week at the most: two or three phone calls and a couple of forms sent by mail."

"Dario—"

I held up a hand. "No, wait, I'm not done. So Brigitte had to take the car on the ferry to the registration office in Vólos, because they insist on actually *seeing* the physical car before they'll register it. She did that: between the ferry and the hotel in Vólos it cost her two hundred and fifty Euros. And they refused to give her any kind of provisional document, said it wasn't possible. This is a sixty-five year-old woman who lives up a hill and needs a car to get around. Imagine.

"The papers got sent by mail from Vólos to Athens to be stamped, then back from there to Vólos by mail, and then to her on Alónissos: total time, almost a month. She went to the insurance agent with the papers, and guess what? Now they wanted to see her residency permit. Of course, they hadn't mentioned that before. And this is an EU citizen who's lived here twenty-eight years and was married to a Greek! She'd never got a residency permit because she'd never needed one.

"So she goes to the police station on Alónissos. The police say, 'very sorry, Brigitte, but you have to go to Skópelos to get your residency'. She comes to Skópelos, does all the paperwork, and they tell her they'll have it in a week. She calls them a week later and they say to come and collect it. But of course when she comes to pick it up—that was last week—it's not ready, and Stávros at the police station tells her to come back in *another* week. By now she's been renting a car at her own expense for over six weeks, and she still has no idea when—or if—she's going to get this fucking residency card.

"So tell me, Yiánnis, how can anyone in their right mind put up with this shit on a daily basis? With your help and the KEP's, I'm sure we could eventually get Linda's residency. I imagine we can lie and bribe our way to a business license so she can make soap. Maybe we can make a decent living and eventually even buy a house. But every single time we sell something, or receive a bill, or try to get something done, it's going to be a headache, all the way to the grave. And much as we love this place, we can't help but wonder if anything is worth that level of daily stress." I took a deep breath. "Do you understand?"

"Eh, yes." Yiánnis spread his arms wide. "I do not see that there are so many difficulties, but what can I say? I hope that you and Linda will not leave, because we like you very much and we want you to stay on Skópelos."

I hugged him, and Yiánnis returned the embrace. "Thanks, Yiánnis," I said into his shoulder, "we love you guys too."

I turned to the workbench. I had a box ready for the signs, and started to pack them, slipping a sheet of butcher paper between each. "*And* it's my bloody birthday tomorrow," I said. "Fifty-five. They just come too damned fast these days."

Yiánnis laughed. "Happy birthday, Dario! I hope very much that you will be happy."

"Me too," I said, though I had serious doubts. "Me too."

OF COURSE, TROUBLES don't go away just because of a birthday. All I'd wanted was for us to pack a picnic, spend the afternoon at the beach, and go out for a nice meal in the evening. It was warm enough to dine outdoors, and I'd been wanting to try Alexander's, the colorful taverna on the corner up the street from Sofía's house. With its picturesque walled courtyard and mature olive trees interspersed between the tables, it looked very inviting.

We'd promised one another no serious birthday presents, so I was delighted to receive the jumbo bag of Starbursts—my favorite chews—that Linda had got her sister to send.

We were just getting ready to leave when Yiánnis called. He'd been thinking about our problems and launched at once into a pep talk: Linda must do *this* to sell her soap, I had to do *that* to sell my painting work, and we should think *this*, and not think *that*, and so on, for a full fifteen minutes. It was well-intentioned and I didn't have the energy to argue, so I just let him roll and said *yes* and *thank you* in all the right places. I finished by asking him to promise to keep our previous day's conversation to himself. We didn't need the whole island knowing our business.

"Save us from friends who want to help," I told Linda, when I hung up. I related the conversation.

"I know he means well," she said, "but I really don't need somebody trying to micromanage my decision-making right now. I need space to think."

"I agree. He can't understand that people might not want to spend their whole lives fighting this ghastly system. To him, we're just not trying hard enough, and not being realistic."

"I'd like to know what experience he has in marketing, too—he's a *doctor*, for crying out loud!"

I chuckled. "Yiánnis doesn't need experience, he has opinions."

WE SET OFF around noon, taking the hill path to Glyfonéri. We were only a few hundred yards up the hill from our house when I asked Linda if she'd had any more thoughts about what we should do about our plight.

My question provoked a frustrated response. "Look, it's your birthday, and I want it to be a nice day. Can we just let go of the subject for today?"

I agreed, and apologized. We held hands and made our way up the switchbacks where my favorite wild oregano plants grew between the stones of the old retaining walls.

But I couldn't let it go.

Before long I said, "Sweetheart, I *have* to talk about our predicament, birthday or no. It's the proverbial elephant in the room—I can't ignore it, and I'd feel better if we talked about it. We have to come to some kind of decision."

We'd come to a bend on the path where the trees gave way to rough pasture, and the harbor view opened out to include the whole of the Skópelos plain to the south.

Linda stopped and gazed out towards the water, hands on her hips. "Well, what's your thinking?"

I took a deep breath. "I think we should go back," I said. "To the 'States. I hate the idea, but I think it's our only choice."

Her eyes remained on the view, one of the most striking on the island. "That's the way I'm looking at it too. If there were just *something* that was working for us here. But it's all so fucking difficult."

I put my arm around her. The water was calm, luminous. "Even if you get your residency and we get through the first year or two, the problems are never going to stop."

"And heaven help us if we ever tried to build a house."

I thought of Sue and her battle over rights of way. Jilly, waiting eighteen months for electricity. "Exactly. In some ways, it might be a blessing that we didn't come with a big pile of money."

"Like Alice and Joe. Alice told me they're completely broke."

I frowned. "Bastards milked them dry. We're in a deep enough mess, but at least we can go back and we've just lost a year and maybe sixty thousand bucks. But heaven knows how much they spent building that house, and they're still no closer to Alice getting her residency. And they're older than us. They have no choices at all."

We started walking again, up the last, steep incline before the sharp turn where the path leveled out towards Glyfonéri.

"So you think so too?" I said. "That we should go back?"

She shrugged. "I'm like you. I hate the idea. I mean, look at the place!" She gestured at the landscape. "We live in a paradise. We've only been here six months and we've made so many friends—*real* friends, good people. But the crappy things aren't going to change. I don't want to spend my whole life fighting a system that won't even let me earn a living."

We were quiet a few moments. "When?" I asked.

"I'm thinking September, after Lucy and Robert's visit. At least we'll get to enjoy the summer."

"I'd like that. I was thinking around then, too. Also the Warmboard work will be probably be slowing down by then."

"And we'll have time with friends before we leave," said Linda. We'll get to leave on an upbeat note." She thought a moment. "Maybe we can even leave at the same time they do, and spend a day or two in Athens together."

I thought a while, looking at consequences and fallout. "Of course, we'll be breaking our two-year lease on both the house and the workshop."

"I think the Balabánises and Tsoúmases will understand," said Linda. "We could always offer them an extra month's rent or something."

"The Balabánises will probably be fine; the Tsoúmases, I don't know. We need to give them both plenty of notice."

Linda put a hand on my arm. "But let's wait a little, okay? I don't want to announce it to everyone right away." My wife knew me too well.

"When?"

"Another month or so. Mid-July. If we leave mid-September, that still gives them two full months. I just don't want to feel pressured while we refocus and start planning, you know?"

"Like Yiánnis telling us how to sell soap, and how to fight, and why we mustn't go."

"Exactly."

We reached level ground and looked out toward the harbor again. The wildflowers had almost all gone, and the ground was hard and dry. It had only rained on six or seven days during the entire winter, and only twice had the rain come hard. I wondered how long these islands could withstand the drought.

I drew a deep breath. A weird sense of unreality had stolen over me. Calm on the surface, I felt as though something inside were crumbling like a sandcastle before the tide.

"I'm glad we talked about it," I said. "At least we have a decision. Once we know where we're going to land and what the plan is, I'll call Aris Export and we'll start figuring out how we're going to do this."

I heard the words coming out of my mouth as though a stranger were speaking them. I couldn't believe we were going back.

I turned to Linda and saw tears running down her cheeks.

THE REST OF the day passed uneventfully. I felt lighter, and I think Linda did too. The fear of going into a winter here with no work and our money running out had given her a good many sleepless nights as well.

We got dressed up, had a cocktail around nine-thirty, and strolled down to the restaurant. About a dozen of the fifteen or so courtyard tables were taken, mostly by English or German couples and quartets. The night was warm, with just a breath of honeysuckle-scented air. We ordered and chatted to the owner in Greek, and got a big smile and a complement. All that work we'd done learning the language, and for what? But you can't judge the value of an experience until long after. Easy to think it had all been a failure, but I recognized the dangers of going down that road. We were made of tougher stuff than that.

Little did I know how our toughness would be tested over the weeks to come. Making the decision to leave was hard; actually leaving would present almost insurmountable challenges.

From Linda's Journal, June 3, 2007:

What should have been a day of celebration was in fact a solemn birthday with a hike to the beach, discussing what if any future we had in Greece. I have always tried to make decade and mid-decade birthdays special, but I met Dario's 55th with the lack of energy that comes from despair. It feels as though the Greek gods have played out their amazing game and we are the losers. Although I can't think of a more beautiful place for a birthday beach picnic, I desperately want to offer my husband something more—a solution, hope that we can make it work. I can only offer up tears.

I am struck by the simplicity of our decision to leave. In a few short minutes, a few short sentences, our life in Greece has been swept away. Our year of Greek lessons, our money, our planning, our Aegean dream will vanish as if one simply pulled the plug on a drain and the swirling vortex took it all away.

I can't imagine how to put my life back together. I no longer have the time or optimism of youth. People have always remarked on my resiliency, but I no longer have it. I can't keep starting all over, and here in Greece, I can't even buy a lottery ticket for those few hours of hope that my world will change.

The air is cool today and our birthday picnic doesn't include a swim or even dipping our toes in the water. I'm angry at the crystalline sea, the Greeks, the bureaucracy, my husband, but most of all myself. I am such a fool.

The thought of packing, moving, and once again having the house decorated in early box museum style depresses me. But having made our decision to leave, we give ourselves permission to simply enjoy what time we have left.

On one of my frequent late night messenger sessions with my sister, I bemoan the fact that now having received the long sought after FedEx package, with my so-desired draperies, the curtains will never hang in a Greek window. I will be leaving in a few months.

But Barbara puts it back into proper perspective: hang the curtains she says. Live well for three months.

I take her advice and hang the Aegean blue fabric on my windows.

A Plague of Celebrities

YIÁNNIS CALLED AGAIN next morning. This time he got Linda. She was amazingly patient with him, even though I could tell she was getting Morale and Marketing 101. Her head bobbed, and she made all the right noises. She tried to mount a small objection, but quickly gave up. She rolled her eyes, and sat down, phone glued to ear. I made her more coffee.

"Jesus Christ!" she said, after over half an hour, "he just doesn't *get* it, does he? I mean, I know he's trying to help, but—*aaargh!* Leave me alone!" She shook her head.

"That's Yiánnis. I'm going to have to ask him to back off, because he just won't quit otherwise. I'll be very nice about it," I added. "I know he wants to help, and he's doing it because he's our friend. And he doesn't know we've already made our decision. But he needs to stop."

So I sent Yiánnis a brief email, thanking him for being such a good friend and for all his help and good advice, but explaining that we really needed some space to weigh the matter without feeling pressured. Email can be a tricky medium even without the language barrier, and misunderstandings are easy. I hoped I'd phrased it well.

We discussed where in the US we might live. We were agreed on not moving back to the Bay Area. It would be too great a step backwards.

Linda favored New Mexico. She'd lived in Taos for a time and loved it there; I knew the area somewhat, and I liked New Mexico a good deal. The Albuquerque metro area was affordable, with some job opportunities. Linda's daughter, Lisa, lived there, as did some very good friends of Linda's. They had a large house and no children, and Linda thought they'd gladly put us up for a few weeks while we got our feet under us. Not an ideal situation, but the way things were looking, we didn't have a lot of choice.

OUR DECISION TO leave affected me strangely. I felt dissociated, as though I were seeing everything through a filter. Shock, perhaps, or some protective mechanism. But life nonetheless went on.

The village was starting to positively bustle with activity. Everything was open now, and oddly-dressed strangers stalked our once-quiet streets. The *paralía* had become a sprawl of tables and chairs, racks of trinkets and beach towels. The giant whiteboard outside the bus station—formerly showing just two departures a day to Glóssa and back—was crowded with freshly-scrawled times and destinations.

And my! but the days were heating up. The sunshine, recently gentle, was rapidly moving toward seriously hot, and we were glad our exposed location generally guaranteed a good breeze. We enjoyed our roof terrace daily, taking drinks and meals up there at every opportunity and watching the growing traffic in the harbor. Super-luxury yachts were starting to appear, and the glass-bottomed excursion boat was making daily trips around the islands. Beaches beckoned.

As long ago as March we'd heard rumors that there was going to be a major movie made on the island later in the summer; the grapevine said Meryl Streep was involved. Now the rumors had solidified: the production was to be a movie version of the hit musical 'Mamma Mia!', and it would star Meryl Streep, Pierce Brosnan, and Colin Firth. The last name gave Linda a case of the vapors, as it would any woman familiar with the British star's performance as the proud and complicated Mr. Darcy in the BBC production of Jane Austen's classic, 'Pride and Prejudice'.

Vasílis, as always, had his ear to the ground. He told us there were already production assistants on the island, organizing this and booking that. The little group of villas high on the east end of the island—where our friends the Coopers would be staying—had already been booked for the stars; the producers had also secured the entire Élios hotel, a big, well-designed complex on the harbor beach owned by the Tsoúmas family. Outdoor locations had been scouted, and a good deal of the shooting was going to take place at Kastáni beach, just near Miliá.

The Friday following my birthday brought further excitement. Yiánnis called us at ten a.m. to tell us that President Bush (the father, George Herbert Walker, not the current one) was visiting our tiny island for the day. He and Barbara and son Jeb, together with a few hangers-on, were cruising the area on billionaire Spýros Látzis's yacht. "It is anchored outside the harbor," said Yiánnis. "If you go up on your roof, you will see it."

Yiánnis was right. There was indeed a yacht—a small ship, really—at anchor a quarter-mile or so beyond the harbor entrance in the direction of Glyfonéri beach, but it was end-on to us so that you couldn't see much. A long, gray shape, a Greek navy cutter, was docked in the harbor.

I grabbed the camera and binoculars and started off up the road to get a better look. About fifteen minutes later, sweating in the sticky noon, I had a good side view of the yacht. It was a monster, black-hulled, with five decks and a helicopter pad on top. No sleek siren of the seas, this, but an uncompromising statement of power. I kept looking for gun turrets. Our local coastguard vessel was cruising a short distance away.

I heard the distant whump of helicopter blades off to my right, and turned to look. A large, black chopper was approaching the ship from the Skópelos plain (I later discovered that the Bushes had gone to visit the famous monastery of Ághios Rigínos). I watched, fascinated, snapping pictures for our blog as the craft swung in and settled on the yacht's helipad.

A big Zodiac inflatable, nose high as it ripped through the water, was circling the yacht in an irregular orbit. Inside were four or five gray-clad figures, private security, or perhaps Secret Service agents. The Zodiac came alongside the parent vessel, cables were attached, and the whole thing, guards, twin outboards, and all, was winched up onto the deck. The inflatable looked tiny against the yacht. The thing must have been over three hundred feet long.

I heard the clank of anchor cables and the yacht began to move, its bows turning in the direction of Alónissos. The navy cutter slid from the harbor, following in the wake of the Látzis yacht at a distance of a half-mile or so. The Skópelos coastguard vessel moved ahead towards the islet of Ághios Giórgos in the strait, doubtless to ensure no terrorists were lurking in ambush in one of its rocky coves.

Later on, we discovered from Brigitte that it wasn't the former president's first visit to the Spórades; he and the First Lady were aficionados of the Aegean. And the same yacht had carried Prince Charles and Camilla through these islands on the occasion of their honeymoon.

Between royal and presidential visits, and the cast and crew of what would doubtless be a Hollywood blockbuster, it seemed that Skópelos was quite the place to be.

THE CAD WORK kept coming, and I'd been working full-bore for weeks, sometimes ten or eleven hours a day. With the awful ergonomics of our computer setup—a narrow wood and cane taverna chair in front a round plastic table—my neck and lower back were giving me a lot of trouble. Daily walking and exercise helped, but Linda had to adjust me every couple of days to keep me from falling apart.

I'd settled into a routine with the CAD work, getting up at six-thirty in the morning and working solidly through to around eleven, by which time I was more than ready to stretch my legs. I'd walk down to the village, do the shopping, and put in another two or three hours until the noon heat had passed and we were ready for the beach. Work another hour or two before dinner, and then again after, while Linda read or watched a DVD.

We were very fortunate that Glyfonéri beach was only about a twenty-minute walk. The return took a little longer because of the steep hill up from the beach, but by then the day had cooled; in any case we enjoyed both the scenery and exercise.

Glyfonéri was something of a well-kept secret and, with the season still young, we rarely saw more than five or six other people on it. Most people went to Stáfilos, Pánormos, and the various beaches on the south side of the island. But with the warming weather the winds had turned southerly, leaving the water at north-facing Glyfonéri calm and unruffled.

Beach days were a major reason we'd come here, and since we would only get to enjoy this one summer, we were determined to make the most of it. Glyfonéri did not disappoint. The sweeping, pebbled bay was guarded to the west by a steep, forested hillside. Nearby tavernas offered food and drink. And, as everywhere on these islands, the water was a miracle of clarity. Now, by mid-June, it had warmed to the point where even Linda only hesitated a moment before fully immersing herself. We lay in the sun and talked and picnicked and swam. But even the brightest days had become shadowed by the knowledge of our leaving.

The Secret

ON THE FOURTEENTH Brigitte had to go to Vólos on another errand and asked Linda if she would like to join her for an overnight stay. I saw them off at the port in the early afternoon. The humidity was through the roof and the weather felt positively tropical. We'd been hoping for a thunderstorm for days, but the few promising cumulus clouds that occasionally loomed over the hills failed to deliver any reprieve.

Back at home, I did a few more hours' work and, a little before six, sent the job off to California so it would be on the design director's desk when she arrived at work. I poured myself an *oúzo* and wrote a blog entry.

The phone rang. It was Rita, wondering if we wanted to go and have a drink in the village with her later on. I explained Linda was out of town but that I'd love to go. Excellent. She would stop by and pick me up after she closed the shop, around nine-thirty.

The mercury was still in the eighties and the night sticky as we strolled down into the village together. Just near Rita's house, a familiar throaty exhaust note made us turn: Tákis, shoulders low and arms spread out over the clip-on handlebars, perpetual cigarette hanging from his grinning mouth, coolly threading his big Ducati motorcycle through the crowd of evening strollers.

He and Rita exchanged a few words of Greek, and I wondered again at the failed chemistry between these two, and Cupid's poor aim. They really made a handsome couple. Both were strikingly attractive, with Rita's full curves matching Tákis's sculpted muscles. Both exuded the kind of smoldering sexuality that ought to come with a fire hazard label. But it wasn't going to work: he liked these skinny, complicated girls, and Rita would never be more than his close friend from childhood.

Tákis gave the throttle a little twist preparatory to his departure. Turning to me, he said, "So, Dario, I will see you later on?"

"That would be great! I'll be around."

Rita and I stopped first at Gorgónes, chatted a little over *ouzo* and *mezés*, then decided to go down to Ánemos and the bright lights of the *paralía*. In her slinky dress, Rita looked very fetching. I could tell she had plans for partying late in the bars, where she was sure to run into a bunch of her friends. In the meantime, since everyone was out on the streets, we could have a little fun with the locals. I offered her my arm. "Shall we start some gossip?"

Rita took my arm with a wicked smile. "Let's," she said.

We were sitting on the bench in front of Ánemos, drinking beer and people-watching, when Tákis caught up to us. Around eleven-thirty, Yiánnis cruised by, looking a little the worse for wear. He seemed amused to see me with Rita and Tákis. Linda and I always marveled at the fact that people young enough to be our children seemed to enjoy hanging with us. *We* certainly enjoyed it, but wondered sometimes what they got out of it.

Yiánnis stayed a few moments, then wandered off to the next bar, the good doctor making his evening rounds. Rita met a girlfriend, and they went off together to cause trouble somewhere. Tákis came out with another couple of beers.

"So how's your love life?" I said, now that Rita had gone.

Tákis laughed. "Ah, Dario!"

"Well?" I said.

"Eh. I have finished now with Yeléna."

I peered at him over my glasses. "Again?"

"No, this time I really make the finish. Also her mother was visiting her house. One night at ten I go there and I ask to speak with the mother. I say to her many things, like 'why you do not let your daughter live her own life? Why you call her every day and tell her what to do, and say bad things for me? You are a very bad person!'"

I clapped my hands in approval. "Very good! What did she say?"

Tákis shook his open palm as though he'd touched a hot plate. "Eh, they could not say anything. Her mouth was open. I tell her all this and many more things, and then I say goodnight and I leave the house."

I slapped him on the back. "Well done! I wish I'd been there to see it! So, uh, is there anybody else in your life?" I wanted to say *so what about Rita, you idiot,* but I knew it would do no good. He'd had every opportunity under the sun to seduce her and never done so. Wasn't gonna happen.

Sheepish grin. "Yes, there is one girl I see, but we are only friends. We will see for this."

We sipped on our beers. "Tákis," I said, "when you are fifty, I will tell you the secret that is only told to men when they reach that age." I wouldn't be here for his next birthday, let alone in another twelve or thirteen years, but I promised myself I'd follow through, by telephone or email if necessary. He needed to know.

"There is a secret?" he said.

"Yes. There is a secret."

He made an impatient gesture. "Eh. Why you do not tell me now?"

"Because you are too young. The secret is not for the young."

Tákis laughed and shook his head. "Ahh, Dario!"

The Secret had first been mentioned to me in a very similar conversation by my wily friend Sid in California. Older than me by several years, Sid is a Sicilian from Brooklyn. He loves to tease, or 'fuck with people's heads,' as he puts it, and had once made me a very similar pitch to the one I'd just made Tákis. I believed him for an hour or two—hell, who *wouldn't* want to believe there was such a thing as The Secret—before realizing he was just fooling around.

Fifty came and went, and Sid never did tell me any secret. But just a year or two later, I discovered it for myself, the profound and illuminating truth that would finally make sense of relationships, and to some extent, life in general. It came in a burning flash, hard and shiny as a fresh-cut diamond. I recognized it at once for what it was. Like all truths, it had a deceptive simplicity, the very quality which would make it of little value to the young. And I promised myself that I would pass this secret on to my closest friends when they reached their half-century milestone.[20]

A few minutes later, Rita came back. "I thought you were gone for the evening," I said.

---

[20] So you really want to know The Secret? Are you a man over fifty? Okay. The Secret is simple: stop competing against your partner, and accept the simple truth—that she is your Goddess, your Muse, your Boss. Get it through your thick, male skull that resistance is futile—you can love or you can compete. Choose *one*.

"No, I have to work tomorrow," she said. "I think I'm going to go home to bed."

"I'm about ready to call it a night, too," I said. "I'll walk you home."

We said goodnight to Tákis, who was just getting started on his evening. Away from the *paralía*, the streets had emptied out. I gave Rita a hug outside her door and made my way up the hill.

I met Linda at the harbor the next day. I took her shopping bag, heavy with goodies, and we walked slowly home in the sultry noon.

Back home, we unpacked her purchases like Klondike miners picking gold nuggets from the pan. There was mozzarella and Parma ham, and three more pounds of Starbucks coffee. Something clanking in there, too.

"And these are from Brigitte," said Linda, pulling out a four-pack of draught Guinness in the special cans with the miraculous floating widget.

"Oh, bless her!" I cried. I'd more than once expressed my longing for a draught Guinness, but hadn't thought of it on our own recent trip to Vólos. "That is *so* sweet of her!"

A Small Ceremony

YIÁNNIS TOOK THE hint about not pressuring us. When I bumped into him in the street a few days later and he asked how we were doing he wasn't able to resist adding, "You asked me to not say anything, so I will not comment."

I put my hand on his shoulder. "Thank you," I said. "I know you want to help. We just need some space to think clearly right now."

Linda had stopped making soap, and was mostly keeping herself busy about the house. Jacqui and Léo invited us to the beach with them every day, and while I sometimes was too busy with CAD work to accept, I always encouraged Linda to go. I was worried about her. I felt her unspoken anxiety; and those hours playing in the water, especially with a fellow *Amerikanída*, did her no end of good. I never resented those times I couldn't go. I'd had a lot to do with getting us into this predicament, and I would do anything I could to get us out.

I called Isaac at Aris Export, our shippers in California. I explained our decision and asked if he could get us quotes on shipping our belongings back to the 'States, Oakland or Houston, we weren't yet sure which, probably around the middle of September. He expressed his sympathies that our plans hadn't worked out and told me he'd get back to us within two or three days.

A week later I still hadn't heard anything, so I called him back.

"I'm sorry, sir," he said, unfailingly formal in his thick Israeli accent, "but I'm still looking for a company that will handle the paperwork in Greece. The broker I contacted hasn't called me back. I will contact them again. It will be a few more days before I know anything."

I assured him that wasn't a problem, and that we had time enough. Isaac was a good guy. It would be fine.

But events would again prove me wrong.

BRIGITTE HAD TO go to Athens for a couple of days to meet her grandson, Alexis, who was coming to spend the summer, and asked if we'd house-sit her property and take care of the cats during her absence. We jumped at the offer. I'd worked ten days straight, and had CAD jobs in the queue for the coming weekend. It was time for a break.

We arrived in Alónissos on Tuesday evening and I took Brigitte down to the harbor the next morning. My driving skills seemed to still be intact.

I did a little shopping, and we took lunch on the terrace with the million-dollar view before setting off for the beach at Kokkinókastro, the Red Castle, so called for the sculpted bluff of orange-red soil that encircles it.

There were a few people on the beach, and the water was crystalline and welcoming. A small, thatched cabana offered drinks and kayak rentals. The Greek flag flew proud from a tall bamboo pole. We swam and read and lolled about in the hot sunshine. It was the first time in many days that—except when deeply involved in a design—I was able to put aside my worries.

A few hours later, back at Artemis, I completed a mission almost a decade overdue.

Among the many boxes we'd shipped to Skópelos was the one containing the jar with my mother's ashes, accompanied by a small casket with the cremated remains of her faithful dog, Tanya, and an even smaller, decorative cardboard box with the ashes of her cat,

Cinders, a name impossible to mention without a morbid chuckle after the poor creature had emerged from the pet crematorium.

The question of my mother's mortal remains had been a vexed one for the entire nine years since her death. Her instruction to me had been to place her ashes in the vault in the small Italian town of Ivrea where my grandmother lay at eternal rest in her lead-lined coffin. My mother had expressed this wish more than once over the last decade of her life, and I thought little of it at the time: it seemed a simple enough request.

Following my mother's death, I'd asked a lawyer friend in Ivrea if she could look into the matter for me and advise me what I needed to do and whom to contact in the municipality.

Of course, since civil servants were involved, it turned out to be anything but simple: it was, in fact, impossible.

"There's no way around it," the lawyer concluded after a string of inquiries. She was clearly embarrassed at her inability to help. "Unless the deceased is a resident, the town council won't allow them to be buried in Ivrea."

"But my grandmother was a resident," I said. "We're just asking to put an urn in the vault with her."

"I told them that, but they just won't budge. I'm sorry, Dario, there's nothing I can do. It's in the town's bylaws."

I called the town council a few names; the lawyer agreed. Where were the town's bylaws, I wondered, when the Nazis arrested my great-grandmother and kept her for months in a filthy cell in Ivrea's red-towered castle before shipping her off to Auschwitz? It was only ten or twelve years since the town had erected a small monument to her and Ivrea's other unfortunate Jews. You'd think they could have bent their damned rules a little by way of apology.

I briefly considered the possibility of entering the cemetery at night with a few tools—the marble front of the vault was held on with four big, slot-head screws, I'd seen them installed—and doing the business myself. The cemetery was walled, and my grandmother's vault was at the back, away from the road. Nobody would see me, and besides, what would they do even if they caught me? It was laughable.

My only concern was access, since her slot in the vault was about eight feet off the ground. Even if I could find a ladder, it seemed a little dicey. And what if there wasn't room beside the coffin? The weight of the lead-lined, mahogany coffin, and the impossibility of sliding it out and balancing it while I unscrewed the lid so as to scatter my mum's ashes inside… Besides the physical challenges, it seemed more than a little macabre. In the end, I decided I'd have to find some alternative rest for my mother. She really should have looked into the matter a little more thoroughly. But, bless her heart, that was never her way.

In life, my mother had possessed—or perhaps been possessed by—an unbridled love for Greece, matched only by her feelings for the Andalusia region of southern Spain. I'd seen her go all fey and swoony at Granada's Alhambra castle and at the Acropolis, and she was convinced she'd lived past lives in those places. And now here I was in Greece, with her ashes.

I'd thought of casting them into the Aegean from the ferry, but the wind would be a problem: I always remembered my friend Nico's account of pouring his father's ashes (as per his wishes) from the Golden Gate bridge into the waters of the San Francisco Bay, and how the bulk of the gritty remains had been blown back into four lanes of traffic, over horrified passers-by, and into his own face and mouth. Besides which, there were very explicit signs on the ferry warning of the penalties for dumping anything into the sea.

Eventually, I decided Mum would be happiest right there at Artemis, on one of the lower, pine-clad terraces facing the Aegean and the million-dollar view. The place was warm and shady. And she dearly loved Alónissos.

After some little difficulty prying open the dog's casket, we walked out to the spot and, with a few simple words, scattered the contents of all three containers onto the soft carpet of pine needles. I pictured those ashes sinking into the soil to break down, becoming part of the pines and the bushes and the earth of this magical place.

You couldn't wish for a better end.

Roasted Alive

WE SPENT THE next two days reading, eating, swimming, and relaxing on the Artemis terrace. We fed the cats and watered—probably overwatered—Brigitte's garden. Years of drought had reduced the landscaping at Artemis to a shadow of its former lushness. Brigitte had satellite TV, and we watched some newscasts in English. There were strikes in France, and Americans were getting killed in Iraq. The world out there hadn't changed much.

On our second evening we drove up to the *hóra* for dinner.

The old village of Alónissos was largely destroyed by a 6.0 earthquake in 1965, the year before I first visited with my parents. Fortunately, the temblor had struck in mid-morning, when most people were out of doors. Only one person had been killed.

Rather than rebuild the *hóra*, the government had rehoused the entire population in a hastily-constructed complex of generic concrete boxes near the port of Patitíri. Not everyone welcomed the idea, but with the authorities refusing to provide electricity to what was left of the village, resistance soon evaporated.

The village lay abandoned for a decade or so until a few adventurous foreign visitors, recognizing a good deal, started to acquire and rebuild some of the ruined properties. This process accelerated through the 'seventies and into the 'eighties, until the new townsfolk—mostly Brits and Germans, who just came for the summer—were able to persuade the authorities to reconnect the electricity supply and reinstate the bus service. Now, decades later, the old village was alive with shops, activity, and nightlife, although barely a handful of Greeks lived there.

Friday was dry and unusually hot. Even by the water, where we had a small cove all to ourselves, the heat was ferocious, with no breath of air to cool us. We spent a long while in the water, snorkeling along the rocky shallows in either direction and slathering sun lotion over ourselves.

Before we left on Saturday, Linda made a cheese and spinach quiche to save Brigitte from having to cook after the long journey, and left it in the fridge with a 'Thank You' note on the fridge door.

THE DAY HAD started hazy. Back on Skópelos, a ghostly veil clung to the land, heralding the approach of serious heat. Sure enough, it was a sweltering day—upwards of 105—and we closed the windows and turned on the air conditioning, which kept the living area to a comfortable 80 degrees. About nine, we took our dinner up to the roof. A light breeze provided some relief from the day's heat.

We were just finishing our meal when Spýros and Mára appeared, and we invited them to join us for a drink. As we chatted under the stars, the wind turned southerly, bringing sudden, extraordinary torrents of hot, dry air that left us all astonished, a blast-furnace heat I'd only ever felt in California's Central Valley and in Morocco. It was almost eleven at night, and the temperature was *rising*. I put a thermometer out on the porch. An hour later, when the Balabánises left, it was 98 degrees. We were profoundly grateful for the small a/c unit in the bedroom.

From the Aegean Dream blog:

Meltdown!
June 27, 2007

Don't go outside. It's like the surface of Mercury out there.

> *In tropical climes there are certain times of day*
> *When all the citizens retire to tear their clothes off and perspire.*
> *It's one of the rules that the greatest fools obey,*
> *Because the sun is much too sultry*
> *And one must avoid its ultry-violet ray.*

We've had daytime shade high temperatures of around 44 C (112 degrees F) for four days now, and Noel Coward's 'Mad Dogs and Englishmen' is constantly playing in my head. The shopkeepers who have air conditioning keep their doors wide with the a/c on full blast, perhaps to entice overheated tourists into their shops.

> *At twelve noon the natives swoon and no further work is done*
> *But mad dogs and Englishmen go out in the midday sun*

And I must confess we have both gone out in it: Linda actually walked uphill from the village with shopping at around noon yesterday, to the consternation of our friend Vasílis who offered her a ride home about ten times before conceding that she was clearly beyond help.

Mad dogs and Englishmen go out in the midday sun.
The smallest Malay rabbit deplores this foolish habit.

Last night at 10:30 Linda and I walked down to the harbor for a breath of air and a cocktail. It had cooled a little, to perhaps 90, and there were at one moment a half-dozen drops of rain. But around midnight, just as happened Saturday, the previously gentle breeze began to deliver a furnace-like heat. I looked up, thinking one of the outdoor space heaters had gone on. Nope. Forest fires approaching the village? Nope, not that either. It's supposed to get cooler at night, not hotter!

Back home, the thermometer on our porch read 97 degrees at one in the morning. It was the same at 8 a.m. when we got up.

This can't go on. Today's forecast to be the hottest day of the week.

In the mangrove swamps where the python romps
there is peace from twelve till two.
Even caribous lie around and snooze, for there's nothing else to do.
In Bengal to move at all is seldom ever done,
But mad dogs and Englishmen go out in the midday sun.

Dario

ON THE SECOND day of the heat wave, I noticed that the lower parts of the dining room curtains were soaked through, and there was a big puddle of water on the tile floor around it. Air conditioning sucks moisture out of the air, but the a/c unit above the window had been poorly installed, so that it sloped slightly inward rather than out. Instead of dripping onto the balcony outside, the unit was steadily dripping moisture onto the drapes, which was why we hadn't heard it.

Asking Spýros to fix this was unlikely to yield results, considering that our toilet still leaked seven months after we'd first mentioned the issue. Eventually, we solved the problem by balancing a quart Tupperware container on the curtain pelmet directly under the drip. It took about four hours to fill, and the steady drip-drip sound added an extra dimension of torture to my work. But given the stone-age ergonomics of my workstation and the abominable heat, it hardly mattered.

One afternoon, we decided we *had* to have ice cream, and would probably die without it. But how to get it back? The nearest store—Chrístos Manólis's little 'Potámi' market, was only five minutes' walk each way, but no way would our favorite vanilla/chocolate cones make it in this heat.

So it was that a short while later I walked into the store with one of our small ice chests prepped with a couple of frozen ice packs and a bag of ice cubes for good measure. The Manólis family, wilting at the cash register, were both amused and impressed.

The heat was killing during those five days, too hot to even go to the beach. I heard from Yiánnis that an old man had died of heatstroke. By day, the streets were deserted. We kept the house cave-like, with windows and shutters closed and the a/c in the dining room/hall area on from morning till night, and prayed the heat would abate before Friday, when Linda's friend and ex-colleague Shari was due to visit with her fiancé, August. We'd booked the *mílos* for them, and it had no air conditioning.

I called Brigitte to see how she was coping.

"I give the cats water with ice cubes three times a day, and they drink it all immediately!" she said. "But my big fear is that we will have forest fires."

With a lot of CAD work coming in, *my* biggest fear was a prolonged power outage. Greece was short of power stations to begin with. We'd read an article a few months ago in the New York Herald Tribune about the country's inability to keep up with its mushrooming electricity needs. Greece's coal-fired plants also produced the dirtiest power in Europe.

With so many people now using a/c units (the tavernas and storekeepers used them indiscriminately, set to maximum, with doors and windows open) I couldn't believe the grid would hold up. Amazingly, it did. Whichever Greek God—probably Hephaestus, God of the forge—held dominion over electricity production, he must have been working those bellows with a fury only an Olympian could command.

ALONG WITH THE heat, a new problem had come to devil us: Spýros had started renting out the *mílos*, the tower dwelling on our roof.

At the onset of the heat wave, in the dead of night, I heard footsteps over our bedroom. When I went up the next morning to investigate, I found a crowd of grumpy, sleep-deprived Italians—two thirty-something couples and a number of small children—stumbling around the roof terrace in swimsuits. Their laundry hung on our line, their beach bags sat on our teak table. The chairs had been pulled out and left at odd angles, one clearly as a foot support.

I was mightily irritated, not just at the invasion of our space—I have always been territorial—but also at Spýros's failure to ask them not to use our table and chairs. The *mílos* had its own little table and chairs, as well as the largest shade umbrella I'd ever seen, in the corner by the disused bar area. But it wasn't as nice as ours, nor as well-placed for enjoying the view.

Reminding myself it wasn't their fault, I introduced myself to the least grumpy-looking woman and her partner. We chatted in Italian. Their accent was southern: they were Calabresi, or Pugliesi. They complained about the terrible heat, and the lack of air-conditioning in the *mílos*. I sympathized.

I politely pointed out that we'd be using our table and chairs that evening, and that the *mílos* had its own. The man looked sour and wandered off; the woman apologized.

"No big worry," I assured her, "I'm sure Spýros would have mentioned it, but the language is a problem."

"It doesn't matter," she said, "we're going to move anyway. None of us slept a wink last night."

I nodded understanding. It wasn't nine yet, and the heat was already oppressive. "And it's forecast to get hotter," I said.

I can be a bastard.

Friends and Families

THE HEAT BROKE Thursday, the day before Shari and August were due to arrive. I gave myself a good talking-to, vowing to put my anxieties about our predicament and the logistics of returning to the US on hold during the course of their visit.

With the Italians gone and the *mílos* booked for our friends, Mára dropped off the key—six inches of hand-crafted black iron, a century old—so that Linda could set things up for them. We'd booked a car for their stay, and drove it to the big Día supermarket where we bought a case of spring water and a few other bulk items.

You entered the *mílos* via a small wooden door built into the thick wall. The cramped interior was almost impossibly romantic, full of gold-tinged light from the rich pine ceilings. It could have been the sentry-tower at the border of Faërie.

The main room was about fifteen feet in diameter, with a varnished stone floor. It contained a low bed, a small fridge, a floor fan, a tiny wardrobe, and a table with a hot plate. Across the room, a small chest sat below the pine casement window with its two-foot thick sill and view of the roof terrace and harbor beyond. Garish ropes of artificial pink-flowered Morning Glory hung on either side of the window. On the wall above the bed was draped a large needlepoint tapestry of a northern European village idyll, a cutesy composition of which Thomas Kincaid, Painter of Light®, would certainly have approved. A three-quarter length mirror and a few folk prints adorned the surrounding wall surface.

The ceiling beams were curvy and knotted, clearly the hand-dressed trunks of small pine trees. Both they and the boards of the floor above were the deep amber-gold of ancient pine, and heavily varnished.

To the left of the entrance, a narrow stone stair hugged the circular wall. The second storey contained another low bed; above that was a sleeping loft about five feet high containing two mattresses and two windows, one looking to the harbor and the other towards the Skópelos plain. The views from this height, some twenty feet above the terrace, were exceptional.

Linda has a talent for making guests feel welcome and pampered. She bustled around with linens and towels, and stocked the refrigerator with bottled water and *oúzo*. A gift bag of soaps and a loaner clock went on one bedside table, a box of tissues and a decorative candle on the other, as well as a folding hand-fan and a small flashlight: the *mílos* had no bathroom, but there was one a few yards across the terrace by the old bar. On the table by the fridge she set a bowl filled with assorted teas and sachets of sugar. Glasses and cups, as well as a half-pound of ground Starbucks coffee and a drip cone, she placed nearby, along with a bag of pistachios.

The next day was also Tákis's birthday. Linda baked him a carrot cake in the evening and iced it next morning. After piping in orange decorations on the side of the white frosting, she wrote a birthday greeting—in Greek, no less—across the top in orange icing. When she was done, she called me in. There, across the top of the cake in bright orange icing, was the greeting:

$$\mathrm{E}\upsilon\tau\upsilon\chi\iota\sigma\mu\varepsilon\nu\iota$$
$$\Gamma\varepsilon\nu\varepsilon\vartheta\lambda\iota\alpha$$
$$\mathrm{T}\alpha\kappa\iota$$
$$\alpha\pi\o$$
$$\eta\ \Lambda\mu\varepsilon\rho\iota\kappa\alpha\nu\iota\delta\alpha$$

which translated as, 'Happy Birthday Tákis, from the American Woman'. Linda broke into song as I read it: "*American Womaaan! Stay away from me-eee!*"

"Do you think he'll get it?" she said, when we'd stopped laughing..

"I don't doubt he will. And I think he'll appreciate the humor."

She always had a way of winning people's hearts.

AFTER LINDA TOOK the cake to Takis's shop, we walked down to the *paralía*. The Flying Cat wasn't due for almost two hours, but we were wild with excitement over our friends' impending arrival, and it felt wonderful to be outdoors after days trapped inside by the heat. The temperature was back in the high eighties, with moderate humidity and even a light breeze. A perfect day.

We had a croissant and coffee at Karávi, then paced the harbor. The minutes crawled by; the hydrofoil would never arrive.

Finally, we heard the distinct roar of the Cat's huge engines beyond the breakwater, and a few moments later the big red-and-white vessel swung into the harbor, its bow coming level as it slowed.

Moments later, Linda and Shari were hugging on the dock as August came down the gangplank with the suitcases. An all-American boy, tall and good-looking, with an open face. We liked him right away.

Fifteen minutes later we were sitting on our terrace in the warm sun, enjoying *oúzo* and *mezés* and hearing about our friends' adventures in Venice, Rome, Florence, and Athens.

"My God! You did well," I said. It was true: neither of these two

AEGEAN DREAM | 273

young people had traveled outside the US before, and they'd just navigated their way around several cities and a bewildering assortment of conveyances over the course of just nine days.

"So," said Linda, "What do you want to *do*? I know you've been up since five this morning. Do you want to take a nap or have some downtime?"

"We want to go to a beach!" said Shari.

August agreed. "After touring all those cities, a beach sounds *really* good."

This was music to Linda's ears. Our beach bag was always packed, and the heat wave had made her miss almost a week of beach time. A little over an hour later, we arrived at Miliá.

Shari had told Linda that she liked beaches but 'wasn't big on ocean swimming.' But the cold, murky waters of the central California coast are so unlike the waters around Skópelos that it's hard to believe they're made of the same stuff. Within minutes, both the 'kids' (as we affectionately thought of them) were frolicking and swimming in the warm, buoyant Aegean.

Night found us dining on our roof. Our friends had taken a nap, and I'd got a few hours' work done while Linda prepared dinner. It was a storybook evening: candlelight, good company, moonlight on the still harbor water, the mouth-watering smell of roast lamb.

We had some idea August worked in finance, but hadn't realized quite what a phenomenon this soft-spoken young man was. At twenty-six, he was Chief Investment Officer of a fast-growing financial institution in Southern California. He was invited to speak at conferences; he'd already published one book on investing, and was starting on another. The world was his oyster, and he had both the brains and the humility to handle it.

This was what was possible, I reflected. And couldn't help but chew over how dismally I had failed in my own life; how badly I'd let my wife down.

With an effort, I forced my funk back into its cellar. The evening remained joyful, one of the best I can remember. We were delighted to see Shari so happy. These two had everything going for them: they were young, smart, attractive, and successful. They were completely in love, and both had enough prior relationship experience to handle it. I prayed life would treat them well. Perhaps their stay in our delightful *milos*—Linda called it 'Rapunzel's Castle'—on this magical isle would weave a lasting enchantment about them, a protection from the cruelties of this world, so they might enjoy the happily-ever-after they so deserved.

WE RETURNED TO Miliá the next day. We lunched on the beach, and drank Smirnoff and Bacardi coolers from the small cabana-bar on the beach. Linda and I had come to know the owner, a young couple with two small children. As we were leaving, they called us over to the bar and poured us four shots of Tequila on the house.

"We need to hang around with you guys more often!" Linda joked to our friends.

Linda and I had talked about going for a midnight swim. Tonight, with the moon full and the company of friends, seemed the perfect occasion.

We had dinner at the little taverna at Agnóndas, wearing our swimsuits under our clothes. We drank *tsípouro* and watched the sunset.

Around eleven-thirty we drove to nearby Pánormos. The tavernas were full, with light and music spilling out across the sand. We parked in the shadows just beyond the last taverna and walked out onto the beach. A large log lay on the sand near the water, and we made this our base, piling our clothes on top and our shoes and towels next to it.

The night was starting to cool. The moon, halfway up the sky, unrolled a wide ribbon of silver on the black water. Muted voices and bouzoúki music reached our ears. The air carried a faint scent of roasting fish.

We stood at the water's edge and hesitated. The sea was *awfully* dark. Anything could be in there.

August and I went in first, wading into the warm, silky water. Linda and Shari were a while getting their courage up before finally tiptoeing in, hand in hand.

I swam out, committing to the deeper water. The moonlight was bright enough that I could just see my limbs in pale silhouette against the black.

And then I saw it, a sparkle around my leading arm. I waggled my hands around. Pinpoints of light glimmered in the disturbed water.

"I can see it!" I cried to the others. "Bioluminescent plankton!" I'd told Linda about seeing it all those years ago, on my first trip to Alónissos, and she'd been spellbound. Now she was experiencing it too.

In a moment, we were all twisting and turning in the water, fascinated by the silvery sparkles in the darkness surrounding us. Some areas were richer than others, and we swam around, finding the best spots, entranced by the fairy coruscations of light our efforts produced.

There are moments of pure magic in every life, glimpses of beauty no grief can tarnish, that live on in the sheltered niches and alcoves of memory. This was one of ours. Remember these places and their treasures, that you may find your way there whenever the darkness of the world presses too close.

THE NEXT DAY, Monday, was August's last on Skópelos. He'd taken all the holiday he could, and would leave on Tuesday at noon. Shari would remain an extra two days, and then fly back on her own. I had designs to turn in, and stayed home that day while the others went to the beach, so that I could spend time with them that evening.

I missed quite a scene:

From the Aegean Dream blog:

Incident at Glyfonéri
July 5, 2007

Linda Speaks

Picture this: Three Americans at a predominantly local Greek beach. Swimming, having fun... but getting a little hungry. August, gentleman that he is, agrees to walk up to the nearby taverna and grab some sandwiches and beer. Shari and I await our refreshments.

After what seems like hours (Shari and I actually thought about rescuing him, he was gone so long—seems he had trouble navigating the language!) the tall, blond, handsome, obviously American hunk returns with our repast. We settle on the beach to enjoy our 'toast' and beer.

So do the wasps. At times, the wasps of Skópelos can make eating anything a true challenge. They buzz us, land on our towels and sandwiches, flit about, call over the whole hive, and before long we become quite frustrated. Shari in particular is being hounded relentlessly.

August becomes severely annoyed and defensive. He swats and waves at the pesky critters, which of course makes them more aggressive. August starts to emit some sort of anger pheromone and the wasps begin to take his attempts at smacking them personally.

The battle instinct of the American male kicks into overdrive, and August grabs one of Shari's flip-flops. He stands up, ready to fight, flip-flop in one hand, beer in the other.

The battle begins! August swings the flip-flop in one hand, precariously balancing his precious beer in the other. The wasps launch a counter-attack. August is enraged as they swoop and dive for his face. The battle is in full swing.

The wasps gain the upper hand and soon the strong young man is in retreat, running backwards into the Aegean, flip-flop fending off the leader wasp, beer in the other hand.

The leader wasp is in attack mode, following August into the water. The flip-flop flails. The beer is barely above the water line. August is nearly submerged. This wasp is out for blood.

Strange, guttural battle sounds come from August. The entire beach full of Greeks watches in amazement. And suddenly, after a howling battle cry and a fist pumping in triumph, man prevails over beast.

I glance over at the local Greeks on the beach. I am laughing uncontrollably, THEY are laughing uncontrollably. The Greeks have been entertained in a fashion that would do credit to the most serious of Greek dramas. I offer our neighbors an apology, explaining that we are American and this is a native ritual. They laugh even harder.

At last, August emerges from the water, beer clenched in one hand, flip-flop in the other. The wasp is securely squished on the back of Shari's flip-flop. He proudly displays the spoils of his victory.

We have confirmed what the Greeks have always thought. Americans are crazy. The village is still talking about it. August has provided a newsworthy event for them to gossip about far into the future. I LOVE AUGUST!

Linda

AFTER DINNER THAT night, we decided to hit the bars. Shari and August wanted to try the extraordinary 'ship' bar on the harbor beach, where a full-size replica of a pirate ship, with a stair leading from the hold to tables on the deck, stood propped up alongside the road.

It was almost midnight, and the place was just waking up. We bought a round of tequila shots. As soon as we'd finished, the barmaid refilled our glasses on the house: it was our week for free shots of tequila, it seemed. We thanked her, took a bowl of munchies, and climbed the stairs to the deck.

The tables at deck level were still empty. What a place to enjoy drinks! The deck of a pirate vessel, a world of dark, varnished wood, with barrels and lanterns and coils of rope all around. Above us, the full moon shone down through the rigging. Below, beyond the gunwale, a pleasing view of the three wenches behind the bar, who seemed to have been hired to keep things hopping. Not young, but very shapely, the three were always in motion, pouring drinks, lighting candles, snapping and popping to the music. All showed plenty of cleavage.

Linda laughed. "Rode hard, put away wet," she said. "Ya gotta love it!"

Now, boarding a pirate ship without climbing the rigging didn't seem right, and August and I were soon clawing our way upwards toward the masts. We'd only gone a few yards when the girls, convinced this wasn't a safe activity, implored us to come down, and we let ourselves be persuaded. We really should have had a third shot before making the attempt.

After seeing August off on the big Cat next morning, I returned to work. I had a full schedule, and it would be nice for Linda and Shari to have some girl time. We'd returned the car to the rental office, and the girls were just packing their things to walk to Glyfonéri when Jacqui and Léo called to say they were going to rent a boat at Pánormos, and did the girls want to join them? I insisted they had my blessings to have all the fun they could handle.

I worked solidly the rest of that day and got an early start the next morning; so when Jacqui and Léo decided an encore of the previous day's fun was on the agenda, I went along too.

We'd told Shari and August of our decision to return to the US, but nobody on Skópelos knew. Still, it was easy to set my worries aside, puttering around the coast and stopping to swim and snorkel at secluded coves with carefree Captain Léo, his young godson Vangélis, and three cute blonde *Amerikanídes*. Time enough to resume worrying after Shari left on the morrow.

I KEPT WORKING hard on the computer, ceding it to Linda for a couple of hours every evening for a fix of YouTube and her IM sessions with Barbara. Both Linda's sisters had been terribly sweet these last few months, especially given the occasionally difficult relationship between the three siblings.

I'd never understood the flare-ups between Linda and her sisters. An only child of only children, I idealized sibling relationships and often wished for brothers or sisters of my own (I have a half-sister, but she's thirty years younger than me and we've only briefly lived in the same city). But when I looked at Linda's and some of my friends' families, I saw that these relationships were generally awkward and contentious, with the much-vaunted 'unconditional love' nowhere to be seen.

As if to underscore the truth of this, my stepmother picked this period to go strange on us and cut off communications. She'd disapproved of our move from the beginning. Given her visceral dislike of the Mediterranean in general and Greece in particular, I wasn't at all surprised that the only times she ever commented on our blog were those rare occasions when we expressed frustration and difficulty with our home in the Aegean.

Ironically, I wasn't currently of a mind to take exception to some of her comments about Greece. When she declared, 'Greece is the worst member of the EU,' I couldn't disagree.

LINDA CONTACTED HER friends in Albuquerque about our proposed return. Their reply was gracious and immediate. They would love to see us, and we were welcome to stay with them for as long as it took us to get sorted out. They had lots of room and would have the 'guest quarters' ready for us.

Linda had been consulting Craigslist and realtor.com, and Albuquerque did indeed look good. There were jobs, and very affordable housing. "Look at this!" she said more than once, calling up photos of brand-new, three-bedroom houses with all appliances, renting at around a thousand dollars a month.

"Dishwashers," I whimpered. "Storage! I bet the toilets don't even leak!"

"When we get out of the hole, we could even afford to buy there," she said. "Two hundred thousand gets you into a new three-bedroom home. That's doable."

I agreed. Albuquerque it would be then. I could do Warmboard work from anywhere, and I knew from past experience I could find high-paying decorative painting work in any large urban area.

Isaac, our shipper, emailed me to say he'd need an inventory of our belongings for the customs broker in Greece. I followed up the next day with a phone call.

"They also want a—" he spelled out the Greek word as best he could—"a declaration that there are no prohibited goods in the shipment. Alcohol, drugs, antiquities, things like that. They said you have to make this at a police station and get it stamped there."

I groaned. "Okay. I can probably get that done. Do we have a ballpark yet?"

"I am trying, but it's so difficult to get anything definite out of these people. Never I have had such problems!"

"Tell me about it," I said.

A COUPLE OF days after Shari left, I went out for drinks one night with Tákis. It was time to let those closest to us know what was going on in our lives.

We went to the Plátanos bar down on the *paralía* and sat under the giant plane tree facing the water. Christine, our friend who worked at the Gorgónes café in the winter, was waiting tables, and brought me an *oúzo* three times larger than I was used to drinking. I wasn't surprised to find that she and Tákis had some minor relationship history.

I broke our news to Tákis. He seemed less shocked than Yiánnis had been; I don't think he believed we were really going to leave, rather that I was just grumbling.

"In my opinion you can succeed," he said. "Maybe Linda's soap will not be enough, she must have some other products, and also it will take three or four years. But she can have a good business. And for you also, with the furnitures. In the winter we can try to do something more traditional, that will sell to many people."

"I don't see it, Tákis. We don't want to spend our lives fighting the system. And Linda won't do business without being legal. Her heart's gone out of it." I'd finished my *oúzo* and felt a little lightheaded. Tákis ordered a beer, and I did the same.

He lit a cigarette. "Eh. Linda must not worry so much about this license. Yes, she must be careful, but the tax people will not be a problem at the beginning unless someone makes trouble for her."

Christine arrived with our beers, and Tákis went on to explain the game the Greek tax authorities played.

"In the beginning they let your business grow. For two or three years they will not bother you. Then one inspector from the office here will come to you and tell you that there can be problems with your books. So you give him some money, and he goes away.

"After another two or three years, your business will be bigger, and now the tax officer from Vólos will come to you and tell you that you can have problems. So now you must pay them money, and of course it will be more."

I sipped my beer. Though my brain was fogging up, I could see where this was going.

"After some more years, your business is very strong. And now you will have a visit from the big people in Athens, and they will make big problems if you do not give them money. Of course, you will: this is how it is in Greece," he concluded, grinding out his cigarette. "But for now, Linda must not worry. In the beginning, they will leave her alone."

We finished our drinks and walked to another bar. I was having trouble walking a straight line, and drank only Pérrier for the rest of the evening. Eventually, we climbed on the Ducati and Tákis—who by now was showing signs of serious wear himself—gentled the beast along a series of deserted backstreets and alleys, wisely avoiding the main road all the way up to the Hotel Denise and home.

Léo and Jacqui had taken to inviting us out pretty much every day. They were great company. Even with the flood of work, I managed to join Linda for beach time every second or third day; the four of us took long, leisurely swims, often staying in the water an hour or more. Jacqui and Linda had really bonded and were a frisky, funny pair to hang out with.

Jacqui and Léo lightened our days in that dark period. Especially as one of our beach days was Linda's birthday.

From the Aegean Dream blog:

July 18, 2007
Birthdays!

Linda Speaks:

July seems to be the month for birthdays around here.

First our friend Tákis had a birthday. Then a few more friends had birthdays. Then it was MY turn! I had a great birthday. I received several e-mail greetings and my sisters have sent me a package that I anxiously track via Fed-x!

Friends took us to the beach and we played in the water. And Dario took me for a lovely evening meal. I LOVE being spoiled.

And….I got a card! In the mail! I actually got something addressed to me! The text of this wonderful card from my dear friend Lucy summed it all up:

Life shouldn't be a journey to the grave with the intention of arriving safely in an attractive and well-preserved body, but rather a skid in sideways, champagne in one hand, body thoroughly used up and worn out, screaming, "WHOO-HOO, what a ride!"

Linda

Going Public

WE'D BEEN DREADING telling Spýros and Mára we were leaving, but we could delay no longer. It was now mid-July, and we wanted to give them a good two months' notice. I'd signed a two-year lease and was about to break it. Would they understand? Would they be able to find another renter?

Linda called Mára in the morning to see if we could meet with them that evening. Mára agreed, and asked if everything was okay, whereupon Linda—a firm believer in rapid Band-Aid removal—broke the news.

"How did she take it?" I asked, as soon as Linda hung up.

"She said she was very sorry, but she understood. Anyway, they'll come 'round at seven."

"Do you think they expected it?"

Linda thought a moment, gave a small shrug. "No. But I don't think she was *entirely* surprised. I mean, they knew we'd been having trouble with my residency. But she sounded genuinely sad."

"I feel like shit," I said.

"Don't. It'll be okay."

I wished I had Linda's strength. I was thoroughly dispirited at our plight. We'd not only failed ourselves but our friends as well, all these good people who had opened their doors and hearts to us.

I kept replaying the sequence of events of the last several months and looking for alternate paths our story could have taken. However I turned it around, the core error was my own impatience to make a change in our lives. Sure, Linda had wanted to come as well, and had been more than ready for a change. But the bottom line? Our finances had been utterly inadequate for the undertaking.

And our business plans? Had those just been pipe dreams, vague, impractical notions? I asked Linda these questions, afraid that I would make myself seriously depressed or even ill if I didn't move past this phase of self-blame.

"I think we prepared as well as we could," she said. "Some things you just can't know until you're on the ground. Yeah, we could have come with more money, but how much is enough? Look at Joe and Alice. They came with probably close to a million bucks and they're no better off than we are."

"Worse, in fact," I said.

"Exactly. I knew it wouldn't be easy, even without the bureaucracy, but I figured we had at least a fifty-fifty chance. We couldn't have known the deck would be so stacked against us."

I struggled, the sadness and regret crushing. "Linda, I'm *so* sorry! I feel—"

"Don't." She rested a hand on mine. "I knew what I was buying into. I wanted it too."

AROUND SIX-THIRTY we headed up to the roof to wait for Spýros and Mára. The sun was low enough that the umbrella wasn't needed. A light breeze took the edge off the still-hot air.

We hugged our friends as they arrived. Linda had prepared some snacks and we fetched these, along with *oúzo* for Spýros and myself and *retsína* for Mára and Linda.

We explained our predicament. The Balabánises listened quietly, occasionally asking questions. When our ex-lawyer's name came up, Spýros shook his head and muttered darkly in Greek.

"I don't understand," I said, "why the good people of Skópelos, uh…" I flipped through the dictionary until I found the word, "…*tolerate* this man. Nobody says anything good for him."

Mára nodded agreement.

"Because he is a Skopelíte," said Spyros.

Because he is one of us. It figured. In a tiny community such as this, you had to live with your neighbors even if you didn't like them.

I began to apologize about the lease; Spýros waved the matter away. "You are our friends. It's not a problem."

"Life is too difficult sometimes," said Mára. Turning to her, I was surprised to see her normally merry expression gone, replaced by a mask of fatigue. She looked suddenly vulnerable. Her chin trembled. "We don't want you to leave."

Linda reached out and touched her arm and in a moment they were both crying and hugging one another. I felt my own throat tighten. I looked at Spýros and a current of empathy passed between us. After a moment, he sighed and looked out to sea.

"How will you get all your things back?" said Spýros.

I was glad of the distraction. "I'm not sure yet. I will ask Goúmas." Goúmas was Skópelos's local moving company, the ones who'd trucked our goods from the harbor up to the house in their dump truck.

We moved on to discuss minor arrangements. We would be selling appliances, and could they keep their ears to the ground for buyers? Possibly also the table and chairs we were sitting at, and the big china cabinet we'd bought from Tákis.

Mára asked when we planned to leave. We'd already booked the *mílos* for Lucy and Robert in September, but since we planned to move out on or around the fifteenth, Linda had another idea. Could we rent *both* Ánesis cottages for the five days of their visit, one for us and one for our friends?

"Of course," said Mára. "They'll be free by then. But where will you stay after your things are gone?"

"Our friends come the nineteenth," said Linda, "we think we will go to Alónissos for a few days."

Mára nodded. "If you want, you can stay in the *mílos* as our guests. It will not cost you anything."

We moved on to lighter talk. The Balabánises had been working long hours, as they did every summer. Both Ánesis cottages were rented, as well as the *kalívi*. In the daytimes, Spýros had his work and Mára had the house, as well as taking care of a sick and disabled father.

I asked how things were going between Anna and Strátos. We knew there'd been some tension in the family over Strátos's younger brother, Kósmos. With his attitude and spiky hair, Kósmos was the poster boy for rebel angst. And though everyone liked him, Anna was becoming very frustrated by Kósmos's failure to earn a living while Strátos worked two jobs to help keep him.

"Ah!" said Mára, "things are much better now. Kósmos has a job."

I was amazed. "Really? Where?'

"At the Día supermarket," said Mára. "For more than a month."

"So it is not a big problem with Strátos and Anna now? Said Linda.

Spýros did the head-raising Greek 'no'. "*Ólos íne kalós, Dario.*" Everything is all right. He grinned and raised his glass in a toast. I saw it was empty, and topped us up. Even Mára, who drank very little, seemed thirsty tonight.

"*Yámas!*" called Spýros, as we clinked glasses. "*Ólos íne kalós!*"

"*Me to Théos,*" added Mára, laughing—with God. Yes indeed.

"When summer's over," said Spýros, glancing across the terrace, "I have to start work on Anna's house again."

"And when she gets married," said Mára, turning to Linda, "I'm going to pay for one of your tickets to come for the wedding!" We laughed and clinked glasses again.

"And we will come," said Linda, "we will come! *Yámas!*"

From the Aegean Dream blog:

SKI CON 5

Linda Speaks

Our friends Scott and Gretchen developed a code, years ago, to assign, numerically, the conditions for water skiing and wakeboarding. Voice mails would be left on home and work phones with the code. This code indicated the importance of planning for boat time on any given day. It went something like this:

Ski Con 1—Not lookin' so good. Keep on working.

Ski Con 2—Iffy. But keep checking water/wind conditions.

Ski Con 3—Lookin' good. Leave work early.

Ski Con 4—Lookin' REALLY good. Fake an illness.

Ski Con 5—GOTTA splash the boat! Quit your job!

So folks, we're at SkiCon5..... and we are headed home.

It's been an adventure. Skópelos remains one of the most beautiful places we have ever seen, but we simply can't navigate the waters.

Sometimes you take a big fall. And you can only hope...

That someone will offer you a beer...

Give you a tow...
Keep an eye out for you...
And hold you close.

We are fortunate. We have lots of people holding us close. We have a wonderful support system. Our friends are unfailingly kind, supportive and generous. Thank you Scott and Gretchen. Thank you Bryta. Thank you Tony. Thank you Barbara. Thank you Brigitte. Thank you Cheryl and Ray. Thank you April and David. Thank you Blunt. The list could continue forever....

When we write our version of A Year In Provence, I believe our dedication page will be full, as are our hearts.

The toilet still leaks.

Linda

I WAS WORKING on a CAD layout one afternoon when Linda got home. "There are jellyfish in the water!" she said. "Jacqui swam right into one and got stung!"

I'd seen one a few weeks previously while out snorkeling, a red-orange bell about the size of a grapefruit. "As long as it's just one or two," I said, "there's not much chance of running into one. Jacqui must just have been unlucky."

As it turned it, it wasn't just one or two. Within a week, just at the height of the summer, there were enough of them in the water that neither Jacqui nor Linda were keen on going in anymore. Some beaches were worse than others: Pánormos, which Jacqui and Léo favored, was one of the worst; Glyfonéri, perhaps because of its northerly exposure, was reasonably free of the things.

After poring through descriptions and photos of jellyfish online, Linda found a match. "Sea Nettles!" she said, pointing to the monitor. "That's what they are."

Further research revealed they were common, that the sting could run anywhere from mild to severe, that warm waters tended to attract them. In 2006, many of the Spanish and Italian beaches were so infested by the things that bathers spent just a few seconds in the water at a time, so frightened were they of running into one. Some experts blamed global warming; others insisted the event was regular and cyclical. Whoever was right, it certainly put a damper on the main activity that helped keep our spirits up.

Not long after, a second, uglier, jellyfish began to appear in truly prodigious numbers. The Greeks called them 'Saloúfa'. They looked like fried eggs, and ranged in size anywhere from a couple of inches to a foot or more across. The Saloúfa lacked ordinary tentacles, but sported masses of little worm-like things instead. "Fish lay eggs inside them," someone told us, "and when they hatch, the Saloúfa dies." The girls and I were disgusted. Léo wasn't bothered at all.

It was the end of July, and time to start packing up our belongings. I began scavenging boxes whenever I passed a store that had some empties. Electronics cartons were highly prized, as they tended to be the sturdiest, and would serve particularly well for china and glass. We'd also kept a few empty boxes and a fair amount of bubble wrap at the workshop.

My worry about getting our belongings out of the country was ripening into full-blown fear. Isaac had reached an impasse with the Greek company he'd been talking to. Unwilling to settle for just the paperwork part of the job, they wanted the whole shipping contract start to finish. All or nothing.

"Why did you move there anyway?" Isaac grumbled. "Greece is so difficult, they want so many papers just to ship belongings *out* of the country! Yes, I'm still looking, but nobody wants to do this procedure."

THERE WERE OTHER people to inform about our decision.

I stopped first at the accountant's and asked Pávlos to present us their bill and to close our TEBE insurance. We had two months' TEBE due at the end of August—another three hundred Euros—and I was sorely tempted to just leave without paying it.

"They will give you many problems," he said. "First, a letter. After this, they will be difficult."

"Pávlos, we'll be gone four weeks later. You think they'll move that fast?"

"Eh, no. But if you do not pay this, they can make big problems for you. Also you can not close with TEBE if you do not pay. "

Since there was really no way of knowing what the fallout from stiffing the bastards would be, should we ever return to Greece, I decided to settle. As for Pávlos and Kléa's bill, they would just charge us three hundred Euros, which was half of what they had quoted us as their standard charge for a year's accounting. It was more money wasted, but I was grateful—they'd certainly worked for it, and put up with my irritability and impatience. Not their fault we'd thrown in the towel.

I next went downstairs to Próton to see Lázaros. He was stacking shelves at the back of the store.

I apologized, explaining we'd decided to return to the US at the end of September, and that we'd be having to leave the workshop.

Lázaros cocked his head. "Ah. Why?"

"We have very much problems with licenses. Also with Linda's residency. Too many laws. It is very difficult to make work in Greece."

An ironic, knowing smile of which I wouldn't have thought him capable split Lázaros's usually bland expression. "The bureaucrats. They do not want anybody to work."

"Yes! Exactly! They do not want to work, they do not do anything! But if you want to make business, they make everything difficult!"

"I understand. I am sorry."

"We are *very* sorry," I said. "And I know we have a lease with you also. Perhaps we can pay for one extra month?"

He waved the offer away. "You have enough problems. Do not worry."

I thanked him, relieved by his reaction, moved by his kindness. Try breaking a lease in the 'States.

And we were going back there.

III

PRISONERS IN PARADISE

When I think back on how hard we worked to realize our dream, I wonder if we would have the energy to do it all again. I think perhaps we would. The question is, could we ever regain the faith and optimism we had then?

Coffee, Casein, Codeine

WE WERE READING about the subprime mortgage crisis looming in the US, and I'd noticed that Warmboard work had begun to slow down. I wondered if the two were connected.

With less CAD work to do, I had more time for packing, and boxes started to pile up in the living room. My old friends John and Sylvie were due to arrive with their family on the fourth of August, and we wanted to get ahead on the packing so we could enjoy their visit and spend time together. "These are the best kind of English people," I assured Linda. "You'll like them." And they were bringing vital supplies, like Cheddar and Brie and good coffee.

I called Isaac to see if he was making any headway. He was both embarrassed and frustrated. "I've tried two other companies, but they don't reply to emails, so I have to get them on the phone. With the ten-hour time difference, it is almost impossible. They are so unprofessional, and they make me look bad! Anyway, I have now asked the steamship line if they can help me."

"The steamship line?"

"We do all our business with this one line. I send hundreds of containers a year with them, mostly to and from the Middle East. I have asked them to put me in touch with someone who will be able to just do this damn paperwork for us. I hope to have something for you in a few days."

"Isaac, I'm so sorry this is such a headache. I know you're trying to get us a good deal. I really appreciate the trouble you're going to for us."

"Thank you, thank you. I just hope that we can find someone!"

So did I. This was turning out much harder than I'd imagined. If Isaac, with all his experience, couldn't find someone to handle the paperwork, what the hell would we do? If we had to use a Greek company for all the shipping arrangements, they'd have us over a barrel. We might not be able to even afford to get our things back.

AS IF THE grief of giving up our dreams wasn't enough, the strain of these added difficulties was starting to tell. We began to lose sleep, waking in the bitter watches of the night. Sometimes one of us would get up and take a spell at the computer, while the other lay staring into the darkness. Other times we just tossed and turned until dawn.

The whole concept of an unbroken night's sleep is actually a modern idea. Before the introduction of electric lights, working people would routinely go to bed soon after sunset, sleep a few hours, then rise for a time around one or two in the morning. With the children sound asleep, this was a popular time for lovemaking, mending clothes, reading (if you were literate), or just quiet conversation. After a couple of hours awake, a second period of sleep would ensue until daybreak. These distinct rest periods were referred to as 'first sleep' and 'second sleep'.

But we weren't getting the second sleep, and after several nights, the vicious cycle of insomnia set in, so that the very anxiety of not being able to sleep kept us awake. We were both sick with worry. On top of that, I suffered almost incessant headaches from the hours spent at the computer, and my neck hurt all the time. Ordinary painkillers barely touched the pain, and the codeine tablets we'd bought in London— illegal in Greece unless prescribed—had run out.

It was time to see Yiánnis.

One of the hateful things about the modern world is that addicts have given all drugs with the potential for abuse a bad name. Greece is even more deranged than America on this issue, to the point where the florists can't even get poppy pods to use in dried flower arrangements, but are forced instead to use imitations, silly-looking white resin cups on long plastic stalks. My God.

I was a little wary of asking Yiánnis to write me a prescription. How ironic! Twenty years ago, few doctors—least of all a friend—would have thought twice about writing a prescription for painkillers or tranquilizers. But the insane, decades-long War on Drugs had brought us to the point where many doctors worried more about getting into trouble with government watchdogs fighting drug abuse than they did about the comfort of their patients. As usual, the innocent paid for the guilty.

I explained the problem and asked Yiánnis if he would write me a prescription for codeine and tranquilizers. He listened carefully, agreed I was a legitimate case, and promptly wrote me up a prescription.

I thanked him. Even sharing the tranks with Linda, it would get us through this difficult period.

WE WERE NOW looking forward to our friends arriving with the most important drug of all—caffeine, in that most ineffable, seductive, and potent form known as Starbucks French Roast. Our supply from Linda's Vólos trip was almost exhausted.

John and his family were due to arrive on Saturday afternoon. But in the late morning, John called to tell their Volvo had broken down in central Greece. The repair had only taken a few hours, but they wouldn't make it to Vólos on time for the ferry. "The power to the cooler was out for a few hours," he explained, "but I think your cheeses will be okay."

When the family showed up at our house the next day, we thought Christmas had come. More than Christmas—the Coopers had brought a cornucopia of food that would have provided a feast for a score of hungry Roman senators. And neither Linda nor I had ever seen a whole wheel of Brie before.

"Actually," said John, "I had to slice it in two to get into the cooler!" It was enormous, the size of an extra-large pizza. We could stop worrying about getting our belongings back to the US, because we'd soon be dead of cholesterol poisoning.

The cheddar was another shock. I'd never seen a block of cheese so large: it was like looking at the side of an alp! I burst out laughing. "John," I said, "when I asked for 'a piece of cheddar', I was thinking of perhaps a pound or so."

John's brow furrowed. "Yes, well, I wasn't sure. But I thought, better too much than not enough, eh?"

I shook my head in wonder. The Brie smelt incredible; the Cheddar—I could tell at a glance—was of the very best, with occasional traces of veining, and a cloth-wrapped exterior. Between that and the

Brie, we must have been looking at a hundred and fifty Euros of cheese alone. Another reason to stop worrying about the shipping: by the time we'd added up the bill for all this bounty, we wouldn't be able to afford to ship anything!

The other items, fortunately, came in predictable quantities: five pounds of Starbucks French Roast coffee, a one-pound tin of *paté de canard*, and a bottle of absinthe that glowed emerald in the sun-drenched confines of our tiny kitchen. *Remember the Titanic!* All we needed now was a band and evening attire.

To my astonishment, John—perhaps aware that he'd gone mildly overboard—insisted on making us a present of the cheese. We tried to argue, but he held firm. It was a kingly gift.

Over the next few days, we showed the Coopers Pánormos beach, took them to Apostólos's taverna on the *paralía*, had them to dinner at our house (where we were forced to eat indoors because the *mílos* had been rented out again), and joined them for dinner at their villa on the hill.

We'd been curious about these five villas since our arrival. Located halfway up the hillside across the harbor, this little gated development included the most expensive rentals on Skópelos. The going rate in mid-season was three hundred Euros a night, and you could buy one for a mere half-million Euros. Each villa had a private pool, and (if you believed the online description) full broadband Internet access. To my purist's eye, the development, with its geometric layout and bland, contemporary architecture, was a vicious scar on the landscape. I'd been staring at it from across the harbor for nine months and hated it.

Linda was also curious about the villas. According to Vasílis, Colin Firth and the stars of the 'Mamma Mia!' movie would be staying here. Linda had more than once joked about planting webcams about the place before Mr. Firth's arrival, and scouting out good blinds in the shrubbery.

The villa's interior was well-decorated and furnished, the aesthetics a blend of modern and traditional. As our hosts showed us around, however, it became apparent that the project—just like Spýros's work on Anna's house—was a result of design on the fly rather than at the drawing board.

Sylvie showed us into the kitchen first. "For a start, the Internet connection doesn't work; that's not a big deal. But look at this," she said, indicating the cabinetry, "how's anyone supposed to get up there?"

We saw her point: the kitchen appeared to have been built on a vertical rather than horizontal axis, with a good two-thirds of the storage well out of reach for anyone but a pro basketball player. The builder had opted for lots of windows in an already open-plan area, and—on finding there was little wall space left for cabinets—just went ahead and installed them in a double stack above the cabinets, so that the uppers were fully eight feet off the ground.

Further evidence of the same cheerful faith in the power of spontaneity was everywhere: the bedroom off the kitchen and living area was just a walled-off section of the space, without a ceiling of its own; another bedroom featured a glass shower cubicle placed in a corner of the bedroom itself; you could only access the pool and patio by going through the master bedroom; and—most bizarre of all—in the master bedroom, a door in the middle of a wall by the bed opened not onto a storage area, but instead into a sinister expanse of chill, black water.

Linda peered into the yawning blackness of the water tank. "I think I'd be afraid to sleep next to that."

John laughed. "That's right—you don't know what might come out of there in the middle of the night, do you? It's like the Creature from the Black Lagoon!"

"I think I'm starting to understand," I said. "A generation ago, if a Skopelíte built a house, the layout was pretty standard. You put up the walls and roof, divide the small interior into three or four tiny rooms, put a fireplace in the biggest, and it's done. An electric stove and a tub can go anywhere.

"But now they're building twenty-five hundred square foot villas with central heating and custom kitchens, swimming pools and Jacuzzis, and they haven't realized that they actually need to draw a floor plan first. I mean, even if you're not going to hire an architect, at least sketch it out on a cocktail napkin, guys! It's not rocket science."

There was general laughter, and our hosts led the way around the bed and out to the pool patio. But my own laughter died on my lips as a sudden guilt assailed me: I shouldn't be making fun of this culture we had so wanted to be part of. Cut them some slack, for God's sakes, and stop being so superior. I remembered Pávlos's hurt pride, and Yiánnis's remarks: *Greece is a poor country. This is not California.*

My guilt lasted all of two seconds. I loved Greece and its people, but their mendacity appalled me. Why was it okay to build wacko, unplanned structures—however nice the pool and view—and expect to rent them for three hundred Euros a night? *Milk the foreigners, boys! They can afford it!*

I realized with a shock just how angry I had become. Angry at greed, ignorance, and malicious bureaucracy. We'd come to this land with a dream and were instead dying the Death of a Thousand Cuts. Perhaps I'd been naïve to expect anything different, but was it so wrong to think that individuals and civic agencies might show some basic ethics and integrity? Or had this sickness taken over the whole world?

Disgusted at myself, at Greece, at the universe, I shook my head and followed Linda onto the patio.

A WEEK AFTER the Coopers left, we had a big dinner up on the roof. We invited Rita and Sofía, Jacqui and Léo, and the entire Balabánis clan. I was by now fully infected by an unshakeable melancholy that colored everything; though our departure was almost two months away, I felt as though we were hosting a wake.

Fortunately, amusement was always close at hand.

"Did you hear about Tákis?" said Rita, as soon as she arrived.

"No," said Linda. "What's happened?" Behind Rita, Sofía made a half-amused, half-exasperated face. I couldn't begin to imagine how much she'd heard about Tákis over the last several months.

"Last night he went swimming in the harbor, naked! In front of everybody!"

Linda and I started to laugh. "You're kidding," I said.

"No! He'd been drinking in the bars, and he took off all his clothes and dived in the water. Right in the harbor, with everybody there!"

"Quite a treat for the girls," said Linda. Sofía nodded vigorously.

We'd put our table and the Balabánises' together on the roof and scrounged up all the chairs we could. Everybody brought food and drinks; but though we drank and ate and talked late into the night, the anticipation of our departure chilled the party like a cold current beneath warm surface waters.

Tákis Lends a Hand

ISAAC HAD CONTACTED the customs brokers in Athens recommended to him by the steamship line, but they hadn't replied to his emails.

"This is so difficult!" he complained. "In thirty years I never dealt with people like this, even in the Middle East! If I can just find someone to do the damned paperwork, everything else is easy. For renting the container, you can guess maybe four and a half thousand dollars; then about seven hundred in terminal fees and maybe two to three hundred for the customs broker. In all, about six thousand maximum. Anyway, I will keep trying. We still have time." The doubt in his tone rattled me. I needed to start investigating options.

I contacted a major international moving company with offices all over the world. They could only accept delivery in Athens, and quoted us nine thousand dollars, including customs brokerage in Greece. If we wanted everything picked up in Skópelos, we could add another three thousand.

Twelve thousand total. It was double what Isaac was quoting, if he could only find a broker to do the damn paperwork.

It was also more money than we had. We'd be putting plane fares on our plastic and needed to keep a little credit available for the first weeks back in the US.

I researched some more shippers and agencies online, made calls to Athens and Houston and L.A. No dice. I was at my wits' end.

"What if we just can't crack this problem?" I said to Linda. "Should we consider storing everything on the mainland, go back to the US, and have it shipped in six months or a year, when we've settled and we're earning again?"

Linda gave me a look. "How's *that* going to be any easier?"

"It solves the immediate problem," I said. "But—"

"There wouldn't *be* a problem if we didn't have so much stuff," she said. I noted the tone in her voice, and it scared me.

"How much money have we spent over the years storing boxes of crap that you never even open?" she went on. "Stuff you brought from England twenty years ago. Boxes of unsorted photographs, school notebooks, unfinished projects, pieces of old lamps…"

"Sweetheart—"

She cut me off with a gesture. I braced against what was coming.

"In Santa Cruz we could hardly get into the garage because it was full of crap. For years I asked you to sort through it. I begged you to let me help. Then when we decided to move, I—"

"I threw out a *lot* of stuff while I was packing!" I said. "At least a dozen—"

"Then why do we still have so much fucking crap in our lives?" she shouted. "We're going to go back penniless—homeless, if it wasn't for my friends—and spend the little we have left getting boxes and boxes of junk shipped back!" She clapped her hands to her head. "My God! What happened to our life?"

I stood frozen in the face of her anger. I *did* have an awful lot of stuff that served no use, that I never even looked at, but couldn't bear to part with. But not that much, not even a third of what we owned.

Linda's face was stone. She'd reached the end of her rope. "I could leave." Her tone was flat. "I could leave now. Everything that matters to me in the world I could fit into two suitcases. Furniture? I don't care. I can buy new. Books? Sometimes I think you care more about your books than you do about me."

I closed my eyes. Unfair as it was, the truth pierced me like a knife-point. My possessions owned me, not the other way around.

An image flashed into my mind: the Devil card of the Tarot. Trump sixteen.

Years ago, I'd studied the Tarot in some depth. The most popular deck portrays the Devil as a huge, bat-winged creature, half goat, half man, perched on a block of black stone. Before him stand two figures, a man and a woman—Adam and Eve after the fall, perhaps. Each is shackled by the neck to a great metal ring set in the Devil's throne. But the chains on their necks are loose: they could easily slip them off and be free, but instead appear resigned to their captivity. The card represents the tyranny of the material, our willingness to remain in thrall to it.

We don't own things, they own us. I knew this to be true, but was powerless to do anything about it.

"I'm sorry," I whispered. It was all I could do.

Linda nodded. The lava of her anger had chilled, congealed at the brink. "It is what it is."

EVERY DAY NOW came freighted with sadness and grief. Linda showed more buoyancy than I, but seeing her own sadness sawed at me like a knife. As we dismantled and repacked our lives, I felt the dark-plumed wings of the angel of depression fold tighter around us.

I hadn't spoken to Tákis in a few days, and I needed to tell him about our decision. He might also have some thoughts on getting our things to the mainland. But he'd been on the go twenty-five hours a day since starting some new construction work at the *épipla* to add an extra floor where the terrace of the defunct Bábalos night club had been.

After waiting a while at the store, I managed to pin him down, and broke the news that we were leaving. I asked if he could make inquiries with the local moving company—of course, he knew them well—and try to get us a good price on delivering our belongings to Piraéus.

Tákis made a call. "Two thousand Euros," he said, when he hung up the phone. "That is just to take the things, not to load the container."

I rubbed my eyes. I hadn't slept well in days, even with Yiánnis's pills. "That's about what I was quoted," I said. "I can't believe it's so expensive. I should probably try Andréas, the trucker, again."

"Tell me," he said, lighting a cigarette, "why you must take everything to Piraéus? If you can get one container from Thessaloníki, I can take your things for you."

I stared at him. "You're joking."

"No, this is not difficult. You say you want to go at the middle of September. If you can do this about the time I must go to Thessaloníki to get the furnitures, we can take everything in my truck. We will get on the ferry, and I will help you to load the container. Also I have friends there who can help us."

"I can't believe… Tákis, that's the kindest offer! I mean… We'd want to pay you for the gas and the ferry, of course."

He waved a hand. "I must take the truck anyway, and always I go empty. But of course I prefer that you and Linda do *not* leave," he added, wagging a finger. "And I think you will decide not, and that it will be all right."

"We would prefer so too, Tákis," I said, past the lump in my throat, "we really would. But I'm not optimistic." Who was I kidding with this half-assed attempt to soften the truth? Was it for Tákis's sake, or mine? Nothing was going to save us at this point.

He showed me the truck, and I took some measurements. "I think we can get everything in," I said.

"Of course. It is very big. There will not be a problem."

I emailed Isaac and told him we could probably get the goods to Thessaloníki, and could he arrange a container there. He said he'd look into it.

A few days later, Isaac called just before three in the afternoon, which was one a.m. in California. He was beside himself with frustration.

"*I am so angry*! Finally I was able to talk to the broker for the steamship line. I had to keep calling until he was in the office. I can't believe these people! They are so rude, so unprofessional, so *greedy*. They have no values. They don't believe in ethics, they don't believe in God! I think they are barely human!"

The short of it was that, like the other people he'd spoken to in Greece, this broker wanted the whole job or nothing. Isaac had told them we'd gladly pay a premium for them simply handling the paperwork, to no avail.

I could hear the defeat in his voice. "I don't know what I can do for you anymore. I do so much work with this steamship line, but still their broker will not help me! Without somebody to do this paperwork, we are not going to be able to get your things out of Greece."

I wanted to climb the walls. We'd have to use the big moving company, nine thousand dollars from Athens. How the hell would we get everything there? And it would completely max out our remaining credit.

Trying to leave this country had become a nightmare. We were out of options. We couldn't get our belongings out, and Linda was going to be fined when we left, and have to deal with God-knew what unpleasantness. I wanted to scream, maybe have a complete breakdown. Check out of reality altogether.

We'd become prisoners in paradise.

That evening I went back to speak to Tákis. I explained the problem, and asked if he'd be willing to drive the hundred and fifty miles to Athens so we could deliver the goods there. Of course, we'd pay for the extra expenses involved.

He was dismayed. "Dario, I can not do this. I do not have the license. If the police stop us, I will have big problems."

"What license?" I asked.

"Eh." He lit a cigarette. "I have the license only to carry my own furnitures, and only on the road for Thessaloníki. If I am going to

Thessaloníki and the police stop me, I can say your boxes are my things from the factory I buy from; also the ferry takes us direct to Thessaloníki, so we will drive only a few kilometers. But in Athens I do not have business. It is a long way, and it is easy to be stopped by the police."

I stared. "You need a special license to carry someone else's things? You can't do a favor for a friend with your own truck?"

"Eh, no. Not in Greece."

"But a *license*? It's not just an insurance issue?"

He shook his head. "It is not the insurance. When you have a truck, you must say exactly what your business is, and where you go, and the police give you a license only to carry things for this."

I slumped back in my chair. "Tákis, this country is incredible. The Chinese will bury you. Christ, even the Albanians will bury you!"

"Yes, I believe this," he said. He fiddled with his cellphone, lost in thought. "Tell me, you trust this person in California?"

"Isaac? Absolutely. I'm sure he's done everything he can. The problem is that nobody here wants to just do the customs work; they want the whole contract."

"Eh, of course they will want. But I do not think this is so big a problem." He reached for a notepad. "Now tell me where you want the container to go. I will talk to my friend in Thessaloníki. He knows some people who make this shipping work. Perhaps he will help."

THAT EVENING, LINDA made pizza. She'd frozen some of her superb dough from the last time, and the convection oven was perfect for the job, since good, crisp pizza requires seriously high temperatures. She cut a few slices and put them on a plate for me to take to Tákis.

Tákis's face lit up as I handed him the still-warm plate. "Mmmm, beautiful!" he said, picking up a slice. "Also I am hungry!" He bit into the pizza and his eyes widened. "Linda, she make this?"

I chuckled. "Everything. Even the bread part."

He shook his head in wonder. "Never I tasted pizza like this! Tell her thank you, and that she is a fantastic cook!"

The next day, Tákis called me in to the shop. His friend had put him in contact with a shipping company in Thessaloníki. "They can do everything," he said. "They can supply the container for us to load in Thessaloníki, they will make the papers, and send it on the ship. Then your Mr. Isaac will make the American papers, and everything will be good."

I sagged. They wanted the whole job. "Getting the container isn't a problem," I said. "We really only need them to do the paperwork here."

"Yes. But I think they will give us also a good price for the container. What price did they tell you in America?"

"Um. Let's see what this man offers us first."

"Ah. Yes, this is good." Tákis dialed a number, there was a fast exchange of Greek. "*Periménete*," he told the voice at the other end: wait. He covered the phone.

"He says about three thousand five hundred dollars. About."

It was a moment before I could speak. "Dollars, not Euros? For *everything?*"

Another quick exchange. "Dollars, yes, for everything, until the container arrives in the Oaklands or Houston."

I felt like a man crossing a desert, afraid to believe the sudden oasis isn't just a mirage. I said, "Tákis, please thank him and tell him we'll have a reply for him tomorrow."

"Do you think we can trust these people?" I said, once he'd hung up.

Tákis dipped his head in the 'yes' gesture and lit a cigarette. "He has give us the price. I do not think this will change."

"I mean, with all our things. Everything we own in the world will be in that container."

"Ah. For this, I do not know. But if you say 'yes' for the price, then I will see to find if it is an honest company."

I told Linda the news. If Tákis's contact was on the level, and they could deliver on the offer, the price was better than we'd dared hope for: even adding in the charges at the US end, we were looking at a total of forty-five hundred dollars, or about fifteen hundred below our previous best-case. There had to be a catch.

I ran the numbers past a very surprised Isaac. "They must be getting a better price even than I can on the container. Ask them what steamship line they use. But really we have no other options. If they can get you the container when you want it, and do the paperwork, I think you should use them."

We gave Tákis the go-ahead, conditional on a firm price quote and the container being available to load in the middle of September, just before our friends Lucy and Robert arrived. If everything looked good, we would send a deposit immediately.

In typical Greek fashion, no deposit was required: I should simply bring the sum in cash when we went to load the container. Worryingly, no written confirmation was forthcoming either.

"I really want this price in writing," I told Tákis.

"It is not the Greek way," he said. "In Athens, yes; but in Thessaloníki, we are still honest in business, and we just shake the hands. I do not think there will be a problem."

The steamship line checked out. "It's the same line we use," said Isaac. "I don't know how they're getting this price, but I am very happy you have found someone to help you."

It was time to take a chance and trust Tákis's judgment. After nine months, I'd finally got it: if you need something done in Greece, ask a Greek.

Lies, and Damned Lies

ASSUMING OUR SHIPMENT went off smoothly, the only other big concern was Linda's passage through Greek passport control. Apart from the twelve-hundred Euro fine, she'd discovered the Schengen countries had an agreement whereby anyone overstaying their entry visa in one could be denied entry to other Schengen member countries.

I suspected this sanction was reserved for the worst offenders, but there was no telling with officials. By the time we left, Linda would be seven months over her ninety-day permit. The full fine, over sixteen hundred dollars at current rates, would almost certainly be levied; and if we refused to pay it—it was hard to see how they could enforce it, unless they were willing to detain an American citizen—Linda could well be blacklisted. The possibility of her being refused entry to Italy, France, Spain, and just about every other EU nation other than Britain in the future gave us pause.

Brigitte—who had finally received her residency card—suggested I should at least try to have my own Greek residency settled by the time we left; it might give us a better chance with passport control on exiting. But after applying two months ago and being told my residency would take no more than a week, I still hadn't heard anything. I'd since been to the police station on two occasions: each time I'd waited in a daunting line of people waiting outside Stávros's office to complete interminable procedures, and each time I'd been told it would be completed very soon, and they would phone me. Greek official time moved on a geological scale, if it moved at all.

Next day, I made a point of rising early so that I could be at the police station first thing. Stávros looked up as I entered his office, He smiled.

"Please, do you have my residency permit?" I asked.

His head twitched backwards, eyes blinked shut in the *no* gesture. "Why?"

He leaned back in his chair and clasped his arms languidly behind his head. "A new law has been passed, and we haven't received the new permit cards. We will have them this week or next week."

"Stávros, I give you papers in June. You say me one week only for residency. Then you say me, wait just few days, we telephone. Two times."

He shrugged. "Yes. But there is a new law. I must wait for the new cards."

I gave a bitter laugh. "Thanks, Stávros. *Yássas.*"

He nodded his head and gave me a smile that I took for satisfaction at yet another job successfully postponed. "*Yássas.*"

Back at home, Linda and I discussed the problem a little more. "Maybe the KEP office can write us a letter," she said. "Or even the Mayor."

"Saying…?"

"Well, that I applied in good faith but that our lawyer screwed up. That we thought my application was being processed, whereas in fact he hadn't even filed a proper application."

"Which is actually the truth."

"Exactly."

I called Iliána, the mayor's daughter, at the KEP office and asked if they could write us what Linda later came to call her *cat-ate-my-homework/get-out-of-jail-free* note. After just a moment's hesitation—I wondered if she shared the general opinion that we were worrying far too much about the Letter Of The Law—Iliána said she could, and would have it in about ten days.

WE'D BEEN SEEING a lot less of our friends since the summer season had begun. Vasílis's shop was open until nine every night and Lítza worked until midnight at the news stand. Rita worked until ten every night. Our English friend Sue had extended her stay in Austria following surgery on her ankle, where an MRI had revealed more serious injuries than a simple sprain. Yiánnis and Mina had a never-ending stream of family staying with them.

Fortunately, both Jacqui and Léo, as well as Alice and Joe, were free a good deal of the time, and their good company helped keep us halfway sane.

Still, August was grim. We kept packing, the pile of boxes kept growing, and the jellyfish kept us out of the water. We decided to leave Skópelos with Lucy and Robert when they left on the 24th of September, thinking this would make for a more upbeat exit. We'd enjoy a day in Athens with them—Brigitte had offered us the keys to her apartment, to save us hotel costs—and fly out the next day.

I was still nervous about whether the shipping arrangements would pan out. After a couple of emails asking the company in Thessaloniki for written confirmation, I received a laconic 'Mr. Dario, container is okay for September 17.' It was the best assurance we would get.

With the island full, the *milos* was rented through much of the month and our gorgeous roof terrace had become hostile territory. It seemed so unfair that on top of all the grief we were struggling with, we couldn't even enjoy our terrace during our last weeks here. I would find strangers sitting at our table, or the chairs moved to the parapet. Linda wanted to move our table and chairs down to the landing by our front door; there was no view, but it would at least be a private place to sit and dine out of doors.

One *milos* renter, a young Greek woman, had moved one of our chairs to the parapet where she spent hour after hour reading and smoking. After several reconnaissance trips up the stairs I finally found her gone, probably to the beach. At last I could sneak our table and chairs down to the front door landing. She could use one of Spýros's ratty old chairs in the future.

Two days later, I went up to water the planters early in the morning and found scores of cigarette butts piled among the geraniums which Linda had so lovingly tended over the months. Putting cigarettes out in planters was a particularly foul habit all Greeks seemed to share: I'd seen

Spýros do the same thing. I damned and cursed the woman for her ignorance. Burning with fury, I picked all the cigarette butts from the planters and dumped the lot at the door to the *mílos*. Some saner part of me knew it for the petty action it was, but baser instincts were running the show.

"I think you might be going a little overboard," said Linda, after giving me a while to cool off. She was right, and I saw now that I'd simply needed a target for my frustrations and grief. I went back upstairs, collected the butts, and dumped them in the trash instead. The woman's behavior was ignorant and disrespectful, no doubt about that, but I really didn't want to make trouble for Spýros.

Even *Skópelites* had issues with the way Greek tourists behaved; and in the high season, most of the island's tourists were Greek.

"It's no good," said Vasílis, when I stopped by his shop one day to ask how business was. "The island is full, but they're all social tourists. They don't spend any money."

"*Social* tourists?" I said. "What do you mean?"

Vasílis puffed at his cigarette. "In Greece, if you're below a certain income, or you have a large family, the Government pays for you to go on holiday. Not all of it. I think they pay about sixty percent of your accommodation for two weeks."

"That's great for the poor," I said. "At least they get a holiday with their families. And it circulates money through the economy."

"Yes, but what about us shopkeepers? These people come with their cars, they cook their own food, and buy a couple of postcards. Ha! It doesn't do us any bloody good at all."

ILIÁNA CALLED FROM the KEP office to tell us they had Linda's letter from the mayor and we could pick it up anytime. When we stopped by the next morning, we found Stávros, the young clerk from the police station, chatting to Iliána. I gave him a terse nod as Iliána greeted us.

Linda took the letter and thanked Iliána for all her help. I did likewise. Iliána expressed her regrets that we were leaving, and wished she'd been able to do more for us.

Stávros had enough English to catch some of this exchange. He said something to Iliána, who explained we'd decided to leave because of Linda's residency problems.

Stávros turned to me. "I can make you permit today," he said. Then, in Greek, "We have the new cards. And then your wife can get her residency permit. It's not a problem." He gave a small shrug, as if to say, *no big deal.* He actually smiled.

I stared at him, thunderstruck. My face heated and my vision narrowed until it was like looking through a rifle scope at his brown eyes. This young, gray-uniformed man embodied everything that was wrong with this country. A little jerk with a power complex and a job for life in the pus-filled system that had poisoned our dreams. I wanted to scream obscenities; my hands itched to hurt him.

I took a deep breath instead.

"It's too late, Stávros," I said, in English. "We're going home. Back to America."

I felt I was in a diorama. Time might have stopped. Stávros and I stared at one another. Nobody moved. Iliána was standing stiffly, face rigid.

It was Linda who broke the silence. She thanked Iliána again for everything she'd done for us. Iliána seemed relieved and mumbled something I didn't catch—I was still staring down Stávros. A second later, he broke eye-contact with me and turned away.

The Titanic Sails at Dawn

BY THE TENTH of August, our plans were made. We would land in San Francisco and stay with Linda's sister Barbara. We'd get a couple of cellphones and buy a used car. Friends had offered us loaners until something came up. And if Warmboard was at all busy, I'd rent a laptop, load my CAD software, and resume work at once.

If everything went well, our shipment would arrive two or three weeks after we did. We'd rent a U-Haul truck, load everything on it, and set off for New Mexico, with Linda driving the car and I, the truck.

Once in Albuquerque, the plan was to put everything into storage and go to Linda's friends' house. As soon as Linda found fulltime employment we would rent a place to live and set up home. As deep a hole as we were in, I thought we had enough skills that we could, with moderate good fortune, dig our way out in a year or two.

Nonetheless, we had no illusions that life would be easy upon our return—the news from the US was not encouraging. The subprime lending crisis was widening, and looked ready to balloon into a general slowdown, perhaps even a recession.

I remembered an amusing news item, published just after the Falklands War between Britain and Argentina in the early 'eighties. A young British couple, convinced that a nuclear war was imminent, decided to leave England for somewhere less likely to be vaporized when Armageddon occurred. They did their research, looking for places with the best chance of getting through the ensuing fallout and nuclear winter. In the end, they settled on the Falkland Islands, a sleepy, self-reliant, out-of-the-way place in the southern hemisphere, about as safe as you could be anywhere. They packed up home and moved there with their children. Just a month later, Argentina invaded the islands and the Falklands War began.

I wondered if we were about to do something very similar.

WE CALLED TÁKIS to see if he wanted to join us for dinner that weekend. "My cousin Theodóros from Thessaloníki is here; I will bring him also," he said. "He is a very good artist, you will like him." The Greek assumption that any invitation naturally extended to friends or family still made me smile.

That afternoon, I ran into Tákis and his cousin outside the Ánemos bar. Tákis introduced us, and we confirmed arrangements for that evening. It was about four p.m. They were drinking cocktails, and Tákis was looking a little blurry.

"Now we will go to the beach and make a little swimming," said Tákis; his cousin looked dubious. "Then we will see you tonight. Also," he put a hand on my shoulder, "I have one idea to discuss with Linda. I think it is a very good idea. Perhaps you will not have to leave. I hope, I hope."

I squeezed his shoulder right back. "I look forward to hearing it," I said. It would take a miracle to save us now, but who knew? Sometimes miracles happened. "You're a good guy, Tákis."

Damn, I was going to miss him!

Still following our 'Titanic' model—when you're going down, you should always go down in style—Linda cooked another extraordinary meal, and our guests ate with relish. After the first course, Tákis lit a cigarette and announced, "So, Linda: I have one idea for you to stay in Skópelos and make a good work."

I took this as a cue to refill wineglasses. Linda smiled at him. "Oh, Tákis! We really don't want to leave. I hope it's a very good idea!"

"It is very good. So, this is my idea. I think you are the best cook on Skópelos. This pizza you make—everything you make—is fantastic! And I am thinking, how can I help Linda and Dario to stay? So I have one idea." He took a draught of wine. Linda was grinning.

"For a long time, I have think to make a restaurant where was Bábalos, over my shop. Not big to begin, just six or seven tables. I will make the licenses and put in the fridges and furnitures, everything for the restaurant, and you will make the cooking. We begin small, but every night it will be a different menu. This will be something new in Skópelos, very special."

"I think small is always a good way to start," said Linda. "Would you open during the winter?"

"Sure, we can make this very soon. Of course, we begin small. But then when people know this place and comes the summer, we can put more tables."

Theodóros and I listened quietly. Linda sipped her wine and nodded. One of her strongest qualities is always being open to opportunity.

Tákis continued, "The only problem is that I do not know what Dario can do." I opened my mouth for a wisecrack, but he waved the thought aside and went on. "But we will find something for him. Anyways, we will make the half of the profits: half for you and half for me. You do not have to put anything except for the cooking. And of course to decide the menus."

"I can shop," I said, laughing.

"Eh, yes, you can shop. Always there is something to do, anyway. And of course you can paint furnitures for the shop." He stubbed out his cigarette. "So, Linda, what do you think for this?"

Linda smiled, tilting her head. "Ohh… Tákis, you are *such* a dear. I think it's a fabulous idea. I just don't know if it would be enough to get us through this mess. It would be some time before we started to make money."

"Eh, yes, of course. But after one or two years, I think we can have very good business. I have many friends, and they will all come. Then, later, we can bring some musicians also."

"But wasn't it the live music that caused all the trouble at Bábalos?" I asked.

"Yes, but the music there was outside, on the roof. Inside it is not a problem."

Linda excused herself and went to fetch the second course. I reached across the table and put my hand on Tákis's arm. "You're the best friend we could ever have, Tákis. Thank you so much."

Behind him, the growing stacks of boxes in the living room mocked me. *Forget it—you're fucked.*

Theodóros was a graphic designer, and spoke quite good English. Toward the end of the meal, emboldened perhaps by wine, he embarked on a somewhat embarrassing confession of his concerns about Tákis's lifestyle.

"Before few years," he said, "I was in one very bad car crash after drinking too much. I was in a coma and almost I died. Even now, after much time, I have very bad pains. Now I am afraid for Tákis. Like today, he drinks for three hours then gets on the motorcycle to go swimming. Today I was sure we would die! And it is very bad for the health to drink and smoke so much."

I glanced at Tákis. He looked sheepish, but kept quiet. Theodóros went on for a little while before realizing he wasn't getting any traction. In our hearts, we both agreed with his sentiments, but with age comes understanding. Tákis was Tákis, and you had to love him for who he was, even if you feared for him.

When Theodóros was quite done, Tákis expounded his philosophy with admirable calm and only a trace of defensiveness. "Yes, this is true. But I believe when you make very hard swimming and exercise, you can burn away these bad things very fast. When I swim every day for one hour, everything is gone from my body—the drink, the cigarettes, everything. This swimming makes you very strong!"

I hoped he was right, and to this day hope so. I've rarely come to like a person so much in less than a year.

SPÝROS AND MÁRA had moved fast to find new tenants for our house. The first two potential renters passed, but the third, a couple from Vólos with two young children, loved the place. The wife was a teacher coming to do her stint in the provinces, as was normal for all civil servants, doctors, and teachers in Greece before getting a permanent posting. That was how Yiánnis had first ended up on Alónissos, and how Doom, our ill-tempered postal employee, came to be on Skópelos. Often, people serving their time on the island fell in love with one of the natives, or with the place itself; and so they stayed.

We'd planned to have everything packed by the tenth of September and move out of the house on the fifteenth, a day before I was due to take our belongings to Vólos with Tákis. But the new tenant needed to move in earlier, since the school year began a few days into September.

Mára and Spýros were visibly embarrassed about asking us to move out early. We were well ahead on our packing, and I thought we could probably be ready in time, but it would be a scramble. Fortunately, Tákis's big truck was empty, and he'd already suggested that we load our belongings into it a bit at a time as we packed them. The big truck sat locked in the *épipla*'s yard at night, and our stuff would be safe.

"I think we can do it," said Linda.

Mára looked relieved. "Of course, you can stay in the *mílos* until your friends come. It will be free after the twentieth of this month."

"We would like that very much," said Linda. We'd always wanted to stay in the adorable little *mílos*. It would be a romantic ending to our life in the village. "I think just one week will be okay, because we will go to Alónissos for one week before our friends arrive."

"*Kalá, Linda. Kalá,*" said Mára. Good, good.

Sofía had already offered to buy the stove, as well as one of Linda's six remaining containers of olive oil. We wanted to take one or possibly two of the seventeen-liter cans back for our own culinary use, but at ninety Euros a can, we hoped to sell the rest. Spýros and Mára bought the appliances, and we were able to sell the china cabinet—which still looked brand new—back to Tákis for a reasonable price. We had also decided to try to sell a couple of cheap wardrobes we'd only recently bought at the *épipla*, as well as a few of our older items of furniture. To our surprise, Jilly from the grocery store ended up buying all of these at a price that everyone was happy with.

I hated to be selling things we actually liked—again—but it wasn't just a question of money; space was an issue. Tákis's truck would only accommodate about eight hundred cubic feet, and my best estimate suggested our shipment would come real close to that. Besides selling those items of furniture I'd rather have kept, we'd have to abandon our beautiful workbenches as well, and build new ones when we got settled again. They were just too big.

I HAD BECOME expert by now at scavenging boxes. Some days I would stagger up the hill towards home carrying a pile of nested empty cartons picked up from Rígas or Chrístos's little market. I had no doubt that gossip was flying, but at this point I didn't give a shit. I just wanted to get out.

Two weeks before we were due to move, Tákis's helpers came and took the first load of packed belongings from our house to his truck. It was a hot day, and the boys sweated in the sun as they loaded our boxes onto the small truck for transporting to the big truck; although it was just a few dozen yards to the *épipla*, it was easier to drive the load.

I'd built packing crates for the immensely heavy marble top to our dresser and the big, baroque, gilt-framed mirror I'd inherited from my Grandmother. Both were back-breakers, and I was glad that younger bodies were doing the heavy lifting.

A little while after they left, I stopped by to see how the load was looking. With Tákis's help and supervision, they'd done a fantastic job. Boxes were stacked to the ceiling, and I couldn't see a chink of space. The truck was little over a quarter full. We were going to be fine.

All that was left to pack was our bed, dining table, and some kitchen and bathroom essentials. Time, then, to start dismantling the workshop.

But it was mid-August, and by late morning, when the sun began to beat on the front of the workshop, we would be wringing wet. I'd tried to buy a fan during the heat wave, but everyone had sold out. Now it wasn't worth it. We toiled stoically, alternating between iced water and cold beer to keep ourselves cool and sane.

After three days we had a full load for the small truck, and Tákis sent the boys down to collect it. We returned home at lunchtime, and I went to see how the loading had gone. To my shock, less than a third of the space in Tákis's truck remained free. A number of tables and chairs from the *épipla* had been tied into place in front of our boxes and, although well-packed and nested, they took up enough room that I feared there wouldn't be room for our remaining belongings.

One of the boys saw my dismay. They'd seen what was still left in the house and workshop. "Tákis has to take these things back to the factory," he explained.

I could hardly argue. It was Tákis's truck, and he was doing this as a favor. But I wished he'd told me. If we got to the end and something important—like our beloved and expensive bed—didn't fit, what would we do then? It was typically Greek.

"I hope we can get everything else in," I said.

"Yes, yes," said the boy; but his face said 'no'.

A Remarkable Twist of Fate

WITH MOST OF our other friends busy and Jacqui and Léo out of town for a few days, we decided to have Tákis for our last dinner guest before we packed up the kitchen. He'd told me he had a new girlfriend, and of course we wanted to meet her.

We'd moved the table and chairs down to the landing by the front door a couple of weeks earlier. It was much noisier than the terrace, but by the time Linda had set it with candles and silver goblets, the effect was still striking.

Elíza, Tákis's new girlfriend, was delightful: bright and upbeat, with a fresh sort of beauty, she seemed very different to the tense, complicated women we'd seen him with before. Elíza lived in Crete, where she worked as an actress; she spoke fluent English. She was full of questions about us and our lives. When we talked about our experiences and explained why we were leaving, Tákis turned gloomy. "I try to make them change their ideas," he said, "but now I see that they can not. For this, I am very sad."

WHILE WE PREPARED to leave, the rest of the island was preparing for the arrival of the cast and crew of 'Mamma Mia!'. Casting calls for extras had been posted around the village with locations and dates for auditions. Jacqui, Rita, Alice and Joe, Mina and the children, and many of the people we knew were applying. Yiánnis had contacted the production assistants to let them know that he was the island's only private doctor—the only one!

Vasílis, meanwhile, having sold a number of cellphones to the advance guard of production assistants a few weeks earlier, had been approached to be one of the drivers for the cast. At a hundred Euros a day for a twelve-hour shift which would mostly involve waiting while shooting took place, the money wasn't great; but it would help, and Lítza could run the shop in the meantime.

"If you end up being Colin Firth's driver," I said, "Linda will be begging you for an introduction."

Vasílis laughed. "I doubt it," he said. "The big stars have their own drivers. I'll probably be assigned to somebody you've never heard of. Still, I get to drive a Land Rover—they're bringing over a whole fleet of them."

I goggled. "God! No wonder films cost a hundred million to make."

"They've booked more than two hundred rooms for the whole month. It's great for the island's business. Most of the tourists have already left, and by the middle of September there's usually nobody here. This gives everyone an extra month of business. And these people aren't Greeks—this lot will spend money!"

WE WERE GETTING to the putzy stuff now. Linda took care of things at home, packing and cleaning, cleaning and packing, and I spent time in the workshop, sorting through materials and belongings to see what could be got rid of. Amazingly, given the stress of the last few months combined with all the packing and heavy lifting, my back hadn't once gone out. Linda's chiropractic adjustments had kept me whole.

"I wish you were a little less scrupulous," I told her one night. "It's such a sick irony that they won't let you make soap but you could probably make a good living as the island's chiropractor."

"I've thought about it." She shook her head.

"Yeah. Don't let's go there."

"I had another thought, too."

Her eyes danced with that playful light I so loved, and I knew something good was coming.

"What if," she began, "when we get back to the 'States, you write a book about our experience here?"

I shrugged. "Oh, sure. I've been thinking about that."

"And then," she went on, "we begin looking for a new country to move to. We spend a year learning the language and then move there with everything we have. We settle in, make friends, and apply for residency and work permits. And a year later, when it all goes wrong, we move back to the US again and you write another book!"

I stared at her. "Gods! The possibilities…"

She slapped her knee. "Exactly! We get to learn languages, make friends, travel, and make a living, all at the same time!"

"It's brilliant! Life as performance art!"

Linda raised her palms in a gesture of accomplishment. "See? I got it all figured out." She broke into a broad grin. "Now all we have to do is survive this first trial run, and then it's plain sailing."

I PUT THE final coat of varnish on the pine dresser I'd painted for Tákis and packed up my brushes. I took shelves apart, sorted through my boxes of oils and acrylics, and looked wistfully at the workbenches we'd have to abandon. I thought about taking them apart and packing them in pieces, but after another look at the remaining space in Tákis's truck, I decided against it. Perhaps I could give them to someone.

It was the first of September, two days prior to our move-out date. We had set the table on the landing for dinner. It was about eight p.m. I was sitting outside with the last of the absinthe and Linda was taking a spell at the computer. Dinner was on the stove.

Although we were headed for Albuquerque, Linda had that morning sent courtesy emails to business contacts and previous employers in the US. She was good at keeping in touch with people. She also wanted to be sure that they would be available as references when she began applying for jobs.

She came out with a bottle of cold *retsína* and a mischievous smile on her lips. She sat down, filled our glasses, and raised hers for a toast. "So what do you think about moving to Willits?"

The expression on my face must have been priceless. Willits is a small town on Highway 101 in Northern California, about three hours' drive north of San Francisco. Population three thousand, elevation about fifteen hundred.

It was also where Metal FX, the company that manufactured the Warmboard product, was located.

I clapped my hands to my head. "Let me guess. Metal FX has offered you a job!"

She took a gulp of *retsína* and laughed. "I just got an email from them. They just let go of their Head of Accounting this morning. They say the job's mine if I want it."

I clinked my glass against hers. "Oh my God! That's an insane coincidence! Are you going to take it?"

"Well, I want to see what you think first. Also I have no idea what they're offering. It's not going to be anywhere near what I was earning at Warmboard."

"I'd love to live up there!" I said. Once you get about fifty miles north of San Francisco, where the climate and ecosystem change from Mediterranean to temperate, the eucalyptus and palm trees disappear and the dreary brown hills of the Bay Area give way to a greener land of mossy forests, where heavy winter rains feed the mighty Russian river. Pines and redwoods dominate there, and great crags jut from the landscape. A wilder, wetter land, more like the north of England than California, and very much to my liking.

I knew Linda liked the area, too. We'd more than once discussed living north of the Bay, but the collapse of the logging industry in the 'nineties had ruined the local economy. It was a depressed region, with jobs scarce and ill-paying. The kind of place you could only live comfortably if you telecommuted, owned a vineyard, or grew pot for a living, the last being a common occupation in both Mendocino and Humboldt counties.

But I *did* telecommute. And now here was Linda being offered a management job!

I sipped at my *retsina*. "Of course," I went on, "I'm not going to get any high-end painting work up there. But the wine country's not that far; I could probably pick up the odd job in Healdsburg. And hopefully I'll get at least a little CAD work through the winter. More to the point, how do *you* feel about it? Wouldn't returning to California feel like a step backwards?"

"Well, it wouldn't be moving back to Santa Cruz," she said. "At least I wouldn't have to spend weeks interviewing for jobs in a new environment. And one of us would have an income right away."

I nodded. "I think it's a fantastic opportunity. It would give us breathing room. And it's close enough to the Bay Area that we can visit friends. Why don't you see what they're offering?"

In less than an hour, they'd ironed out a deal. The starting salary was modest, but we could probably rent a home for half of what it cost in the Bay Area.

"They want me to start on October fifteenth," said Linda. She looked a little dazed.

"Linda! We're going to be living in the redwoods! You," I said, refilling our glasses, "are fucking awesome!"

"It's kind of amazing how that happened, isn't it?"

"It happened because they remembered how damned capable you were in negotiating with them when you worked for Warmboard. Of course they want you!"

Linda shrugged. "I don't know about that. But it'll be interesting to see what it's like on the other side of the fence."

We sat quietly for a time. "How fast things can turn around," she said. "Just a couple of hours ago we were going to move to New Mexico and hope for the best. Now, out of the blue, I've got a job in California starting two weeks after we get back and I didn't have to do a thing to get it."

"No shit. I'd better post the news on the blog."

Up On The Roof

THE NEXT MORNING, Tákis's boys returned for the rest of our belongings. I helped them load, and soon the house was bare except for our suitcases, a couple of boxes of food, a briefcase full of important papers, a few books and toiletries, and my laptop.

A little later, I walked up to the *épipla* to see how much room was left in the truck. There was space left, but by the time we finished packing up the workshop it was going to be very close indeed. I expressed my concerns to Tákis. His tone was apologetic. "Eh. I must return these furnitures I have put in there," he said. "But it will be alright."

I was glad he felt that way, but he hadn't seen what was still in the workshop.

We spent the rest of the day deep-cleaning the house and touching up holes in walls where we'd hung paintings. I helped Spýros manhandle the appliances they'd bought out of the house and into his storage area. Léo and Jacqui came by to collect Sofía's stove for her.

By the end of the afternoon we were physically and emotionally spent. But the house was spotless, the keys handed over, and ourselves installed in Rapunzel's castle up on the roof, free to enjoy the full use of our glorious roof terrace for the next several days. Being in the *mílos* was like living in a lighthouse—a long-cherished, romantic notion of mine.

We had dinner that evening at Pepárithos, an open-air taverna just a few dozen yards down the ring road from Vasílis's house. We'd meant to try it since it had opened for the season in June, but had somehow never got around to it.

A long, shallow flight of stairs led down from the road to a tranquil, lantern-lit garden setting. The tables were well-spaced, the other diners few. We ate slowly, drawing the time out like reeling silk. Things seemed a little surreal. Emotional fatigue, no doubt. Moving out of the house underscored the reality of our position: we were approaching the very end of our stay on Skópelos, the final and certain abandonment of our dream.

NOW WE WERE out of the house, there were the inevitable accounts to close off. Settling our phone account at OTÉ, to my great surprise, proved easy. The electricity was another matter. The fat slob was gone, replaced by a less obnoxious and more polite functionary. Yes, I could close our account, but in order for the new tenant to not be billed for the outstanding sum, they would have to come to the office with me. I could only guess at the logic behind this, but—apart from not having the language to fully investigate the matter—the *Bastards/Fuck'em/Whatever* rule seemed to apply: there *was* no logic, just the usual arbitrary bureaucracy.

I trudged back up to the house and knocked on the door. There was a heap of empty cartons on the landing where our patio table had stood. A tall man opened. His name was Antónis. He was the new tenant's husband.

I explained the situation as best I could, and Antónis agreed to come along with me to DEÍ, the electricity office. First, though, he had some questions about the house, and asked me in.

It was weird seeing our house with someone else's belongings in it. The living room had been turned into a children's bedroom; two cots with gaily-patterned quilts sat against the right-hand wall. Toys and stuffed animals were strewn about at random.

Pointing to the wall thermostat, Antónis complained that the water never got hot. "How do you get enough for a bath?" he asked. I tried to explain the multiple on-off trick with the heater that fooled the thermostat. "It makes warm with little time," I assured him. Wait until winter, baby.

Next, he showed me into the bathroom. Pointing to a couple of unhappy rags around the pedestal, he said, "The toilet is leaking."

Not wanting to make Spýros look bad, I feigned surprise. "This is a problem," I agreed. "You must tell Spýros. He will make good!"

A few minutes later we stood before the counter at DEÍ. I had noted the electric meter reading, but—even with the new tenant present—they wouldn't let me close our account. The bill would arrive from the mainland office in due time. When I explained that we would be leaving for California in two weeks and could they send us the bill there, the man behind the counter gave me an incredulous grin and a slight shake of his head. *What, are you nuts?* he seemed to say. *It's hard enough billing customers in Greece!*

"I do not want this man to pay our bill," I said, pointing at Antónis.

"No, no. Now you have finished, he will begin a new bill."

"Good," I said. "I will look at the post office for our bill."

Assured that the new tenants wouldn't be hit with our charges, I dismissed the matter from my mind. It probably wouldn't be more than fifty or so Euros anyway.

And of course, Antónis wasn't able to open an account. He had his ID and he had the thirty-Euro deposit. But he didn't have a lease, since Spýros hadn't given them one. After wrangling for a while with the official, he was allowed ten days, after which their power would be cut off if they hadn't supplied a stamped, notarized copy of their lease.

Antónis looked distressed.

"*Ólos íne dískolo stin Elláda,*" I said.

ANOTHER DAY PACKING and sorting at the workshop. Out of our house, with Jacqui and Léo on the mainland for a few days and our other friends still busy, we felt oddly isolated for the first time since we'd come to Skópelos. We took our evening meal down by the harbor and strolled along the *paralía*, window-shopping.

On the way to the workshop on the third morning we stopped by at Vasílis's store to say hello to Lítza.

"Have the beautiful people arrived?" said Linda.

Lítza was wide-eyed "You will not believe!" she said. "Vasílis come ten minutes before with Pierce Brosnan. Here, in the shop!"

"Wow, Lítza!" said Linda. "What was he like?"

"Was he beautiful?" I asked.

"Oh, God! Yes! Very tall, and beautiful! I am so red when he come, I do not know what to say!"

The next morning, we got the full story from Vasílis. "I should have been just one of the pool drivers," he said, "but as it turned out, Pierce Brosnan came on his own, ahead of his family. When they told us he needed a driver, all the others started putting their hands up and shouting, "Me! Me!" I just kept quiet. Finally the boss turned to me and said, 'Vasíli, you drive him.'"

"*Oh, Man!*" I said. "You're James Bond's driver?"

"Well, just until his regular driver arrives tomorrow. Pierce is a great guy, just like you and me! He wanted to know all about me. In ten minutes we were like old buddies. He made me show him around the island, then I took him up to the villa. After that, we went down to the *paralía*, where he insisted on buying me a beer.

"I had to stop by the shop a moment, and asked if he would mind saying hello to Lítza. 'She's a big fan of yours,' I said. 'No problem,' he said. He was so nice about it. So I called Lítza and told her to make sure she looked good because I was on my way to the shop with Pierce Brosnan. She thought I was joking. 'Yeah, yeah,' she said. When we walked in five minutes later, she almost dropped through the floor. He spent a few minutes talking to her and Kóstas. He has a son about the same age."

"What a bummer you don't get to drive him all the time," I said.

"Funny thing: he told the boss he wants me to be his family's driver. Apparently they don't usually provide a driver for the family, that's the actor's responsibility. But Pierce went up to the boss, right in front of me, and said, 'I want Vasílis to drive my family.' And that was that. 'Yes, Mr. Brosnan! Of course!' they said. It was amazing."

I laughed. "Makes sense. The last thing the studio wants is to piss off one of the principal actors. Besides which, it's a drop in the bucket for them to put on an extra driver."

"What are you driving?" said Linda.

"Brand new Land Rover. Great car. It's parked out there, just past the post office."

We were happy for him.

THE FILM PEOPLE were suddenly everywhere. The tavernas and bars, which had all quieted down in the last ten days, were full again. Rented Suzuki jeeps with the top down zipped along the roads, full of immaculately coiffed twenty-somethings in mirror shades looking cool and full of themselves.

Since much of the beach footage was being shot at tiny Kastáni beach, 'Mamma Mia!' HQ had been set up in the pines by adjoining Miliá. Big trailers filled the parking lot of the big taverna down there, and we heard that the studio had installed its own cooks in the kitchens.

But the weather was uncooperative. Just as the cast and crew arrived, the skies had filled with great, looming clouds herded by fitful winds. After weeks of packing and moving boxes in the humid heat, Linda and I didn't mind a bit. It made wrapping up the job a little less painful.

On the morning of Thursday the sixth, we were done. I went down to the workshop at ten and met Tákis's boys there. We loaded all our boxes onto the small truck, along with the little hutch I'd painted for Tákis and one of the four remaining cans of olive oil, and I rode back up with the driver while the other lad squatted in the back, steadying a precarious corner of the load for the brief drive.

Leaving the boys to unload, I carried the heavy can of oil into the store, where a bleary-eyed Tákis, wreathed in bluish smoke, was sipping his morning *frappé*.

"Linda asked me to give you this," I said, setting down the container. "You and your family have been such good friends."

"Oh, Dario!" he said, "it is too much."

"Do you already have a lot of olive oil?" I asked, thinking they might have groves of their own, or relatives who did.

"No, but we must pay Linda for this. This is very much oil."

"She wouldn't take it. We'd be in very deep shit without you."

The boys brought in the parts of the painted hutch and began to assemble it. Tákis was delighted. I was surprised: I'd never thought much of myself as a figurative painter, and other than the antiquing work, all I'd done to this piece was paint on a few olive branches. Admittedly, the olives did look plump and mouthwatering, with a little glistening highlight on each, but still.

Tákis made the boys move the hutch over to the wall near the desk. He lit another cigarette and stood in front of the piece. "This is very beautiful, Dario. Also the older people will like this."

He walked around it some more, touching the surface here and there. "Ah. This is something like I try to find for many years. Even in Mýkonos and Santoríni you can sell this, and for much money."

I smiled at the irony. The copper chest, infinitely more splendid and unusual, still sat in the front of the store. In five months, just one person had shown interest in it, and I suspected it would end up in Tákis's parents house. The big floorcloth I'd finished in faded oriental red and gold leaf detailing had elicited puzzled looks, and comments like, "we do not use these in Greece. They will not know what to do with it."

Tákis went on, "If you stayed here we could have very good business. I can make these furnitures in Thessaloníki for very little money. You would paint them, and I would also pay to make advertising in the magazines. In one or two years we could sell this style all over Greece." He put out his cigarette. "But you are leaving."

My gut churned. He wasn't just saying these things. And I could see that Tákis, like Yiánnis, felt bad that he hadn't been able to help us more, or seen the problems we faced sooner. And I think both of them were ashamed to see people they cared for driven away by their beloved country's toxic bureaucracies.

I shut my eyes. If there was a moment for Linda and I to slip into an alternate reality, this was it. Slip sideways through the veil; turn the clock back, change the outcome.

It should have all worked out for us. I couldn't believe that it hadn't. These people loved us, and we loved them. We had skills to offer this place. Linda could make people clean and sweet-smelling; I could make their homes beautiful.

Shit. Shit. *Shit!*

I STILL HAD to dispose of the workbenches; in the end, Jilly from the supermarket took one and Apostólos, our neighbor above the workshop, the other. And so, the workshop emptied and swept clean, I dropped the keys off at Próton. Lázaros thanked me, and refused my offer to pay for the extra week we'd stayed. Low-key as ever, he wished us well, leaving the rest unsaid.

We'd arranged to meet Yiánnis and Mina for a drink on the *paralía* that afternoon. With everything else settled and us taking off the next day for our week on Alónissos, there really wasn't anything to do but say goodbyes. We wanted to keep our last days here free for Lucy and Robert, with the exception of a farewell dinner invitation from the Balabánises, which they had also extended to our American friends.

We'd just crossed the street from the *mílos* and were starting down the side street by the Hotel Denise when Linda gave a small cry. I turned, reached out. Too late! She had slipped and fallen right beside me. She was sitting upright, but her right leg stuck out beneath her at an odd angle. Disbelief hit me like a fist. After everything we'd gone through, for her to break a leg now was beyond horrible.

I dropped to one knee beside her and touched her arm. "Are you alright?"

She grabbed my hand and put her other palm flat on the stone. She winced, and started to push herself up.

I reached my other arm around her and helped her to rise. "Your leg. Are you okay?"

She was pale, but she was getting up. "I think so," she said.

"God! I thought you'd broken your leg. When I saw it sticking out like that…"

"Me too." She was upright now, her weight on the left leg, the right slightly bent. She reached down and rubbed the knee as I steadied her.

"I was just about to take your hand, too". I always did, on the steep, slippery section, but we hadn't quite reached it yet.

She cursed once or twice as she started to walk, gripping my hand in hers. It had been close, and a miracle that she hadn't broken the leg. Clearly, my wife was a great deal more flexible than I thought. I hoped she hadn't torn anything.

"We need to get you some ice," I said. But our icepacks were in boxes.

"I'll get some at the bar." She was just relieved to be able to walk.

Yiánnis and Mina arrived a few minutes after we did. Ajax and Phílippos, their two boys, were with them, but soon took off to go and play. Linda was holding a bag of ice cubes against her knee. I'd suggested she ask Yiánnis to take a look at it, maybe get an x-ray done before we left, but had backed off at the first warning growl. She hated to be babied.

We ordered drinks and chatted. A miasma of unreality and pathos hung over the table. Was I the only one who felt it? We were leaving, and might never see these friends again, but everyone was trying to be normal and upbeat. I wanted to beat my fists on the table and rail at the universe. When we finally did say goodbye, I was relieved. Sick, sick!

That evening, I bought some food at the garden taverna near Vasílis's house and we ate out on the roof terrace. By ten, there was nothing to do but go indoors and read. Linda's knee was stiff and painful. She took one of the remaining codeine tablets and we settled onto the bed.

We'd been reading for about forty-five minutes when we heard footsteps outside. A moment later, Vasílis's cheery face appeared at the open window.

"Vasíli!" we both cried. "Come on in," said Linda.

He held up a hand. "No, no. It's nice and cool out here on your terrace." He shifted around a bit, settling on his haunches. "I just thought I'd come and say hello." His good-naturedness warmed us like sunlight.

"It's great to see you!" said Linda. "How's the filming?"

"The weather's been a problem. I've been driving Pierce's family around all day. Then tonight I took them all to O Kýpos for dinner. I was trying to make a turn off the ring road. There were cars everywhere and the family were all talking, and Pierce was telling me to watch out for another car, and I turned to him and said, 'look, just shut up and let me drive, will you?'"

We gasped. Vasílis nodded. "I know!" he said. "I started to apologize right away once I realized what I'd said. But he just laughed and said, 'no, you're absolutely right, Vasílis, don't worry about it.' What a great guy! I felt terrible."

Vasílis accepted a glass of *retsína*, but insisted on staying outside. We talked through the open window for an hour, Linda and I sitting on the bed, Vasílis squatting on the terrace. It was a quirky, delightful interlude, and—in the context of our disjointed feelings—as oddly normal as Shakespeare's Pyramus and Thisbe speaking through the chink in the wall.

Eventually, it was time for Vasílis to pick up Lítza and close the shop. We felt thoroughly cheered. We said our goodbyes and agreed to try to meet up with them at least for an evening drink when we returned to Skópelos on the day before Lucy and Robert's arrival.

Farewell to Alónissos

THE NEXT MORNING we packed our cases and bags, cleared out the fridge, and cleaned the *mílos*. I crammed the last of our belongings into a couple of boxes I'd kept aside and walked them up to Tákis's truck. They just barely fit on top of the load, high in one rear corner: incredible. You couldn't have got a bag of groceries in that truck and still been able to close the shutter.

We were booked on the four o'clock Flying Cat to Alónissos. We had arranged to meet Rita on the *paralía* when she finished work and spend an hour together while we waited for the Cat.

At one o'clock we were ready. Linda's knee hurt like hell. I had misgivings about her walking on it, but she insisted she'd take care, and started off for Sofía's house; it wasn't that far, and she'd asked Rita to meet her there from work. They could hang out a bit and Rita could provide a little support, if needed, on the walk down to the *paralía*. I had the cellphone, and the number of one of the island's cab drivers. I would join them at the Karávi bar with our luggage once Mára arrived to pick up the keys to the *mílos*.

I was waiting for the cab and chatting with Mára when Spýros arrived. After confirming the dinner invitation with us and our friends on our return—the occasion was St. Strátos's day and all the family would be there—Spýros rang the doorbell to our old residence.

"He has to meet the plumber," said Mára. "The toilet is leaking."

I allowed a light smile onto my lips. "The toilet has leaked for ten months," I observed.

Mára chuckled. "Yes."

I glanced at Spýros. His expression at that moment reminded me very much of his beloved *seeps*.

RITA COULDN'T QUITE believe we were leaving for real. Like Alice and Joe, she said, "But we'll see you again, won't we?" even though we'd explained we were only coming back for a few days when our friends arrived. It was both touching and irritating.

We talked and laughed over drinks and a snack. I took pictures. Linda held a bag of ice cubes to her knee.

The Cat arrived and Rita helped us across the road to the quay. We hugged her and told we loved her. We promised to meet again, though we had no idea where.

Thirty minutes later, Brigitte met us at the harbor on Alónissos and whisked us up the hill to the sanctity of Artemis. We set our bags down in the guest rooms and joined her for drinks and snacks on the terrace with the million-dollar view. Linda and I were both drained, and happy to be spoilt and taken care of. Brigitte refused help with dinner, leaving us to sit and catch up with the last few days' news from her stack of New York Herald Tribunes by the door. The cats kept us company, lazing on the low wall where they could monitor the activities of small creatures in the bushes on the steep hillside below. The spirits of my mother and her pets were at peace nearby.

Linda spent much of the next day reading while I took myself for a long walk, eventually opening a gate and crossing someone's land to reach a portion of rocky shore a mile or so from Artemis, where a double row of bleached, wave-pitted rocks parallel the coast like a pair of half-submerged whales. It was at this spot I'd taken my first swim in the Aegean forty-one years earlier, when Mános had led me and my parents out here on our first day on Alónissos.

The sea was rough, and the pitted rocks were sharp above the waterline and dotted with sea urchins below. Good timing would be needed to get back ashore uninjured. I hesitated before going in, but it seemed important that I did. Sometimes the past demands that we honor it.

We took Brigitte to dinner that evening at a hotel/restaurant a little behind her house, to which she'd taken us on a previous trip. As during the last weeks on Skópelos, everything we did, every place we visited, was haunted by our impending departure. I could almost *see* the iron-gray pall of melancholy that shadowed us, but somehow never quite doused our spirit. However ugly life gets, you have choices: you let it crush you, or you don't. It was a struggle. But friendship, laughter, and good food still seemed a damned sight better than morbid self-pity.

Brigitte had to take an overnight trip to Vólos for a medical appointment. She'd been putting it off for weeks because she didn't want to leave the cats, but had now booked it for the day after next. This was probably a good thing for all three of us. With Brigitte's rigid ways and routines, occasional friction was inevitable, and I could see I'd upset her by snapping back once or twice over trivialities. Like the time she told me off for forgetting that bottled water for drinking was kept in the fridge, but bottled water for boiling in the kettle went in the pantry. It was, after all, her house; and she'd been single-handedly taking care of a very sick man for eighteen years, an experience which would lead anyone to become set in their behaviors.

The incessantly baying hound was another thing.

One of Brigitte's neighbors had almost finished building an ostentatiously large house on the adjoining lot, some hundred yards away from the building where our little guest suite was located. Near the new house stood a miserable kennel made from an old camper shell and strewn about with garbage and old buckets, the whole circled about with a wire fence. An old wooden pallet poorly secured with wire served as a door to the filthy enclosure.

Brigitte had told us the story. The dog—a German shorthair pointer—had given birth to a litter of puppies a few weeks ago, and the owner, a local taxi driver, came by only occasionally. On one occasion, when the despair in the bitch's howls had become unbearable, Brigitte had gone over and braved the filth and stench to feed and water the starving animals. "I never was so disgusted in all my life," she said. "I washed and washed after, and still I didn't feel clean."

She'd called the police station, but there was nothing they could do: Greece didn't have laws against animal cruelty. A confrontation with the owner in the village streets a few days later only brought a torrent of abuse. A strong, courageous woman, Brigitte nonetheless slept with her doors locked at night. She'd made more than one enemy over the years.

The day that Brigitte left for Vólos, the barking—which we had become more or less accustomed to—turned to nonstop howls of anguish. After a few minutes we could stand no more of it. I walked across to the pen, nervous as to what I might find, or have to do.

Up close, the problem was obvious. The puppies had grown large and curious enough to go off exploring on their own, and discovered they could squeeze between the pallet-door edges and the wire fence and get out of the enclosure; the mother, too large to follow, was going mad with anxiety. It was chaos, with playful pups everywhere—inside, outside, wriggling through the gaps like a circus troupe. It was impossible to even count them. In another context, this might have been amusing; but with the mother chained and the filthy, neglected condition of the place, it was heartbreaking.

I cursed the owner over and over. I'd seen a good many dogs kept chained all day long on Skópelos, but never such mindless ignorance and cruelty. Overcome by anger, I wanted to make the owner suffer in the same way, to chain him up in this filthy pen and leave him uncared for until he begged for mercy. How could a European nation not have laws against this sort of thing? What the fuck did the politicians *do* in Brussels and Athens, day after day, year after year? If they spent a little less time arguing over subsidies and tariffs and instead devoted their attention to animal and human rights in their member nations, the dream of Europe might one day be a thing of pride rather than mere words on paper.

I started to grab puppies, easing them back through the narrow gaps, but the task was impossible: as I went to catch the next, the first one would wriggle out again through one gap or other, escaping as quickly as I could capture them. It was like Sisyphus on fast-forward.

I looked to the pallet-door itself; perhaps if I fastened it securely so that the gaps closed up, I could then just drop the escaped pups back into the enclosure one at a time. I pushed and tugged and tried reattaching wire, but the whole thing was such a lash-up, the pallet ends broken, the fence posts so flimsy, that it couldn't be fixed without tearing the pallet off and starting afresh.

I looked at the bitch. She was a handsome animal, healthy-looking despite her wicked mistreatment. She looked at me with knowing, intelligent eyes.

I shook my head and apologized: sometimes you have to know when to stop. The puppies would go back in when they got hungry. I began to walk away. The bitch stood silent, watching me while her pups frolicked and scampered about.

Brigitte returned the next day. We had only two more days left on Alónissos before my trip to Thessaloníki with Tákis.

Our experiences in Greece, and our decision to leave and cut our losses, had given added material to Brigitte's own speculations as to her future on the island. "Mános always said, 'I am afraid for you Brigitte, after I am gone.' He knew that I would have all these problems with the car, with the taxes, now with the *kástro*. Maybe I will stay, maybe not. I do not know. I do not know."

On the last evening, Brigitte took us to a pizzeria on the outskirts of the old village. The place was owned and run by an Italian, and served real, wood-fired pizza of a quality rarely found outside Italy.

The evenings were cooling now, and we had to think a moment before deciding on an outdoor table. The buildings of the *hóra*, pale cubes silhouetted against the blue-black close of twilight, climbed the hill a few hundred yards away. To the south, beyond the darkening fields, cliffs tumbled down to the inky sea.

We ate and drank, barely touching on the obvious: this was our last night, and very possibly our last ever time on Alónissos with Brigitte. My own association with Alónissos, which had so improbably lasted half a lifetime, was finally at an end.

The Platinum Club

WE RETURNED TO Skópelos early on Sunday afternoon. It was election day, and the cafés were full of people watching the event unfold on television over coffee and *oúzo*. Jacqui met us at the harbor with her car and took us first up to Tákis's house, where we had left a box of foodstuffs, coffee, and the like, and then on to the Ánesis cottages across the bay.

Jacqui had a girlfriend from Nevada visiting, and it was her friend's last day on Skópelos. They invited us to join them for a dip and a drink, but I wanted some time to get myself ready for the trip to Thessaloníki. Linda was willing, though, and a little *Amerikanída* time would be good for her. I kissed her goodbye; she wished me luck, and went off with the girls.

It was a strange feeling, returning to spend our last week on Skópelos in the same little cottage we had rented as tourists two years before moving here. The two Ánesis cottages—little *kalívi*s, really— were identical, and charming. French windows led from the kitchen to a small, tiled and roofed-over patio on which stood a simple table and four chairs, a perfect setting from which to enjoy the view across the harbor to the village. Our old home and the *mílos*—the only big, cylindrical structure in the entire village—were clearly visible.

The ferry to Thessaloníki left at six, and I was scheduled to meet Tákis on the dock at five-thirty. The ferry would arrive in Thessaloníki at three-thirty a.m. I'd originally feared that I'd have to return via Vólos, a long bus ride from Thessaloníki, but it turned out the same ferry was returning to Skópelos the next night, on its way to the Cyclades and Crete. I was in luck.

I'd asked about getting a cabin but Tákis told me not to worry, since truckers automatically had one included with their ticket. We'd be working hard to load the container—we only had two hours in which to do so before the driver returned to collect it—and I wanted to get some sleep beforehand. I'd asked Tákis what we'd do in Thessaloníki until eight in the morning, when the container would be available for loading. "We can go to my house," he said. "We will have coffee and some food, and then we will load."

Tákis picked me up on the dock and we drove out to the end of the quay, where the Thessaloníki ferry would tie up. His father Vangélis arrived a few moments later, and the two smoked and talked together. Spýros rode up on his little Honda with Mára riding side-saddle behind; they were dressed in their Sunday best and had been out for a drive. We chatted until the ferry arrived. It was a beautiful evening for a sea voyage.

Tákis met me up in the lounge after parking the truck. He'd brought his travelling chess set, a handsome bag of wooden pieces and a flexible plastic board which he unrolled on the table. I bought us drinks and we began to play. A little while later, a young woman with a baby arrived and greeted Tákis. A Skopelíte who'd lived in Australia for many years, she spoke fine English. We had a disjointed, three-way conversation while Tákis finished beating me.

We ate in the ship's modest cafeteria, then returned to the lounge to find the woman and her baby still there. Tákis wanted to play more chess. I concentrated on my moves while he and his friend talked and smoked. I won the last game.

About ten-thirty, since Tákis showed no inclination to rest, I had him show me to the cabin. I brushed my teeth and climbed with my book into the upper bunk, happy to get even a few hours' sleep.

Tákis woke me a little after three. The other bed was undisturbed; he'd been up all night talking to the woman in the lounge. He went down to his truck and would meet me dockside. I splashed water on my face, dressed, and left the cabin as the clank-clank-clank of anchor chains announced our arrival.

We drove out of the port onto the deserted streets. Tákis lit a cigarette. He seemed more awake than previously, a nighthawk through and through.

"We have four hours until the container will be ready," he said. "I am thinking what can we do all this time."

"I thought we were going to your house."

"Also I was thinking this. But it is on the other side of Thessaloníki, and there will be very bad traffic to come back." He looked around as he drove. "What we can do?" he repeated to himself.

"Is there a bar or café on the way?"

"Yes, but from four o'clock, it will be a long time to wait."

We drove a mile or so along a wide, empty avenue. The area looked vaguely industrial. A long, boxy structure with illuminated stars on its walls appeared on our left, and Tákis slowed, turning to look at it. His face lit up.

"Ah! We will go to the Platinum Club!" he announced, pulling over to the curb. I turned to look at the building. Other than the stars and a sign with that same name over the doorway, it could have been a warehouse.

"The Platinum club?" I said.

Tákis looked happy. "It is a striptease club, very nice. I think you will like this place."

I laughed. I've led anything but a sheltered life, but I'd never been to a strip club. It seemed somehow old-fashioned, something my parents' generation did, like drinking Manhattans and frequenting Turkish baths.

Tákis had turned the ignition off and was rooting about in his bag. It occurred to me that I was carrying some three thousand Euros in cash to pay the shippers, and that leaving it in the truck wasn't a good idea. I had the cash in a money belt in the front pocket of my pack, and could simply strap it on under my waistband, though I wondered if walking into a strip joint with it was any wiser. I unbuckled my belt, explaining what I was doing. Tákis chuckled as I strapped on the money belt. "Don't worry," he said, "it is a very nice place. Many times I come here."

Tákis paid the admission fee for both of us, a solid thirty Euros each including the first drink. The place was spacious, dim, and smoky. He led us to a couch at the near end of the stage, a big, low platform in a blaze of ruby light where an improbably muscular, near-naked young man slunk panther-like through a swirling fog of dry ice, discarding items of clothing in time to the music. Tákis caught my look. "Eh, yes, also they have men dancing. But the most they are women."

Right on cue, a waitress appeared. She wore little more than lingerie, heels, and a smile. We ordered drinks, our heads swiveling after her—as mens' heads will—as she went to fill our order.

The dancer on stage finished his routine, and I was heartened that he still wore a pouch as well as his jauntily-angled bowler hat. The audience responded with loud applause. He bowed once and left the stage for the smoke-shrouded rear of the building.

I looked around. Despite its location, the Platinum Club was well-decorated and expensively furnished. At four on a Monday morning, the place was at least half-full of well-heeled twenty- and thirty-somethings, not a few of whom were women.

Our waitress arrived with our drinks. She set my drink on the coffee table in front of me before leaning far over to hand Tákis his, straining her demi-cup support architecture to the limit in the process. This motion, barely a foot in front of me, made me feel a little faint. Tákis fished out a tip, and I did the same, in return for which we got a brilliant smile.

The next dancer—female, I was happy to see—took the stage. Tákis and I talked a little, sipping our drinks while we watched the show. She swayed, she stretched, she rolled around on the stage, she wrapped her legs around the poles at each corner of the stage, riding the shiny metal suggestively. Occasionally an item of clothing came off. The routine was polished to the point of perfunctory. It was more athletic than sensual, and the platform-soled, thigh-length latex boots looked silly. A caricature, almost an abstraction of sexuality, rather than anything visceral. I'd expected more.

As the dancer left the stage in boots and a g-string to the audience's applause, two striking young girls wearing no more than did the waitress approached us. One made for Tákis, trailing her arm around his shoulders as she walked around the couch. The other sank onto the couch at my side, making sure I noticed her cleavage. It would have been hard not to: it was a particularly noticeable cleavage, with very little fabric to conceal the smooth globes surrounding it.

It's difficult to ignore an approach of this sort. The girl had good English, and of course asked me to buy her a drink; the waitress appeared as if by telepathy, and I complied. Tákis ordered also.

The next dancer came onto the stage. I strained to keep some decorum while my uninvited partner snuggled up to me and slipped her hand onto my thigh. Tákis looked perfectly calm and cool.

The drinks arrived. I winced at the price: thirty Euros for a single cocktail! I was glad I hadn't ordered one for myself as well. The girl melted against me, tracing a finger along my jaw and making small talk. I had no idea what to do: the situation was awkward rather than erotic. I made small talk back and hoped she'd just go away.

Within about five minutes she'd finished her drink. "If you will buy me another drink," she whispered, "we can go to the back, and I will make you a private dance." I politely declined the offer. After a brief attempt at further persuasion, she smiled and thanked me before rising to leave. Tákis's partner drained the rest of her drink and followed a moment after.

I turned to Tákis. He raised an eyebrow from within his cocoon of smoke.

"This place could get expensive," I said. "Thirty Euros a drink! I can't imagine there's much alcohol in them, either."

He chuckled. "One time I come here, I spend six hundred Euros."

My jaw dropped. "Six *hundred?*"

"Ehh! All night I drink with this one girl. Very beautiful. In the end, at six o'clock, she is coming home with me. But now I am so drunk, I can not do anything!" He was laughing. "You can understand this, Dario? So I tell her, 'Go home, go home! I can not!' Ahh!" He threw up his hand in a gesture of exasperation.

We chuckled about this. Another girl came on stage and did her routine, followed by a male dancer.

The place had emptied somewhat. Across the stage from us were two young couples on a couch. The last time I'd looked, one couple had been locked in a long, sensual kiss. Now I saw that the woman, fully clothed, had straddled her partner, whom she was still kissing, and seemed to be trying to grind him into the couch like a handful of spice in a mortar. The couple beside them were laughing. Passionate folk, these Greeks.

Eventually, the house lights brightened and an amplified voice announced the end of the floor show and the imminent closure of the establishment. It was five forty-five.

"So," said Tákis, "we pass two hours. Now we will find one place for breakfast and then we go to load the container."

Mission Accomplished

WE DROVE FOR a time, passing through more residential areas until we reached a small, brightly-lit corner café with sidewalk tables. Tákis pulled the truck up on the sidewalk a few yards away and reached into his bag for the chess set. There was light traffic, the advance guard of the morning commute. It was still dark.

We ordered coffee and some oversweet, fried pastries which Tákis assured me were a traditional specialty, and sat outside, playing chess as the stream of cars intensified and the sky lightened about us, the night's cool yielding to the promise of a warm day. We were both tired. I was looking forward to getting this job done.

At seven-thirty we packed up the chess set and got back in the truck. We drove for a while before turning off the road onto a narrow street, more of a long alley. To the right ran a row of low, scruffy, light-industrial buildings; on the left was an acre or so of waste ground dotted with scrub and thin grass, beyond which loomed low-rise housing projects.

Tákis eased the truck onto the waste ground and drove a couple of dozen yards before stopping by a clump of bushes facing the projects. If I hadn't known him well, I'd have feared for my life, especially given the cash I was carrying: the place was the perfect location for a crime.

Tákis switched off the ignition and lit a cigarette. "Eh. Now we will wait," he said.

I looked at my watch. It was ten to eight. "They're bringing the container here?"

"Yes. We are near the lahanágora, the vegetables market. Also my friend who makes the furnitures has his business here." Tákis gestured toward the industrial buildings along the alley.

The minutes passed, and no container appeared. I got out and stretched my legs. A pickup drove over the scrub towards us, and Tákis clambered out of the cab to greet the driver, a slight, friendly-looking man in his thirties. His name was Theodóros, and he owned the company that made Tákis's furniture.

They began to chat. Eight-thirty came and went, and there was no sign of the container. Theodóros left us for his workplace across the road. I was getting impatient.

Tákis made a brief call. "They say the container is coming," he told me. "I will get us a coffee."

Tákis walked across the road to Theodóros's workshop. I waited in the truck and tried, unsuccessfully, to read. Would the container really come? What the hell would we do if it didn't? It was all very Greek.

A half hour later, Tákis returned with our coffee just as a big rig carrying a rust-red container turned into our alley from the main road and lumbered across the dirt to park beside us.

I perked up, my fatigue sloughing off as purpose took over. Tákis went to greet the driver. A few moments later, the driver had deposited the container on its chassis, swung the big doors open, and left us to it.

We rolled up the shutter on the truck and I guided Tákis back to within three feet of the container. We placed a metal ramp across the gap, changed into shorts (it was getting hot) and started to load.

Before long we were both sweating and shirts came off. Tákis stacked and arranged the load, carefully selecting and positioning boxes so as to fill the space floor to ceiling and wall to wall, allowing no room for the cargo to shift. Despite the short night's sleep and the hours of hanging around, I was happy and full of energy—the goal that just a few weeks ago seemed to be slipping toward impossibility was now within reach. Once this was done, our only worry would be Linda's long-expired permit.

In less than two hours, we were done. We secured rope and straps to anchor points on the container walls, crossing and tightening them until we'd stretched a taut web against the wall of boxes to prevent them tumbling into the empty rear third of the container. I slapped Tákis on his sweaty back and hugged him. What a friend!

I'd brought with me the very padlock we'd used on our container coming out here. When the driver returned, he closed and latched the doors, and I attached the padlock and snapped it shut. He placed a tamper-evident plastic seal to the lock and gave me the address of the office where I was to go to sign papers and make the payment. We shook hands and he eased the rig off the patch of waste land and back onto the road. If all went well our container would be loaded onto a shuttle vessel to Piraéus the next day and then join hundreds of others on the sturdy deck of a container vessel for the transatlantic voyage.

The next time I would see our belongings would be six weeks and six thousand miles away.

WE DROVE BACK across the street and backed the truck into the forecourt of Theodóros's workshop. Tákis looked exhausted. I helped him unload the items of furniture he was returning and we drank a coffee in Theodóros's cluttered little office.

The shipping office was in the very center of town, some twenty minutes' drive away, and Tákis and Theodóros had business to do. Theodóros drove me out to an intersection on the busy arterial road nearby, and we set about the daunting task of trying to find a taxi to take me downtown.

Getting a taxi in Greece requires an extreme combination of timing, persistence, and luck. Rarely will the taxi you hailed actually stop; the Greek cabbies' preferred *modus operandi* is to slow to a crawl just long enough for you to shout your destination at them through the open passenger-side window. In almost all cases, this elicits either a frown, laughter, incomprehensible mutterings, rude gestures, or total indifference, followed by a screech of tires as the cabbie hits the gas before you can make a grab for the doorhandle. Almost to a man, they take a perverse delight in refusing fares for any number of reasons. If you aren't going in the direction they want to go in, forget it; if you're going too far, forget it; if you're not going far enough, forget it; if they don't reckon on a good chance of finding a second or even third passenger along the way—every passenger is charged on a solo basis, even on shared journeys—forget it; and so on.

It took us half an hour and a score of refusals before we found a driver willing to take me downtown. The driver was a woman, thirtyish and intelligent-looking. I was amazed to find her both cheerful and polite.

As she drove, I expressed my gratitude for the ride and aired my frustrations about Greek cab drivers in general. She was sympathetic. "Many of them are pigs," she said, matter-of-factly. "My father was a cab driver all his life. He would always try to take people. He had a good business."

Most of all, she obviously enjoyed her work, and drove with such skill and confidence that I didn't fear for my life once during the entire journey. I tipped her generously, and she gave me her business card. "My name is Antónia," she said. "If you need a taxi again, call me."

I jumped at the chance of not having to go through the whole ghastly routine again. "I'll need one as soon as I'm finished here... Perhaps in an hour?"

She smiled. "Call me when you have finished. If I am near and I can come, I will."

The shippers' office was located in a small, second floor suite above a shop in the city center, a refreshingly upscale neighborhood after the variety of seedy places I'd frequented over the last several hours. I gave the contact's name—Níkos Paskalídis—to the receptionist and she directed me around a corner to an adjacent office.

Níkos was young, perhaps Tákis's age, with smooth manners, a ready smile, and good English.

"Everything went well," he said, "our driver told me. Your container will leave for Piraéus tomorrow."

"Thank you," I said. "That's *such* good news."

He showed me into a bright corner office, where an older and much rounder man was engaged in an animated phone conversation. The older man grinned and waved me to a seat.

"You would like a Greek coffee?" said Níkos.

"I'd love one! *Skéto, parakaló*." Unsweetened, please.

Níkos broke into a grin. "Ah, you speak Greek. *Kalá!* This is my father," he said, gesturing at the man on the phone. "He has had the business many years. He will only be a minute."

The father's desk was thick with tidy stacks of files and papers; on the walls hung framed photos of bulk carriers and container ships. The place was clean and wholesome.

Níkos returned with three coffees, and Mr. Paskalídis senior finished his call. He gripped my hand, and I introduced myself in Greek. He flashed me a gold-toothed smile, and apologized that he spoke no English. There was something extremely likeable about both father and son: both had a piratical air, and though I didn't doubt they were canny businessmen, I felt immediately that I could trust them.

Mr. Paskalídis pulled my file from one of the stacks on his desk and handed me various papers to sign. One was the faxed copy of my inventory. Níkos explained the others, and I added my signature to those. There was no mention of notarized declarations about the lack of guns and contraband. Níkos went next door, photocopied everything, and handed me the copies. The whole process took just a few minutes.

I counted out the cash and asked Níkos to check it. Everything added up, there were big smiles all around, and the dad wrote me out a receipt, signing and stamping it with a practiced flourish. I thanked him and turned to Níkos.

"Please tell your father," I said, "how happy I am to have found you." I went on to explain the problems Isaac had had trying to find a customs broker to handle the Greek end of things. As Níkos translated, both father and son started to grin.

I was puzzled. "Níkos, you're both smiling. Now tell me: why wouldn't anyone deal with my shipper in California? He's a very experienced, honest man. What's the story here?"

Níkos shrugged, still smiling his piratical smile. I looked from him to his father and back. "Come on," I insisted, "why is it so difficult to find somebody to do this?"

Níkos spread his palms. "This is Greece," he said. "Tell your shipper that if he has problems here, we will be happy to help him. Why not? Why not?" His smile grew broader than ever. Across the desk, the father chuckled. No English indeed! I shook my head and threw up my hands, and all three of us began to laugh.

A PHONE CALL and twenty minutes later, Antónia picked me up on the same corner she'd left me at and dropped me off at Theodóros's workshop just as they were finishing their morning's business. "So, you are ready to take lunch?" said Tákis. "There is one very good place near here."

I clapped him on the shoulder. "More than ready—I'm starving! And lunch is on me."

We walked a short distance to a nearby taverna. The neighborhood was a cheerful brawl of activity, like London's East End, or a market district in any metropolis.

We sat at one of two small tables on the busy sidewalk. I was in high spirits. The food was wonderful, the beers cold. We toasted the completion of my quest.

Tákis was staying in Thessaloníki a couple of days before loading up for the return trip. We left the truck at Theodóros's workshop and Theodóros drove us several miles across town to Tákis's parents house, with Tákis fast asleep for the entire ride.

The Doúkas family apartment was on the sixth floor of a 1960s block overlooking a busy avenue in a fashionable district. It was big and tastefully decorated. Máhi, Tákis's mother, gave me a warm hug and showed me around. Tákis grinned as I admired the shelves of swimming trophies in his bedroom.

We sat on the spacious balcony, enjoying the rest. It was about three-thirty and my ferry sailed at seven. Máhi brought us coffee and cakes. While she and I chatted, Tákis was mostly quiet, smoking and smiling the silly smile of someone so tired they barely know what day it is.

Máhi was a city woman through and through. She had a quiet, radiant kind of dignity and an aristocratic bearing. I remembered Tákis's refined table manners, and wished for the thousandth time that my Greek had been good enough to really get under the surface with these people, to understand their past and the influences, both coarse and subtle, that made them who they were. It would never happen now.

Máhi confirmed my impression of her as a city person. "I prefer the life in Thessaloníki," she said. "There's nothing to do on Skópelos." I could understand the attractions: the city below pulsed with life and energy; Vangélis, her husband, loved his *hórta* and Tákis his swimming, but Máhi needed the city to make her feel alive. And though she clearly doted on her son, I also wondered if she needed the weeks away from Vangélis.

The time was pleasant and I felt a deep nostalgia for the balcony days in Italy, where, from my earliest childhood all the way through my twenties, I would spend months every summer with one or other set of grandparents. Whether overlooking empty meadows in Northern Italy or a hillside on Capri, balconies were an anchor of those years, places where time became formless and benign, where card games and reading, laughter and aperitifs, aunts and gossip, all swam together in the endless afternoon of the sticky Italian summer.

Towards five Máhi offered to drive me to the port. Tákis had settled onto the couch and turned on the TV, clearly headed for a solid sleep. I hugged him goodbye and hoped to see him in Skópelos before we left for good.

In the elevator, Máhi told me how sorry she was to see us leave, though she understood our reasons. "You must do what is right for you. A few years ago, I had breast cancer. Now I live every moment of every day."

"I didn't know," I told her, feeling it was a lame reply.

"Eh, yes," she said, and shrugged.

Máhi's car was a cute Renault, new-looking and spotlessly clean. I remarked on it. "It was a birthday present from Tákis," she said.

"He's a good son."

She smiled. "I am very lucky."

I WALKED DOWN the jetty and boarded the ferry, climbing to the top deck, where I stood, waiting for our departure and admiring the view.

A row of ancient warehouses, long rendered obsolete by containerization, marched for hundreds of feet along the wharf. The low sun cut through decades of grime, making the brickwork sing russet and brown and restoring dignity and beauty to the long, many-windowed façade. A luxury cruise ship was moored a short distance away, making a perfect composition. As I reached for my camera I noticed a young woman further along the rail taking a picture of her friend against the same backdrop. A trio of nuns climbed onto the deck and sat themselves in a silent, tidy row.

The sun was close to setting as we cast off. I remained on deck several minutes longer, soaking in the beauty of the scene. Happy to be done, sad in the knowledge we would be leaving this country for good in just over a week.

The purser wouldn't give me the key to the cabin for which I'd paid sixty Euros. The cabins were for two people; they didn't know if I had to share yet, and would have to see if another occupant turned up. Unable to grasp this logic, I tried to impress on him that I was deeply tired, needed a good night's sleep, and was liable to turn homicidal if I didn't get my cabin in an hour or so, when I returned from dinner.

After a drink in the bar and a so-so meal in the same functional cafeteria as before, I returned to the purser's office to find nobody there. Muttering slurs about the man's ancestry, I went out onto the deck.

The black, warm night was alive with the cries of gulls. The lights of Thessaloníki twinkled amber in the distance. I moved to the rail and saw a rippling river of seagulls keeping pace with us, flapping along just a few feet above the ship's side wake. It looked like fun, but after a few moments I began to wonder at the strange expenditure of energy in this profitless pursuit.

And then I saw it: a flash of silver leaping out of the frothy wake only to vanish in mid-arc as an open-beaked seagull perfectly intercepted it. I gaped. A few seconds later I saw it happen again: fish! The seagulls had been following along, knowing, I supposed, that sooner or later the ship's wake would pass through a shoal of fish. Quite why the fish left the water I wasn't sure, but the gulls were quick at spotting their prey and expert at catching them in mid-leap.

The whole, streaming flock of birds had dipped now, and was barely skimming the waves. I watched, rapt, for several minutes, as the gulls worked the wake. Every time a gull 's beak closed on a fish, the bird would peel away from the flock and settle on the water nearby to enjoy its supper.

In time, the catch thinned, and after a few minutes in which no further fish appeared, the gulls reluctantly, by twos and threes, wheeled away, until the only sounds were the modulated churning of the wake and the steady thrum of the ship's engines.

The purser was there when I returned, and a few moments later I was in my tiny cabin. I had about eight hours until the ferry docked in Skópelos at five a.m., and I chuckled to myself as I curled up with my book. The container was loaded, the sea was calm, Linda was waiting for me at the cottage, and our friends were arriving the day after next. Life, sometimes, was good.

IT WAS A little before dawn as I walked along the jetty toward the paralía, passing several opulent yachts. On some, crew were just beginning to stir; on others, people were still partying from the night before. I stopped and had a croissant and an espresso at the Kohíli bakery before making my way up the hill.

We had no plans that day, but ended up having an ad hoc dinner with Alice and Joe down on the paralía. We'd known them for less time than all our other friends on Skópelos; perhaps because of that, and the parallels between our situations, I felt oddly strange saying goodbye, as though we were running out on them.

As we ate, I saw Mr. Haralámpos, the lawyer who had given us the second opinion on Linda's residency, take a seat at a nearby couch.

Joe grimaced. "That's the lawyer who's supposed to be doing Alice's residency," said Joe, inclining his head slightly in his direction.

"Why don't you go over and ask him how it's going, Joey?" said Alice.

"He said he'd have it at the end of this month," Joe replied.

Alice rolled her eyes. "He says that every month. Go on, Joey, ask him."

Joe eased himself out of his chair and walked over to Mr. Haralámpos with evident reluctance. The lawyer smiled, and they spoke for less than a minute before Joe turned to rejoin us.

"Well?" said Alice.

"He says he's waiting for the papers from Vólos. He still says we should have everything by the end of the month." Joe looked unconvinced.

Alice rolled her eyes again. We made sympathetic noises.

An hour or so later, as we all prepared to leave, Alice said, "we'll be seeing you again, won't we? You're here another five days, right?"

We gently reminded her, as we had Rita, that we had friends arriving tomorrow and would be pretty well booked until we left with them a few days later.

The goodbyes weren't getting easier.

Leaving on a High Note

From Linda's Journal, Sept 19, 2007:

Our dear friends Lucy and Robert are arriving today. It is bittersweet. I have looked forward for so long to welcoming friends to the island. But this is our last week on Skópelos. My heart breaks a little, but I am thankful to have the companionship of two very dear people as I navigate my way through the turmoil of what is ahead. Bless them for coming.

Dario and I awake early and restlessly wait for the Dolphin to arrive. We are SO ready to see them. But we have over an hour yet, so we sip coffee on the rear deck of the Ánesis cottage while we plan our week of adventures.

A casual glance at the water reveals a Flying Dolphin entering the harbor... What? Early? Yikes! We make a mad dash to the rental car, jump in, and Dario drives like a Greek to the harbor, dumping me off at the landing area while he goes to park. We stand at the exit ramp, *excited as kids at Christmas, camera in hand. But no Lucy, no Robert. Where the heck are they? Well of course, on the Flying <u>Cat</u>. In our childlike enthusiasm we of course forget that this is the earlier Dolphin. Jeez…*

An hour later, and they're here! I have so missed these dear friends. Hugs abound, we stow the luggage in our little rental Fiat, barely give them a chance to rinse their hands at the cottage, and of course whisk them off to Miliá beach, as the forecast is for cloud and cool days ahead. We swim, drink, and catch the glorious rays. I will miss this place.

The next day is the name day for Strátos, the Balabánises' future son-in-law. Lucy, Robert, Dario and I join the family to celebrate. There are 20 or so of us. We eat, drink and make merry. Traditional Greek songs are sung. It is the quintessential Greek family gathering. These people are our family. In spite of the language barriers, the cultural differences and the occasional blank stares, I love these people.

The evening comes to a close as a heavy rainstorm lashes the island. I make my way around the table, giving my thanks, saying my goodbyes. I fear reaching Mára at the end. I don't know if I have it in me to hold back the tears. I don't. I can't hold Mára tight enough, can't give her enough thanks and can't come close to telling her how much I love her. Tears come to both of us and flow freely. My heart breaks a little more.

Our adventures with Robert and Lucy continue. We explore the village, hike to Sendoúkia, visit the Roman baths at Loutráki, take fabulous Greek meals and Ouzos in outdoor cafés. We share a late, late night of drinks and laughter at the Café Gorgónes with dear friends Vasílis and Lítza. On our last night, we enjoy an elegant outdoor meal at Perivóli, with none other than Pierce Brosnan and his family sitting at the adjoining table.

It is wonderful, as we prepare to leave, to see Skópelos through the eyes of two of our dearest friends. Lucy and Robert savor every moment. As the days pass, I can see they understand why we risked so much to attempt a life in this most magical and unforgettable place.

WE ROSE BEFORE dawn to catch the seven a.m. Dolphin to Ághios Kostantínos. The morning was chill and windy, and as the sun came up I could see the chop in the harbor and the whitecaps out beyond the breakwater. Marginal travel weather. Marginal.

I was right: an hour later, we drove back up to the cottages and unloaded our luggage from the cars. The Dolphin had been cancelled because of the rough conditions, but the ferry office was confident the wind would die down; besides which, the much bigger Flying Cat, which arrived at four and left for Ághios Kónstantinos shortly after, could handle worse conditions than the little Dolphin.

We went to bed for a couple more hours, then took ourselves down to the *paralía* one last time for drinks and *mezés*. I'd been expecting to run into Yiánnis or Mina or *somebody* we knew at the last minute. It was unusual to spend an hour on the *paralía* without bumping into friends, and strange not saying one last goodbye to any of those closest to us on the actual day of our departure. It was as though they'd all left town.

The Cat pulled out of the harbor. Linda and I sat in a side row, just behind Lucy and Robert, watching the *hóra* slide out of view behind us as the vessel skirted the breakwater and began to pick up speed.

I felt at once both overfull and drained of emotion. Our ten months on Skópelos had been such a rollercoaster of ups and downs, hopes and fears, that it all canceled out, leaving me numb. Somewhere just inside me there had to rage a storm of anger and grief; but the relief and satisfaction of overcoming so many obstacles during these final weeks, coupled with the immense kindness and love shown us by our Greek friends, had gone a long way to calming the waters of my spirit.

In truth, I was in something close to shock, and it would be some time before I could really begin to debrief myself.

Linda, doubtless full of similar feelings, had immersed herself in a book. I turned towards the bar at the rear of the lounge, thinking I might get some iced tea, and saw Pierce Brosnan and his young son buying snacks. I remembered Vasílis telling us Mr. Brosnan had asked him to go to Athens with them on their way back from Skópelos and act as a city guide for the family. But Vasílis was going to take the Land Rover, which meant he'd probably gone ahead on a ferry.

I turned to Linda. "Pierce Brosnan's on the Cat with us, and after we were next to them at dinner last night. Weird, eh?"

She turned, angling to look between the seats. "Oh my God!" she said in a stage whisper, "he's stalking us!" She leaned forward and told Lucy and Robert.

"Well, of course he is," said Robert, laughing. "Who *wouldn't* want to stalk us?"

ABOUT AN HOUR out of Ághios Kónstantinos, as twilight turned the sea to blued steel, we began to close on a slower-moving ferry off to the port side. We were just drawing level with it when our cellphone rang. It was Vasílis.

"Can you see me?" he said.

"I, uh."

"I'm on the ferry! The one you're just passing!"

I laughed. I told him we'd seen Pierce Brosnan on board the Cat.

"Yah," he said. "I left an hour earlier on the ferry. We're supposed to arrive about fifteen minutes after you do."

I passed the phone to Linda, and by the time she said goodbye, the ferry had slipped behind us and the lights of Ághios Kónstantinos were growing closer.

The ferry was dropping anchor and snuggling up to the quay as we disembarked from the Cat and walked the few yards to the waiting buses. It was now dark. A few minutes later, as the bus pulled out of the harbor, we saw a slim figure standing ramrod-straight at the end of the quay, making professional-looking 'approach slowly' gestures with both hands like an airport staffer guiding a plane to the terminal gate.

It was Mr. Brosnan, hamming it up for all he was worth: the concrete quay was his stage, the headlamps of the approaching Land Rover the star's spotlight.

The audience went wild.

AN HOUR LATER, halfway to Athens, the bus swung in to the familiar roadside rest stop.

We'd brought some leftover food from the cottage, but no liquid accompaniment. Lucy saved us an outside table while I tasked Linda and Robert with finding *retsína*, and fast. We only had fifteen minutes, and all of us were in high spirits. I went off to the rest room.

When I came out, the wine-gathering party ran up to me, near panic. "I can't find any *retsína*!" said Linda. "Do you have to ask for it at the counter?"

"Maybe they don't have any?" said Robert.

I snorted a laugh. "We're in Greece," I said. "Of course they have *retsína*."

I glanced about. "Aha!" I said, pointing. No surprise they hadn't seen it. It wasn't chilled, and it wasn't even in a glass bottle, but the label clearly stated it was 'Retsína, Traditional Wine of Greece'. I plucked the squidgy plastic bottle from the shelf and made for the cash register.

Robert looked dubious. "That's *it?*"

I grinned. The golden fluid in the bottle looked for all the world like fresh urine, or perhaps a thin industrial lubricant, and cost even less. Our gourmet friends were about to sample the worst wine-flavored slop that Greece could muster.

Using a disemboweled plastic shopping bag for a tablecloth, Linda and Lucy set out a princely snack of crackers spread with cheap tinned paté, as well as a nice hunk of féta and a few olives. Robert put out plastic cups, I poured, and we toasted one another and celebrated our friendship. The *retsína*—which under other circumstances we'd have poured down the nearest drain—was warm, thin, and utterly delightful. Ten minutes and a liter of the vile stuff later, we climbed back on the bus, laughing and happy. Life was once again good.

Back at the Athens bus terminal, Lucy and Robert found a taxi without too much difficulty and headed off to the St. George Lycabettus. After considerable effort Linda and I managed to find a second one and ten minutes later we were at Brigitte's flat in the old Pangráti district of Athens, located just behind the classical expanse of white marble that is the Panathenaic stadium, built a century ago on the site of the original for the 1896 Olympic games.

We settled our belongings in the apartment, freshened up, made the bed, and went in search of a late dinner. We didn't have to look far: just a few doors away was a typical neighborhood taverna. We ordered wine and *tzatzíki* and *gigantés* beans, and just enjoyed the cool night air.

We had discussed with our friends what to do on our one day in Athens. We would keep the morning free and meet up after lunch for a bus tour out to the Temple of Poseidon at Cape Soúnion, a bit over an hour out of the city and one of the must-see ruins of classical Greece. Despite our many visits to Greece, neither Linda nor I had seen it, and our friends were more than willing. Dinner, of course, was a no-brainer—a table on the sumptuous roof terrace of the St. George Lycabettus.

OUR LAST DAY arrived. I fought to remain calm. Under the thin crust of my composure lay a festering swamp of despair from which, should my control break, I would never get free. Even in the bright sunshine of the Athenian noon I couldn't shake the persistent sense of looming shadow.

We met Lucy and Robert at the bus stop a little before two and were soon gliding by past Glyfáda, the platinum-plated beach resort on the southern outskirts of the city, and the swanky hotels and restaurants of nearby Vouliagméni.

Fifty miles along the increasingly deserted coast we rounded a curve and saw the temple perched high on its scrub-crowned promontory. It was unmistakable: open any guide or picture book of Greece, and you're sure to see the temple of Poseidon surrounded on three sides by scintillating blue water, its thick base supporting stately rows of pale marble pillars,

We climbed off the bus and joined the endless stream of visitors to-ing and fro-ing up the dusty path toward the temple. The afternoon was breezy, the air sparkling.

All the major classical sites I've ever seen have impressed me, but Soúnion especially so; it would be impossible to imagine a more appropriate and dramatic site for a temple to the God of the Sea. Here all the elements—Sun, Wind, Earth, and, above all, Water—seemed in perfect, dynamic balance. Here, with the wind in our face and the faint *kshwwww!* sound of the waves breaking on the rocks below, only a corpse could fail to be stirred.

There were graffiti. *Old* graffiti. There, beyond the low post-and-wire fencing, clearly visible on the columns' bases, were names and dates carefully carved into the weathered marble in steady, accurate roman characters complete with serifs; a tribute to the calligraphy taught in the Victorian era, as well as a clear indication that visitors to the site could do what they wanted in those times. We read the names: R. LAING, ABERDEEN, 1886; GEO. LONGDEN, LONDON; J. DAVIS, H'POOL, 1893; there were many, mostly English, with here and there a Greek name. A nearby sign informed visitors that Lord Byron had carved his name on a column in the temple's interior, which unfortunately was no longer accessible to the public.

We wandered around a bit longer, took some photos, and—far too soon—it was time to return to the waiting bus.

A little after nine, Linda and I left Brigitte's flat and took a taxi to the St. George. Robert had made reservations for dinner at nine-thirty, and we waited in the lobby for our friends to arrive. How fortunate we'd been to have their company these last days: Lucy was empathy and warmth personified, able to settle the most frayed nerves with her gentle heart and patient ear; Robert was mischief and wicked irony delivered with a New Jersey edge that thirty years on the West Coast hadn't even begun to dull. You couldn't stay down for long around these two.

But all was bittersweet now. The St. George had always been one of our luxuries: now, we not only couldn't afford to stay here, but even had to think twice about dining at the pricey roof restaurant, Le Grand Balcon. But it was our last night in Greece, and, really, what difference would a couple of hundred dollars make at this point? We would again go out on a high note, in the best of company, with the band playing.

The four of us emerged on the sixth floor and were shown to our table by the rail on the balcony. Everything was as it should be: we'd dressed up, the table was candlelit, the night warm, the view perfect. If only I could dispel these crushing feelings. Half of me was absent, already grieving for what we were about to leave behind. I tried my best to make light and merry, and I knew it showed; everyone understood.

As Kurt Vonnegut was so fond of saying, *so it goes*.

Exeunt Omnes

I KNEW LINDA was stressed about the upcoming confrontation with passport control from the moment we woke. Being an outlaw—even by accident—goes entirely against her grain, and though I thought the mayor's letter would probably prove sufficient to get her through without paying a hefty fine or being declared *persona non grata* throughout the Schengen countries, I could understand her worry.

Linda dressed in a pinstripe pant suit and white blouse, a professional, even corporate look; I wore pressed slacks and a shirt. Aside from the passport control issue, we always dress well to fly: you generally get better treatment and are far more likely to get upgraded on an overbooked flight. If you look scruffy, as a good many air travelers do, you'll just get bumped even if there's plenty of room in business class.

We left the apartment building at nine-thirty and set off, wheelie suitcases in tow, to find a taxi in the chaos of the bright Athens morning.

The central Pangráti neighborhood with its busy streets, should have been an easy place to find a cab. But after fifteen frustrating minutes watching full taxis muscle their way through the traffic at a promising intersection near the flat, we realized that the morning commute in Athens hadn't yet ended.

We set off towards the main avenue, a third of a mile away, where we would surely find a taxi. It was getting warm, and the narrow sidewalks were obstructed everywhere by parked cars, so that we were constantly forced to go around them, manhandling our suitcases off the sidewalk onto the busy street. Cabs kept zipping by, ignoring our attempts to flag them down. One or two slowed before taking off again on finding we were going to the airport. At this rate, we wouldn't have to worry about passport control because we weren't going to make it to the airport.

Finally an empty taxi slowed. It stopped. This driver was going to take us, I was sure.

"*Poú páte?*" he asked, where are you going?

"*Sto aerodrómo,*" I said.

He made a disgusted face, added an impatient gesture, and stamped on the gas, as if telling a pair of bums to get lost.

Linda exploded.

"*Munákia!!*" she screeched after him. *Pussy!* Or, more appropriately in this context, *cunt!*

I stared. My wife isn't given to this sort of public outburst, but the subhuman behavior of Greek cab drivers would drive a saint to distraction. That even Linda was surprised became obvious an instant later, when—realizing she'd totally lost it in public—she turned around to see if anyone had heard. Sure enough, a woman who'd been approaching close behind was staring open-mouthed and stepping out into the street to make a wide detour around us.

We were almost at the corner of the avenue when another empty cab approached. I hailed it, and the driver stopped alongside us. I told him our destination. He smiled, made the 'yes' head-gesture and flipped open his trunk before exiting to help us in with the luggage. A miracle! I could have kissed him, but decided that a huge tip would probably be more appropriate, and certainly more welcome.

We stood in line forever before finally reaching the check-in counter. Linda's face was tight as we walked toward security and passport control. This was it, the last nightmare headache of our Greek odyssey. One way or another we would get out; but if we came up against a real bastard, I feared Linda would break down. She'd been through too much.

Passport control consisted of a small booth with two young officers, barely out of their teens, each with his own short line. One had a friendly, open face; Linda picked him. Fingers crossed.

She handed over her passport with a bright *'kaliméra!'* The officer took it with a quick smile, saw the long-outdated entry stamp and flipped back and forth through the pages looking for a more recent stamp. He looked up at Linda.

"When did you come here?"

"In November of 2006," said Linda.

The man frowned.

In her best Greek, Linda said, "I want live in Greece. My husband is from EU, but—" a small sigh—"*ólos íne dískolo stin Éllada.*" She fished out the mayor's letter from her purse and unfolded it on the counter. "I have paper from Skópelos."

The officer read it, turned to his colleague, and explained the situation in a few words. "What do I do?" he asked.

The second officer took the letter, read it, and returned it to the first guy with a shrug. "I don't know."

The first officer punched a number. A moment later he was reading Linda's cat-ate-my-homework note to a superior. Clearly neither of these uniformed children wanted to make a decision over this potentially dangerous, if sweetly polite, foreign national.

After a moment, he put down the phone, stamped Linda's passport without even glancing at her, and waved her on. Ten seconds later, I joined her on the far side of the inquisitors' booth.

I smiled at Linda. Before us was an open expanse of generic airport architecture, flanked by windows overlooking the tarmac on one side. I took her hand and squeezed it, and together we strolled away down the empty lounges toward our departure gate.

∾

Epilogue

We couldn't have timed our return worse if we'd tried.

The economy went into freefall within a month of our landing on US soil. Linda's job in Willits quickly went pear-shaped and, despite the geographic splendor of the place, the combination of lack of culture and economic depression made it a grim place to live: during the entire six months of our stay the only friend we made was a nine-year old neighbor boy who liked to hang out with us and brought his friends over as well! But the lull provided me time to write; by April 2008, just six months after our return, I'd finished the first draft of this book and we were desperate to get out.

Two dear friends from the Bay Area, seeing how bad things were for us, took us into their home, where we remained for sixteen months. My work was patchy; Linda's likewise, with intermittent periods of contract work and unemployment. We had no health insurance and were again buried in debt, with weeks when we struggled to put gas in the car. Without the kindness of friends it's conceivable we could have ended up homeless.

In the fall of 2009 we were finally in a position to rent a place of our own. I was getting more work and Linda started a job which turned full-time in early 2011. I founded Panverse Publishing and edited three Science Fiction anthologies. Aegean Dream was in the hands of my agent, but with the chaos and uncertainty in the publishing industry, none of the majors were taking chances. I decided to publish it through Panverse, and the result is the book you have just finished.

Others have had it far worse than us, and we count ourselves fortunate. Our trials have tempered us and made us realize how resilient and adaptable we are. We learned to live for the day, and to be happy with little.

Would we risk such an adventure again?

It's a question we don't dare ask ourselves.

GLOSSARY

Pronunciation notes: the Greek 'd' (delta, or δ) is a soft 'th' sound, as in the English word, then; the Greek letter 'χ' (represented in our text as 'h') is pronounced like the 'ch' in the Scottish word, loch.

AFM, or AFIMÍ	Greek tax number, similar to SSN
DIMARHÍO	Town Hall
ÉPIPLA	Furniture store
HÓRA	Old town or village
KALIMÉRA	Good day/morning
KALLITÉHNIS	Craftsman; Artisan
KALÍVI	Cottage; rural home
KATÁLAVA	I understood; I got it
KÉNTRO IGEÍAS	Public Health Clinic
MEZÉS	Small dishes served with drinks
NE (pron. *neh*)	Yes
ÓHI	No
ÓLOS ÍNE DÍSKOLO STIN ELLÁDA	Everything is difficult in Greece
OÚZO	Anise-flavoured licqueur
OUZERÍA	Bar serving *oúzo* and *mezés*
PARALÍA	Waterfront
PRÁGMATA	Things; goods
RETSÍNA	Dry white wine flavoured with pine resin
SIGÁ, SIGÁ	Slowly, slowly
SÍGOUROS	Certainly; for sure
TEKNÍTIS	Technician

TIRÓPITA	Cheese pie
TSÍPOURO	Strong pomace brandy
TSIPOURÁDIKO	Bar serving tsipoúro and *mezés*
TZATZÍKI	Yogurt, garlic, & cucumber dip
YÁSSOU/YÁSSAS	Hi; hallo (informal/formal)
XÉNOS (XÉNI)	Stranger; foreigner (& plural of)

LINKS

The Skópelos Island Websites

http://www.skopelos.net
http://www.skopelosweb.gr

Skopelos hóra webcam (harbor view)

http://www.skopelosweb.gr/webcam/

Skopelos—aerial tour

http://www.youtube.com/watch?v=_ZI_S9MqKrI

NMPANS (Northern Marine Park of Alónissos Northen Spórades)
http://www.alonissos-park.gr/index_en.html
http://www.youtube.com/watch?v=VooR7qNJobA

Glóssa

Ághios Yiánnis to Kastro

Loútraki

Glyfonéri

Ánesis

Skópelos (hóra)

Miliá

Pánormos

Stáfilos

Agnóndas

Alónnisos

N

THE ISLAND OF SKOPELOS

0   Miles   2

About the Author

Like most writers, Dario Ciriello has lived several lives in one and enjoyed an eccentric career trajectory. He's worked in a warehouse, driven trucks, drag raced motorcycles, had a small import business, enjoyed a twenty-five year career as a decorative painter, and currently divides his time between writing and CAD design.

A graduate of the Clarion West writing program, Dario has been a finalist in the prestigious Writers of the Future Contest, sold several short science fiction and fantasy stories, and edited three critically-acclaimed anthologies for Panverse Publishing. Aegean Dream is his first nonfiction work.